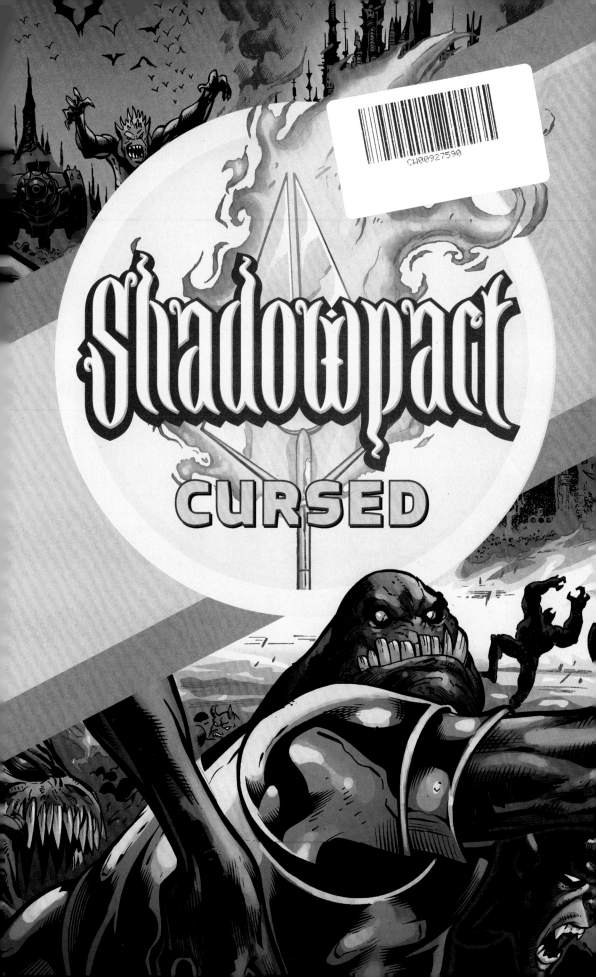

Shadowpact

CURSED

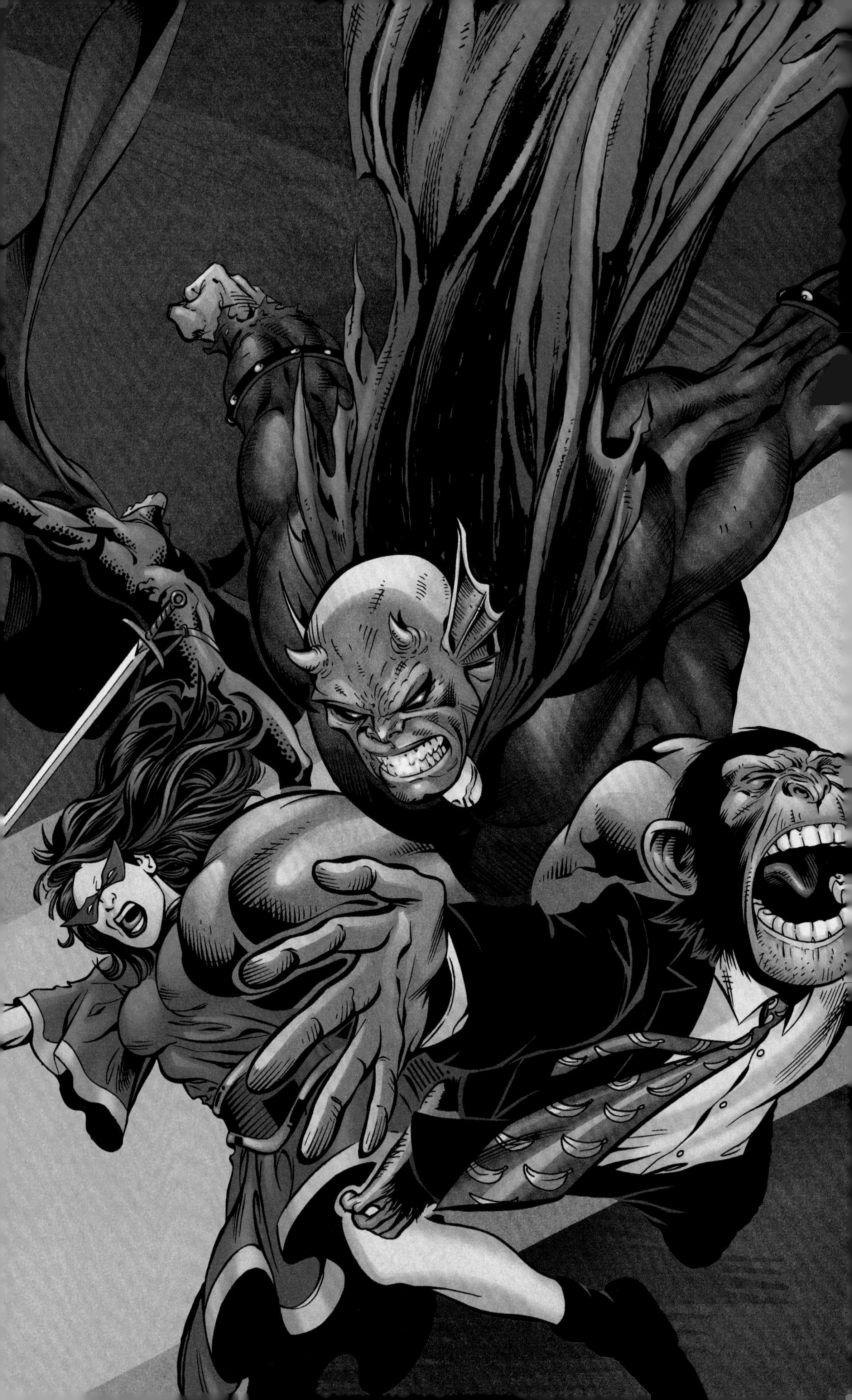

Shadowpact

CURSED

All stories written by **BILL WILLINGHAM**

BLUE DEVIL: A NIGHT IN THE LIFE

Pencilled by **STEVE SCOTT** • *Inked by* **WAYNE FAUCHER**

THE DEMON TRIPTYCH: PARTS 1-3

LIVE BY THE SWORD, DIE BY THE SWORD

Pencilled by **TOM DERENICK** • *Inked by* **WAYNE FAUCHER**

BAD TIDINGS & EVIL DEEDS

Art by **SCOTT HAMPTON**

Lettering by **PAT BROSSEAU**

Color by **MIKE ATIYEH** *and* **CHRIS CHUCKRY**

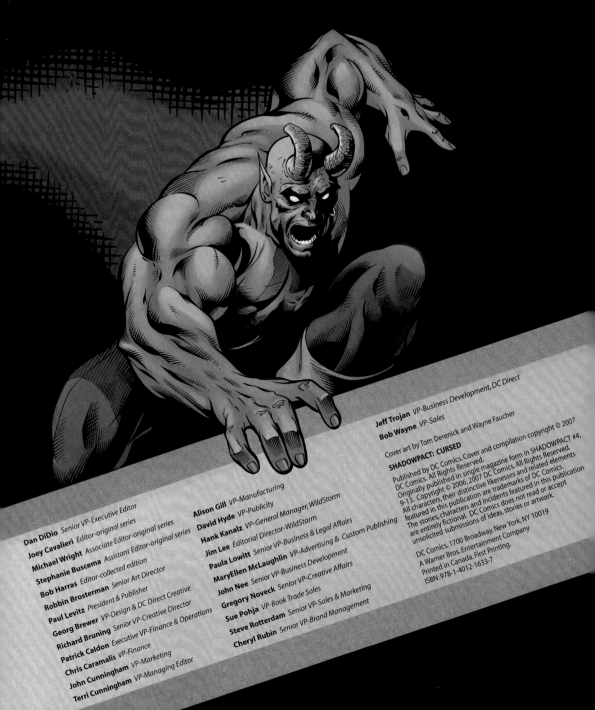

Jeff Trojan VP-Business Development, DC Direct

Bob Wayne VP-Sales

Cover art by Tom Derenick and Wayne Faucher

SHADOWPACT: CURSED

Published by DC Comics. Cover and compilation copyright © 2007
DC Comics. All Rights Reserved.
Originally published in single magazine form in SHADOWPACT #4,
9-13. Copyright © 2006, 2007 DC Comics. All Rights Reserved.
All characters, their distinctive likenesses and related elements
featured in this publication are trademarks of DC Comics.
The stories, characters and incidents featured in this publication
are entirely fictional. DC Comics does not read or accept
unsolicited submissions of ideas, stories or artwork.

DC Comics, 1700 Broadway, New York, NY 10019
A Warner Bros. Entertainment Company
Printed in Canada. First Printing.
ISBN: 978-1-4012-1633-7

THE BLUE DEVIL: A NIGHT IN THE LIFE

cover art by **STEVE SCOTT** *and* **WAYNE FAUCHER**
colored by **MIKE ATIYEH**

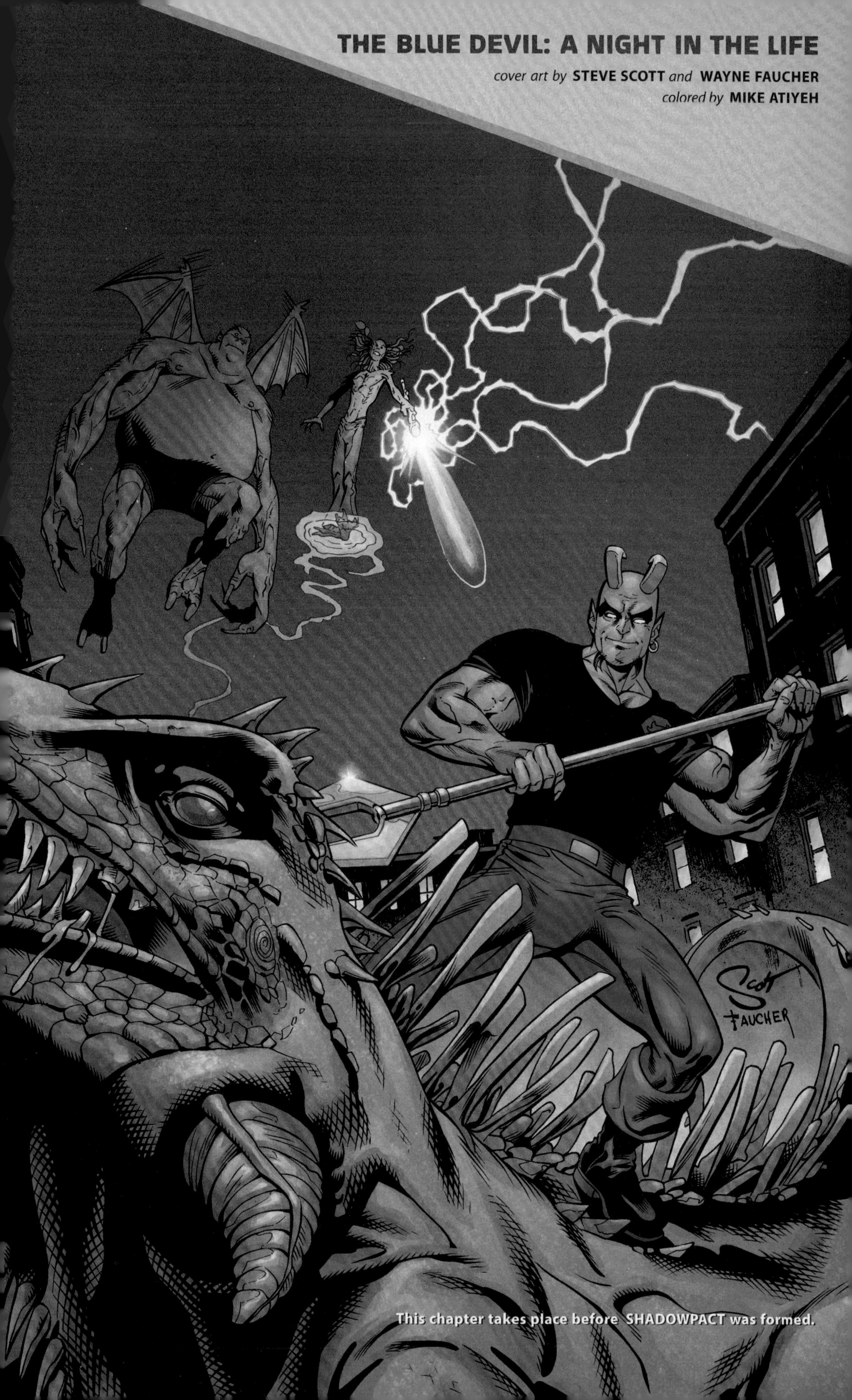
Scott
FAUCHER

This chapter takes place before SHADOWPACT was formed.

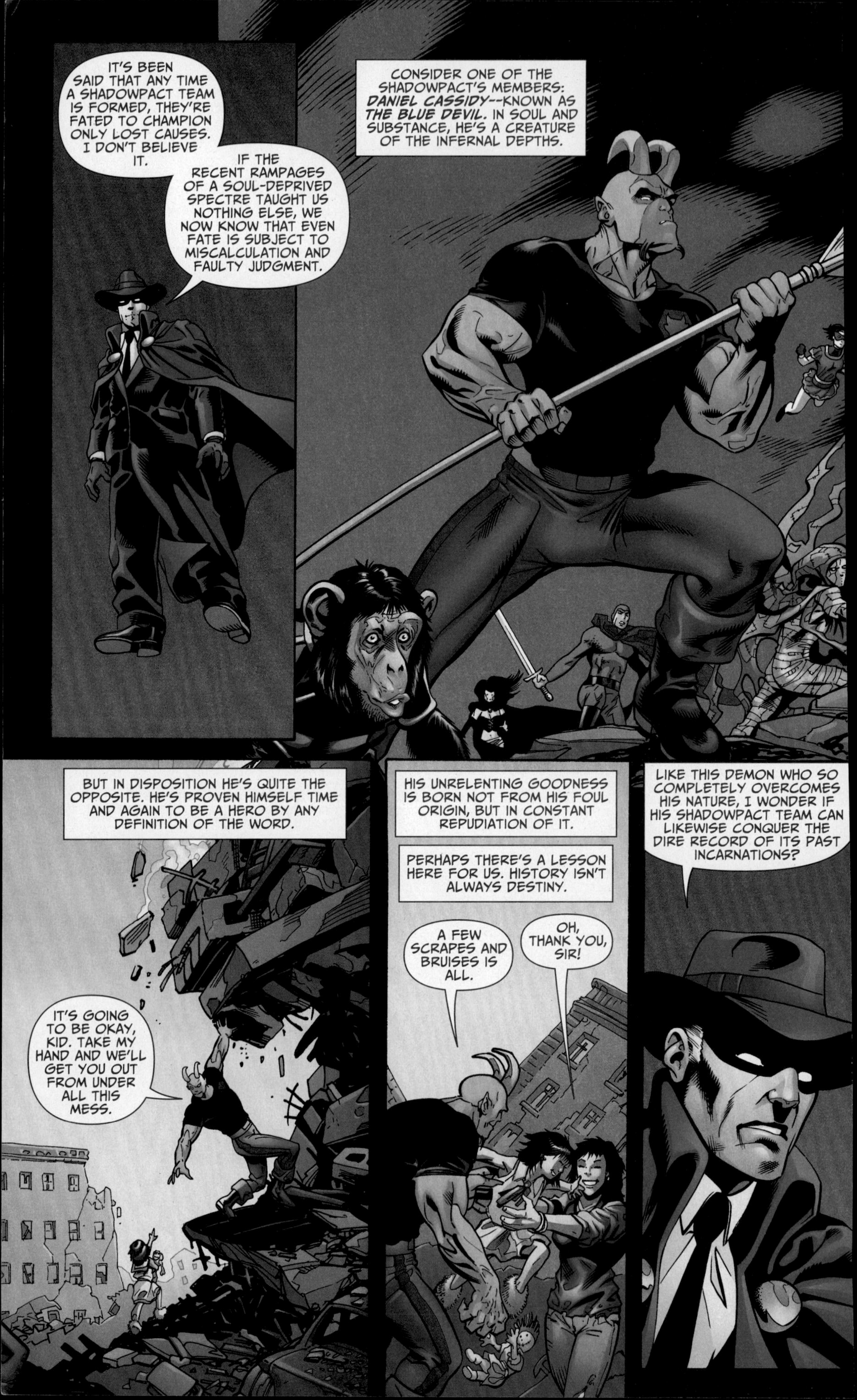
IT'S BEEN SAID THAT ANY TIME A SHADOWPACT TEAM IS FORMED, THEY'RE FATED TO CHAMPION ONLY LOST CAUSES. I DON'T BELIEVE IT.
IF THE RECENT RAMPAGES OF A SOUL-DEPRIVED SPECTRE TAUGHT US NOTHING ELSE, WE NOW KNOW THAT EVEN FATE IS SUBJECT TO MISCALCULATION AND FAULTY JUDGMENT.
CONSIDER ONE OF THE SHADOWPACT'S MEMBERS: DANIEL CASSIDY--KNOWN AS THE BLUE DEVIL. IN SOUL AND SUBSTANCE, HE'S A CREATURE OF THE INFERNAL DEPTHS.
BUT IN DISPOSITION HE'S QUITE THE OPPOSITE. HE'S PROVEN HIMSELF TIME AND AGAIN TO BE A HERO BY ANY DEFINITION OF THE WORD.
IT'S GOING TO BE OKAY, KID. TAKE MY HAND AND WE'LL GET YOU OUT FROM UNDER ALL THIS MESS.
HIS UNRELENTING GOODNESS IS BORN NOT FROM HIS FOUL ORIGIN, BUT IN CONSTANT REPUDIATION OF IT.
PERHAPS THERE'S A LESSON HERE FOR US. HISTORY ISN'T ALWAYS DESTINY.
A FEW SCRAPES AND BRUISES IS ALL.
OH, THANK YOU, SIR!
LIKE THIS DEMON WHO SO COMPLETELY OVERCOMES HIS NATURE, I WONDER IF HIS SHADOWPACT TEAM CAN LIKEWISE CONQUER THE DIRE RECORD OF ITS PAST INCARNATIONS?

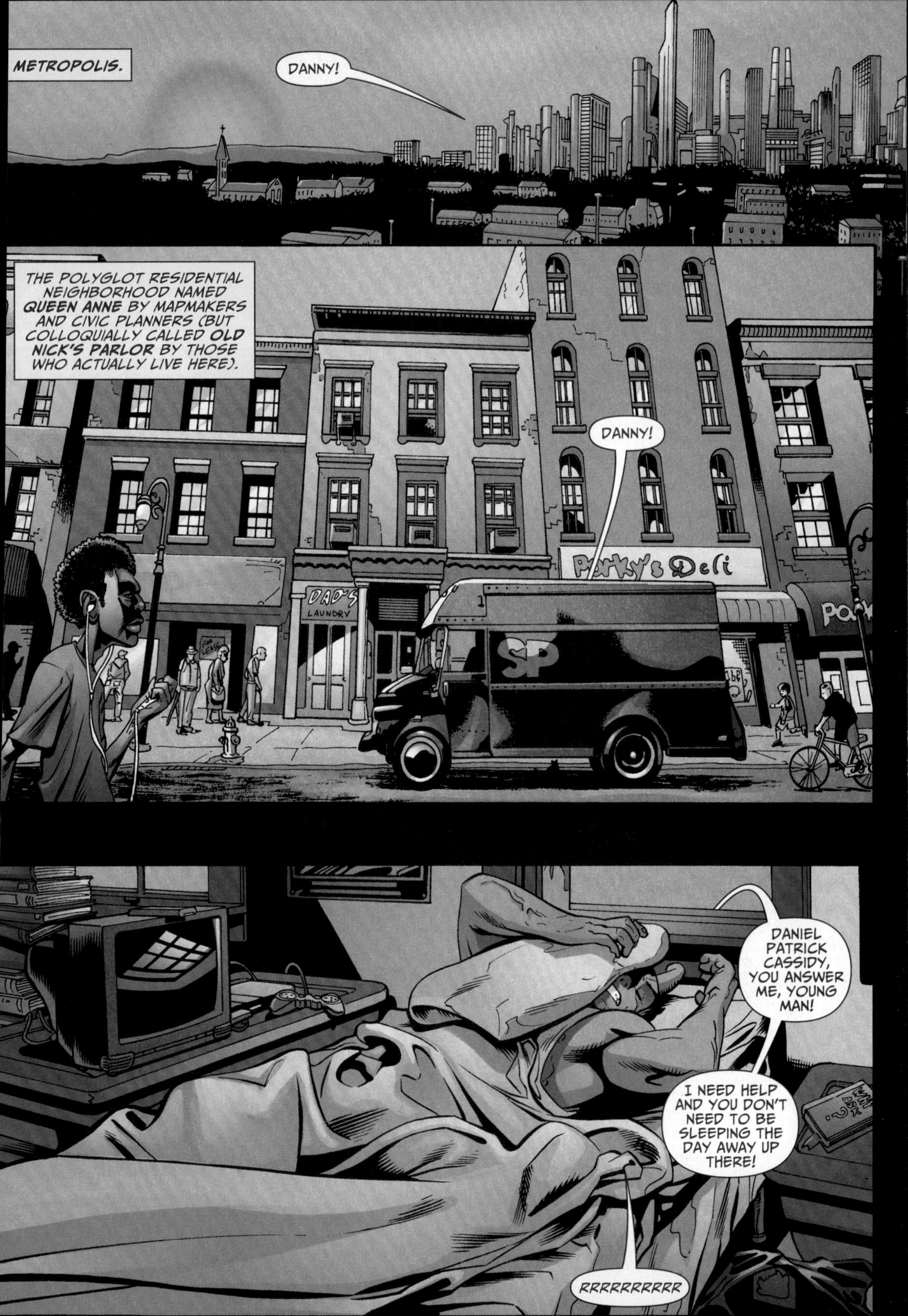
METROPOLIS.
DANNY!
THE POLYGLOT RESIDENTIAL NEIGHBORHOOD NAMED QUEEN ANNE BY MAPMAKERS AND CIVIC PLANNERS (BUT COLLOQUIALLY CALLED OLD NICK'S PARLOR BY THOSE WHO ACTUALLY LIVE HERE).
DANNY!
Porky's Deli
DAD'S LAUNDRY
SP
DANIEL PATRICK CASSIDY, YOU ANSWER ME, YOUNG MAN!
I NEED HELP AND YOU DON'T NEED TO BE SLEEPING THE DAY AWAY UP THERE!
RRRRRRRRRR

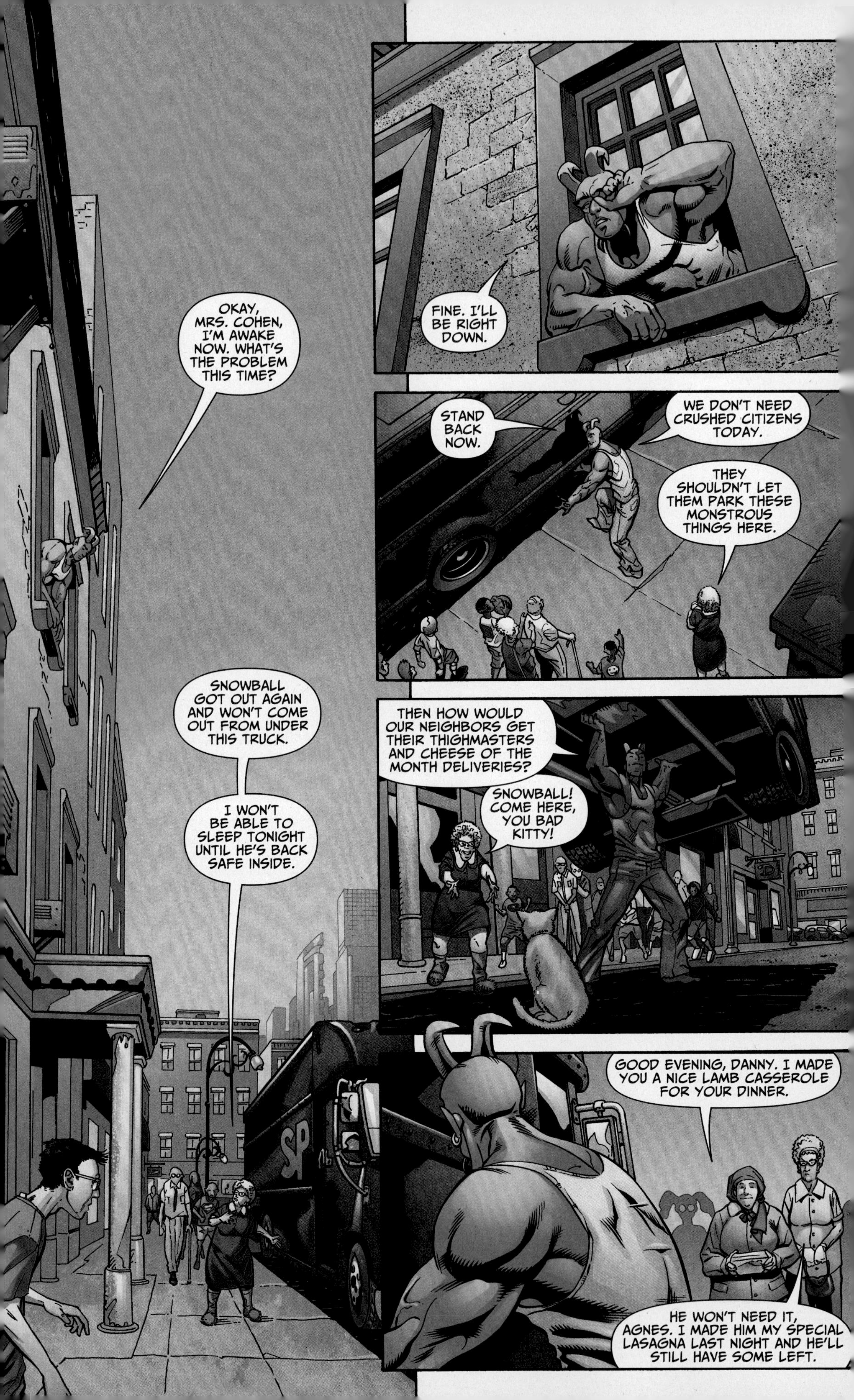
OKAY, MRS. COHEN, I'M AWAKE NOW. WHAT'S THE PROBLEM THIS TIME?
FINE. I'LL BE RIGHT DOWN.
SNOWBALL GOT OUT AGAIN AND WON'T COME OUT FROM UNDER THIS TRUCK.
I WON'T BE ABLE TO SLEEP TONIGHT UNTIL HE'S BACK SAFE INSIDE.
STAND BACK NOW.
WE DON'T NEED CRUSHED CITIZENS TODAY.
THEY SHOULDN'T LET THEM PARK THESE MONSTROUS THINGS HERE.
THEN HOW WOULD OUR NEIGHBORS GET THEIR THIGHMASTERS AND CHEESE OF THE MONTH DELIVERIES?
SNOWBALL! COME HERE, YOU BAD KITTY!
GOOD EVENING, DANNY. I MADE YOU A NICE LAMB CASSEROLE FOR YOUR DINNER.
HE WON'T NEED IT, AGNES. I MADE HIM MY SPECIAL LASAGNA LAST NIGHT AND HE'LL STILL HAVE SOME LEFT.

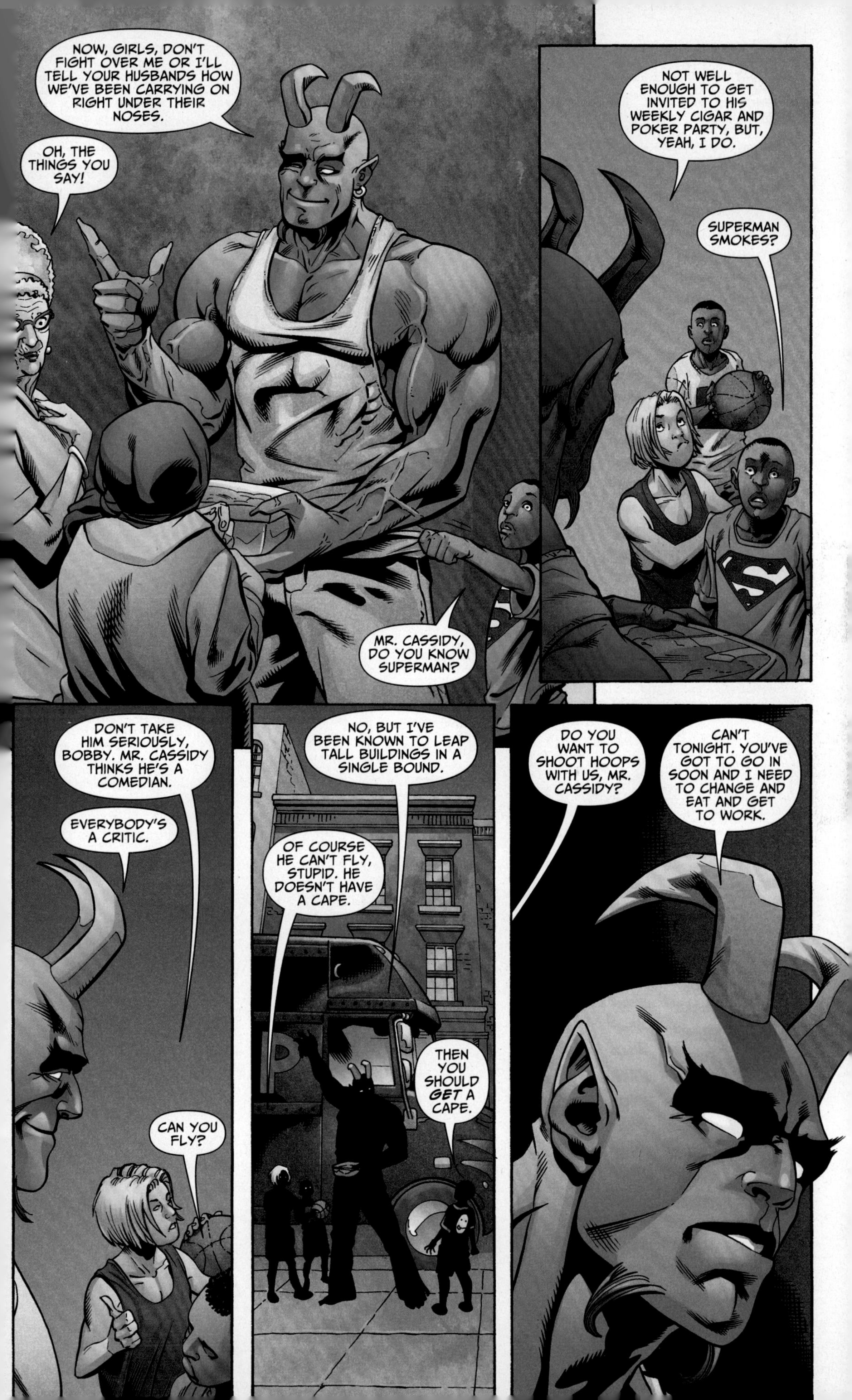
NOW, GIRLS, DON'T FIGHT OVER ME OR I'LL TELL YOUR HUSBANDS HOW WE'VE BEEN CARRYING ON RIGHT UNDER THEIR NOSES.
OH, THE THINGS YOU SAY!
MR. CASSIDY, DO YOU KNOW SUPERMAN?
NOT WELL ENOUGH TO GET INVITED TO HIS WEEKLY CIGAR AND POKER PARTY, BUT, YEAH, I DO.
SUPERMAN SMOKES?
DON'T TAKE HIM SERIOUSLY, BOBBY. MR. CASSIDY THINKS HE'S A COMEDIAN.
EVERYBODY'S A CRITIC.
CAN YOU FLY?
NO, BUT I'VE BEEN KNOWN TO LEAP TALL BUILDINGS IN A SINGLE BOUND.
OF COURSE HE CAN'T FLY, STUPID. HE DOESN'T HAVE A CAPE.
THEN YOU SHOULD GET A CAPE.
DO YOU WANT TO SHOOT HOOPS WITH US, MR. CASSIDY?
CAN'T TONIGHT. YOU'VE GOT TO GO IN SOON AND I NEED TO CHANGE AND EAT AND GET TO WORK.

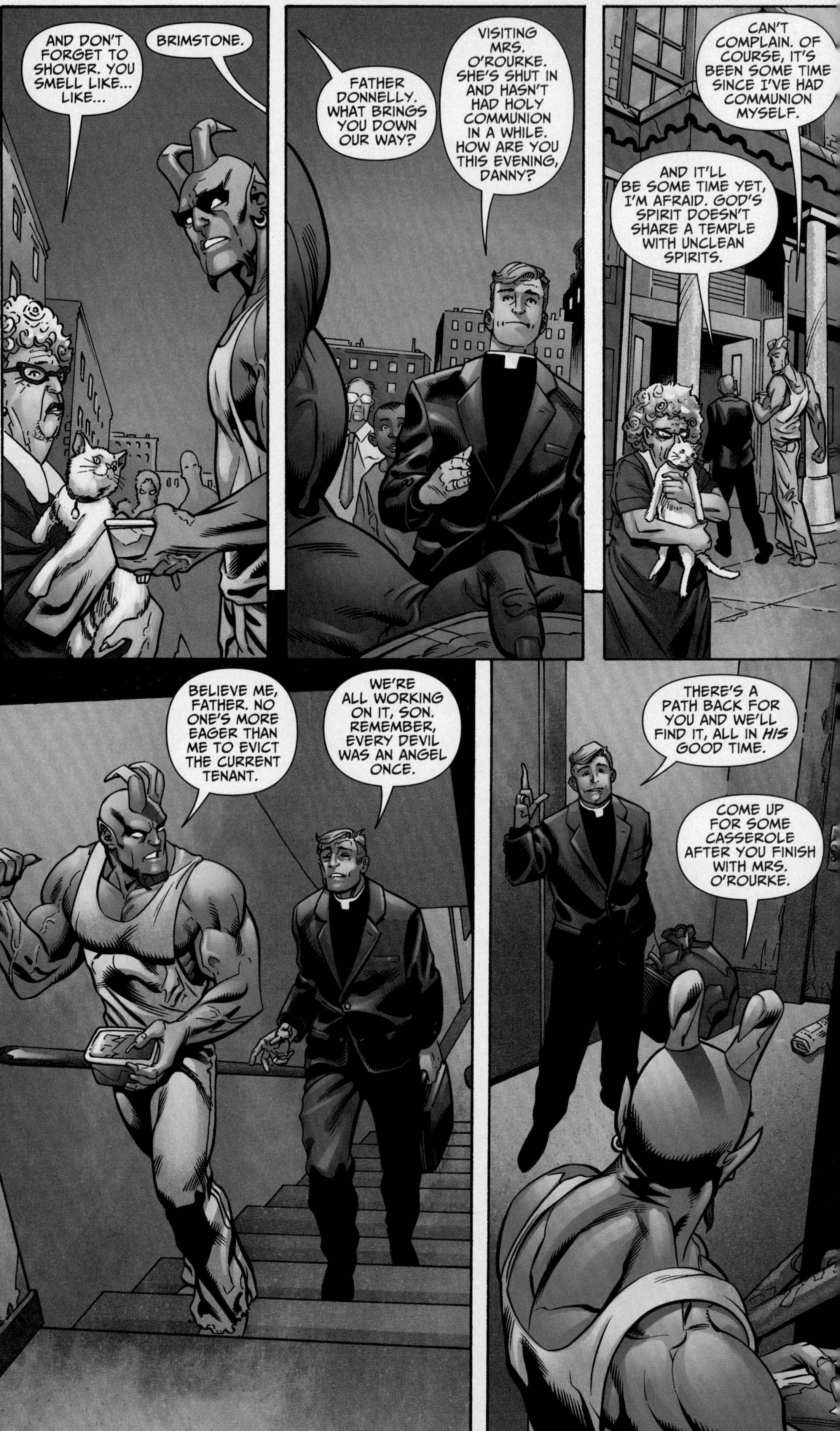
AND DON'T FORGET TO SHOWER. YOU SMELL LIKE... LIKE...
BRIMSTONE.
FATHER DONNELLY. WHAT BRINGS YOU DOWN OUR WAY?
VISITING MRS. O'ROURKE. SHE'S SHUT IN AND HASN'T HAD HOLY COMMUNION IN A WHILE. HOW ARE YOU THIS EVENING, DANNY?
CAN'T COMPLAIN. OF COURSE, IT'S BEEN SOME TIME SINCE I'VE HAD COMMUNION MYSELF.
AND IT'LL BE SOME TIME YET, I'M AFRAID. GOD'S SPIRIT DOESN'T SHARE A TEMPLE WITH UNCLEAN SPIRITS.
BELIEVE ME, FATHER. NO ONE'S MORE EAGER THAN ME TO EVICT THE CURRENT TENANT.
WE'RE ALL WORKING ON IT, SON. REMEMBER, EVERY DEVIL WAS AN ANGEL ONCE.
THERE'S A PATH BACK FOR YOU AND WE'LL FIND IT, ALL IN *HIS* GOOD TIME.
COME UP FOR SOME CASSEROLE AFTER YOU FINISH WITH MRS. O'ROURKE.

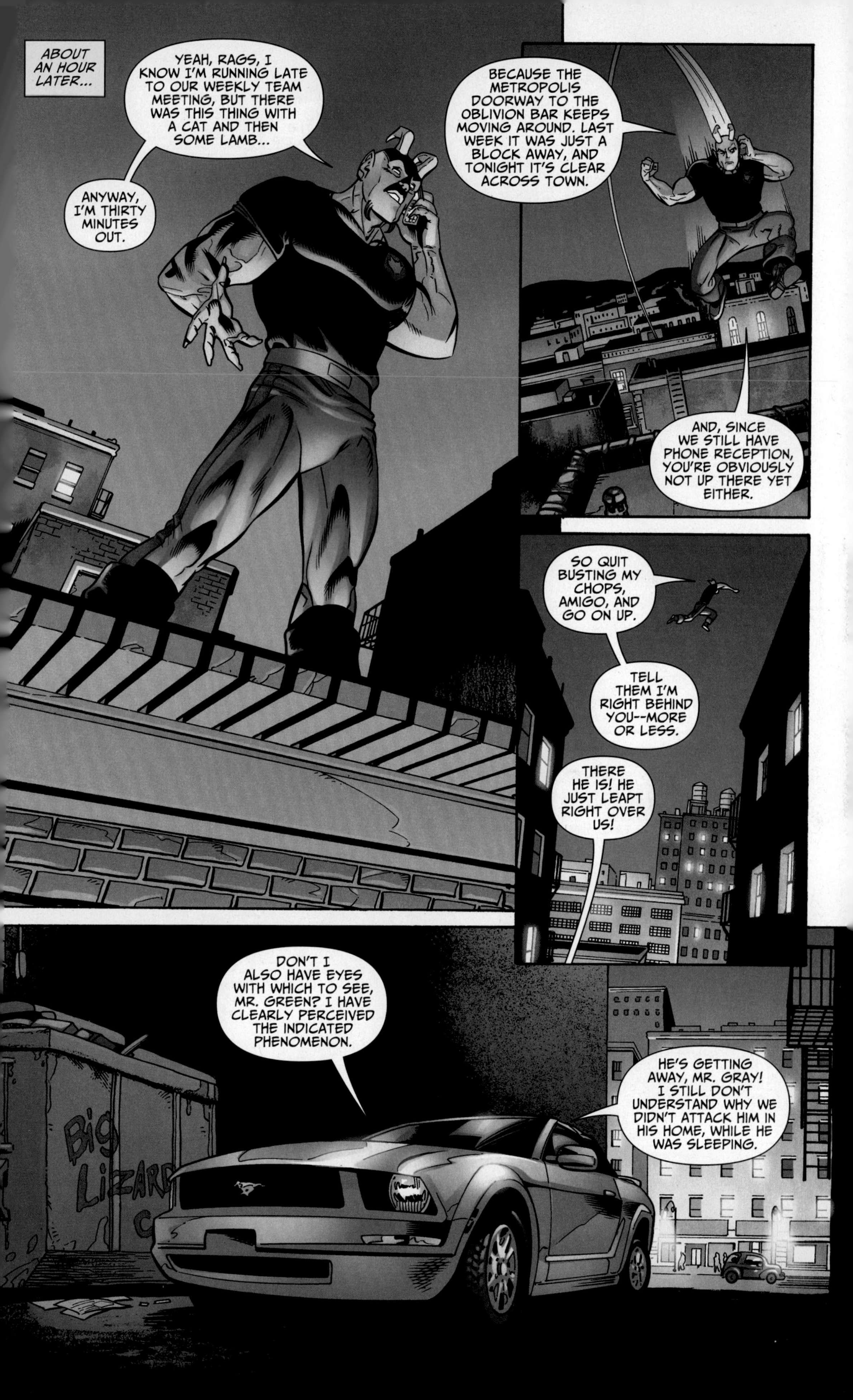
ABOUT AN HOUR LATER...
YEAH, RAGS, I KNOW I'M RUNNING LATE TO OUR WEEKLY TEAM MEETING, BUT THERE WAS THIS THING WITH A CAT AND THEN SOME LAMB...
ANYWAY, I'M THIRTY MINUTES OUT.
BECAUSE THE METROPOLIS DOORWAY TO THE OBLIVION BAR KEEPS MOVING AROUND. LAST WEEK IT WAS JUST A BLOCK AWAY, AND TONIGHT IT'S CLEAR ACROSS TOWN.
AND, SINCE WE STILL HAVE PHONE RECEPTION, YOU'RE OBVIOUSLY NOT UP THERE YET EITHER.
SO QUIT BUSTING MY CHOPS, AMIGO, AND GO ON UP.
TELL THEM I'M RIGHT BEHIND YOU--MORE OR LESS.
THERE HE IS! HE JUST LEAPT RIGHT OVER US!
DON'T I ALSO HAVE EYES WITH WHICH TO SEE, MR. GREEN? I HAVE CLEARLY PERCEIVED THE INDICATED PHENOMENON.
HE'S GETTING AWAY, MR. GRAY! I STILL DON'T UNDERSTAND WHY WE DIDN'T ATTACK HIM IN HIS HOME, WHILE HE WAS SLEEPING.
Big Lizard

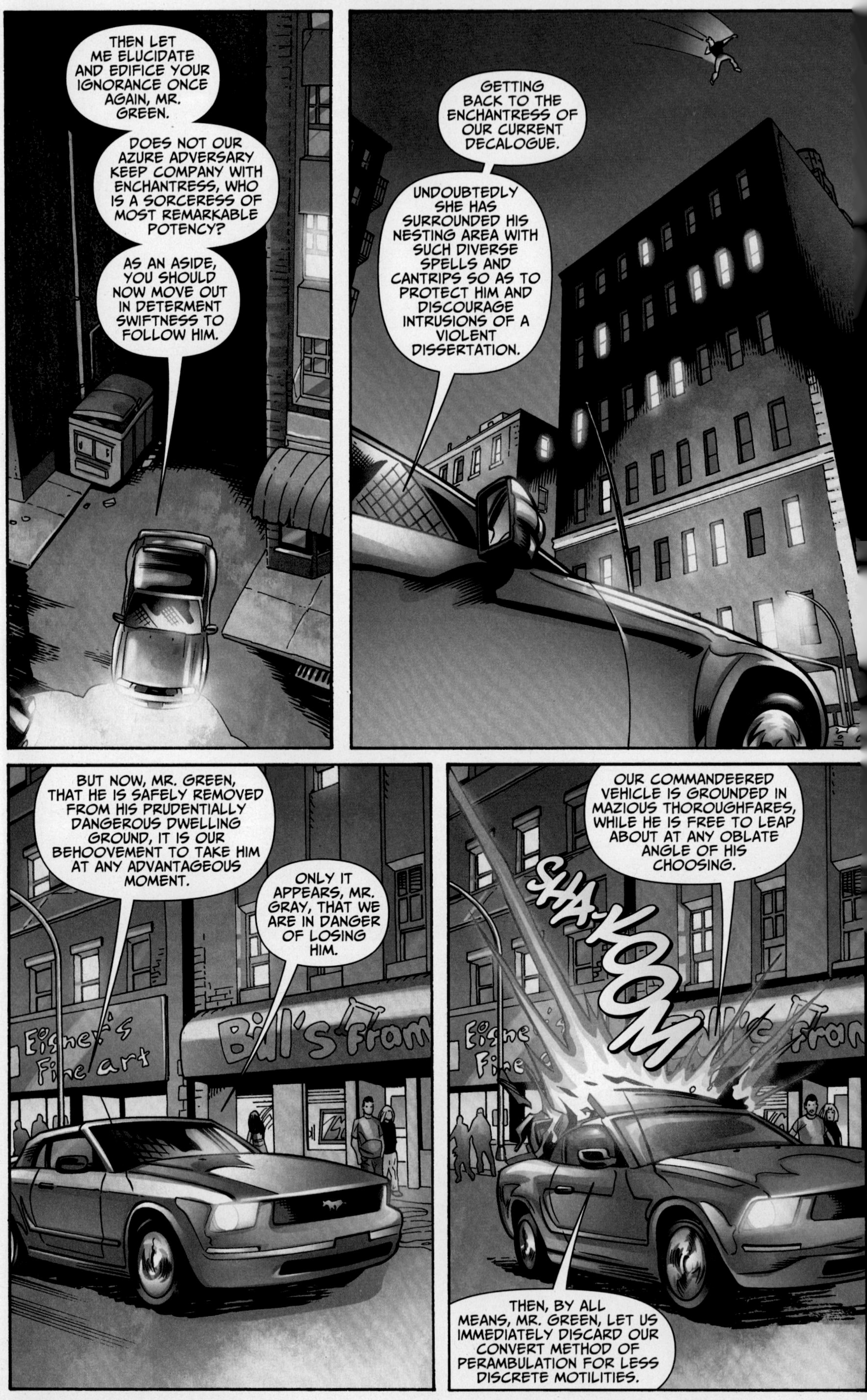
THEN LET ME ELUCIDATE AND EDIFICE YOUR IGNORANCE ONCE AGAIN, MR. GREEN.
DOES NOT OUR AZURE ADVERSARY KEEP COMPANY WITH ENCHANTRESS, WHO IS A SORCERESS OF MOST REMARKABLE POTENCY?
AS AN ASIDE, YOU SHOULD NOW MOVE OUT IN DETERMENT SWIFTNESS TO FOLLOW HIM.
GETTING BACK TO THE ENCHANTRESS OF OUR CURRENT DECALOGUE.
UNDOUBTEDLY SHE HAS SURROUNDED HIS NESTING AREA WITH SUCH DIVERSE SPELLS AND CANTRIPS SO AS TO PROTECT HIM AND DISCOURAGE INTRUSIONS OF A VIOLENT DISSERTATION.
BUT NOW, MR. GREEN, THAT HE IS SAFELY REMOVED FROM HIS PRUDENTIALLY DANGEROUS DWELLING GROUND, IT IS OUR BEHOOVEMENT TO TAKE HIM AT ANY ADVANTAGEOUS MOMENT.
ONLY IT APPEARS, MR. GRAY, THAT WE ARE IN DANGER OF LOSING HIM.
Eisner's Fine art
Bill's Fram
OUR COMMANDEERED VEHICLE IS GROUNDED IN MAZIOUS THOROUGHFARES, WHILE HE IS FREE TO LEAP ABOUT AT ANY OBLATE ANGLE OF HIS CHOOSING.
SHA-KOOM
THEN, BY ALL MEANS, MR. GREEN, LET US IMMEDIATELY DISCARD OUR CONVERT METHOD OF PERAMBULATION FOR LESS DISCRETE MOTILITIES.

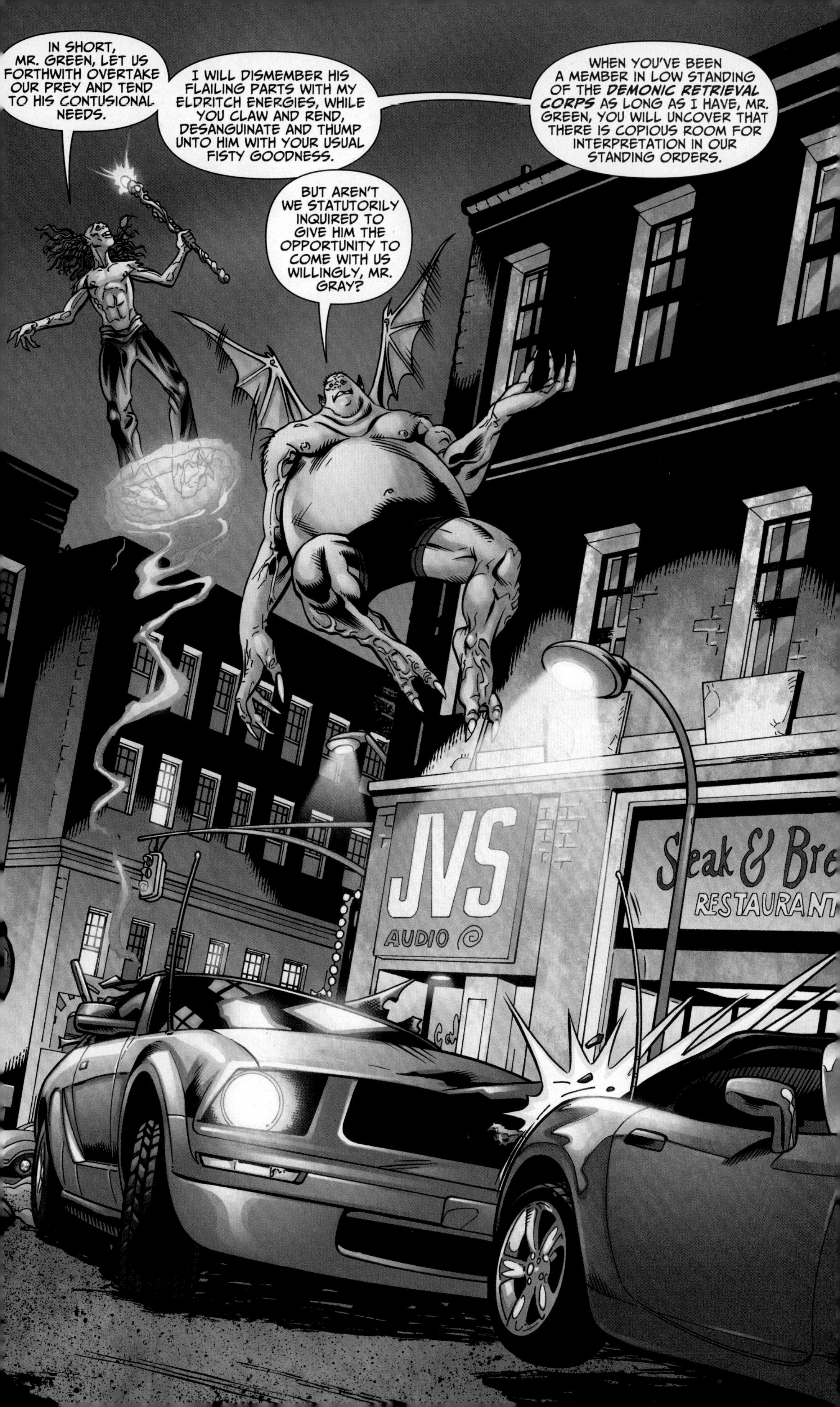

IN SHORT, MR. GREEN, LET US FORTHWITH OVERTAKE OUR PREY AND TEND TO HIS CONTUSIONAL NEEDS.
I WILL DISMEMBER HIS FLAILING PARTS WITH MY ELDRITCH ENERGIES, WHILE YOU CLAW AND REND, DESANGUINATE AND THUMP UNTO HIM WITH YOUR USUAL FISTY GOODNESS.
BUT AREN'T WE STATUTORILY INQUIRED TO GIVE HIM THE OPPORTUNITY TO COME WITH US WILLINGLY, MR. GRAY?
WHEN YOU'VE BEEN A MEMBER IN LOW STANDING OF THE *DEMONIC RETRIEVAL CORPS* AS LONG AS I HAVE, MR. GREEN, YOU WILL UNCOVER THAT THERE IS COPIOUS ROOM FOR INTERPRETATION IN OUR STANDING ORDERS.
JVS
AUDIO
RESTAURANT

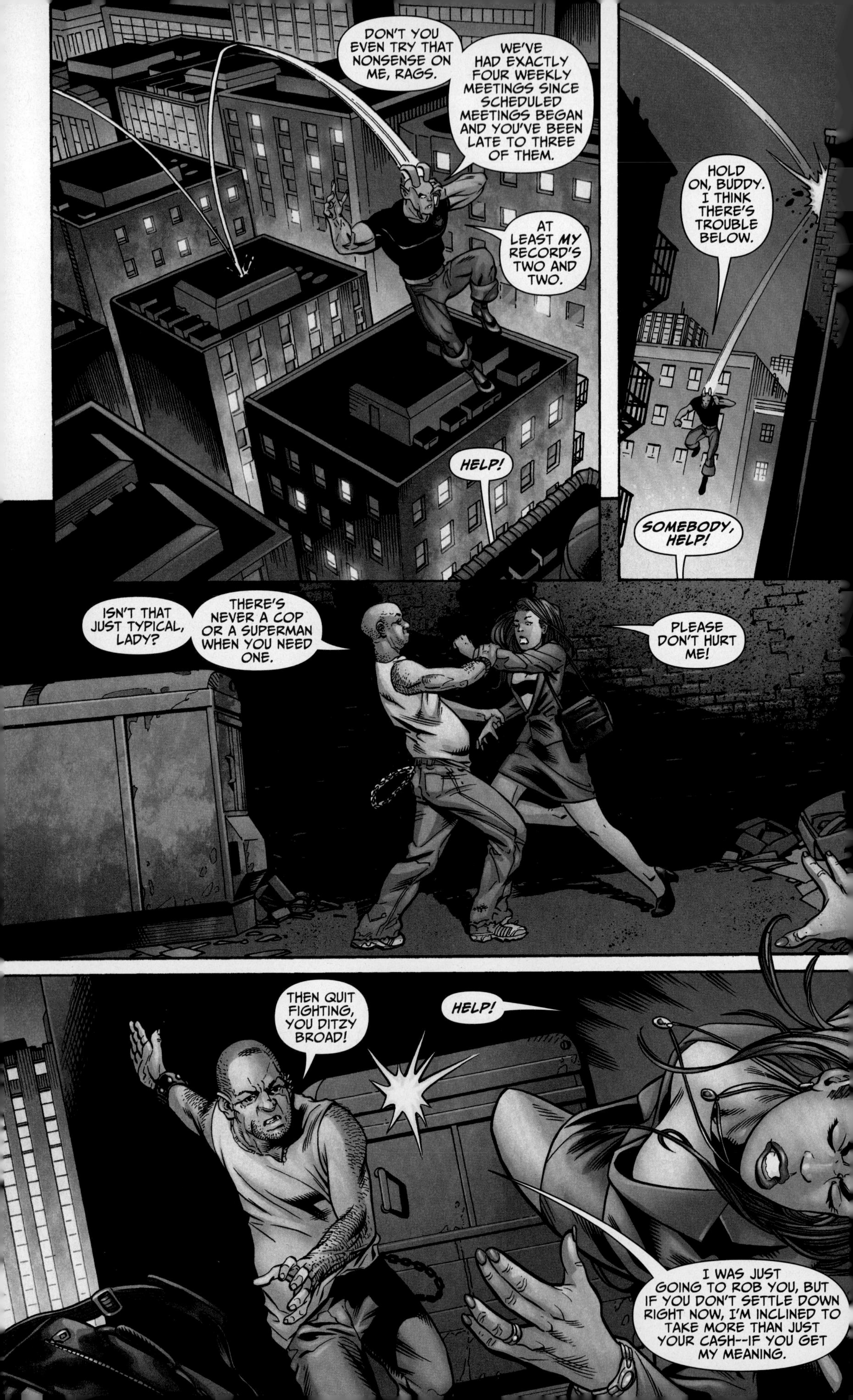

DON'T YOU EVEN TRY THAT NONSENSE ON ME, RAGS.
WE'VE HAD EXACTLY FOUR WEEKLY MEETINGS SINCE SCHEDULED MEETINGS BEGAN AND YOU'VE BEEN LATE TO THREE OF THEM.
AT LEAST MY RECORD'S TWO AND TWO.
HELP!
HOLD ON, BUDDY. I THINK THERE'S TROUBLE BELOW.
SOMEBODY, HELP!
ISN'T THAT JUST TYPICAL, LADY?
THERE'S NEVER A COP OR A SUPERMAN WHEN YOU NEED ONE.
PLEASE DON'T HURT ME!
THEN QUIT FIGHTING, YOU DITZY BROAD!
HELP!
I WAS JUST GOING TO ROB YOU, BUT IF YOU DON'T SETTLE DOWN RIGHT NOW, I'M INCLINED TO TAKE MORE THAN JUST YOUR CASH--IF YOU GET MY MEANING.

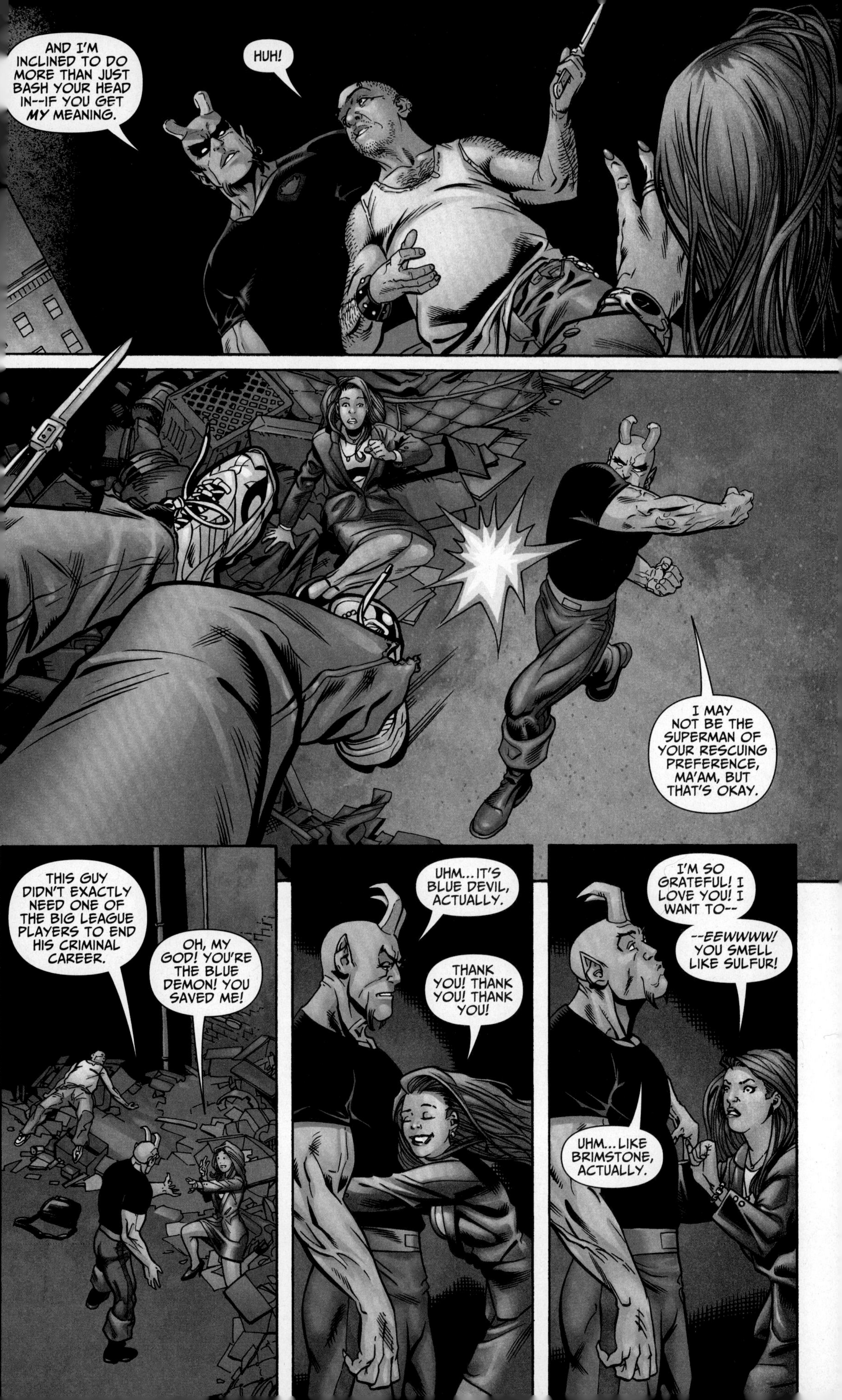
AND I'M INCLINED TO DO MORE THAN JUST BASH YOUR HEAD IN--IF YOU GET MY MEANING.
HUH!
I MAY NOT BE THE SUPERMAN OF YOUR RESCUING PREFERENCE, MA'AM, BUT THAT'S OKAY.
THIS GUY DIDN'T EXACTLY NEED ONE OF THE BIG LEAGUE PLAYERS TO END HIS CRIMINAL CAREER.
OH, MY GOD! YOU'RE THE BLUE DEMON! YOU SAVED ME!
UHM... IT'S BLUE DEVIL, ACTUALLY.
THANK YOU! THANK YOU! THANK YOU!
I'M SO GRATEFUL! I LOVE YOU! I WANT TO--
--EEWWWW! YOU SMELL LIKE SULFUR!
UHM... LIKE BRIMSTONE, ACTUALLY.

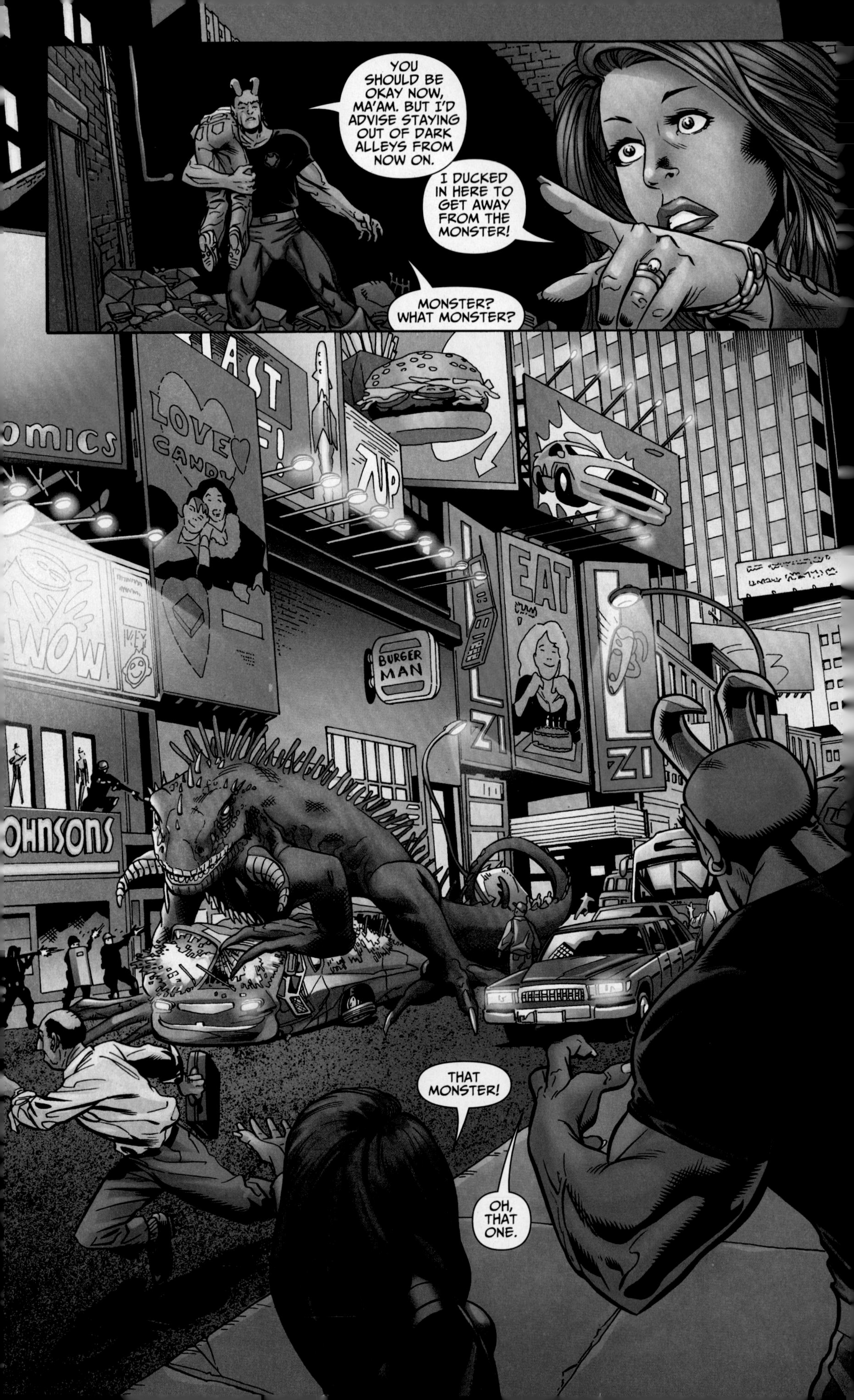
YOU SHOULD BE OKAY NOW, MA'AM. BUT I'D ADVISE STAYING OUT OF DARK ALLEYS FROM NOW ON.
I DUCKED IN HERE TO GET AWAY FROM THE MONSTER!
MONSTER? WHAT MONSTER?
THAT MONSTER!
OH, THAT ONE.

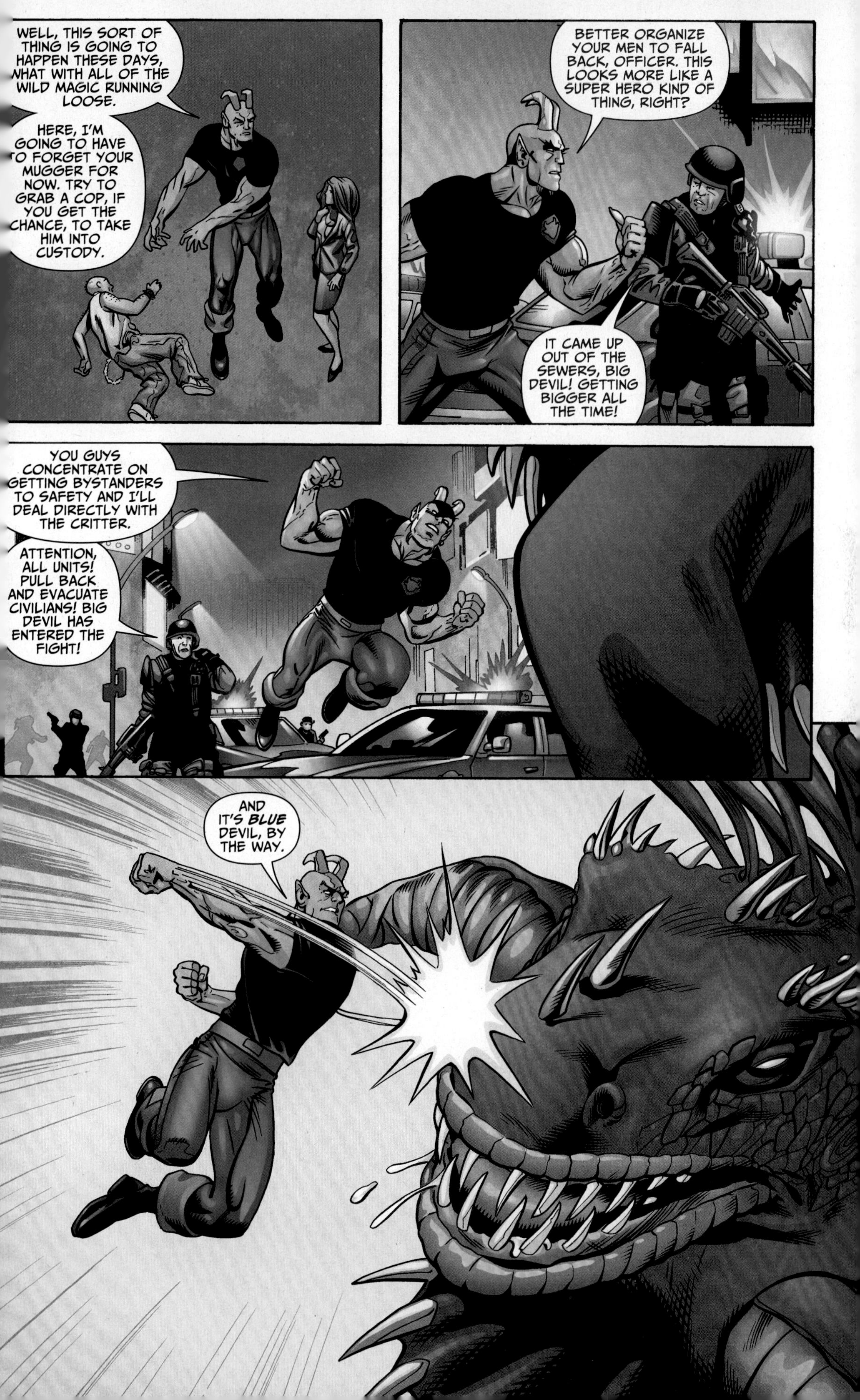
WELL, THIS SORT OF THING IS GOING TO HAPPEN THESE DAYS, WHAT WITH ALL OF THE WILD MAGIC RUNNING LOOSE.
HERE, I'M GOING TO HAVE TO FORGET YOUR MUGGER FOR NOW. TRY TO GRAB A COP, IF YOU GET THE CHANCE, TO TAKE HIM INTO CUSTODY.
BETTER ORGANIZE YOUR MEN TO FALL BACK, OFFICER. THIS LOOKS MORE LIKE A SUPER HERO KIND OF THING, RIGHT?
IT CAME UP OUT OF THE SEWERS, BIG DEVIL! GETTING BIGGER ALL THE TIME!
YOU GUYS CONCENTRATE ON GETTING BYSTANDERS TO SAFETY AND I'LL DEAL DIRECTLY WITH THE CRITTER.
ATTENTION, ALL UNITS! PULL BACK AND EVACUATE CIVILIANS! BIG DEVIL HAS ENTERED THE FIGHT!
AND IT'S *BLUE* DEVIL, BY THE WAY.

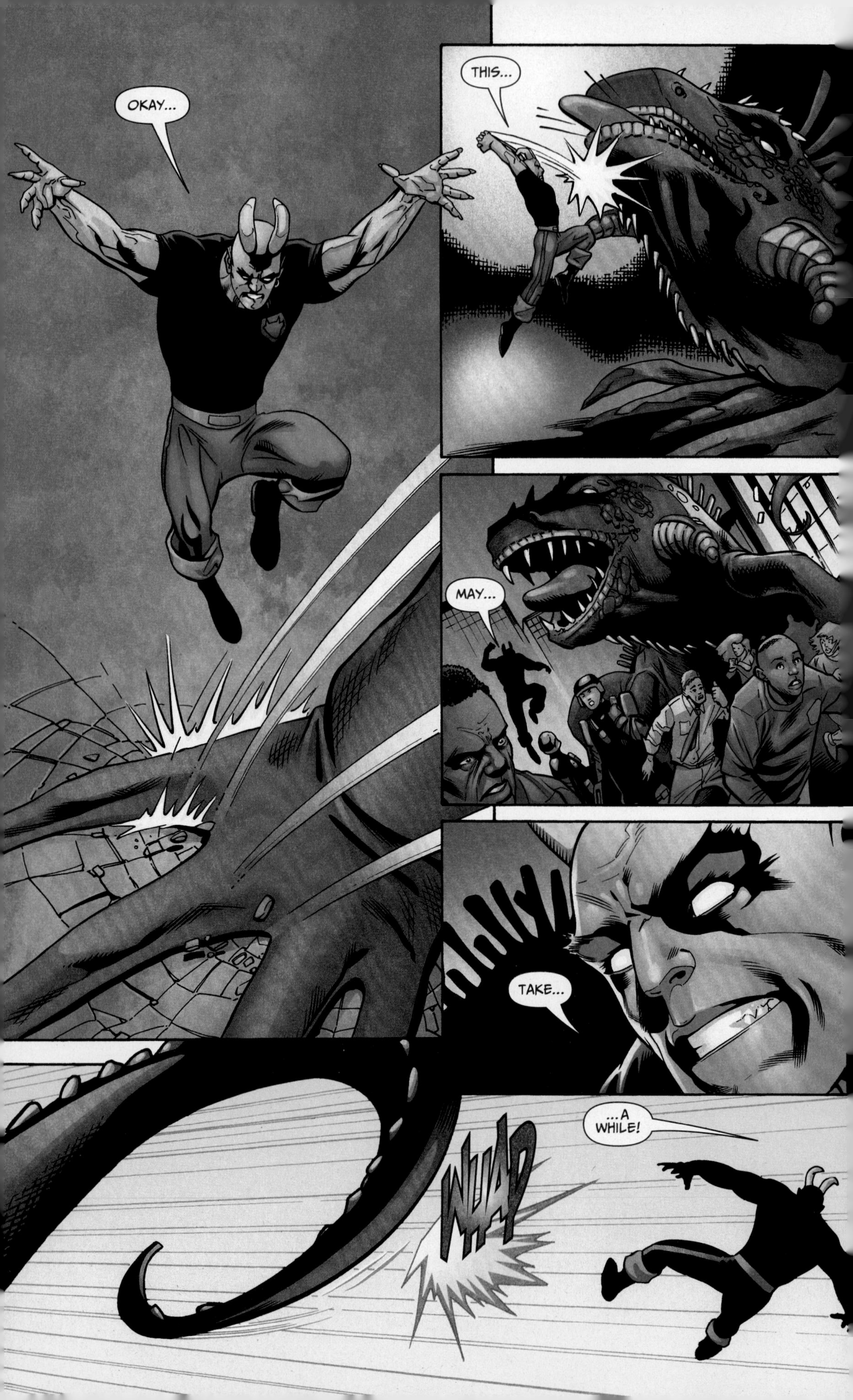
OKAY...
THIS...
MAY...
TAKE...
WHAP
...A WHILE!

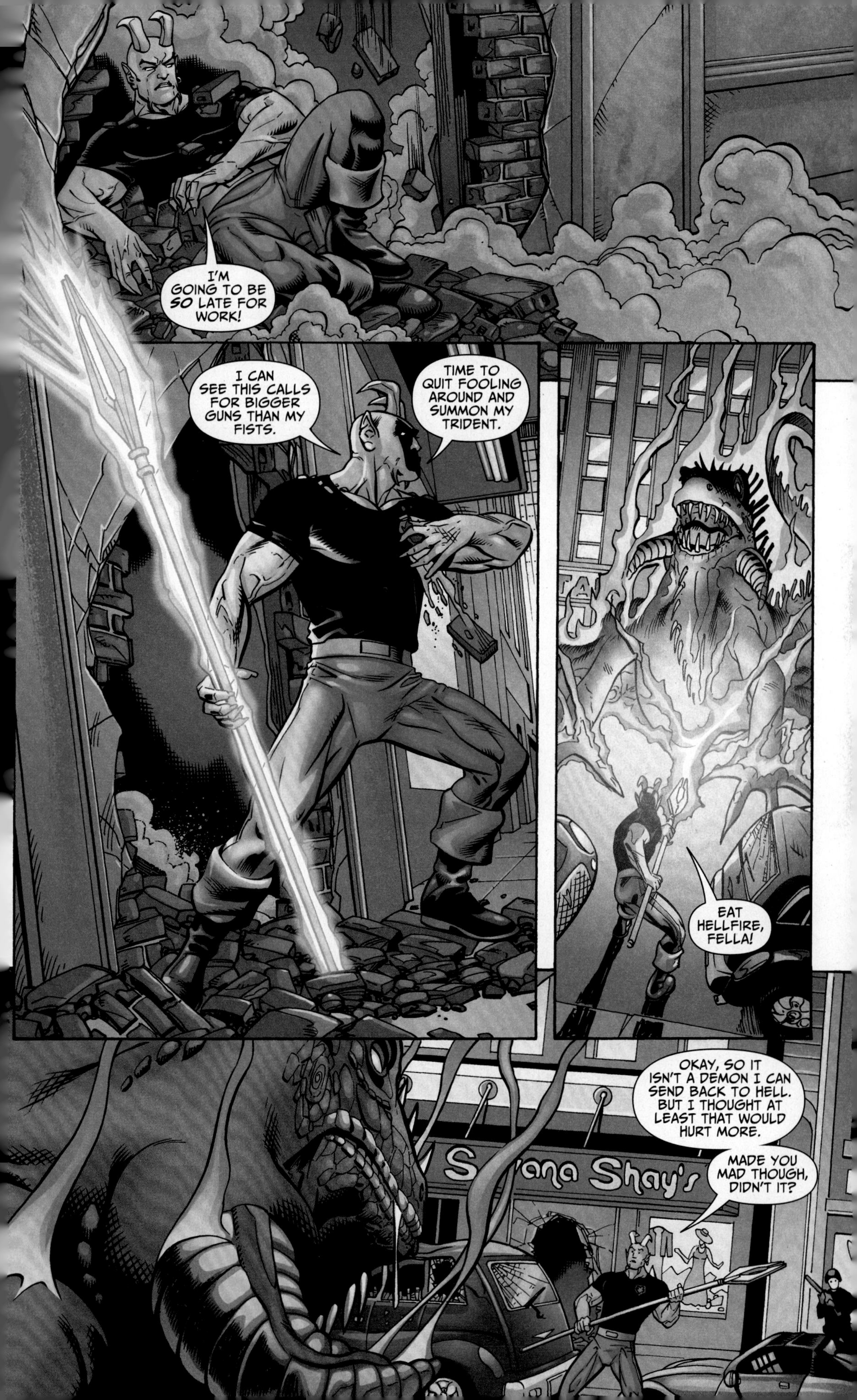
I'M GOING TO BE SO LATE FOR WORK!
I CAN SEE THIS CALLS FOR BIGGER GUNS THAN MY FISTS.
TIME TO QUIT FOOLING AROUND AND SUMMON MY TRIDENT.
EAT HELLFIRE, FELLA!
OKAY, SO IT ISN'T A DEMON I CAN SEND BACK TO HELL. BUT I THOUGHT AT LEAST THAT WOULD HURT MORE.
MADE YOU MAD THOUGH, DIDN'T IT?

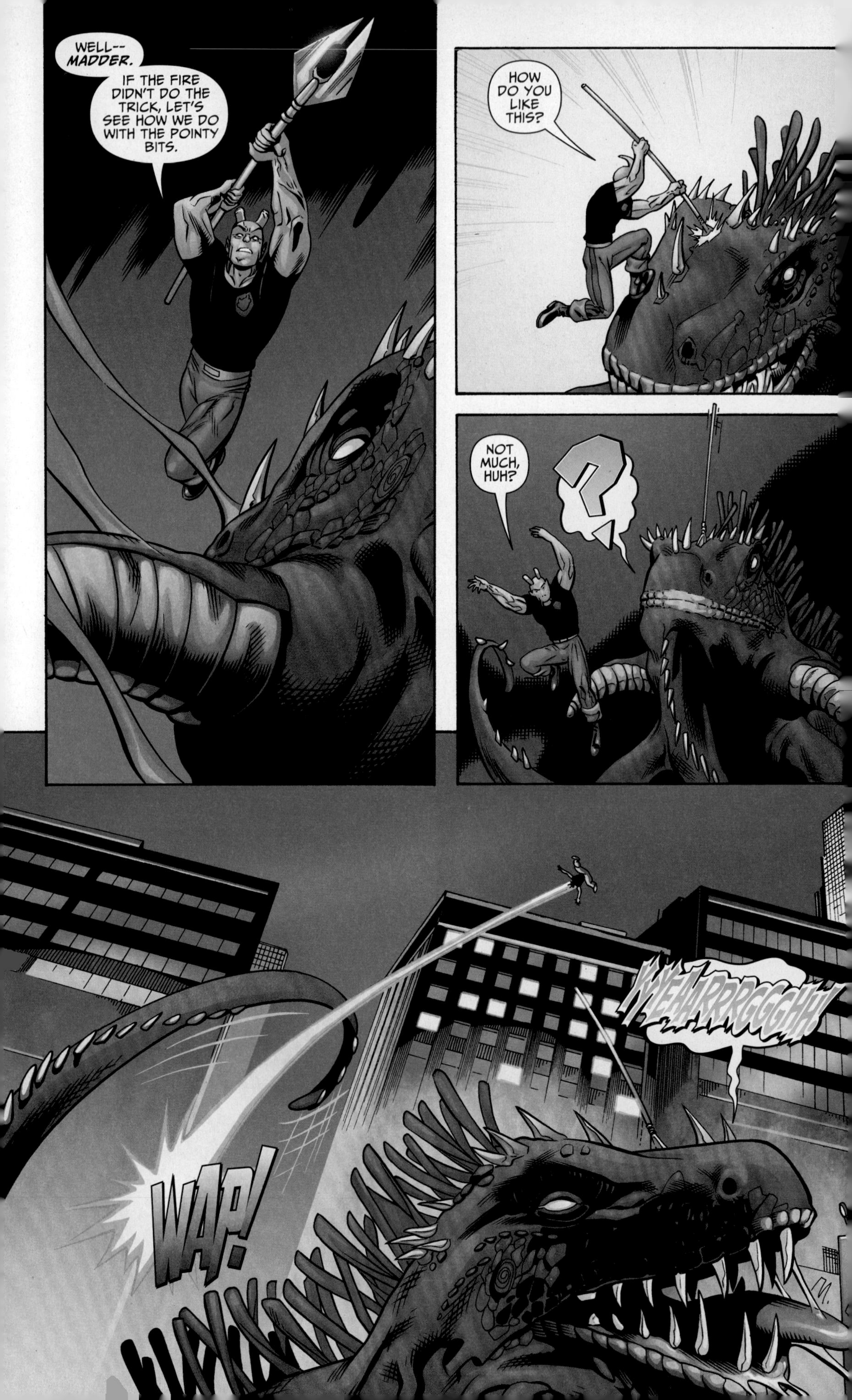
WELL--
MADDER.
IF THE FIRE DIDN'T DO THE TRICK, LET'S SEE HOW WE DO WITH THE POINTY BITS.
HOW DO YOU LIKE THIS?
NOT MUCH, HUH?
?
YYEAARRRGGGHH!
WAP!

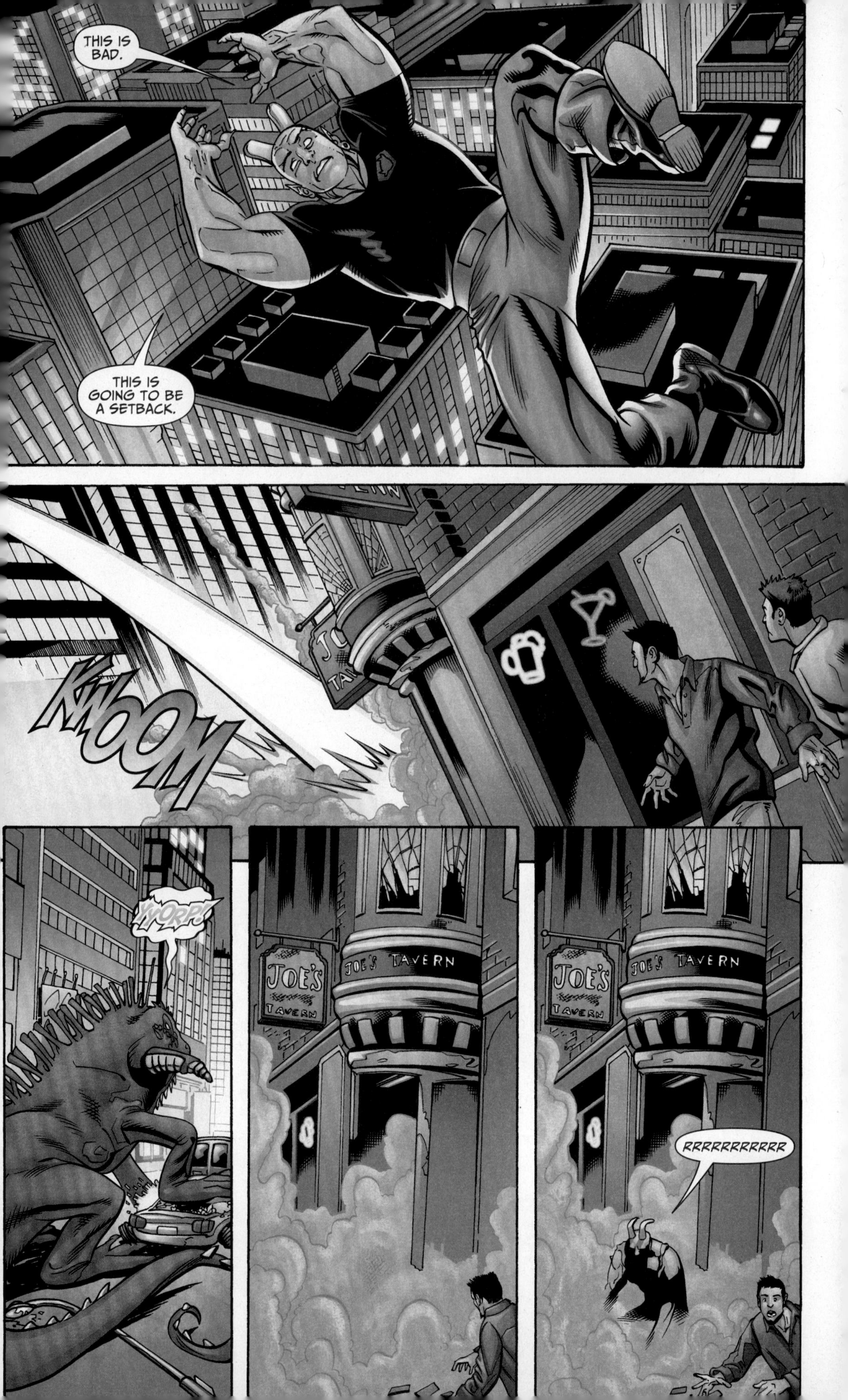
THIS IS BAD.
THIS IS GOING TO BE A SETBACK.
KWOOM
JOE'S TAVERN
YYORP!
JOE'S TAVERN
JOE'S TAVERN
JOE'S TAVERN
JOE'S TAVERN
RRRRRRRRRRR

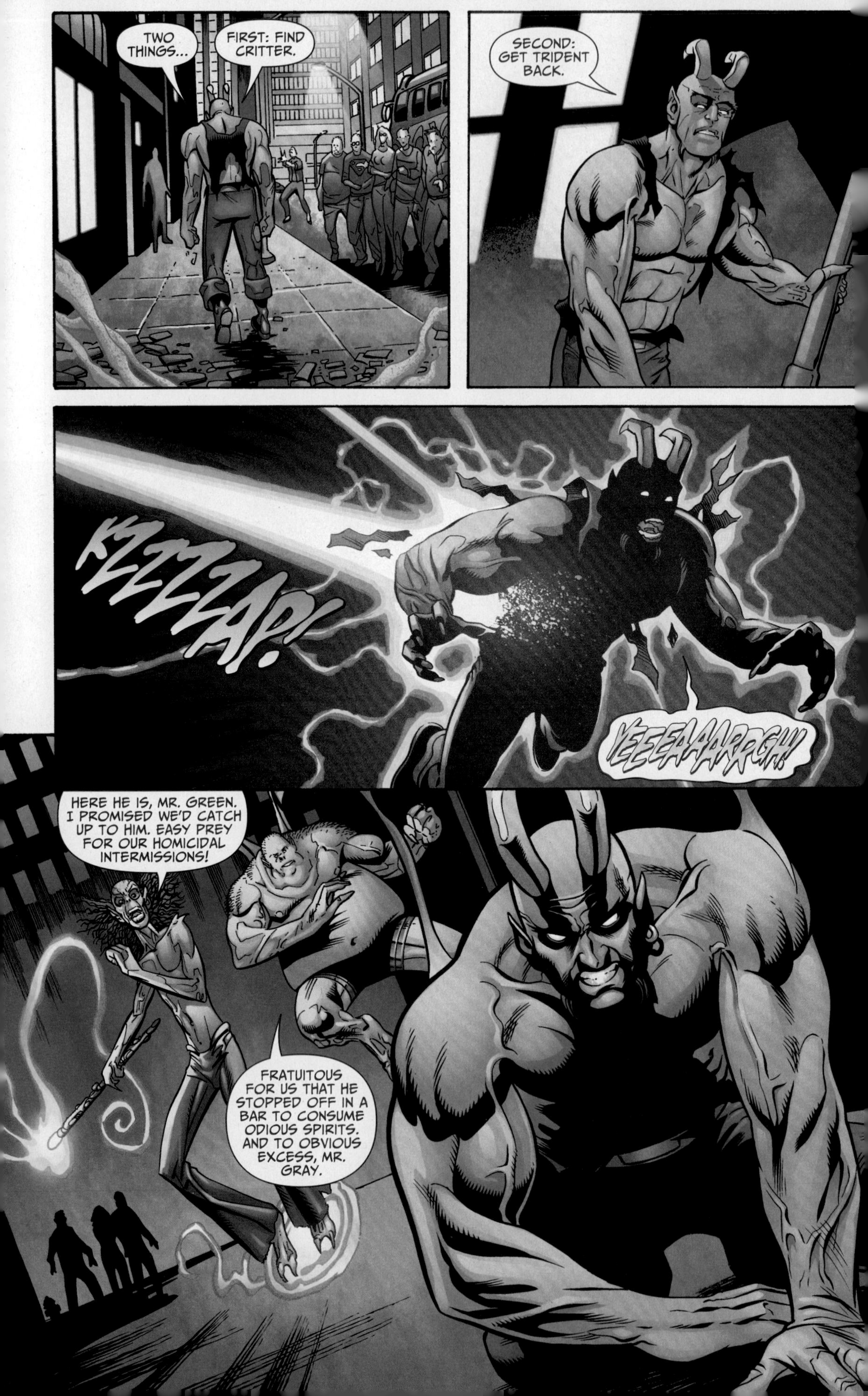
TWO THINGS...
FIRST: FIND CRITTER.
SECOND: GET TRIDENT BACK.
KZZZZAP!
YEEEAAARRGH!
HERE HE IS, MR. GREEN. I PROMISED WE'D CATCH UP TO HIM. EASY PREY FOR OUR HOMICIDAL INTERMISSIONS!
FRATUITOUS FOR US THAT HE STOPPED OFF IN A BAR TO CONSUME ODIOUS SPIRITS. AND TO OBVIOUS EXCESS, MR. GRAY.

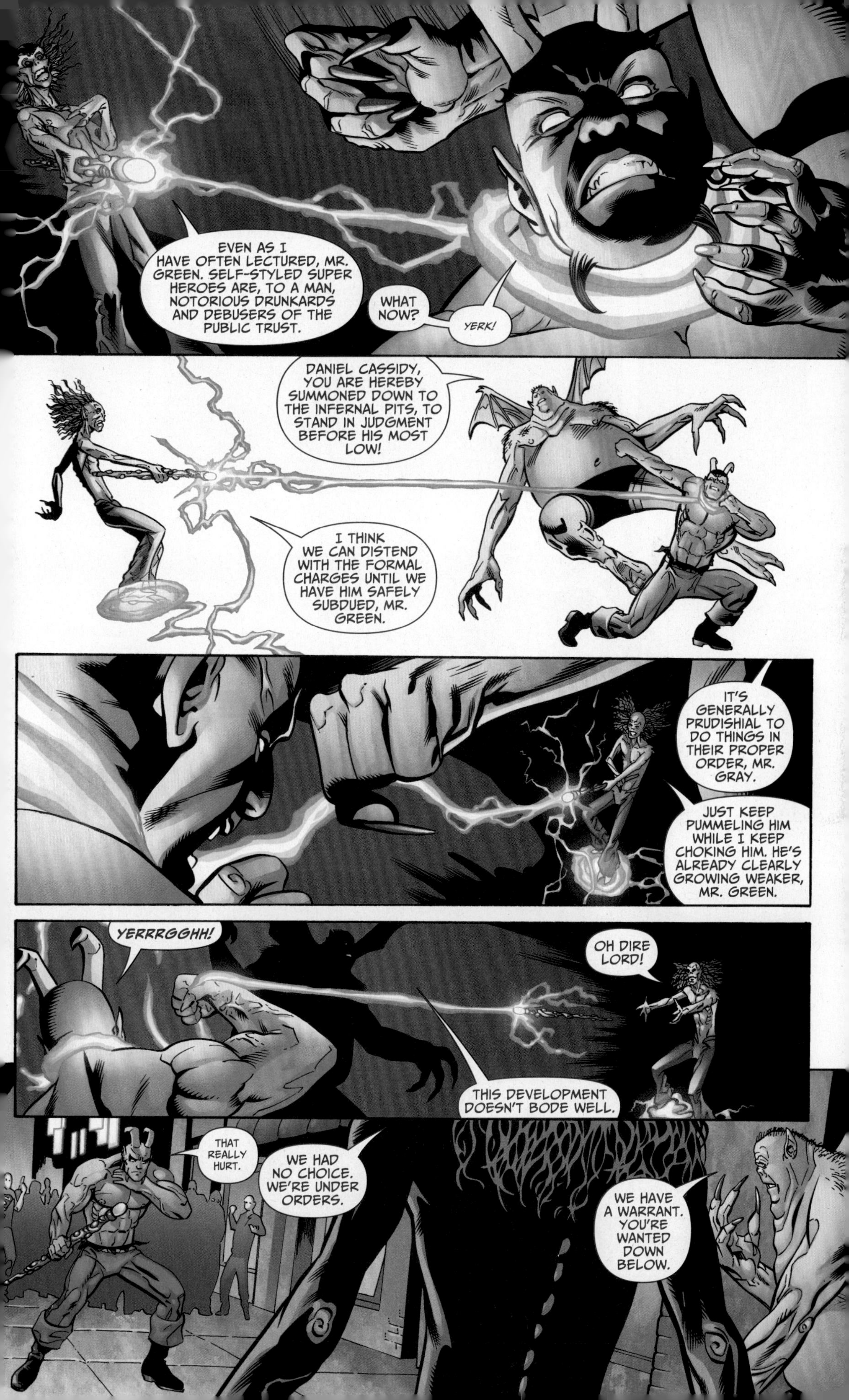
EVEN AS I HAVE OFTEN LECTURED, MR. GREEN. SELF-STYLED SUPER HEROES ARE, TO A MAN, NOTORIOUS DRUNKARDS AND DEBUSERS OF THE PUBLIC TRUST.
WHAT NOW?
YERK!
DANIEL CASSIDY, YOU ARE HEREBY SUMMONED DOWN TO THE INFERNAL PITS, TO STAND IN JUDGMENT BEFORE HIS MOST LOW!
I THINK WE CAN DISTEND WITH THE FORMAL CHARGES UNTIL WE HAVE HIM SAFELY SUBDUED, MR. GREEN.
IT'S GENERALLY PRUDISHIAL TO DO THINGS IN THEIR PROPER ORDER, MR. GRAY.
JUST KEEP PUMMELING HIM WHILE I KEEP CHOKING HIM. HE'S ALREADY CLEARLY GROWING WEAKER, MR. GREEN.
YERRRGGHH!
OH DIRE LORD!
THIS DEVELOPMENT DOESN'T BODE WELL.
THAT REALLY HURT.
WE HAD NO CHOICE. WE'RE UNDER ORDERS.
WE HAVE A WARRANT. YOU'RE WANTED DOWN BELOW.

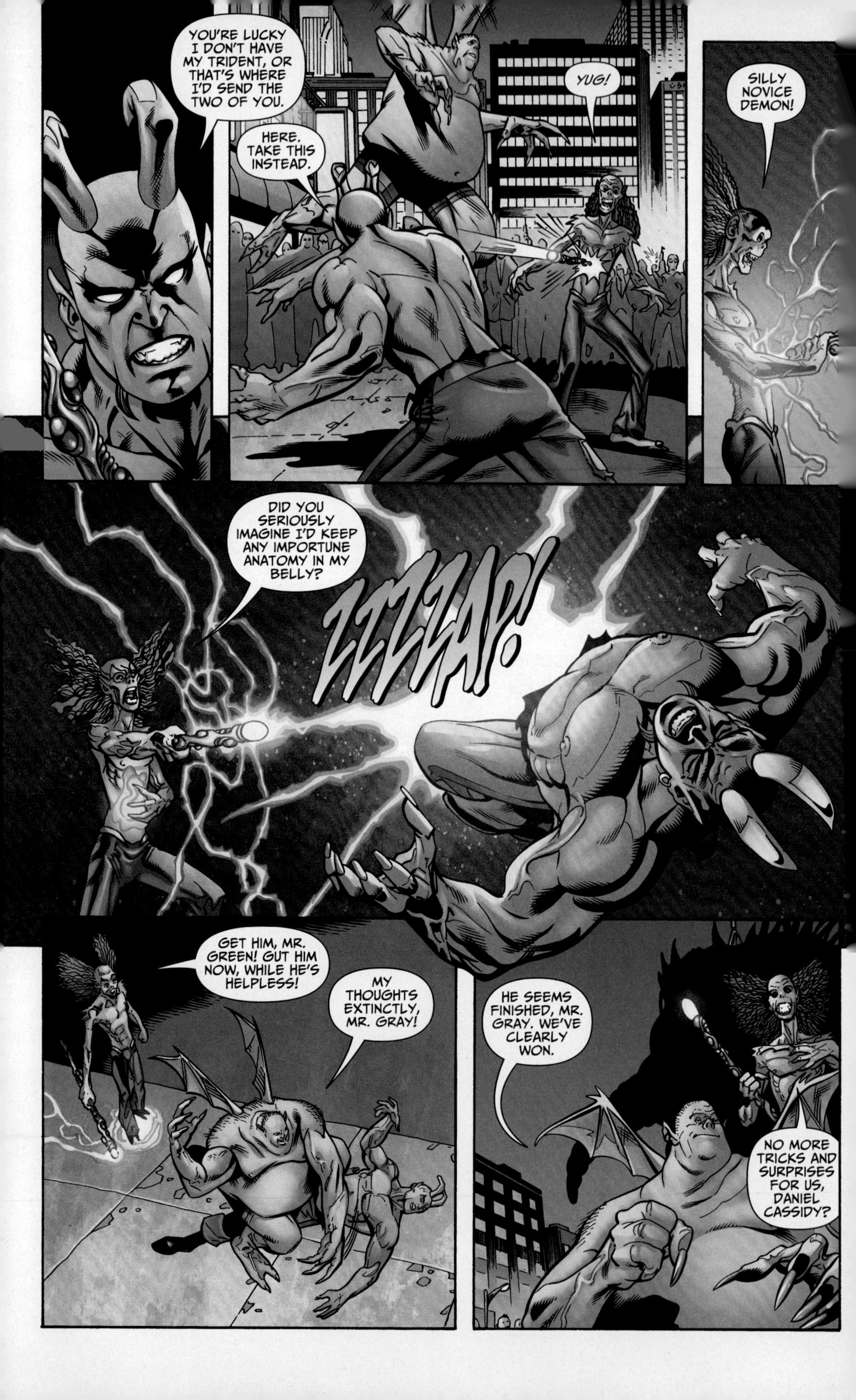
YOU'RE LUCKY I DON'T HAVE MY TRIDENT, OR THAT'S WHERE I'D SEND THE TWO OF YOU.
HERE. TAKE THIS INSTEAD.
YUG!
SILLY NOVICE DEMON!
DID YOU SERIOUSLY IMAGINE I'D KEEP ANY IMPORTUNE ANATOMY IN MY BELLY?
ZZZZAP!
GET HIM, MR. GREEN! GUT HIM NOW, WHILE HE'S HELPLESS!
MY THOUGHTS EXTINCTLY, MR. GRAY!
HE SEEMS FINISHED, MR. GRAY. WE'VE CLEARLY WON.
NO MORE TRICKS AND SURPRISES FOR US, DANIEL CASSIDY?

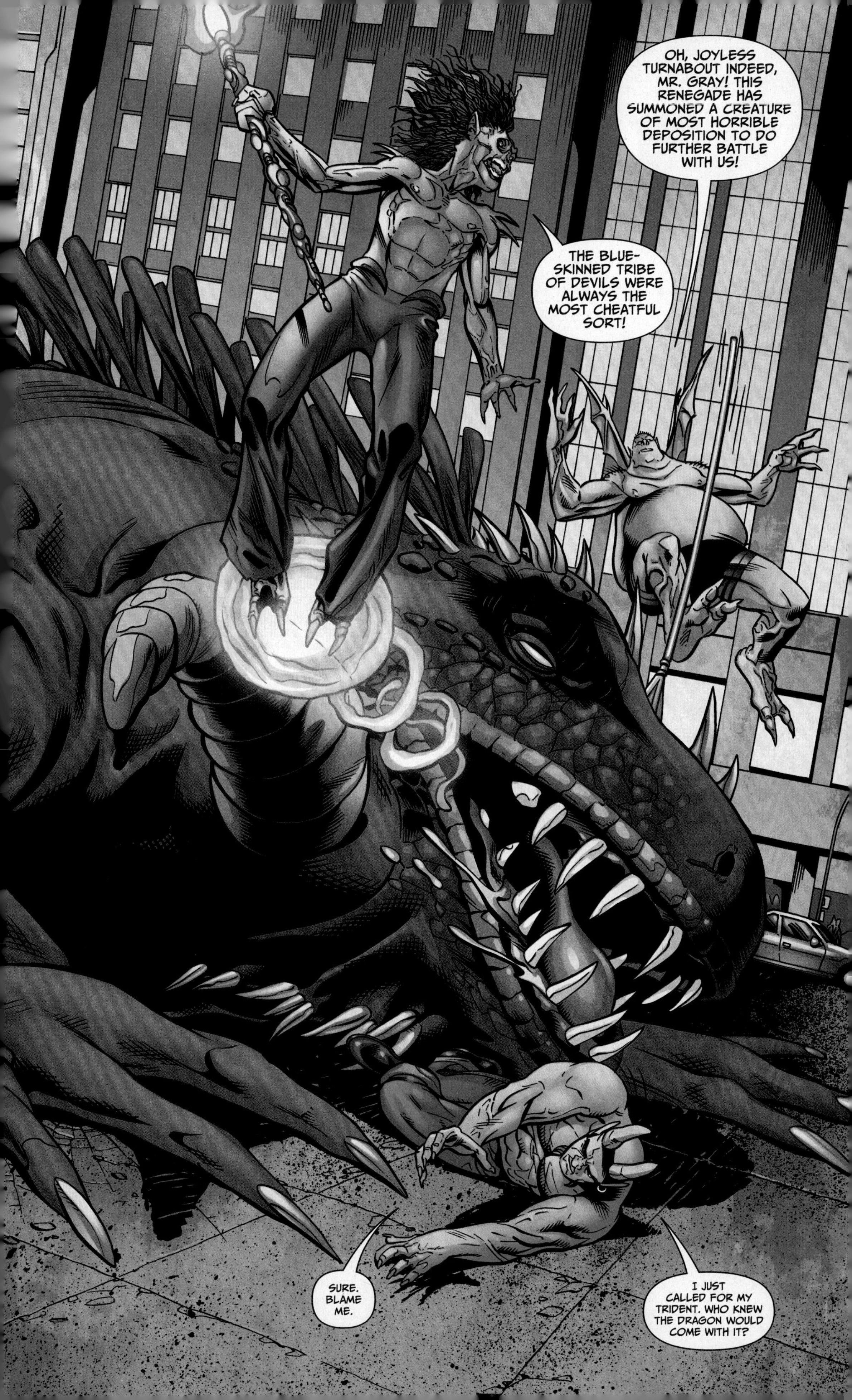
OH, JOYLESS TURNABOUT INDEED, MR. GRAY! THIS RENEGADE HAS SUMMONED A CREATURE OF MOST HORRIBLE DEPOSITION TO DO FURTHER BATTLE WITH US!
THE BLUE-SKINNED TRIBE OF DEVILS WERE ALWAYS THE MOST CHEATFUL SORT!
SURE. BLAME ME.
I JUST CALLED FOR MY TRIDENT. WHO KNEW THE DRAGON WOULD COME WITH IT?

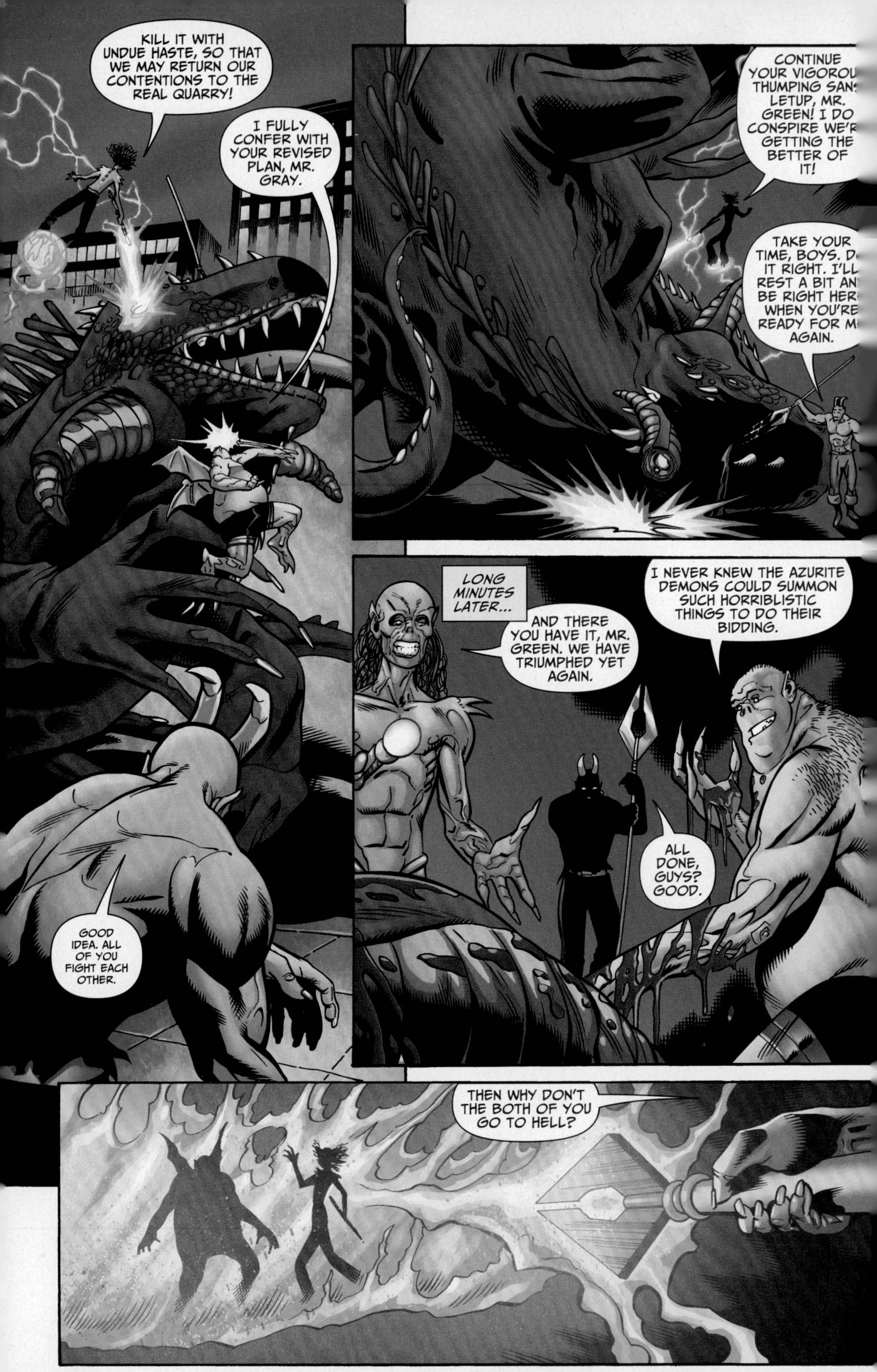
KILL IT WITH UNDUE HASTE, SO THAT WE MAY RETURN OUR CONTENTIONS TO THE REAL QUARRY!
I FULLY CONFER WITH YOUR REVISED PLAN, MR. GRAY.
GOOD IDEA. ALL OF YOU FIGHT EACH OTHER.
CONTINUE YOUR VIGOROU THUMPING SANS LETUP, MR. GREEN! I DO CONSPIRE WE'R GETTING THE BETTER OF IT!
TAKE YOUR TIME, BOYS. D IT RIGHT. I'LL REST A BIT AN BE RIGHT HER WHEN YOU'RE READY FOR M AGAIN.
LONG MINUTES LATER...
AND THERE YOU HAVE IT, MR. GREEN. WE HAVE TRIUMPHED YET AGAIN.
I NEVER KNEW THE AZURITE DEMONS COULD SUMMON SUCH HORRIBLISTIC THINGS TO DO THEIR BIDDING.
ALL DONE, GUYS? GOOD.
THEN WHY DON'T THE BOTH OF YOU GO TO HELL?

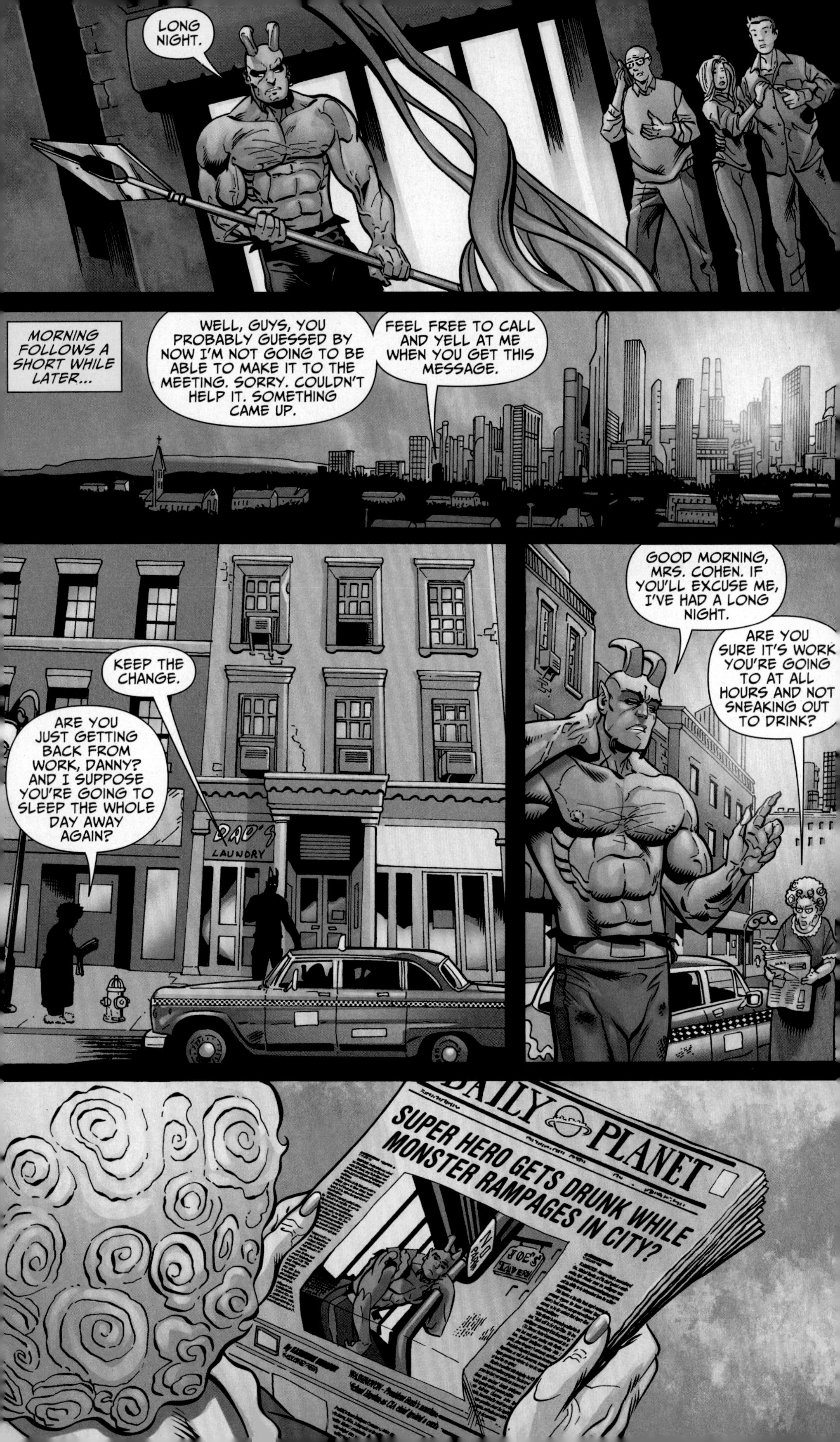
LONG NIGHT.
MORNING FOLLOWS A SHORT WHILE LATER...
WELL, GUYS, YOU PROBABLY GUESSED BY NOW I'M NOT GOING TO BE ABLE TO MAKE IT TO THE MEETING. SORRY. COULDN'T HELP IT. SOMETHING CAME UP.
FEEL FREE TO CALL AND YELL AT ME WHEN YOU GET THIS MESSAGE.
KEEP THE CHANGE.
ARE YOU JUST GETTING BACK FROM WORK, DANNY? AND I SUPPOSE YOU'RE GOING TO SLEEP THE WHOLE DAY AWAY AGAIN?
LAUNDRY
GOOD MORNING, MRS. COHEN. IF YOU'LL EXCUSE ME, I'VE HAD A LONG NIGHT.
ARE YOU SURE IT'S WORK YOU'RE GOING TO AT ALL HOURS AND NOT SNEAKING OUT TO DRINK?
DAILY PLANET
SUPER HERO GETS DRUNK WHILE MONSTER RAMPAGES IN CITY?
JOE'S

THE DEMON TRIPTYCH: PART 1
THREE LAWS SAFE

cover art by **TOM DERENICK** *and* **WAYNE FAUCHER**
colored by **MIKE ATIYEH**

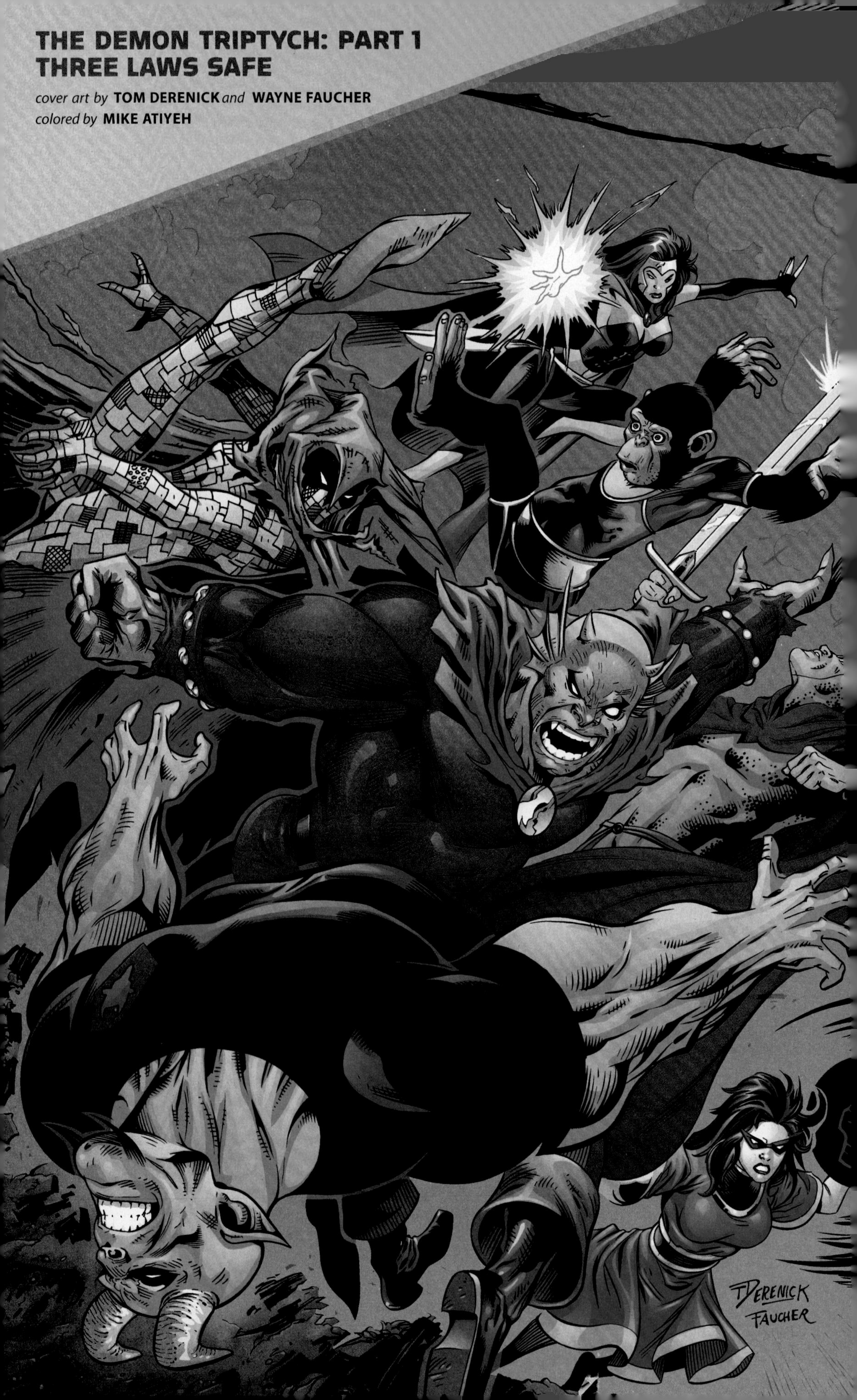
T DERENICK
FAUCHER

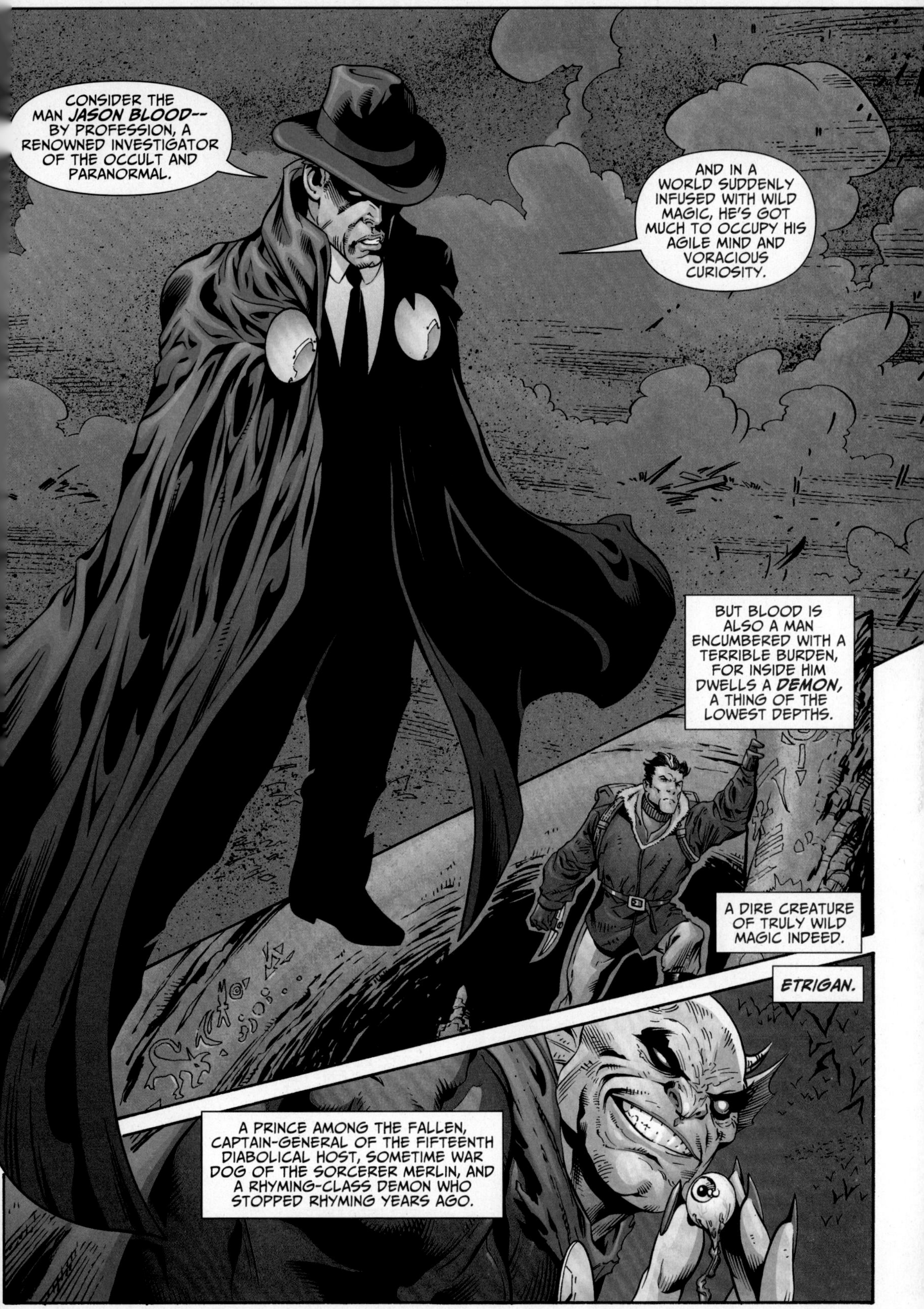
CONSIDER THE MAN JASON BLOOD-- BY PROFESSION, A RENOWNED INVESTIGATOR OF THE OCCULT AND PARANORMAL.
AND IN A WORLD SUDDENLY INFUSED WITH WILD MAGIC, HE'S GOT MUCH TO OCCUPY HIS AGILE MIND AND VORACIOUS CURIOSITY.
BUT BLOOD IS ALSO A MAN ENCUMBERED WITH A TERRIBLE BURDEN, FOR INSIDE HIM DWELLS A DEMON, A THING OF THE LOWEST DEPTHS.
A DIRE CREATURE OF TRULY WILD MAGIC INDEED.
ETRIGAN.
A PRINCE AMONG THE FALLEN, CAPTAIN-GENERAL OF THE FIFTEENTH DIABOLICAL HOST, SOMETIME WAR DOG OF THE SORCERER MERLIN, AND A RHYMING-CLASS DEMON WHO STOPPED RHYMING YEARS AGO.

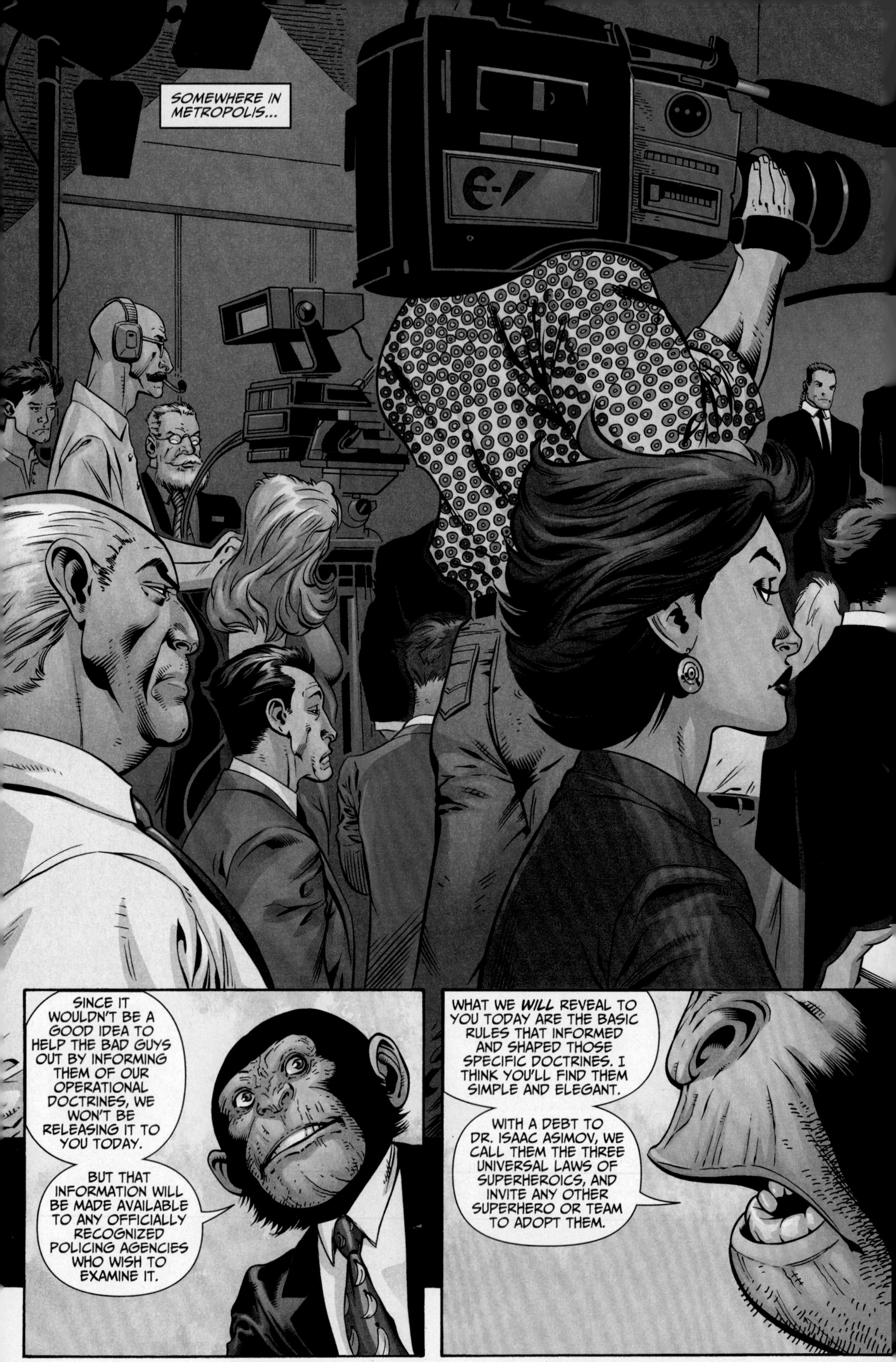

SOMEWHERE IN METROPOLIS...
SINCE IT WOULDN'T BE A GOOD IDEA TO HELP THE BAD GUYS OUT BY INFORMING THEM OF OUR OPERATIONAL DOCTRINES, WE WON'T BE RELEASING IT TO YOU TODAY.
BUT THAT INFORMATION WILL BE MADE AVAILABLE TO ANY OFFICIALLY RECOGNIZED POLICING AGENCIES WHO WISH TO EXAMINE IT.
WHAT WE *WILL* REVEAL TO YOU TODAY ARE THE BASIC RULES THAT INFORMED AND SHAPED THOSE SPECIFIC DOCTRINES. I THINK YOU'LL FIND THEM SIMPLE AND ELEGANT.
WITH A DEBT TO DR. ISAAC ASIMOV, WE CALL THEM THE THREE UNIVERSAL LAWS OF SUPERHEROICS, AND INVITE ANY OTHER SUPERHERO OR TEAM TO ADOPT THEM.

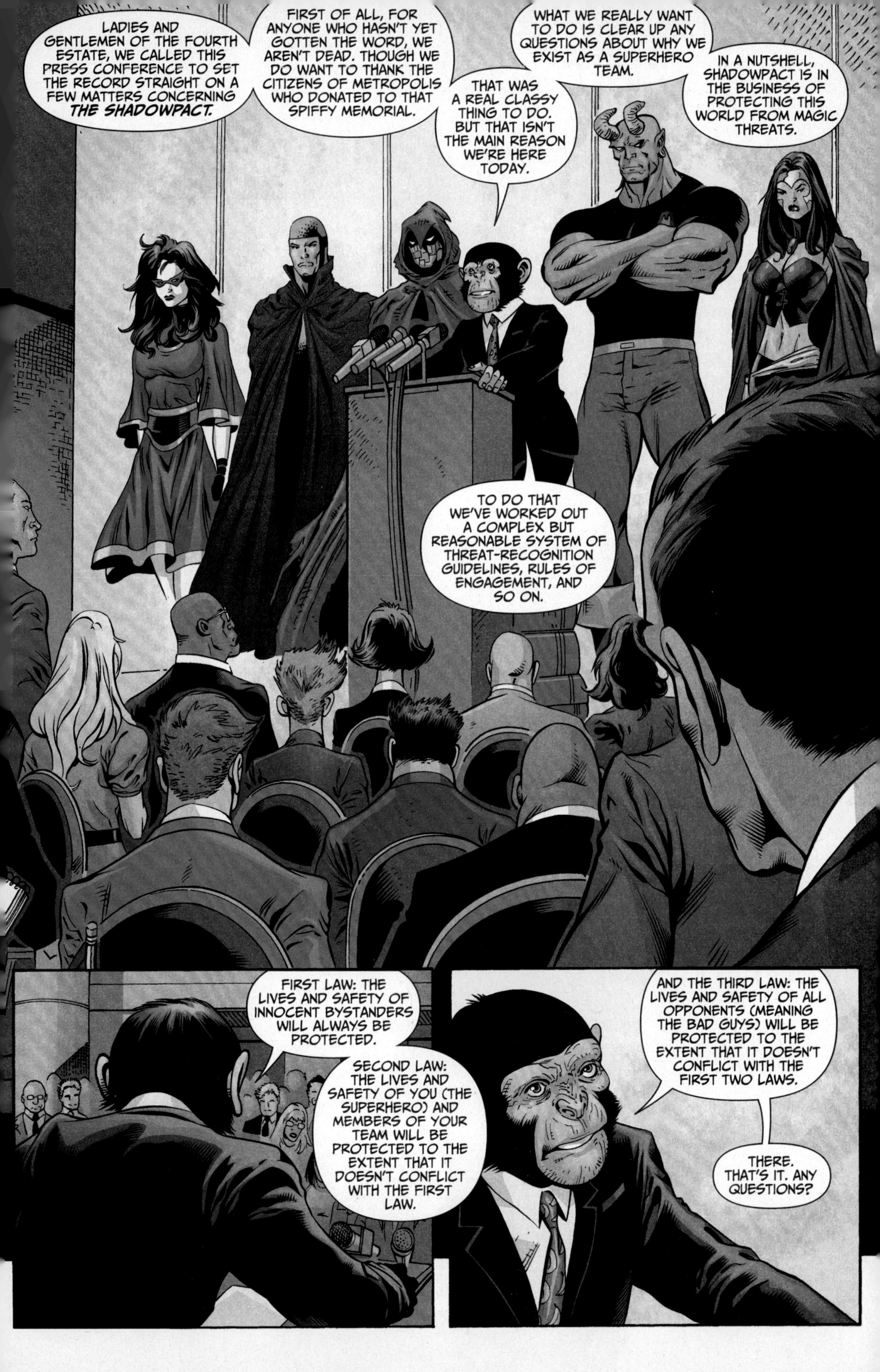
LADIES AND GENTLEMEN OF THE FOURTH ESTATE, WE CALLED THIS PRESS CONFERENCE TO SET THE RECORD STRAIGHT ON A FEW MATTERS CONCERNING *THE SHADOWPACT.*
FIRST OF ALL, FOR ANYONE WHO HASN'T YET GOTTEN THE WORD, WE AREN'T DEAD. THOUGH WE DO WANT TO THANK THE CITIZENS OF METROPOLIS WHO DONATED TO THAT SPIFFY MEMORIAL.
THAT WAS A REAL CLASSY THING TO DO. BUT THAT ISN'T THE MAIN REASON WE'RE HERE TODAY.
WHAT WE REALLY WANT TO DO IS CLEAR UP ANY QUESTIONS ABOUT WHY WE EXIST AS A SUPERHERO TEAM.
IN A NUTSHELL, SHADOWPACT IS IN THE BUSINESS OF PROTECTING THIS WORLD FROM MAGIC THREATS.
TO DO THAT WE'VE WORKED OUT A COMPLEX BUT REASONABLE SYSTEM OF THREAT-RECOGNITION GUIDELINES, RULES OF ENGAGEMENT, AND SO ON.
FIRST LAW: THE LIVES AND SAFETY OF INNOCENT BYSTANDERS WILL ALWAYS BE PROTECTED.
SECOND LAW: THE LIVES AND SAFETY OF YOU (THE SUPERHERO) AND MEMBERS OF YOUR TEAM WILL BE PROTECTED TO THE EXTENT THAT IT DOESN'T CONFLICT WITH THE FIRST LAW.
AND THE THIRD LAW: THE LIVES AND SAFETY OF ALL OPPONENTS (MEANING THE BAD GUYS) WILL BE PROTECTED TO THE EXTENT THAT IT DOESN'T CONFLICT WITH THE FIRST TWO LAWS.
THERE. THAT'S IT. ANY QUESTIONS?

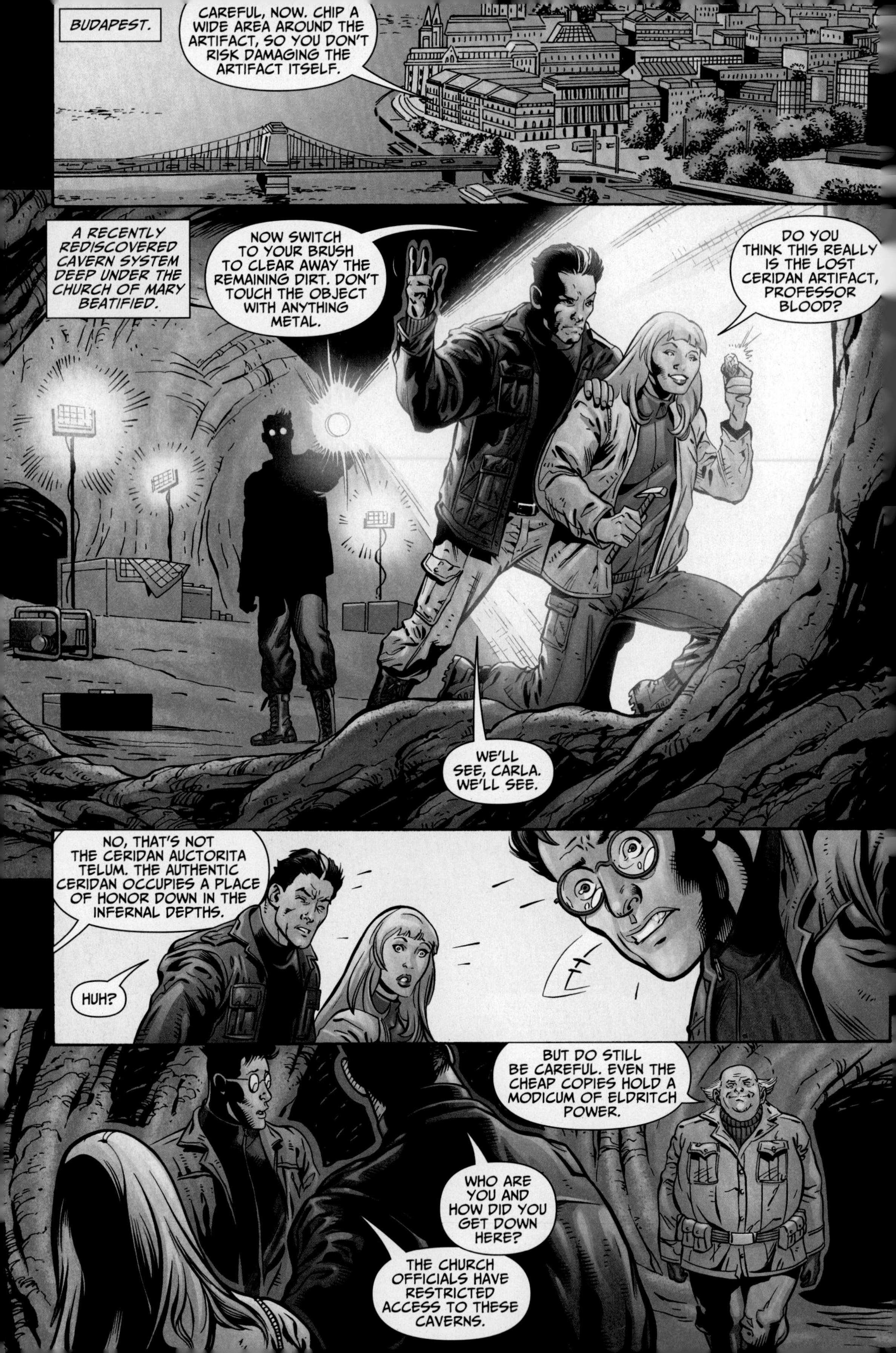
BUDAPEST.
CAREFUL, NOW. CHIP A WIDE AREA AROUND THE ARTIFACT, SO YOU DON'T RISK DAMAGING THE ARTIFACT ITSELF.
A RECENTLY REDISCOVERED CAVERN SYSTEM DEEP UNDER THE CHURCH OF MARY BEATIFIED.
NOW SWITCH TO YOUR BRUSH TO CLEAR AWAY THE REMAINING DIRT. DON'T TOUCH THE OBJECT WITH ANYTHING METAL.
DO YOU THINK THIS REALLY IS THE LOST CERIDAN ARTIFACT, PROFESSOR BLOOD?
WE'LL SEE, CARLA. WE'LL SEE.
NO, THAT'S NOT THE CERIDAN AUCTORITA TELUM. THE AUTHENTIC CERIDAN OCCUPIES A PLACE OF HONOR DOWN IN THE INFERNAL DEPTHS.
HUH?
BUT DO STILL BE CAREFUL. EVEN THE CHEAP COPIES HOLD A MODICUM OF ELDRITCH POWER.
WHO ARE YOU AND HOW DID YOU GET DOWN HERE?
THE CHURCH OFFICIALS HAVE RESTRICTED ACCESS TO THESE CAVERNS.

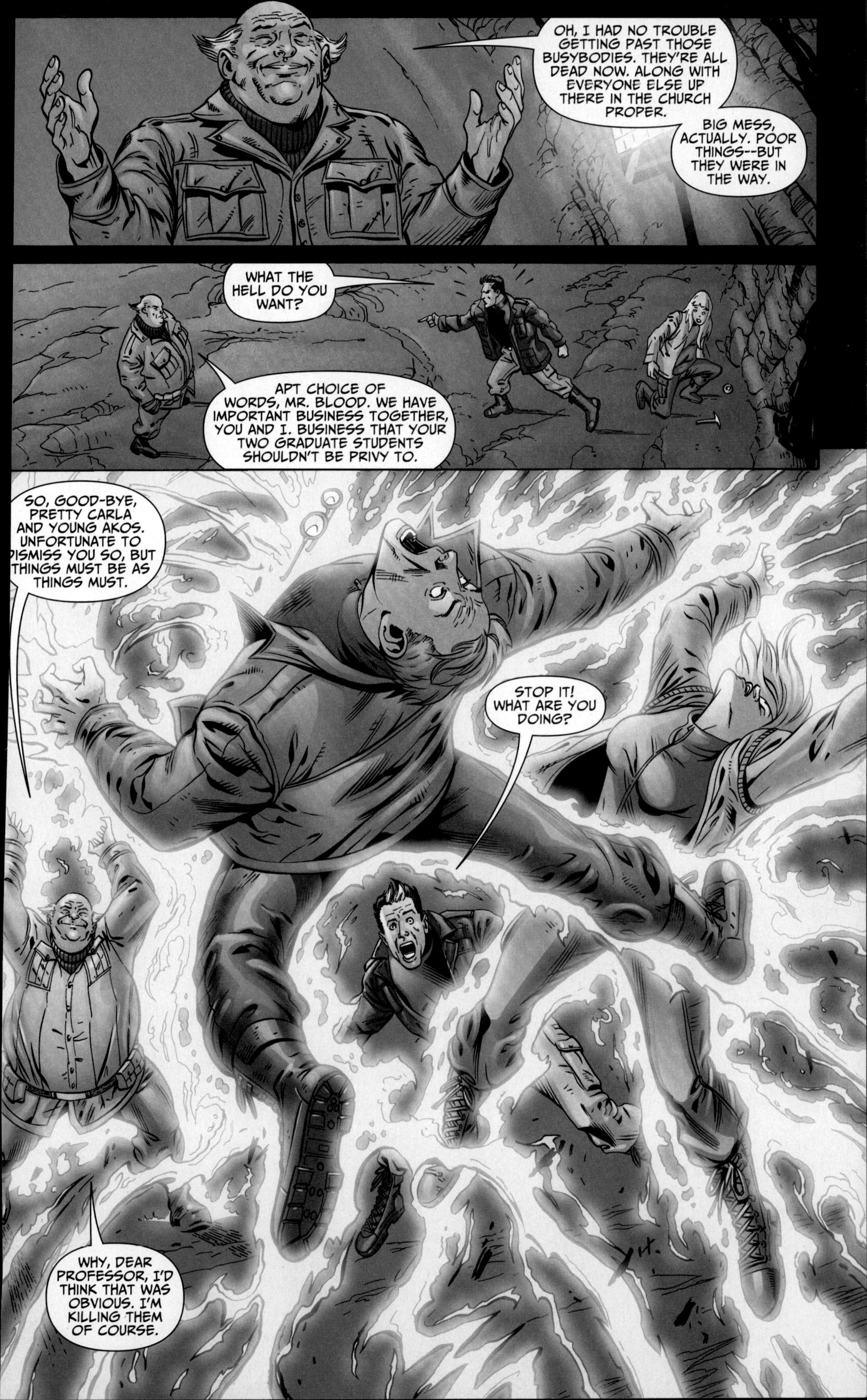
OH, I HAD NO TROUBLE GETTING PAST THOSE BUSYBODIES. THEY'RE ALL DEAD NOW. ALONG WITH EVERYONE ELSE UP THERE IN THE CHURCH PROPER.
BIG MESS, ACTUALLY. POOR THINGS--BUT THEY WERE IN THE WAY.
WHAT THE HELL DO YOU WANT?
APT CHOICE OF WORDS, MR. BLOOD. WE HAVE IMPORTANT BUSINESS TOGETHER, YOU AND I. BUSINESS THAT YOUR TWO GRADUATE STUDENTS SHOULDN'T BE PRIVY TO.
SO, GOOD-BYE, PRETTY CARLA AND YOUNG AKOS. UNFORTUNATE TO DISMISS YOU SO, BUT THINGS MUST BE AS THINGS MUST.
STOP IT! WHAT ARE YOU DOING?
WHY, DEAR PROFESSOR, I'D THINK THAT WAS OBVIOUS. I'M KILLING THEM OF COURSE.

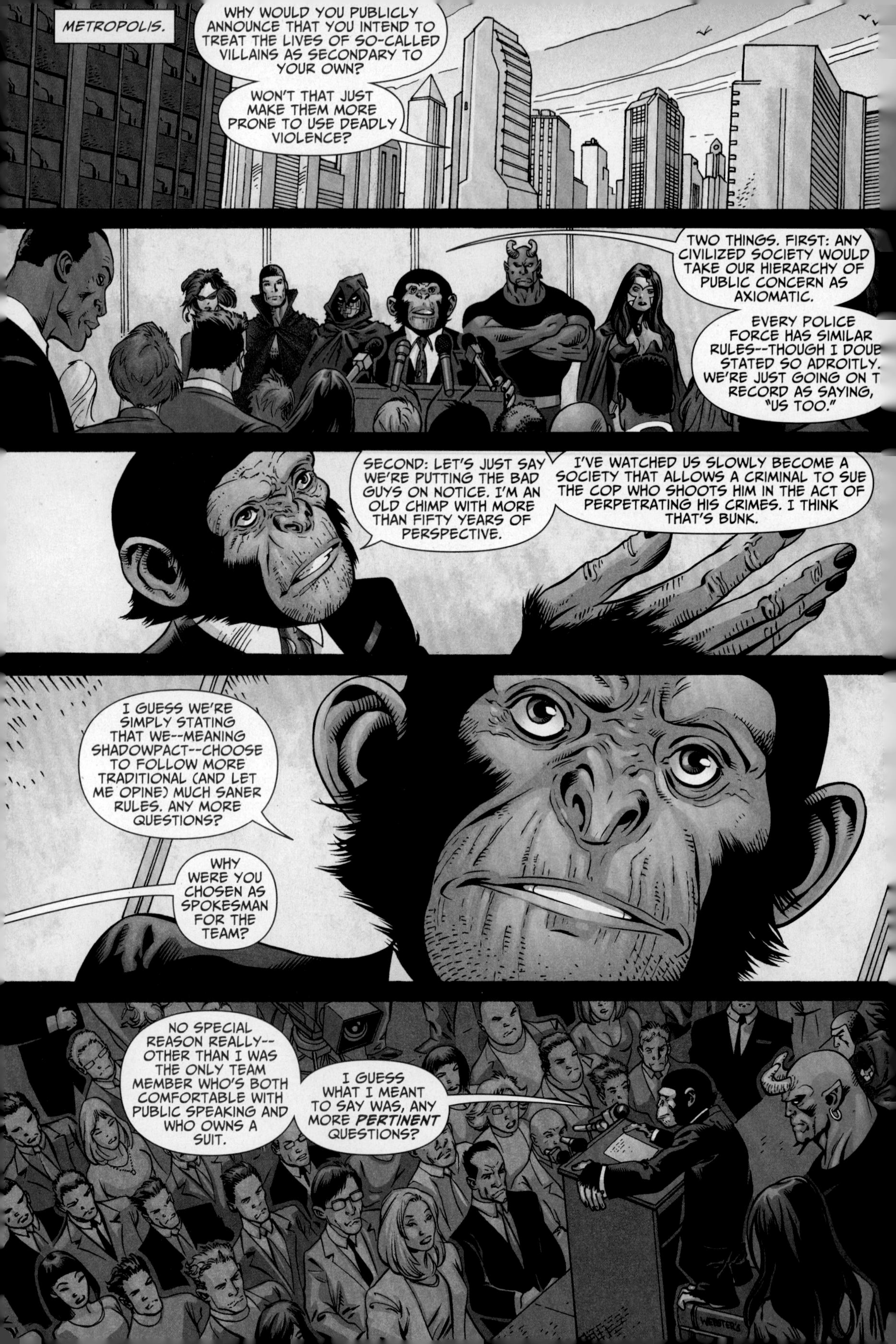

METROPOLIS.
WHY WOULD YOU PUBLICLY ANNOUNCE THAT YOU INTEND TO TREAT THE LIVES OF SO-CALLED VILLAINS AS SECONDARY TO YOUR OWN?
WON'T THAT JUST MAKE THEM MORE PRONE TO USE DEADLY VIOLENCE?
TWO THINGS. FIRST: ANY CIVILIZED SOCIETY WOULD TAKE OUR HIERARCHY OF PUBLIC CONCERN AS AXIOMATIC.
EVERY POLICE FORCE HAS SIMILAR RULES--THOUGH I DOUB STATED SO ADROITLY. WE'RE JUST GOING ON T RECORD AS SAYING, "US TOO."
SECOND: LET'S JUST SAY WE'RE PUTTING THE BAD GUYS ON NOTICE. I'M AN OLD CHIMP WITH MORE THAN FIFTY YEARS OF PERSPECTIVE.
I'VE WATCHED US SLOWLY BECOME A SOCIETY THAT ALLOWS A CRIMINAL TO SUE THE COP WHO SHOOTS HIM IN THE ACT OF PERPETRATING HIS CRIMES. I THINK THAT'S BUNK.
I GUESS WE'RE SIMPLY STATING THAT WE--MEANING SHADOWPACT--CHOOSE TO FOLLOW MORE TRADITIONAL (AND LET ME OPINE) MUCH SANER RULES. ANY MORE QUESTIONS?
WHY WERE YOU CHOSEN AS SPOKESMAN FOR THE TEAM?
NO SPECIAL REASON REALLY--OTHER THAN I WAS THE ONLY TEAM MEMBER WHO'S BOTH COMFORTABLE WITH PUBLIC SPEAKING AND WHO OWNS A SUIT.
I GUESS WHAT I MEANT TO SAY WAS, ANY MORE *PERTINENT* QUESTIONS?

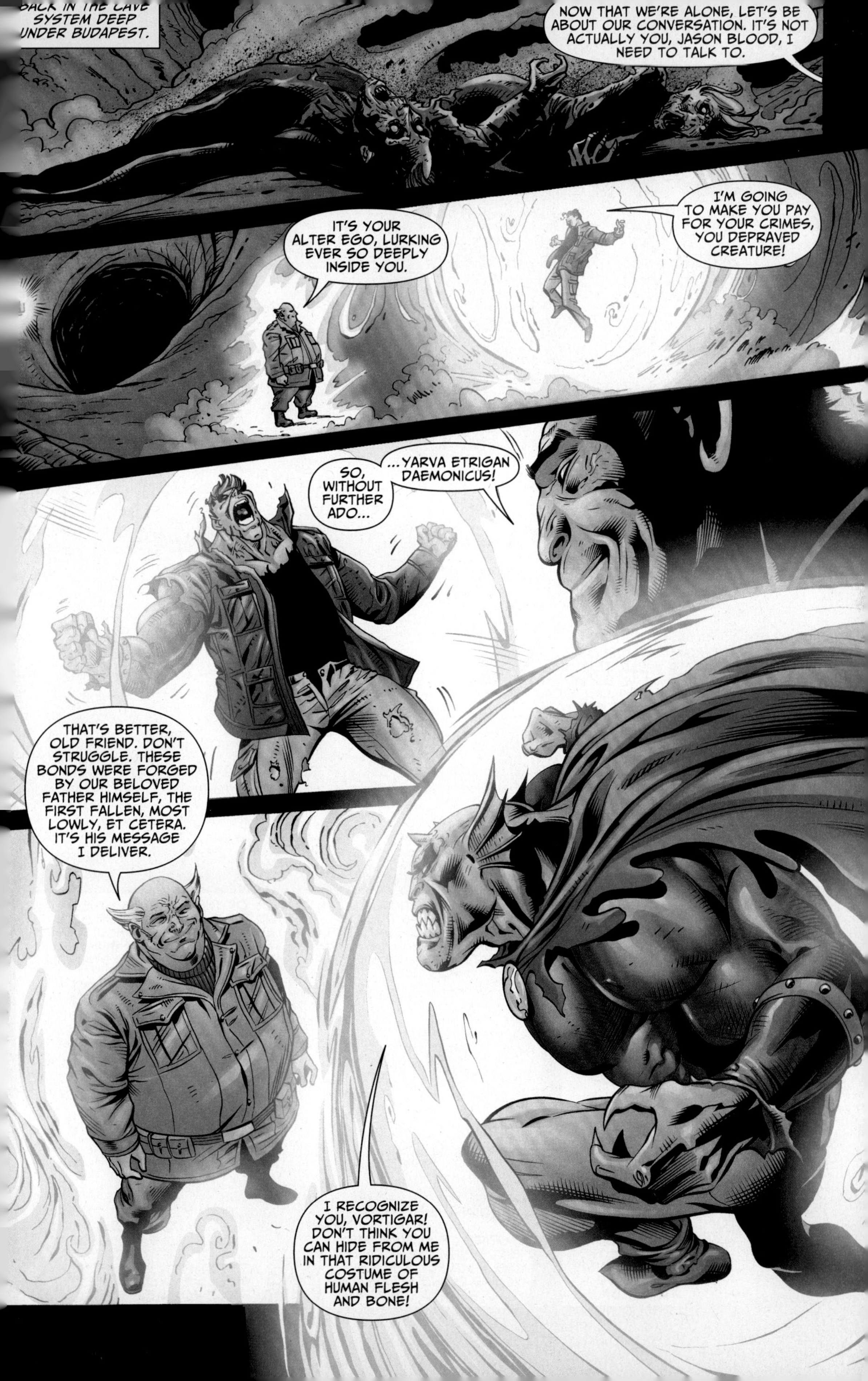
BACK IN THE CAVE SYSTEM DEEP UNDER BUDAPEST.
NOW THAT WE'RE ALONE, LET'S BE ABOUT OUR CONVERSATION. IT'S NOT ACTUALLY YOU, JASON BLOOD, I NEED TO TALK TO.
IT'S YOUR ALTER EGO, LURKING EVER SO DEEPLY INSIDE YOU.
I'M GOING TO MAKE YOU PAY FOR YOUR CRIMES, YOU DEPRAVED CREATURE!
SO, WITHOUT FURTHER ADO...
...YARVA ETRIGAN DAEMONICUS!
THAT'S BETTER, OLD FRIEND. DON'T STRUGGLE. THESE BONDS WERE FORGED BY OUR BELOVED FATHER HIMSELF, THE FIRST FALLEN, MOST LOWLY, ET CETERA. IT'S HIS MESSAGE I DELIVER.
I RECOGNIZE YOU, VORTIGAR! DON'T THINK YOU CAN HIDE FROM ME IN THAT RIDICULOUS COSTUME OF HUMAN FLESH AND BONE!

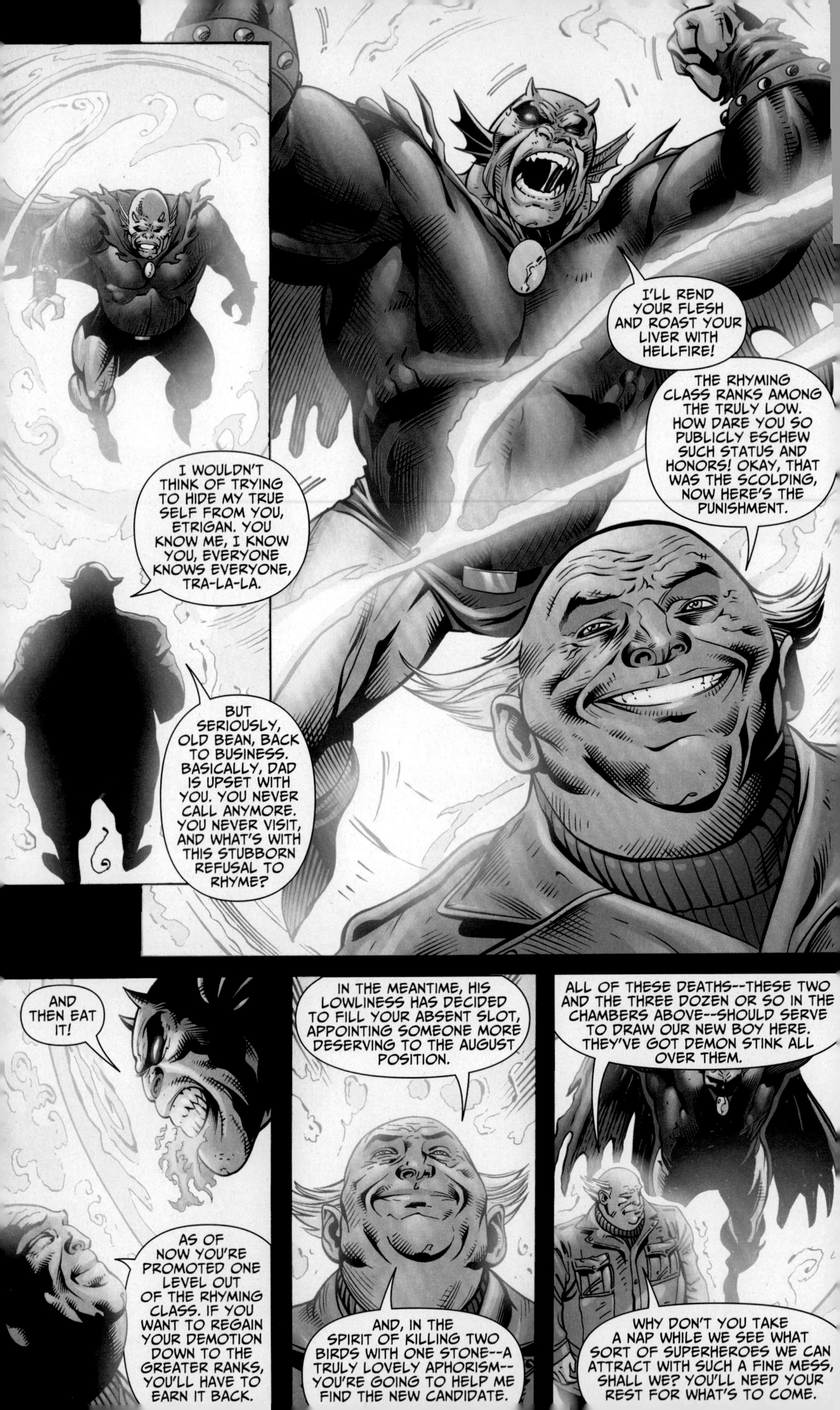
I WOULDN'T THINK OF TRYING TO HIDE MY TRUE SELF FROM YOU, ETRIGAN. YOU KNOW ME, I KNOW YOU, EVERYONE KNOWS EVERYONE, TRA-LA-LA.
BUT SERIOUSLY, OLD BEAN, BACK TO BUSINESS. BASICALLY, DAD IS UPSET WITH YOU. YOU NEVER CALL ANYMORE. YOU NEVER VISIT, AND WHAT'S WITH THIS STUBBORN REFUSAL TO RHYME?
I'LL REND YOUR FLESH AND ROAST YOUR LIVER WITH HELLFIRE!
THE RHYMING CLASS RANKS AMONG THE TRULY LOW. HOW DARE YOU SO PUBLICLY ESCHEW SUCH STATUS AND HONORS! OKAY, THAT WAS THE SCOLDING, NOW HERE'S THE PUNISHMENT.
AND THEN EAT IT!
AS OF NOW YOU'RE PROMOTED ONE LEVEL OUT OF THE RHYMING CLASS. IF YOU WANT TO REGAIN YOUR DEMOTION DOWN TO THE GREATER RANKS, YOU'LL HAVE TO EARN IT BACK.
IN THE MEANTIME, HIS LOWLINESS HAS DECIDED TO FILL YOUR ABSENT SLOT, APPOINTING SOMEONE MORE DESERVING TO THE AUGUST POSITION.
AND, IN THE SPIRIT OF KILLING TWO BIRDS WITH ONE STONE--A TRULY LOVELY APHORISM--YOU'RE GOING TO HELP ME FIND THE NEW CANDIDATE.
ALL OF THESE DEATHS--THESE TWO AND THE THREE DOZEN OR SO IN THE CHAMBERS ABOVE--SHOULD SERVE TO DRAW OUR NEW BOY HERE. THEY'VE GOT DEMON STINK ALL OVER THEM.
WHY DON'T YOU TAKE A NAP WHILE WE SEE WHAT SORT OF SUPERHEROES WE CAN ATTRACT WITH SUCH A FINE MESS, SHALL WE? YOU'LL NEED YOUR REST FOR WHAT'S TO COME.

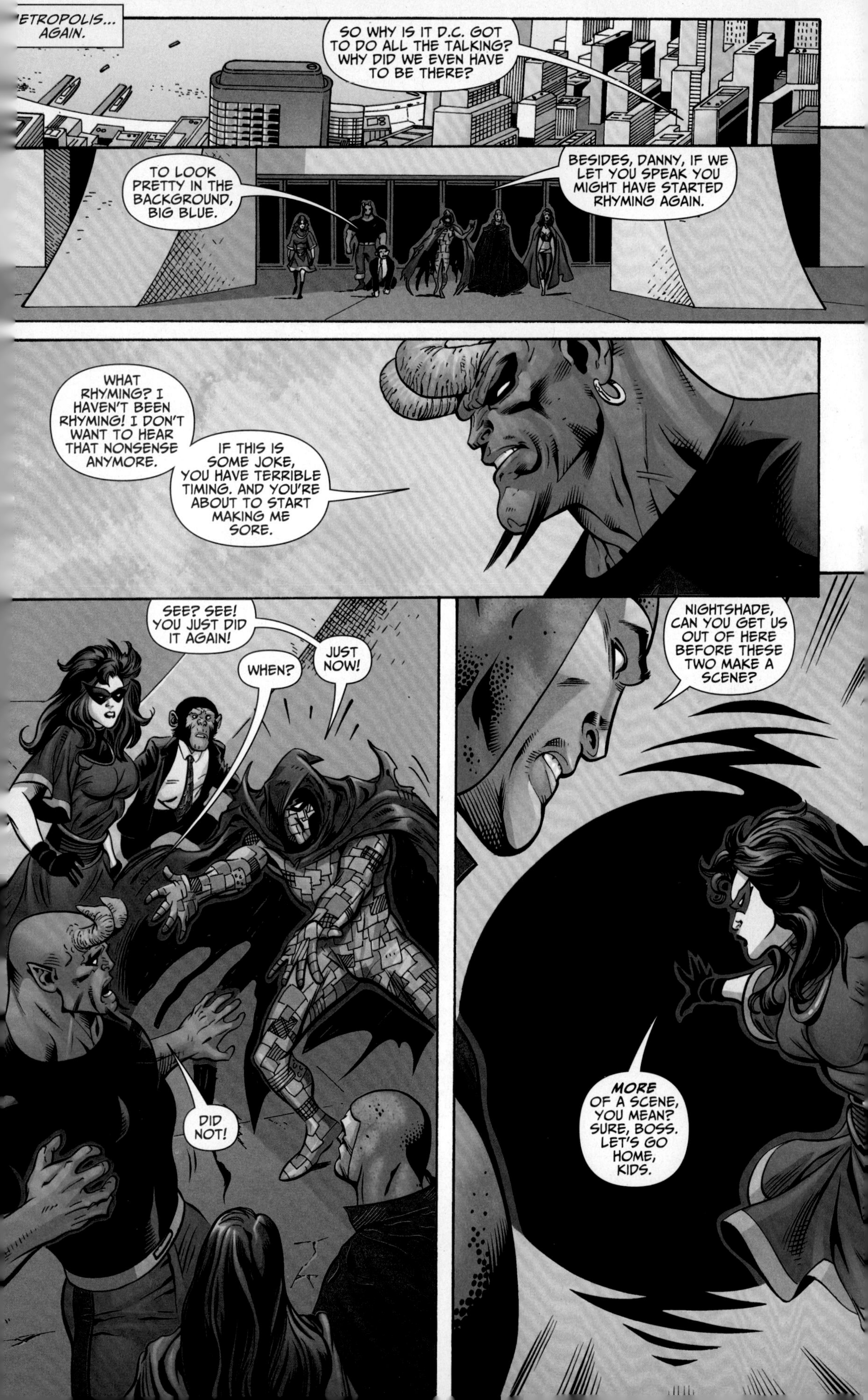

ETROPOLIS... AGAIN.
SO WHY IS IT D.C. GOT TO DO ALL THE TALKING? WHY DID WE EVEN HAVE TO BE THERE?
TO LOOK PRETTY IN THE BACKGROUND, BIG BLUE.
BESIDES, DANNY, IF WE LET YOU SPEAK YOU MIGHT HAVE STARTED RHYMING AGAIN.
WHAT RHYMING? I HAVEN'T BEEN RHYMING! I DON'T WANT TO HEAR THAT NONSENSE ANYMORE.
IF THIS IS SOME JOKE, YOU HAVE TERRIBLE TIMING. AND YOU'RE ABOUT TO START MAKING ME SORE.
SEE? SEE! YOU JUST DID IT AGAIN!
WHEN?
JUST NOW!
DID NOT!
NIGHTSHADE, CAN YOU GET US OUT OF HERE BEFORE THESE TWO MAKE A SCENE?
MORE OF A SCENE, YOU MEAN? SURE, BOSS. LET'S GO HOME, KIDS.

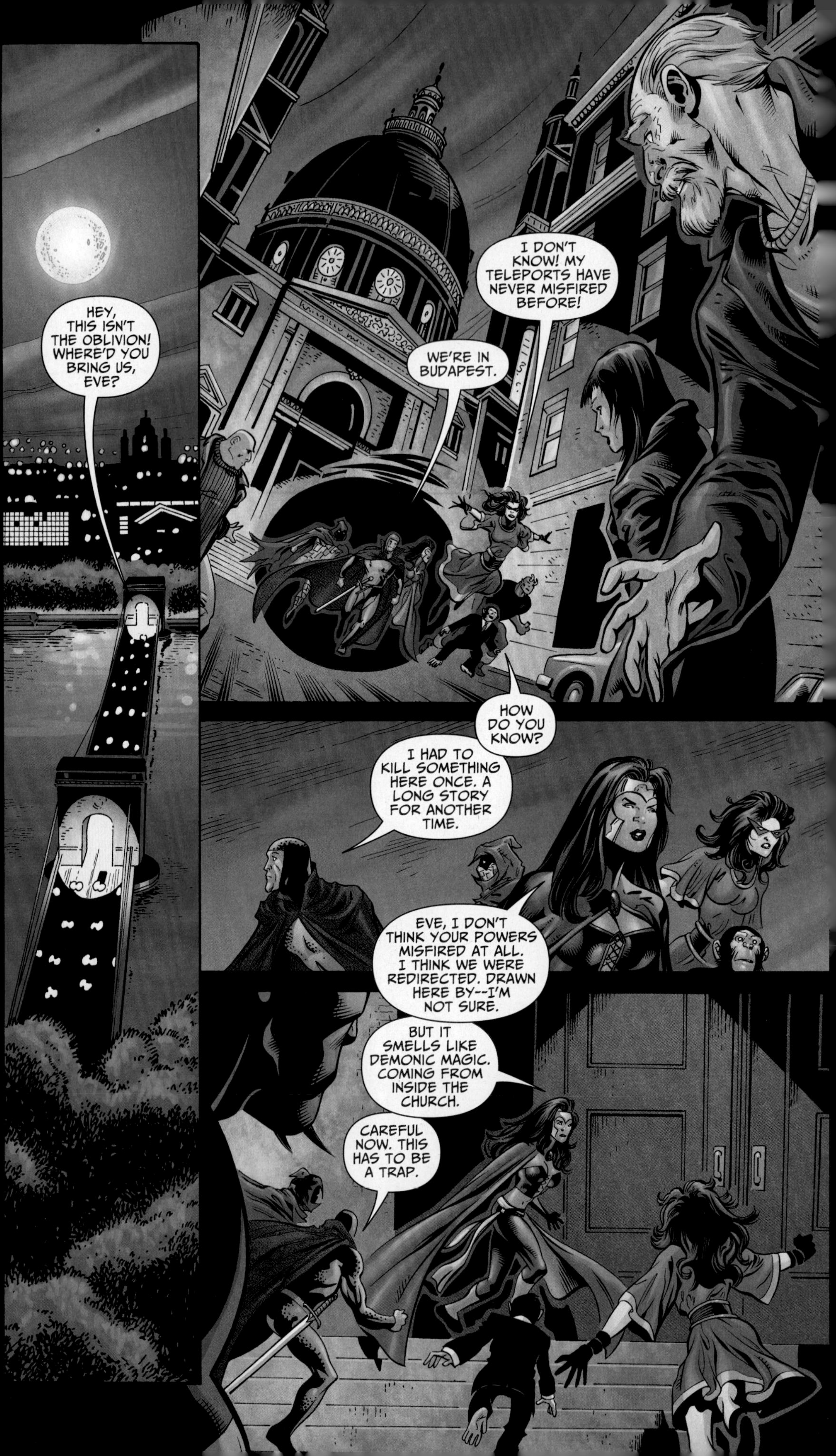
HEY, THIS ISN'T THE OBLIVION! WHERE'D YOU BRING US, EVE?
I DON'T KNOW! MY TELEPORTS HAVE NEVER MISFIRED BEFORE!
WE'RE IN BUDAPEST.
HOW DO YOU KNOW?
I HAD TO KILL SOMETHING HERE ONCE. A LONG STORY FOR ANOTHER TIME.
EVE, I DON'T THINK YOUR POWERS MISFIRED AT ALL. I THINK WE WERE REDIRECTED. DRAWN HERE BY--I'M NOT SURE.
BUT IT SMELLS LIKE DEMONIC MAGIC. COMING FROM INSIDE THE CHURCH.
CAREFUL NOW. THIS HAS TO BE A TRAP.

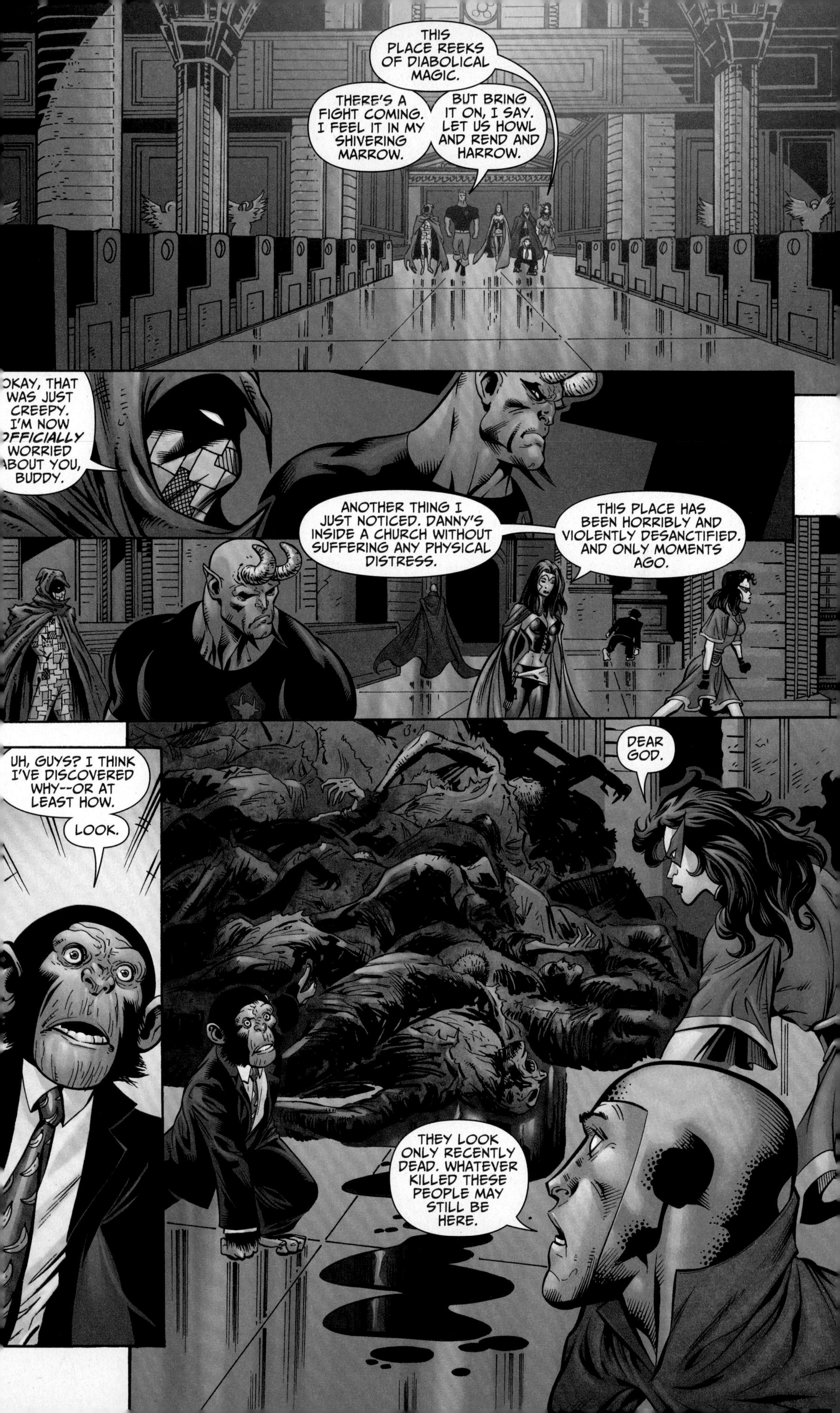
THIS PLACE REEKS OF DIABOLICAL MAGIC.
THERE'S A FIGHT COMING. I FEEL IT IN MY SHIVERING MARROW.
BUT BRING IT ON, I SAY. LET US HOWL AND REND AND HARROW.
OKAY, THAT WAS JUST CREEPY. I'M NOW OFFICIALLY WORRIED ABOUT YOU, BUDDY.
ANOTHER THING I JUST NOTICED. DANNY'S INSIDE A CHURCH WITHOUT SUFFERING ANY PHYSICAL DISTRESS.
THIS PLACE HAS BEEN HORRIBLY AND VIOLENTLY DESANCTIFIED. AND ONLY MOMENTS AGO.
UH, GUYS? I THINK I'VE DISCOVERED WHY--OR AT LEAST HOW.
LOOK.
DEAR GOD.
THEY LOOK ONLY RECENTLY DEAD. WHATEVER KILLED THESE PEOPLE MAY STILL BE HERE.

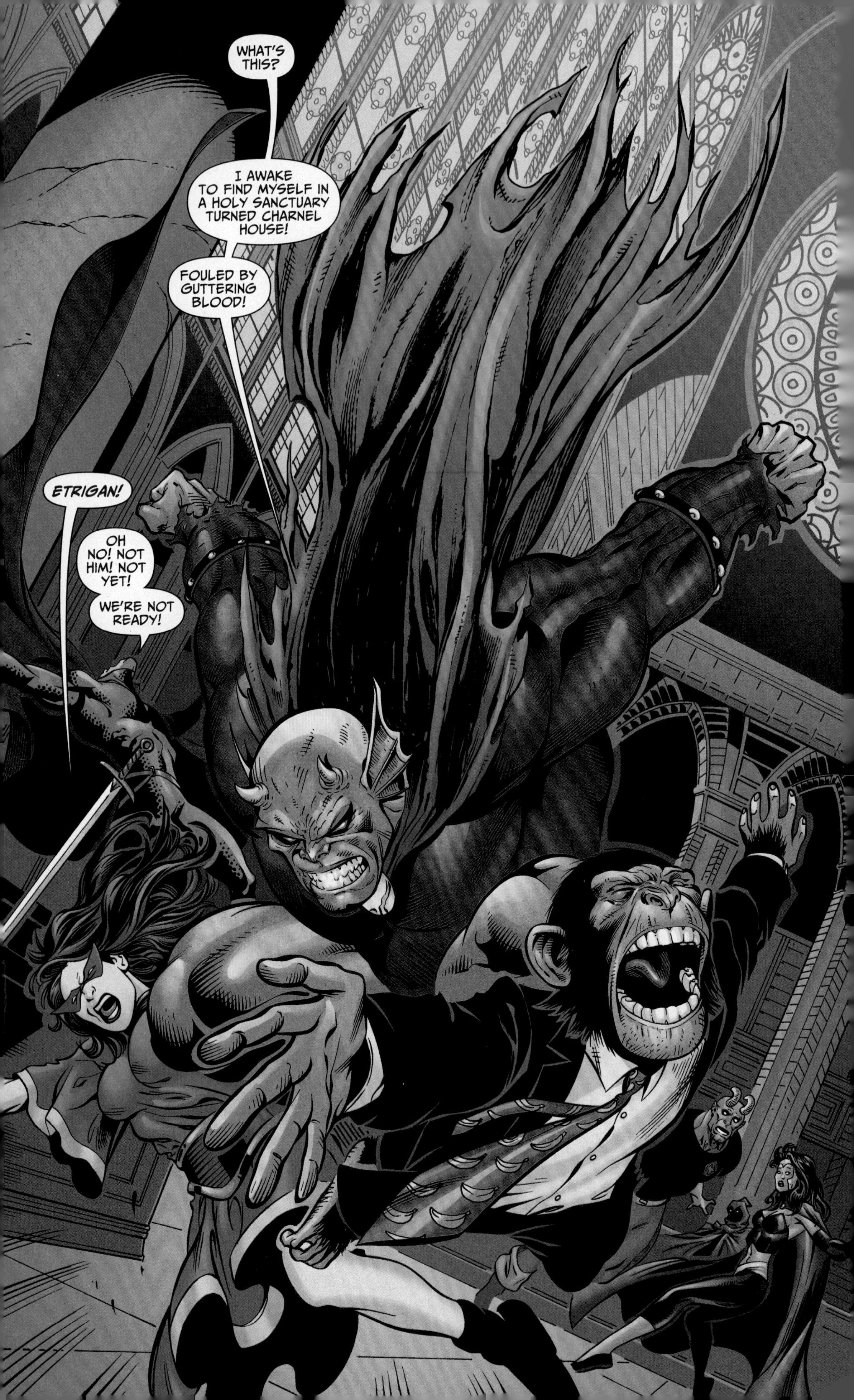
WHAT'S THIS?
I AWAKE TO FIND MYSELF IN A HOLY SANCTUARY TURNED CHARNEL HOUSE!
FOULED BY GUTTERING BLOOD!
ETRIGAN!
OH NO! NOT HIM! NOT YET!
WE'RE NOT READY!

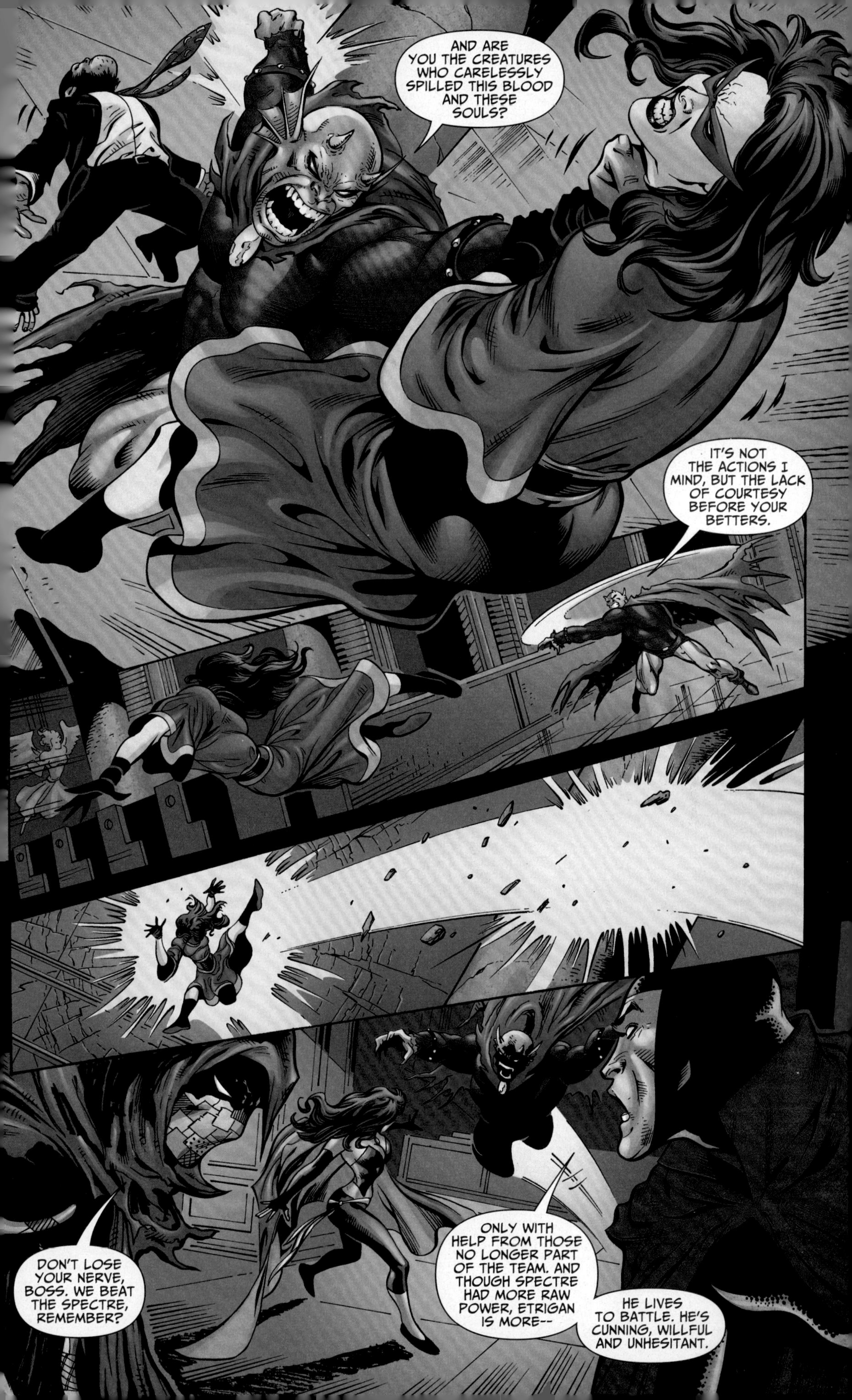
AND ARE YOU THE CREATURES WHO CARELESSLY SPILLED THIS BLOOD AND THESE SOULS?
IT'S NOT THE ACTIONS I MIND, BUT THE LACK OF COURTESY BEFORE YOUR BETTERS.
DON'T LOSE YOUR NERVE, BOSS. WE BEAT THE SPECTRE, REMEMBER?
ONLY WITH HELP FROM THOSE NO LONGER PART OF THE TEAM. AND THOUGH SPECTRE HAD MORE RAW POWER, ETRIGAN IS MORE--
HE LIVES TO BATTLE. HE'S CUNNING, WILLFUL AND UNHESITANT.

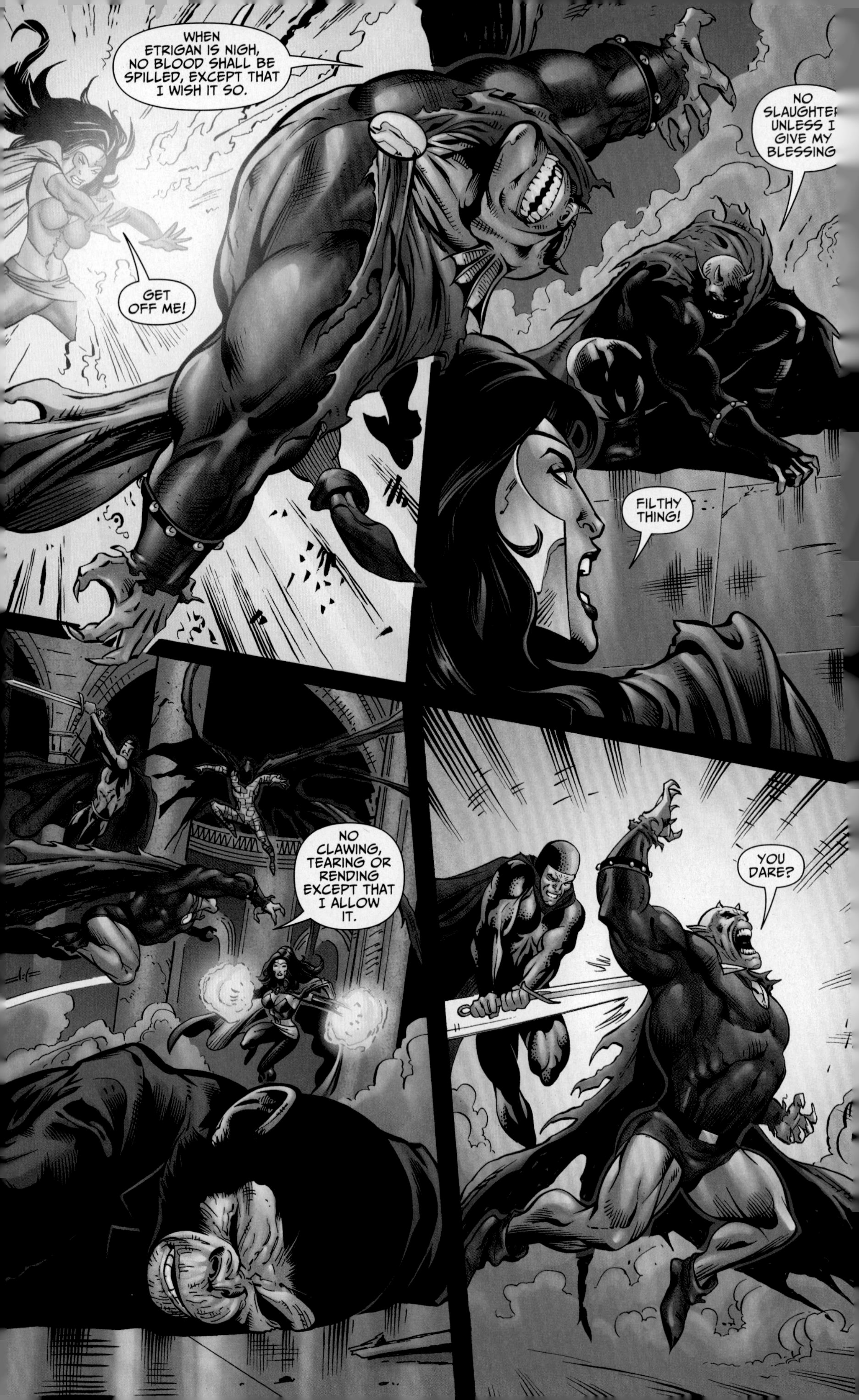

WHEN ETRIGAN IS NIGH, NO BLOOD SHALL BE SPILLED, EXCEPT THAT I WISH IT SO.
NO SLAUGHTER UNLESS I GIVE MY BLESSING
GET OFF ME!
FILTHY THING!
NO CLAWING, TEARING OR RENDING EXCEPT THAT I ALLOW IT.
YOU DARE?

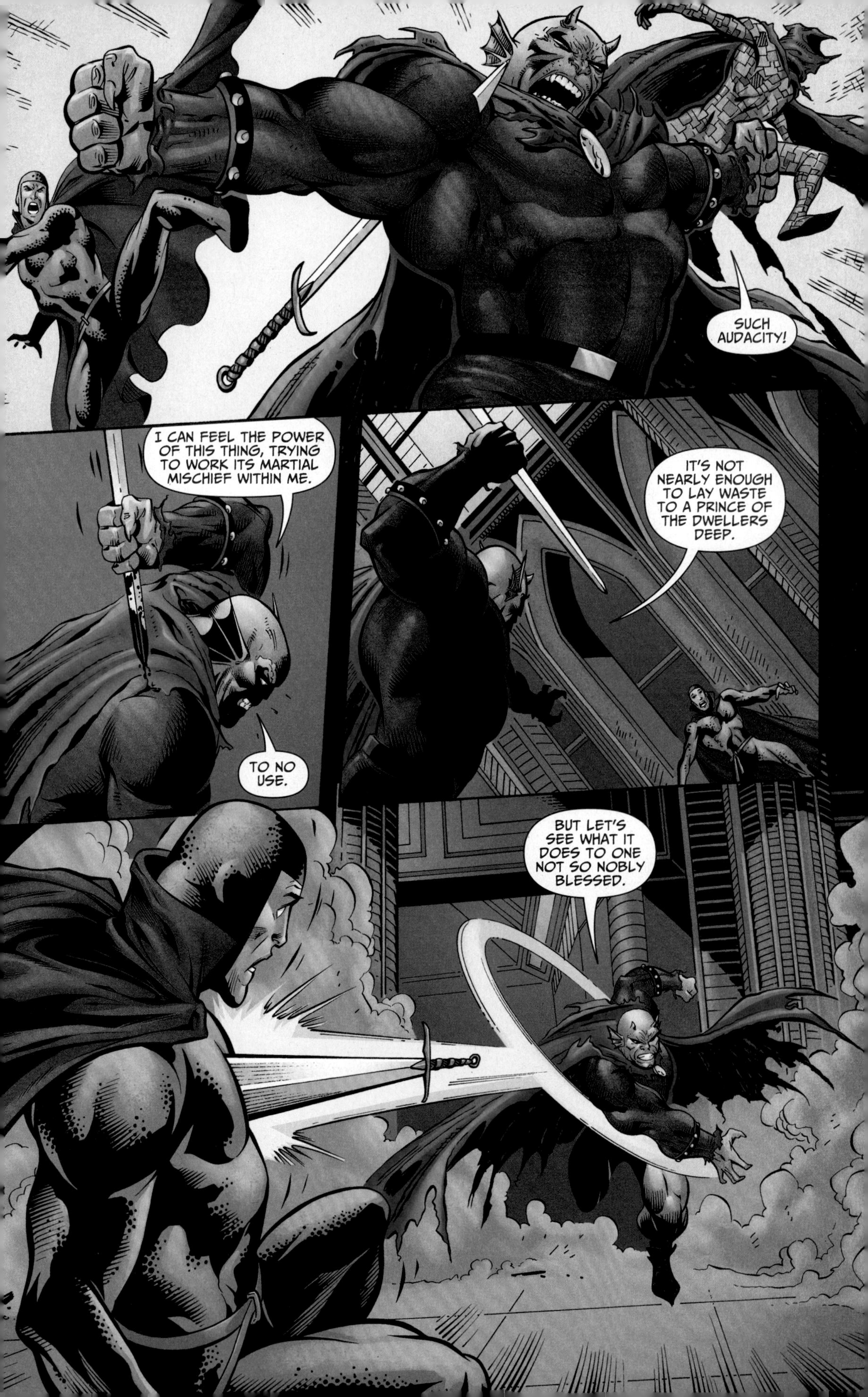
SUCH AUDACITY!
I CAN FEEL THE POWER OF THIS THING, TRYING TO WORK ITS MARTIAL MISCHIEF WITHIN ME.
TO NO USE.
IT'S NOT NEARLY ENOUGH TO LAY WASTE TO A PRINCE OF THE DWELLERS DEEP.
BUT LET'S SEE WHAT IT DOES TO ONE NOT SO NOBLY BLESSED.

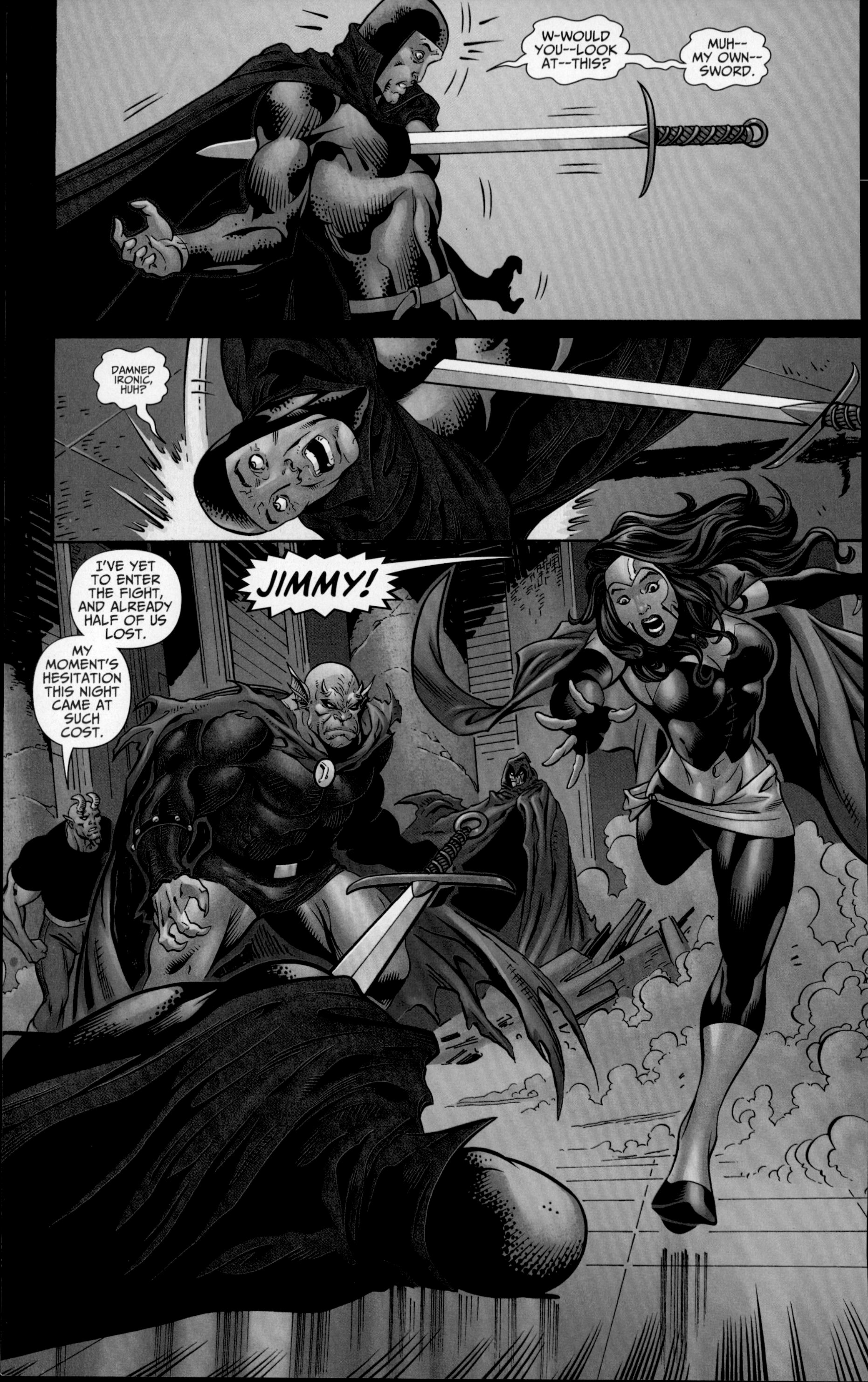
W-WOULD YOU--LOOK AT--THIS?
MUH-- MY OWN-- SWORD.
DAMNED IRONIC, HUH?
I'VE YET TO ENTER THE FIGHT, AND ALREADY HALF OF US LOST.
MY MOMENT'S HESITATION THIS NIGHT CAME AT SUCH COST.
JIMMY!

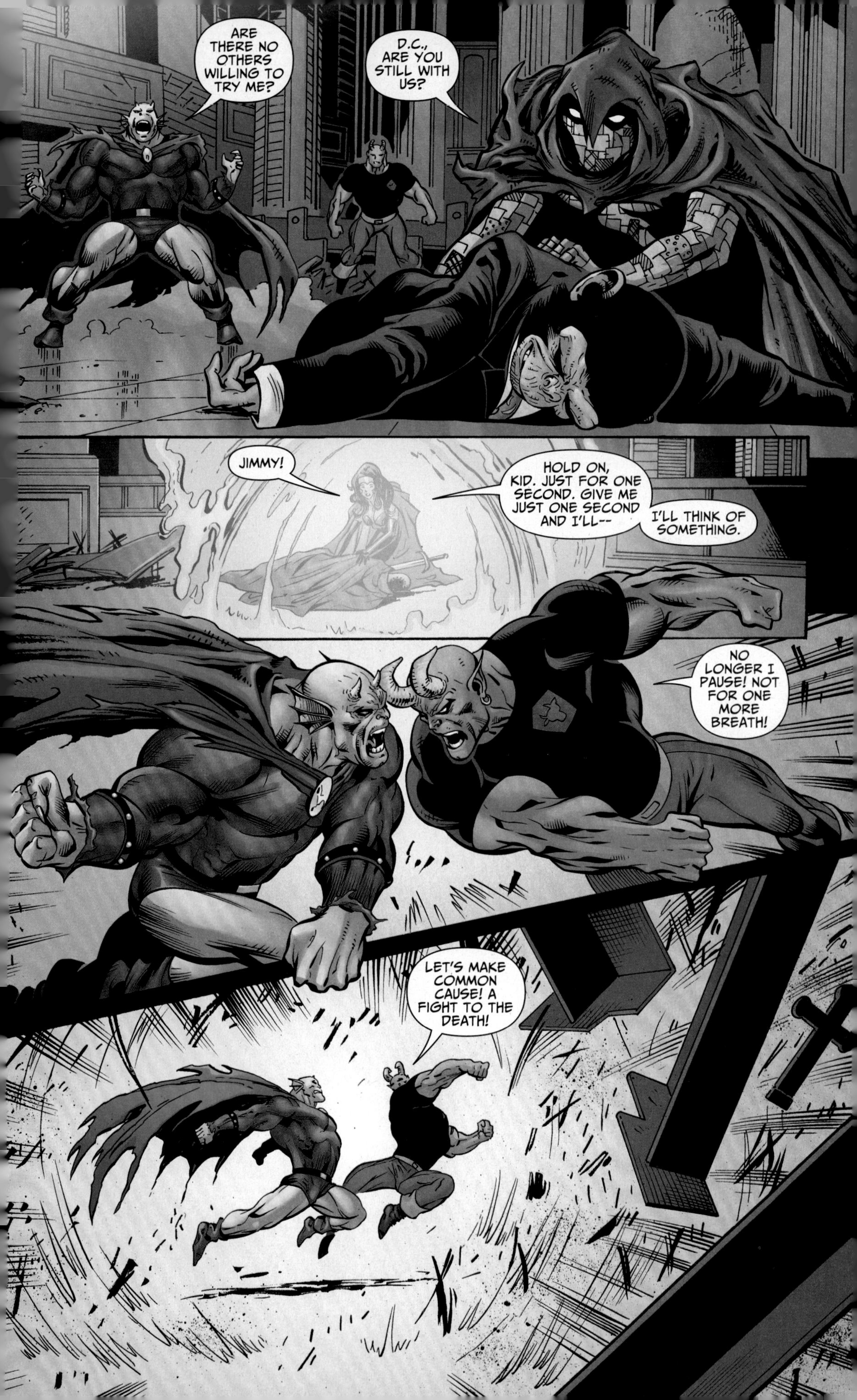
ARE THERE NO OTHERS WILLING TO TRY ME?
D.C., ARE YOU STILL WITH US?
JIMMY!
HOLD ON, KID. JUST FOR ONE SECOND. GIVE ME JUST ONE SECOND AND I'LL--
I'LL THINK OF SOMETHING.
NO LONGER I PAUSE! NOT FOR ONE MORE BREATH!
LET'S MAKE COMMON CAUSE! A FIGHT TO THE DEATH!

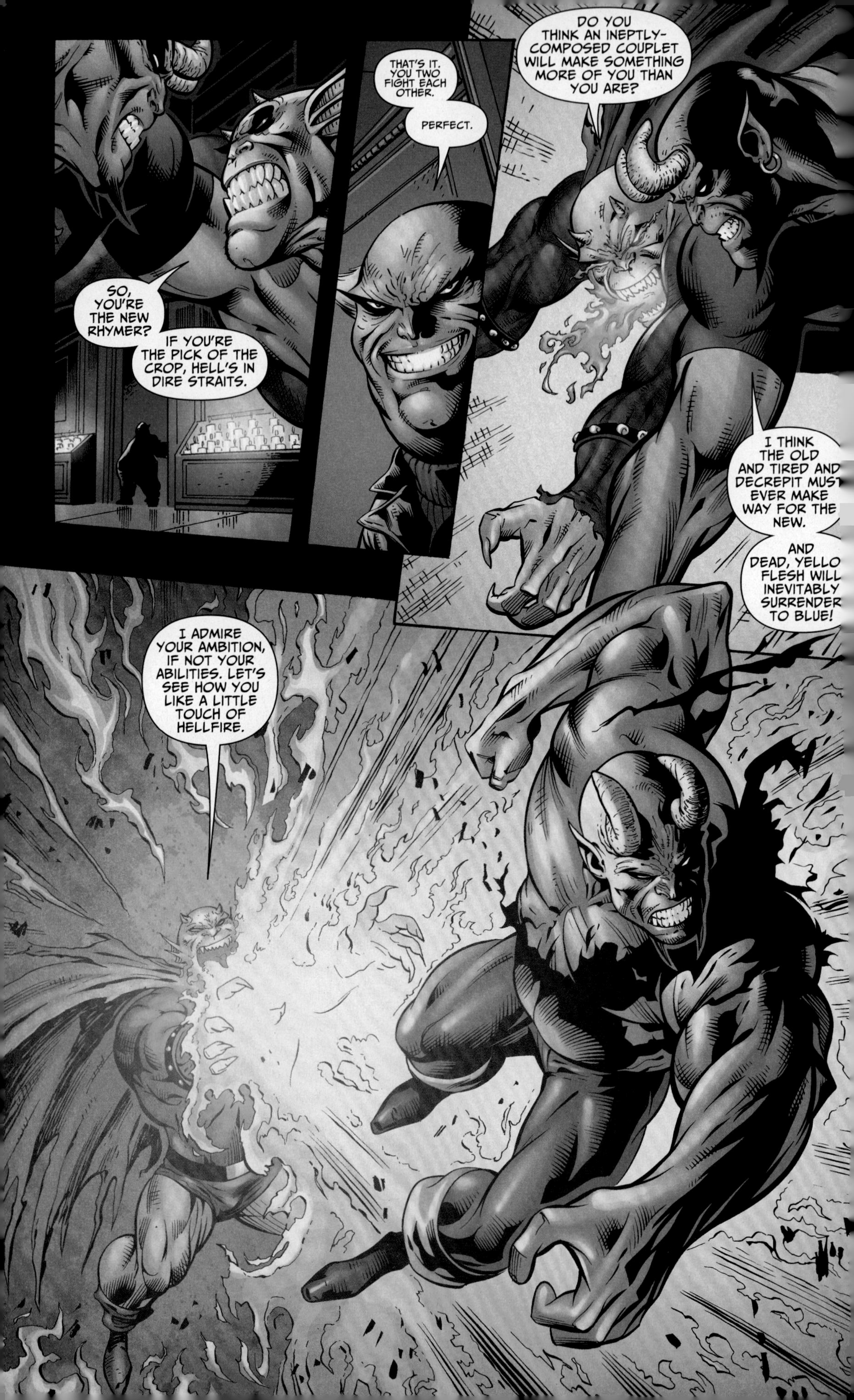
SO, YOU'RE THE NEW RHYMER?
IF YOU'RE THE PICK OF THE CROP, HELL'S IN DIRE STRAITS.
THAT'S IT. YOU TWO FIGHT EACH OTHER.
PERFECT.
DO YOU THINK AN INEPTLY-COMPOSED COUPLET WILL MAKE SOMETHING MORE OF YOU THAN YOU ARE?
I THINK THE OLD AND TIRED AND DECREPIT MUST EVER MAKE WAY FOR THE NEW.
AND DEAD, YELLO FLESH WILL INEVITABLY SURRENDER TO BLUE!
I ADMIRE YOUR AMBITION, IF NOT YOUR ABILITIES. LET'S SEE HOW YOU LIKE A LITTLE TOUCH OF HELLFIRE.

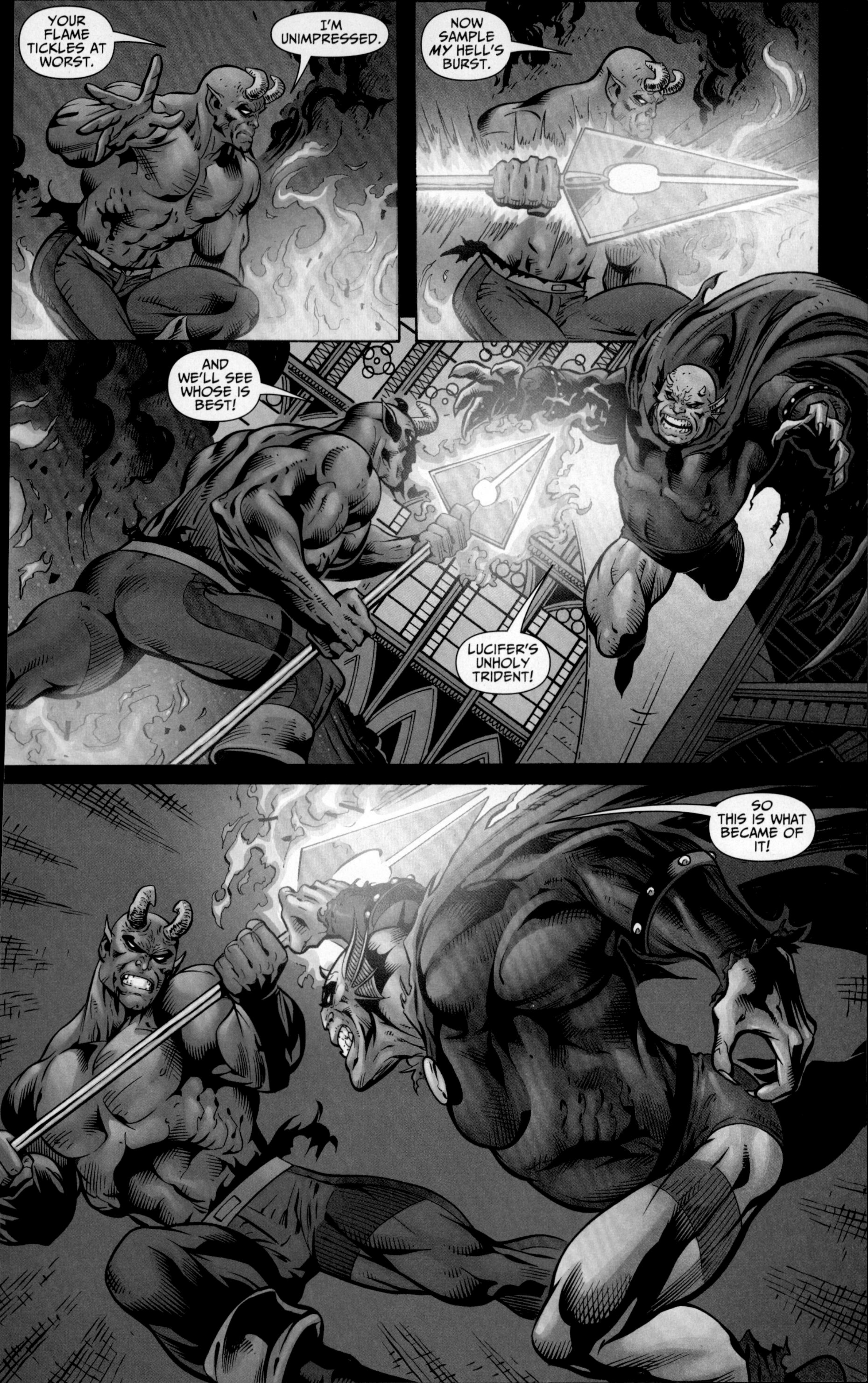
YOUR FLAME TICKLES AT WORST.
I'M UNIMPRESSED.
NOW SAMPLE MY HELL'S BURST.
AND WE'LL SEE WHOSE IS BEST!
LUCIFER'S UNHOLY TRIDENT!
SO THIS IS WHAT BECAME OF IT!

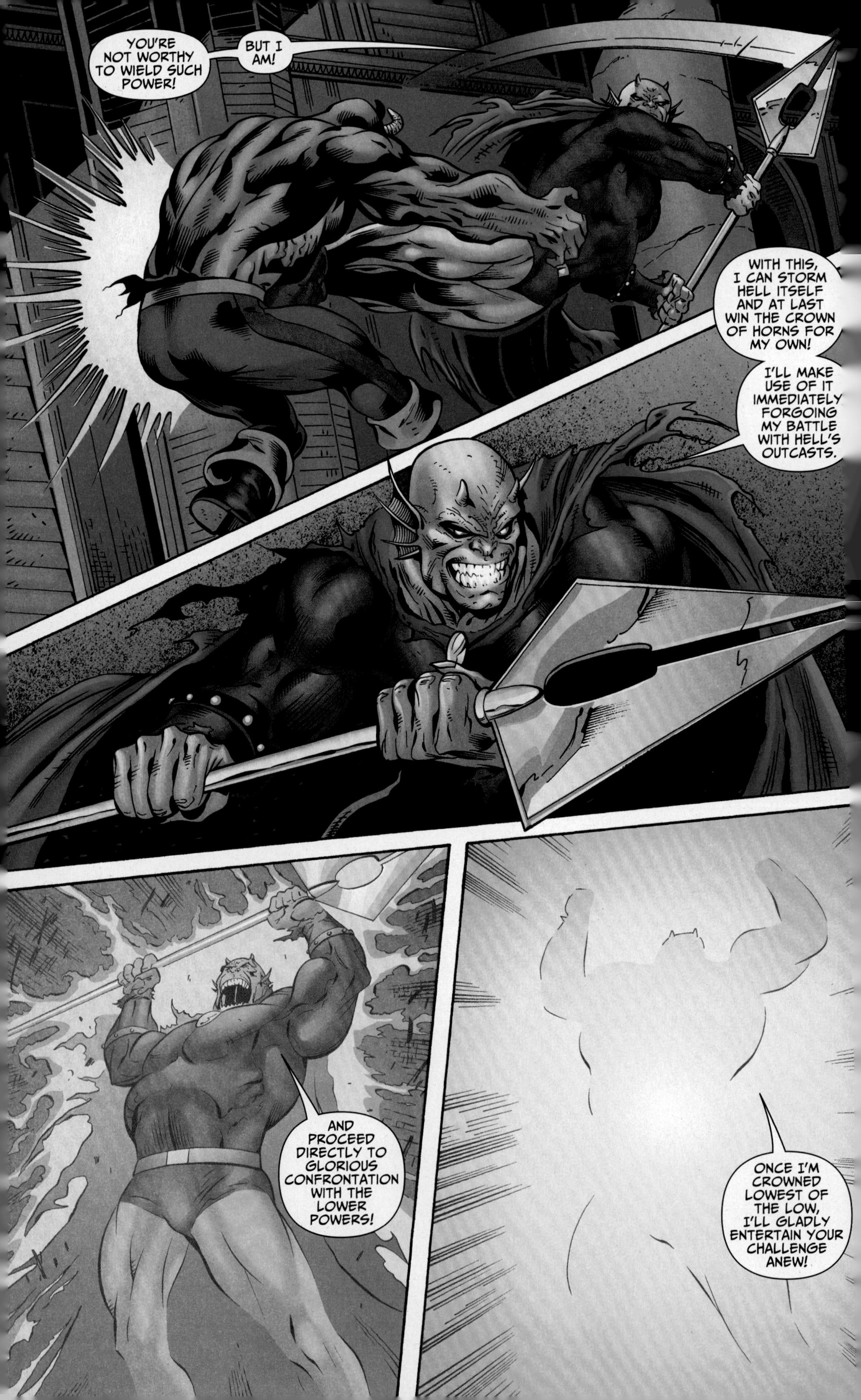
YOU'RE NOT WORTHY TO WIELD SUCH POWER!
BUT I AM!
WITH THIS, I CAN STORM HELL ITSELF AND AT LAST WIN THE CROWN OF HORNS FOR MY OWN!
I'LL MAKE USE OF IT IMMEDIATELY FORGOING MY BATTLE WITH HELL'S OUTCASTS.
AND PROCEED DIRECTLY TO GLORIOUS CONFRONTATION WITH THE LOWER POWERS!
ONCE I'M CROWNED LOWEST OF THE LOW, I'LL GLADLY ENTERTAIN YOUR CHALLENGE ANEW!

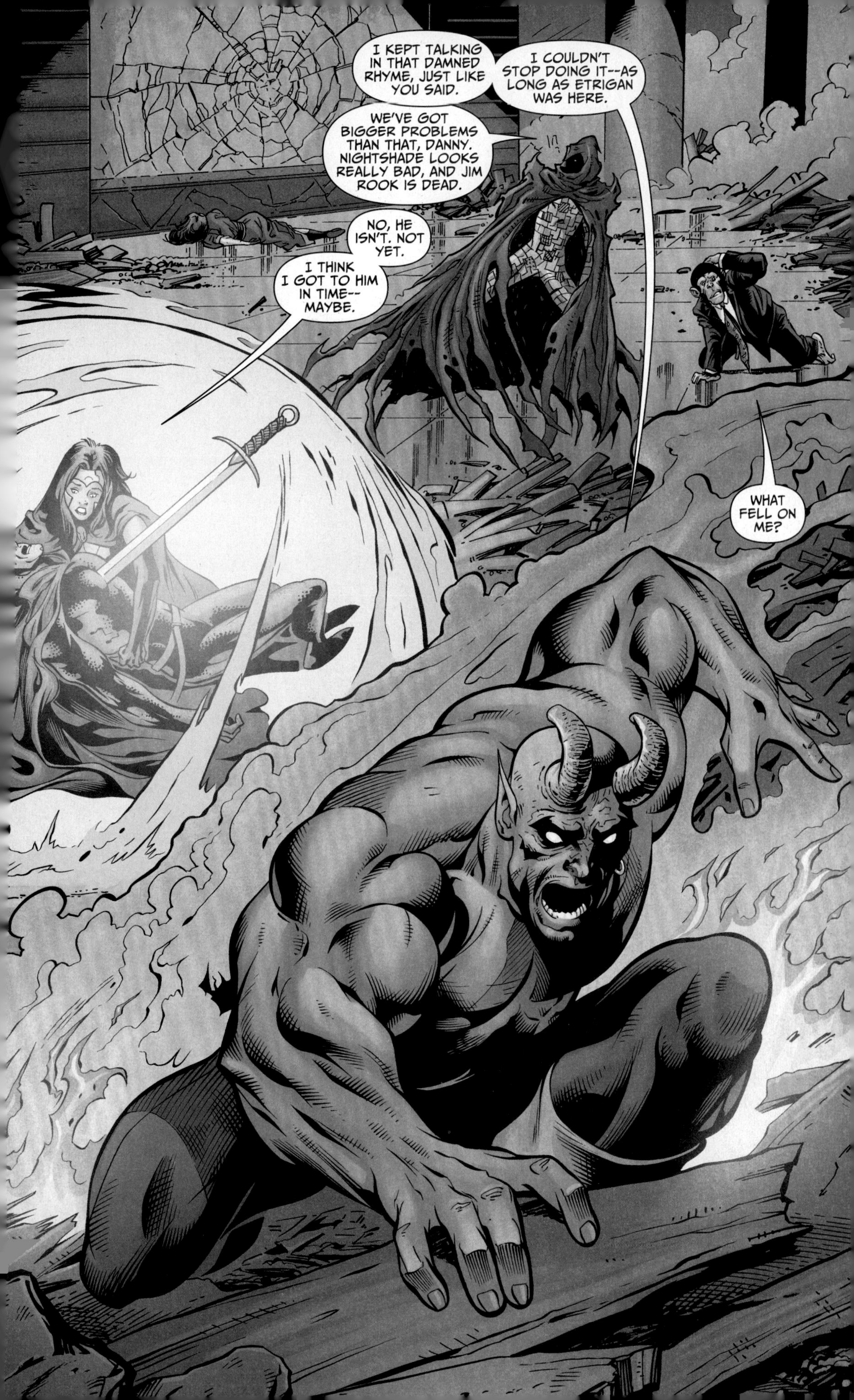
I KEPT TALKING IN THAT DAMNED RHYME, JUST LIKE YOU SAID.
I COULDN'T STOP DOING IT--AS LONG AS ETRIGAN WAS HERE.
WE'VE GOT BIGGER PROBLEMS THAN THAT, DANNY. NIGHTSHADE LOOKS REALLY BAD, AND JIM ROOK IS DEAD.
NO, HE ISN'T. NOT YET.
I THINK I GOT TO HIM IN TIME--MAYBE.
WHAT FELL ON ME?

NIGHTSHADE-- EVE--YOU HAVE TO WAKE UP. YOU HAVE TO TELEPORT US OUT OF HERE.

IS SHE--?

ALIVE, BUT I DON'T LIKE THIS INJURY TO HER HEAD. I KNOW EVEN MINOR HEAD WOUNDS TEND TO BLEED A LOT, BUT--

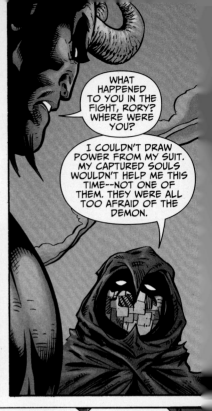

WHAT HAPPENED TO YOU IN THE FIGHT, RORY? WHERE WERE YOU?

I COULDN'T DRAW POWER FROM MY SUIT. MY CAPTURED SOULS WOULDN'T HELP ME THIS TIME--NOT ONE OF THEM. THEY WERE ALL TOO AFRAID OF THE DEMON.

WE SHOULD'VE LISTENED TO THE OTHERS. EVERYONE WARNED US SHADOWPACT TEAMS ARE DOOMED TO FAIL. THEY ALWAYS HAVE.

WE'RE CURSED BY OUR OWN HUBRIS.

STOP IT. NOW'S NOT THE TIME. WE NEED TO GET HOME, CARE FOR OUR WOUNDED AND REGROUP. WE'LL COME BACK FROM THIS, RIGHT?

RIGHT?

THE DEMON TRIPTYCH: PART 2
CURSED

cover art by **TOM DERENICK** *and* **WAYNE FAUCHER**
colored by **MIKE ATIYEH**

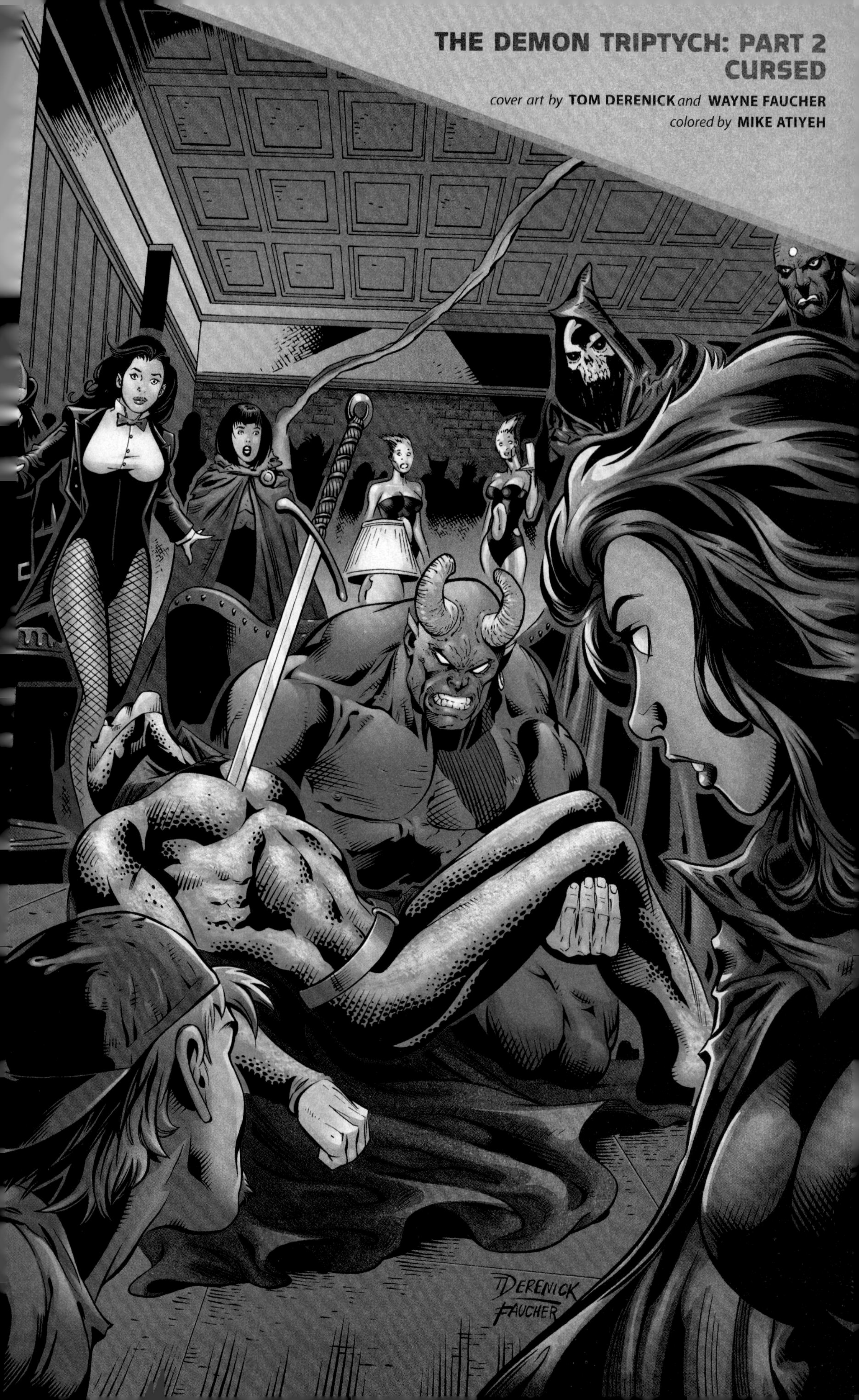
DERENICK
FAUCHER

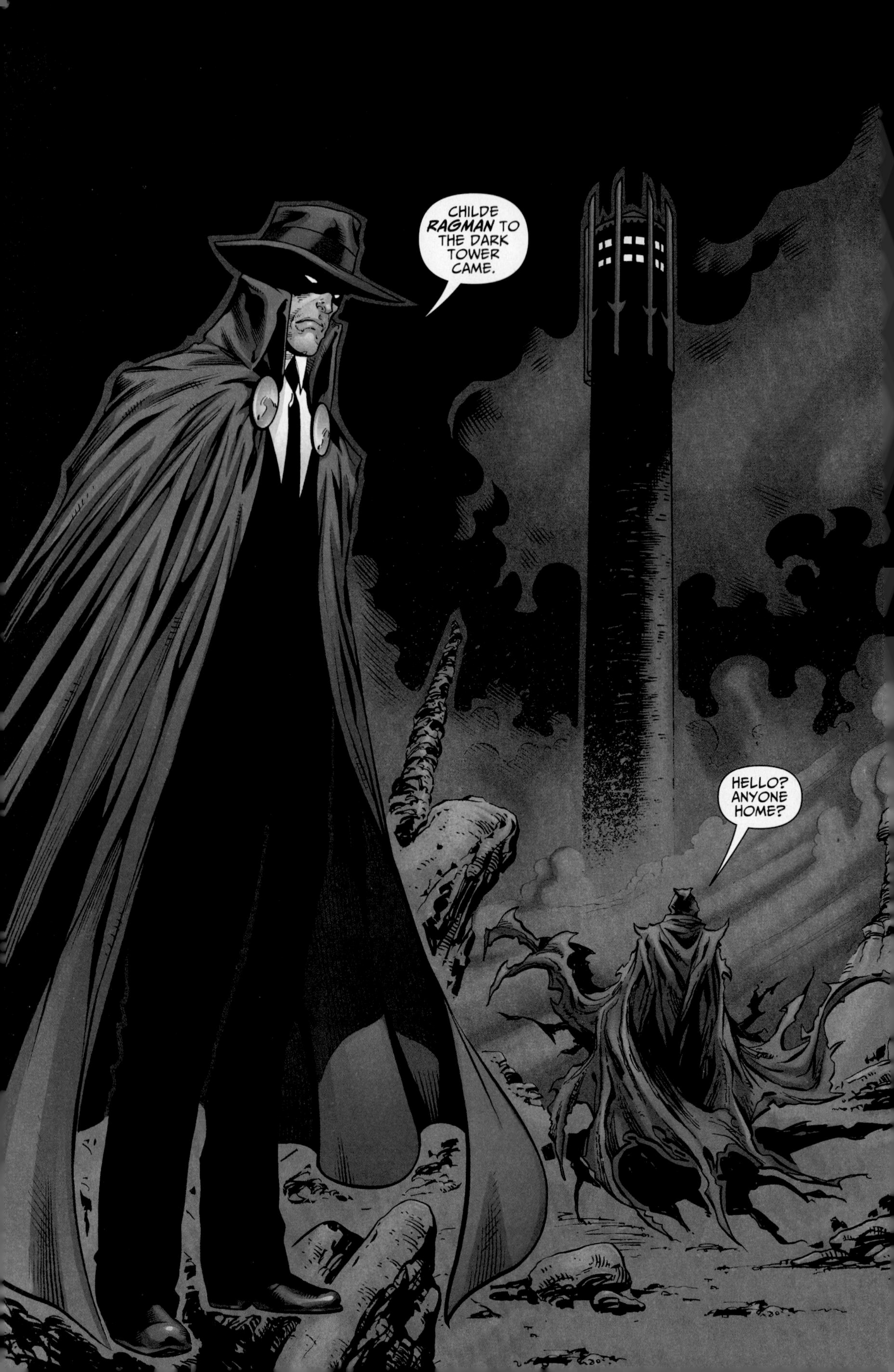
CHILDE RAGMAN TO THE DARK TOWER CAME.
HELLO? ANYONE HOME?

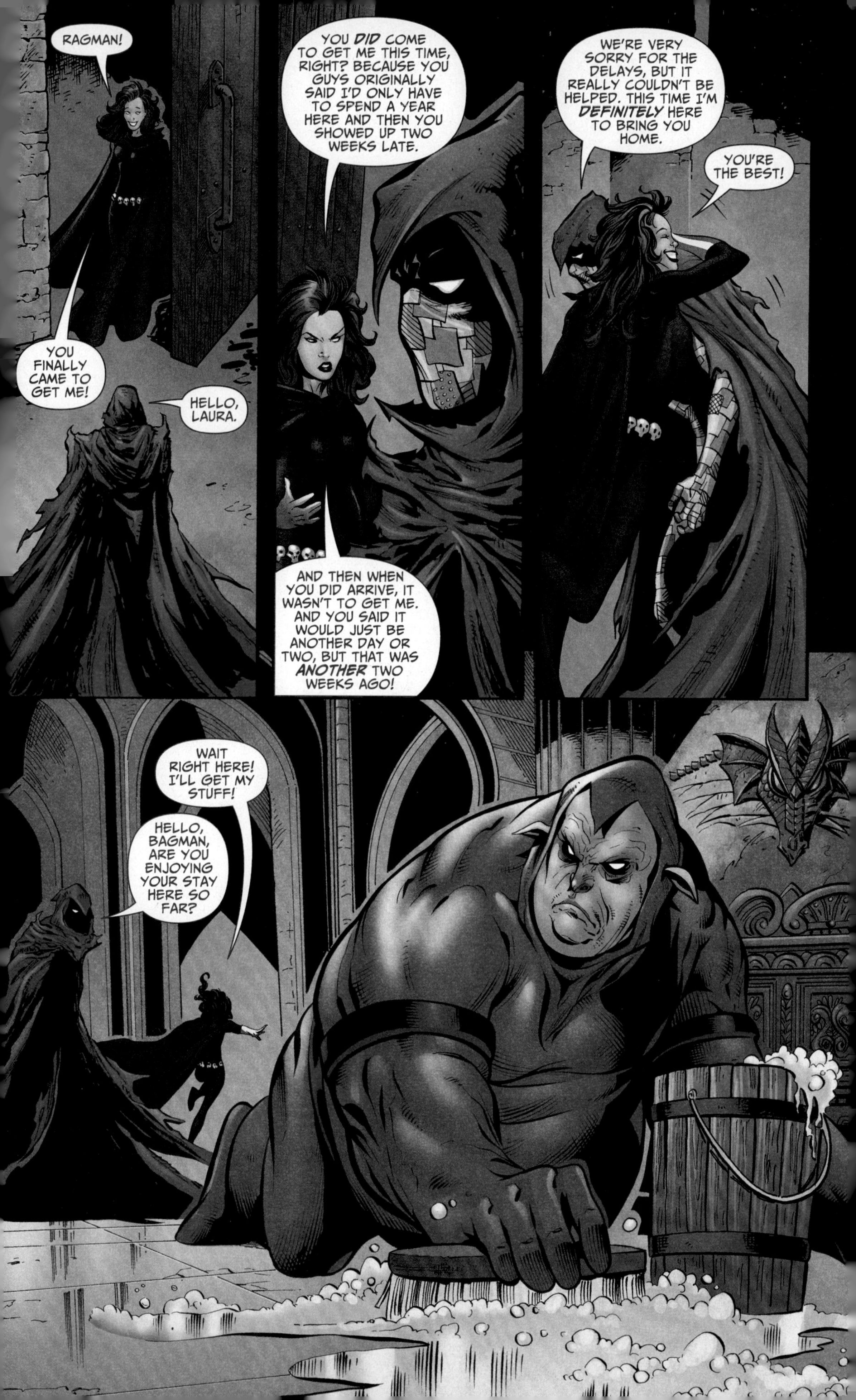
RAGMAN!
YOU FINALLY CAME TO GET ME!
HELLO, LAURA.
YOU DID COME TO GET ME THIS TIME, RIGHT? BECAUSE YOU GUYS ORIGINALLY SAID I'D ONLY HAVE TO SPEND A YEAR HERE AND THEN YOU SHOWED UP TWO WEEKS LATE.
AND THEN WHEN YOU DID ARRIVE, IT WASN'T TO GET ME. AND YOU SAID IT WOULD JUST BE ANOTHER DAY OR TWO, BUT THAT WAS ANOTHER TWO WEEKS AGO!
WE'RE VERY SORRY FOR THE DELAYS, BUT IT REALLY COULDN'T BE HELPED. THIS TIME I'M DEFINITELY HERE TO BRING YOU HOME.
YOU'RE THE BEST!
WAIT RIGHT HERE! I'LL GET MY STUFF!
HELLO, BAGMAN, ARE YOU ENJOYING YOUR STAY HERE SO FAR?

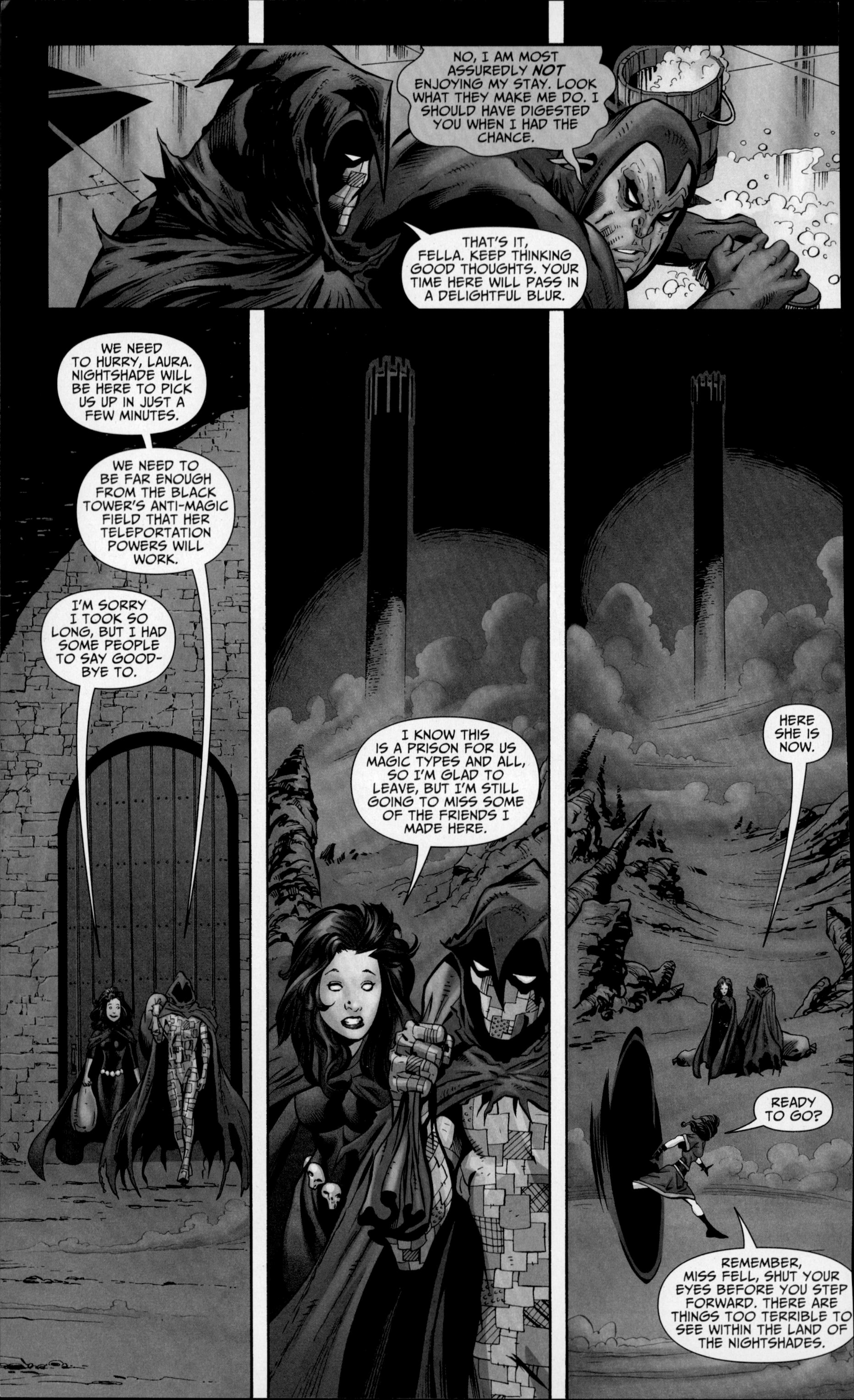
NO, I AM MOST ASSUREDLY NOT ENJOYING MY STAY. LOOK WHAT THEY MAKE ME DO. I SHOULD HAVE DIGESTED YOU WHEN I HAD THE CHANCE.
THAT'S IT, FELLA. KEEP THINKING GOOD THOUGHTS. YOUR TIME HERE WILL PASS IN A DELIGHTFUL BLUR.
WE NEED TO HURRY, LAURA. NIGHTSHADE WILL BE HERE TO PICK US UP IN JUST A FEW MINUTES.
WE NEED TO BE FAR ENOUGH FROM THE BLACK TOWER'S ANTI-MAGIC FIELD THAT HER TELEPORTATION POWERS WILL WORK.
I'M SORRY I TOOK SO LONG, BUT I HAD SOME PEOPLE TO SAY GOOD-BYE TO.
I KNOW THIS IS A PRISON FOR US MAGIC TYPES AND ALL, SO I'M GLAD TO LEAVE, BUT I'M STILL GOING TO MISS SOME OF THE FRIENDS I MADE HERE.
HERE SHE IS NOW.
READY TO GO?
REMEMBER, MISS FELL, SHUT YOUR EYES BEFORE YOU STEP FORWARD. THERE ARE THINGS TOO TERRIBLE TO SEE WITHIN THE LAND OF THE NIGHTSHADES.

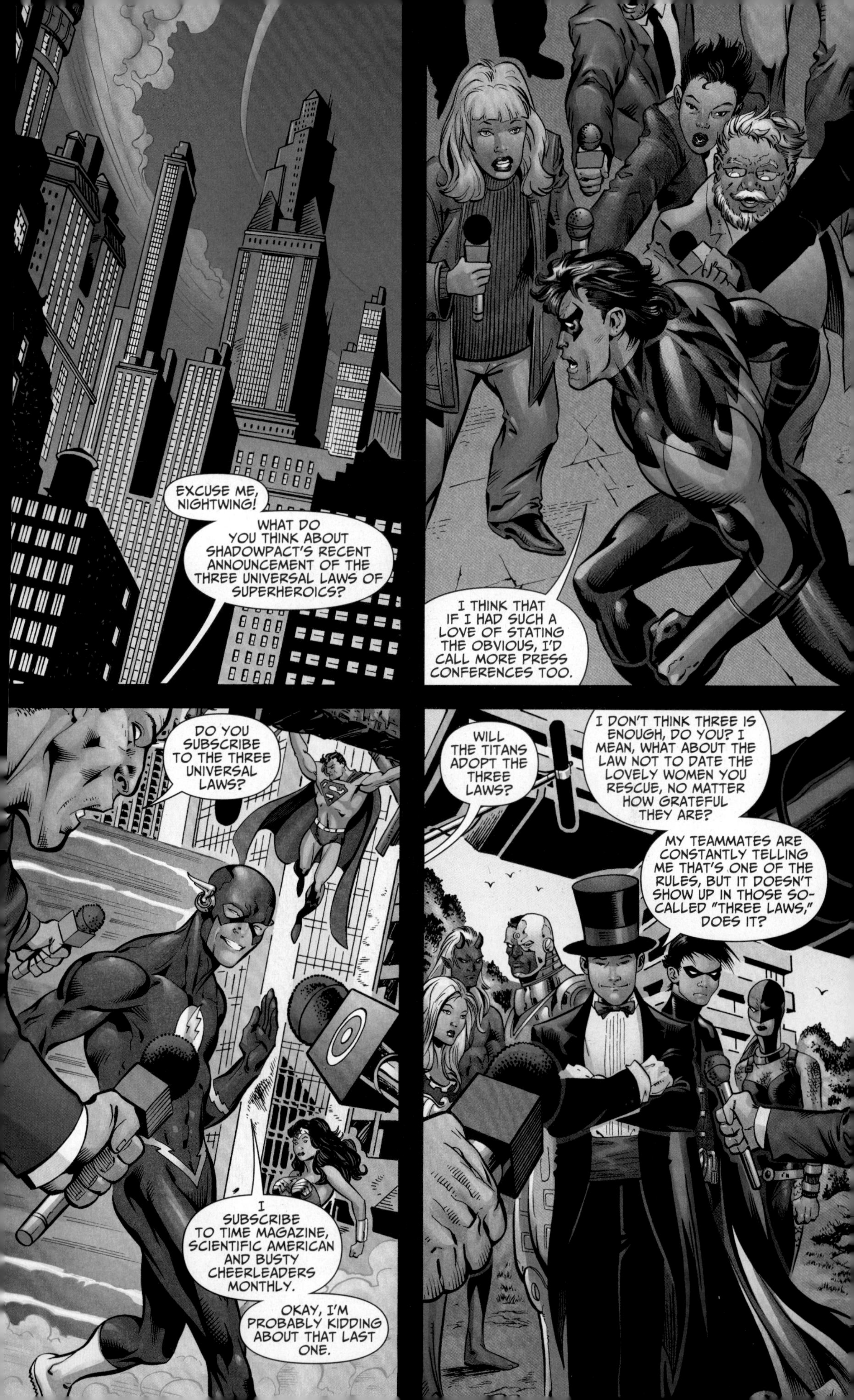
EXCUSE ME, NIGHTWING!
WHAT DO YOU THINK ABOUT SHADOWPACT'S RECENT ANNOUNCEMENT OF THE THREE UNIVERSAL LAWS OF SUPERHEROICS?
I THINK THAT IF I HAD SUCH A LOVE OF STATING THE OBVIOUS, I'D CALL MORE PRESS CONFERENCES TOO.
DO YOU SUBSCRIBE TO THE THREE UNIVERSAL LAWS?
I SUBSCRIBE TO TIME MAGAZINE, SCIENTIFIC AMERICAN AND BUSTY CHEERLEADERS MONTHLY.
OKAY, I'M PROBABLY KIDDING ABOUT THAT LAST ONE.
WILL THE TITANS ADOPT THE THREE LAWS?
I DON'T THINK THREE IS ENOUGH, DO YOU? I MEAN, WHAT ABOUT THE LAW NOT TO DATE THE LOVELY WOMEN YOU RESCUE, NO MATTER HOW GRATEFUL THEY ARE?
MY TEAMMATES ARE CONSTANTLY TELLING ME THAT'S ONE OF THE RULES, BUT IT DOESN'T SHOW UP IN THOSE SO-CALLED "THREE LAWS," DOES IT?

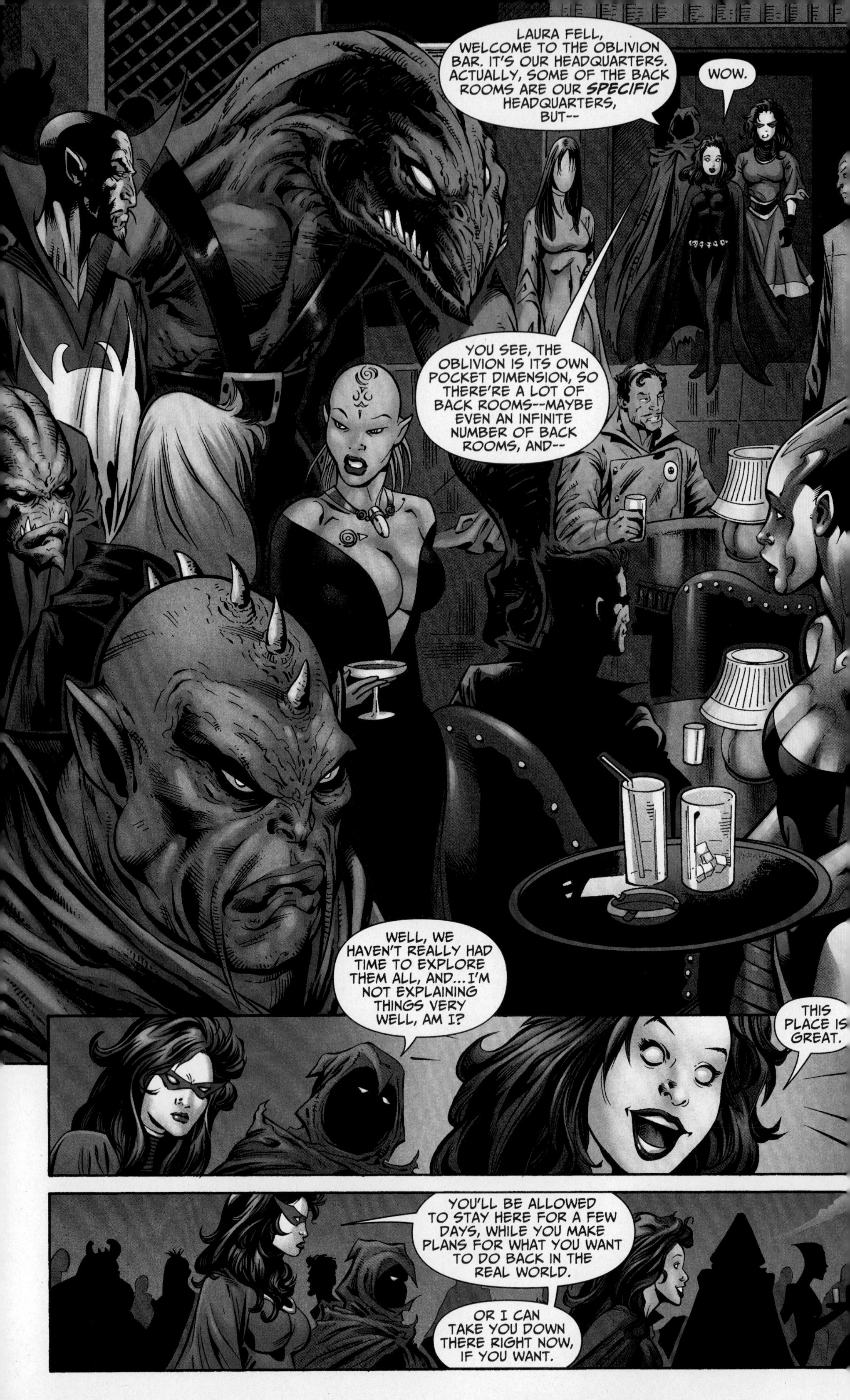
LAURA FELL, WELCOME TO THE OBLIVION BAR. IT'S OUR HEADQUARTERS. ACTUALLY, SOME OF THE BACK ROOMS ARE OUR SPECIFIC HEADQUARTERS, BUT--
WOW.
YOU SEE, THE OBLIVION IS ITS OWN POCKET DIMENSION, SO THERE'RE A LOT OF BACK ROOMS--MAYBE EVEN AN INFINITE NUMBER OF BACK ROOMS, AND--
WELL, WE HAVEN'T REALLY HAD TIME TO EXPLORE THEM ALL, AND... I'M NOT EXPLAINING THINGS VERY WELL, AM I?
THIS PLACE IS GREAT.
YOU'LL BE ALLOWED TO STAY HERE FOR A FEW DAYS, WHILE YOU MAKE PLANS FOR WHAT YOU WANT TO DO BACK IN THE REAL WORLD.
OR I CAN TAKE YOU DOWN THERE RIGHT NOW, IF YOU WANT.

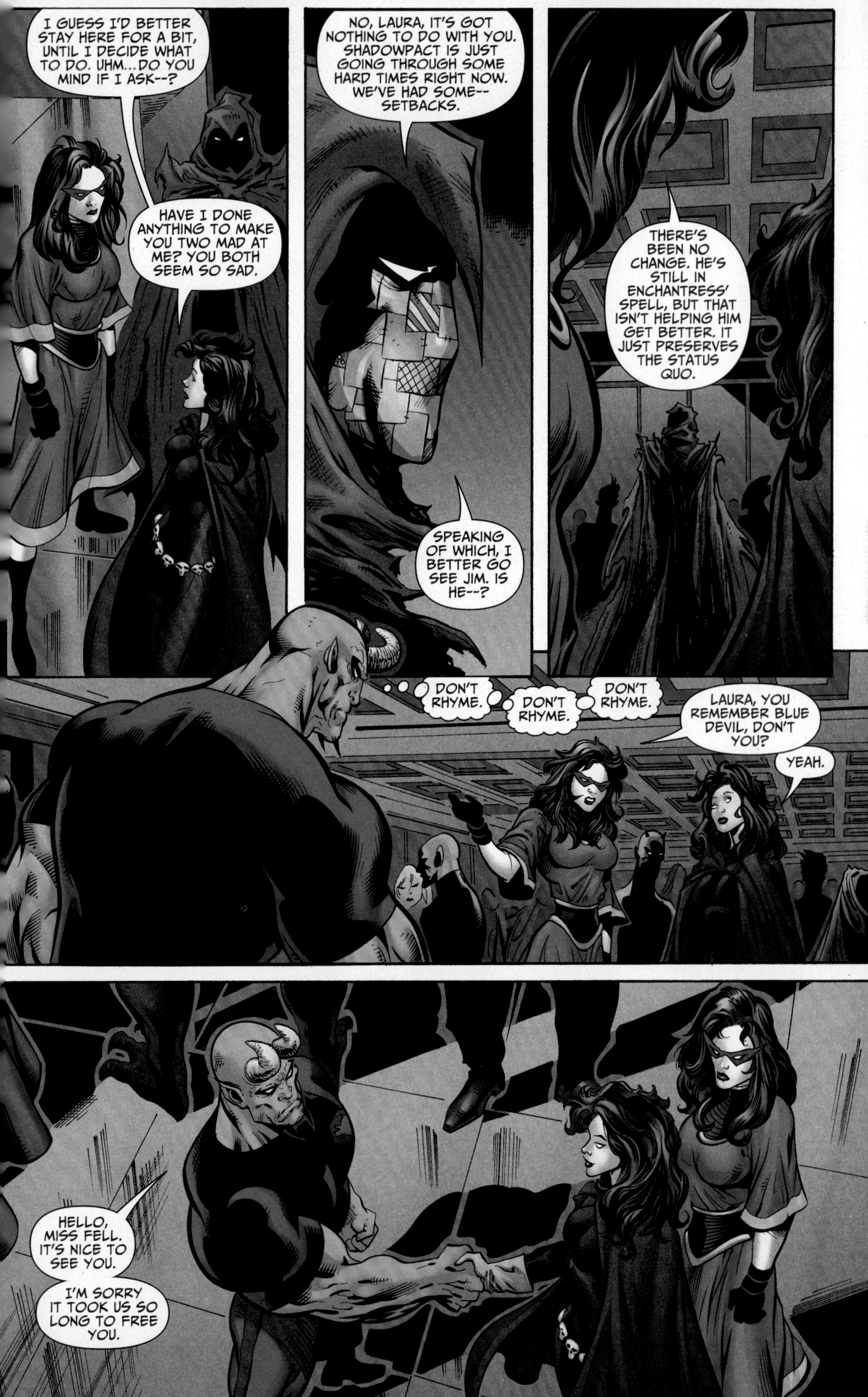
I GUESS I'D BETTER STAY HERE FOR A BIT, UNTIL I DECIDE WHAT TO DO. UHM...DO YOU MIND IF I ASK--?
HAVE I DONE ANYTHING TO MAKE YOU TWO MAD AT ME? YOU BOTH SEEM SO SAD.
NO, LAURA, IT'S GOT NOTHING TO DO WITH YOU. SHADOWPACT IS JUST GOING THROUGH SOME HARD TIMES RIGHT NOW. WE'VE HAD SOME-- SETBACKS.
SPEAKING OF WHICH, I BETTER GO SEE JIM. IS HE--?
THERE'S BEEN NO CHANGE. HE'S STILL IN ENCHANTRESS' SPELL, BUT THAT ISN'T HELPING HIM GET BETTER. IT JUST PRESERVES THE STATUS QUO.
DON'T RHYME.
DON'T RHYME.
DON'T RHYME.
LAURA, YOU REMEMBER BLUE DEVIL, DON'T YOU?
YEAH.
HELLO, MISS FELL. IT'S NICE TO SEE YOU.
I'M SORRY IT TOOK US SO LONG TO FREE YOU.

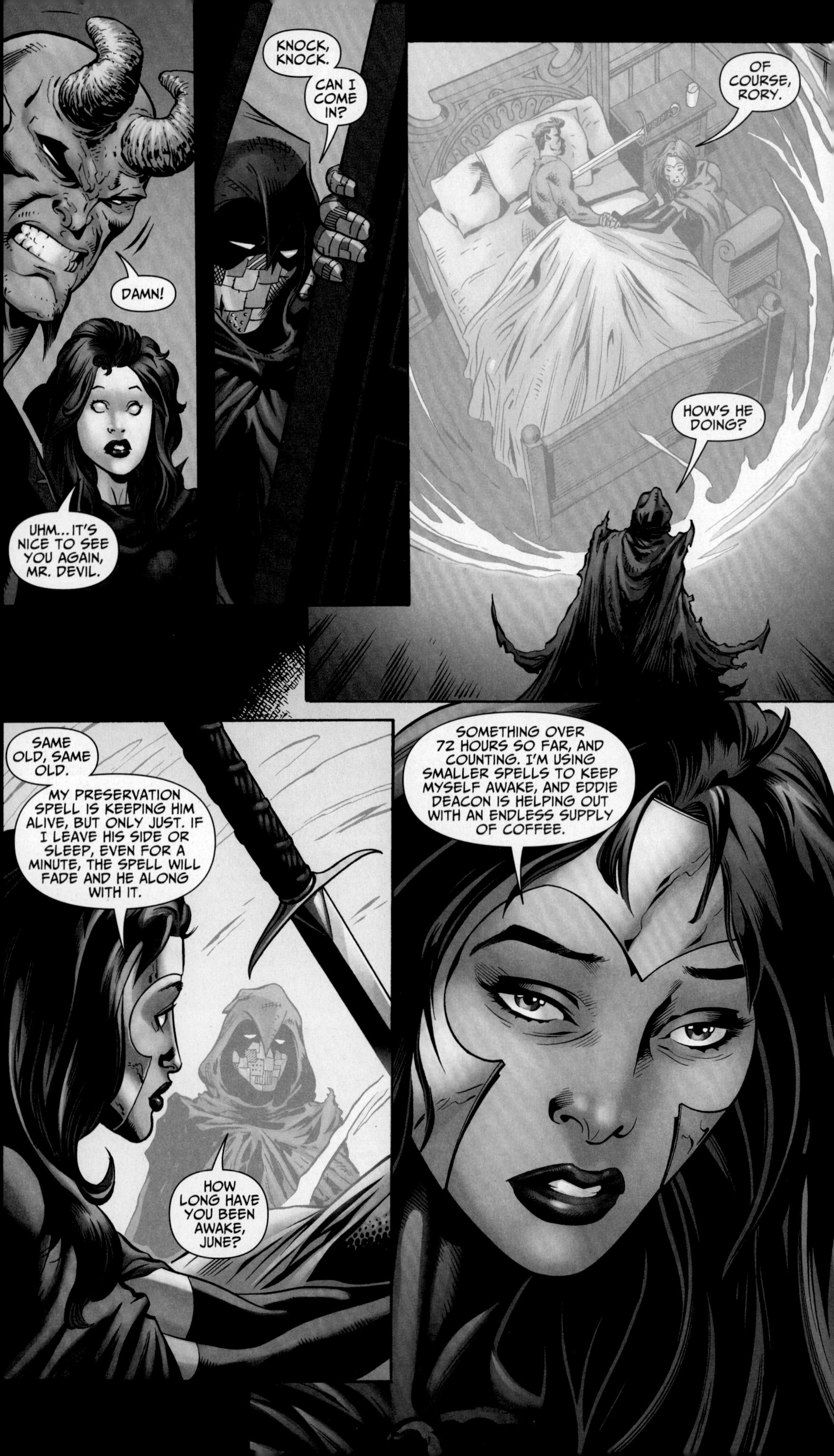
DAMN!
UHM... IT'S NICE TO SEE YOU AGAIN, MR. DEVIL.
KNOCK, KNOCK.
CAN I COME IN?
OF COURSE, RORY.
HOW'S HE DOING?
SAME OLD, SAME OLD.
MY PRESERVATION SPELL IS KEEPING HIM ALIVE, BUT ONLY JUST. IF I LEAVE HIS SIDE OR SLEEP, EVEN FOR A MINUTE, THE SPELL WILL FADE AND HE ALONG WITH IT.
HOW LONG HAVE YOU BEEN AWAKE, JUNE?
SOMETHING OVER 72 HOURS SO FAR, AND COUNTING. I'M USING SMALLER SPELLS TO KEEP MYSELF AWAKE, AND EDDIE DEACON IS HELPING OUT WITH AN ENDLESS SUPPLY OF COFFEE.

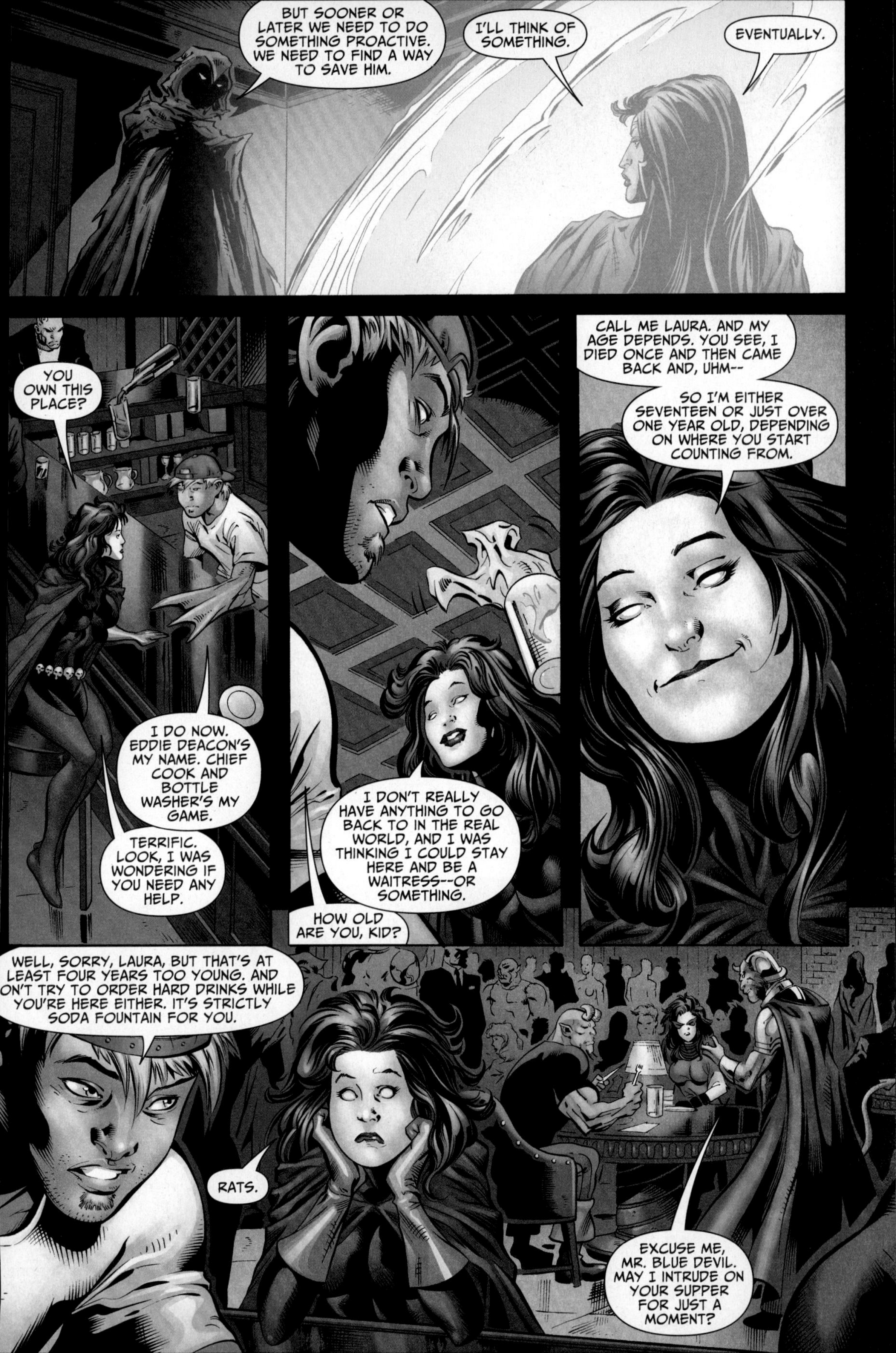

BUT SOONER OR LATER WE NEED TO DO SOMETHING PROACTIVE. WE NEED TO FIND A WAY TO SAVE HIM.
I'LL THINK OF SOMETHING.
EVENTUALLY.
YOU OWN THIS PLACE?
I DO NOW. EDDIE DEACON'S MY NAME. CHIEF COOK AND BOTTLE WASHER'S MY GAME.
TERRIFIC. LOOK, I WAS WONDERING IF YOU NEED ANY HELP.
I DON'T REALLY HAVE ANYTHING TO GO BACK TO IN THE REAL WORLD, AND I WAS THINKING I COULD STAY HERE AND BE A WAITRESS--OR SOMETHING.
HOW OLD ARE YOU, KID?
CALL ME LAURA. AND MY AGE DEPENDS. YOU SEE, I DIED ONCE AND THEN CAME BACK AND, UHM--
SO I'M EITHER SEVENTEEN OR JUST OVER ONE YEAR OLD, DEPENDING ON WHERE YOU START COUNTING FROM.
WELL, SORRY, LAURA, BUT THAT'S AT LEAST FOUR YEARS TOO YOUNG. AND ON'T TRY TO ORDER HARD DRINKS WHILE YOU'RE HERE EITHER. IT'S STRICTLY SODA FOUNTAIN FOR YOU.
RATS.
EXCUSE ME, MR. BLUE DEVIL. MAY I INTRUDE ON YOUR SUPPER FOR JUST A MOMENT?

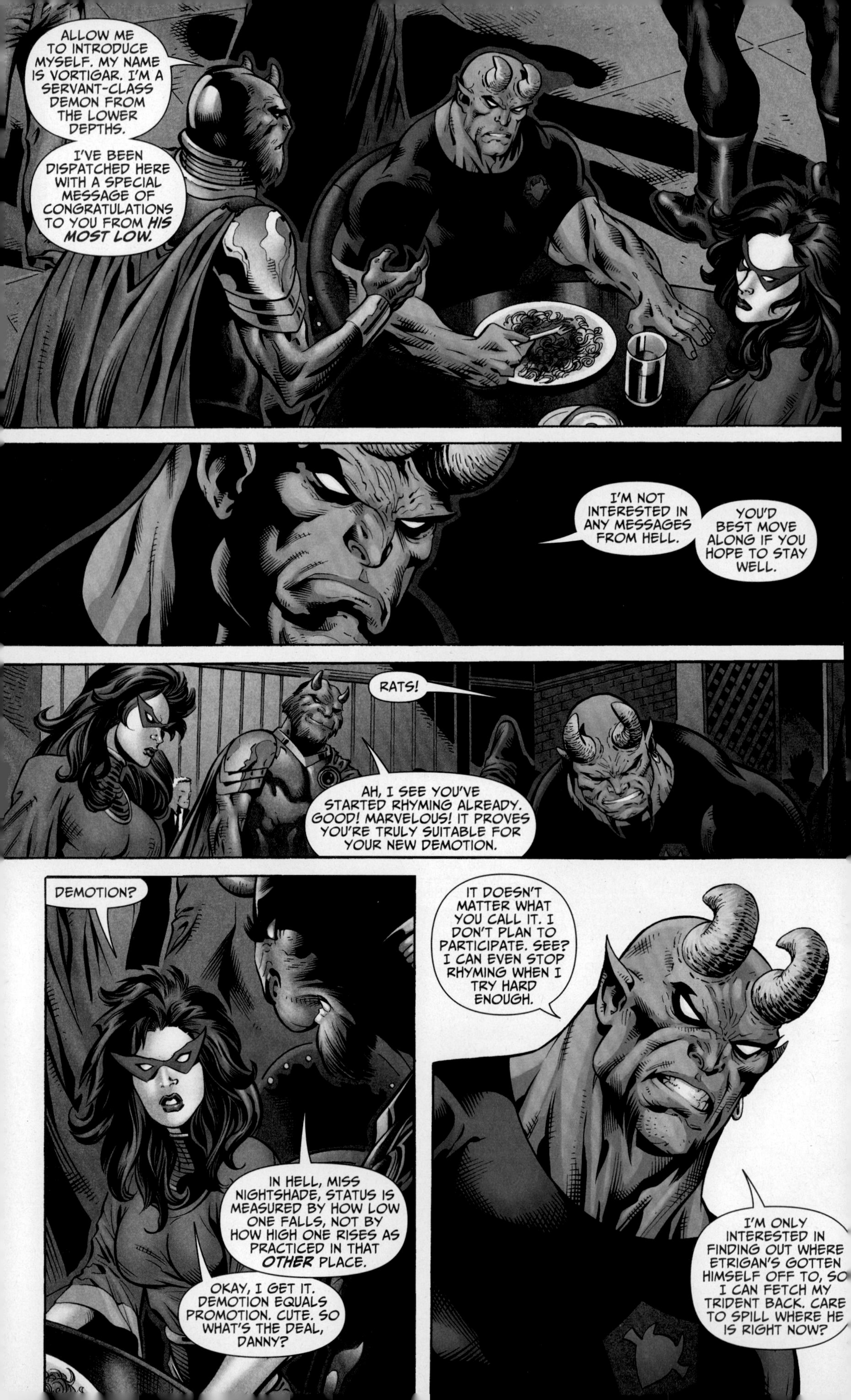
ALLOW ME TO INTRODUCE MYSELF. MY NAME IS VORTIGAR. I'M A SERVANT-CLASS DEMON FROM THE LOWER DEPTHS.
I'VE BEEN DISPATCHED HERE WITH A SPECIAL MESSAGE OF CONGRATULATIONS TO YOU FROM ***HIS MOST LOW.***
I'M NOT INTERESTED IN ANY MESSAGES FROM HELL.
YOU'D BEST MOVE ALONG IF YOU HOPE TO STAY WELL.
RATS!
AH, I SEE YOU'VE STARTED RHYMING ALREADY. GOOD! MARVELOUS! IT PROVES YOU'RE TRULY SUITABLE FOR YOUR NEW DEMOTION.
DEMOTION?
IN HELL, MISS NIGHTSHADE, STATUS IS MEASURED BY HOW LOW ONE FALLS, NOT BY HOW HIGH ONE RISES AS PRACTICED IN THAT ***OTHER*** PLACE.
OKAY, I GET IT. DEMOTION EQUALS PROMOTION. CUTE. SO WHAT'S THE DEAL, DANNY?
IT DOESN'T MATTER WHAT YOU CALL IT. I DON'T PLAN TO PARTICIPATE. SEE? I CAN EVEN STOP RHYMING WHEN I TRY HARD ENOUGH.
I'M ONLY INTERESTED IN FINDING OUT WHERE ETRIGAN'S GOTTEN HIMSELF OFF TO, SO I CAN FETCH MY TRIDENT BACK. CARE TO SPILL WHERE HE IS RIGHT NOW?

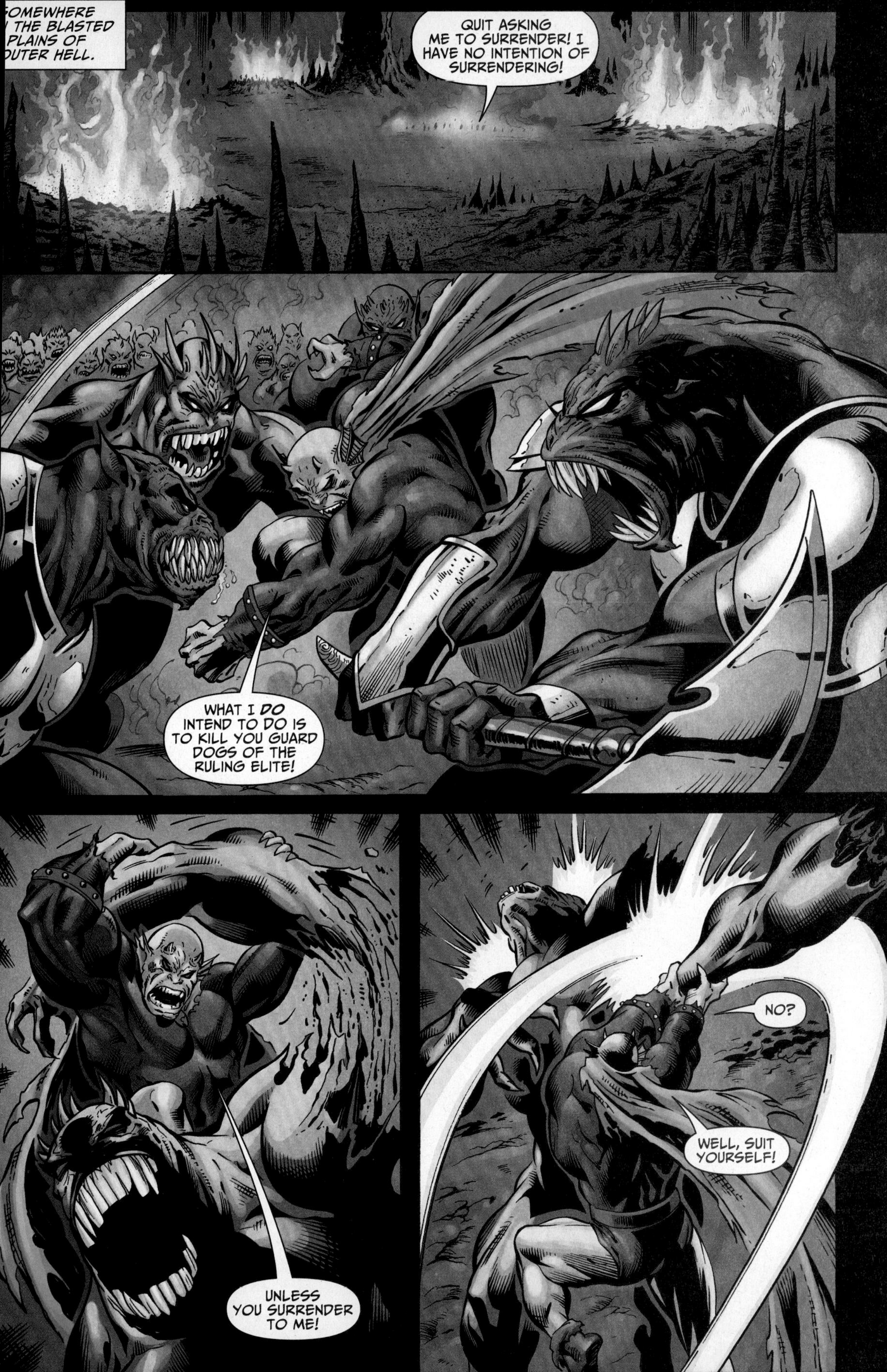
SOMEWHERE IN THE BLASTED PLAINS OF OUTER HELL.
QUIT ASKING ME TO SURRENDER! I HAVE NO INTENTION OF SURRENDERING!
WHAT I DO INTEND TO DO IS TO KILL YOU GUARD DOGS OF THE RULING ELITE!
UNLESS YOU SURRENDER TO ME!
NO?
WELL, SUIT YOURSELF!

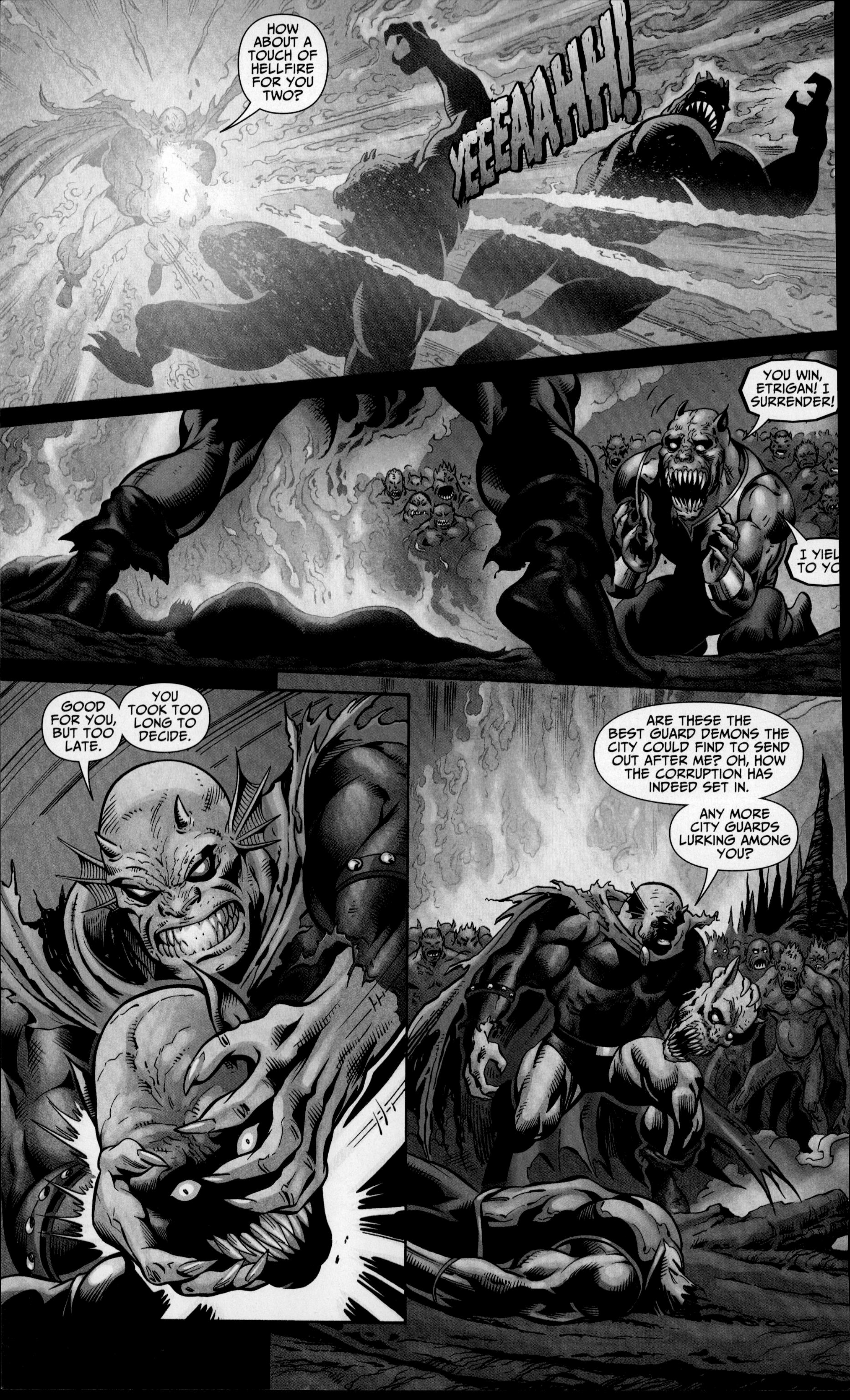

HOW ABOUT A TOUCH OF HELLFIRE FOR YOU TWO?
YEEEAAHH!
YOU WIN, ETRIGAN! I SURRENDER!
GOOD FOR YOU, BUT TOO LATE.
YOU TOOK TOO LONG TO DECIDE.
ARE THESE THE BEST GUARD DEMONS THE CITY COULD FIND TO SEND OUT AFTER ME? OH, HOW THE CORRUPTION HAS INDEED SET IN.
ANY MORE CITY GUARDS LURKING AMONG YOU?

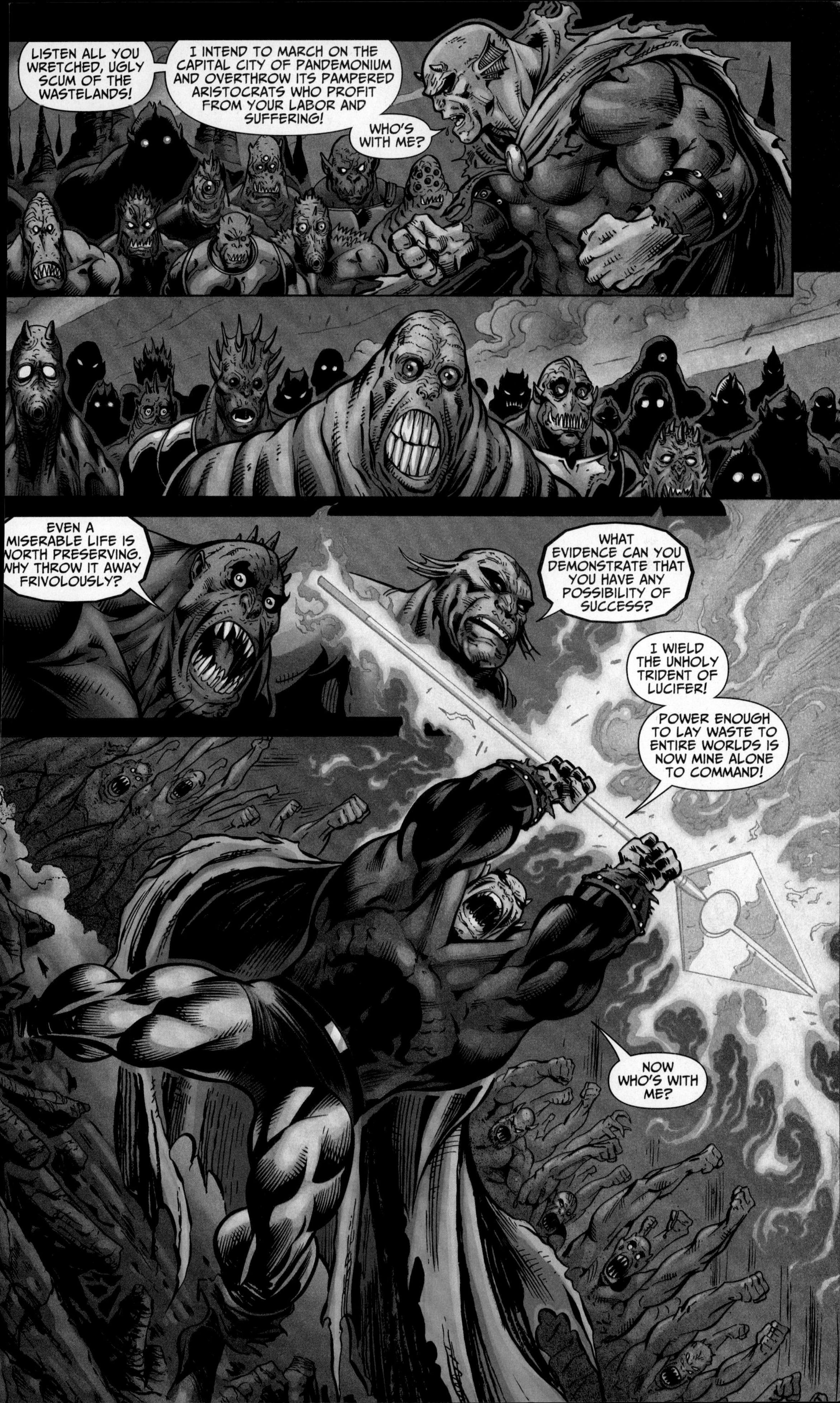
LISTEN ALL YOU WRETCHED, UGLY SCUM OF THE WASTELANDS!
I INTEND TO MARCH ON THE CAPITAL CITY OF PANDEMONIUM AND OVERTHROW ITS PAMPERED ARISTOCRATS WHO PROFIT FROM YOUR LABOR AND SUFFERING!
WHO'S WITH ME?
EVEN A MISERABLE LIFE IS WORTH PRESERVING. WHY THROW IT AWAY FRIVOLOUSLY?
WHAT EVIDENCE CAN YOU DEMONSTRATE THAT YOU HAVE ANY POSSIBILITY OF SUCCESS?
I WIELD THE UNHOLY TRIDENT OF LUCIFER!
POWER ENOUGH TO LAY WASTE TO ENTIRE WORLDS IS NOW MINE ALONE TO COMMAND!
NOW WHO'S WITH ME?

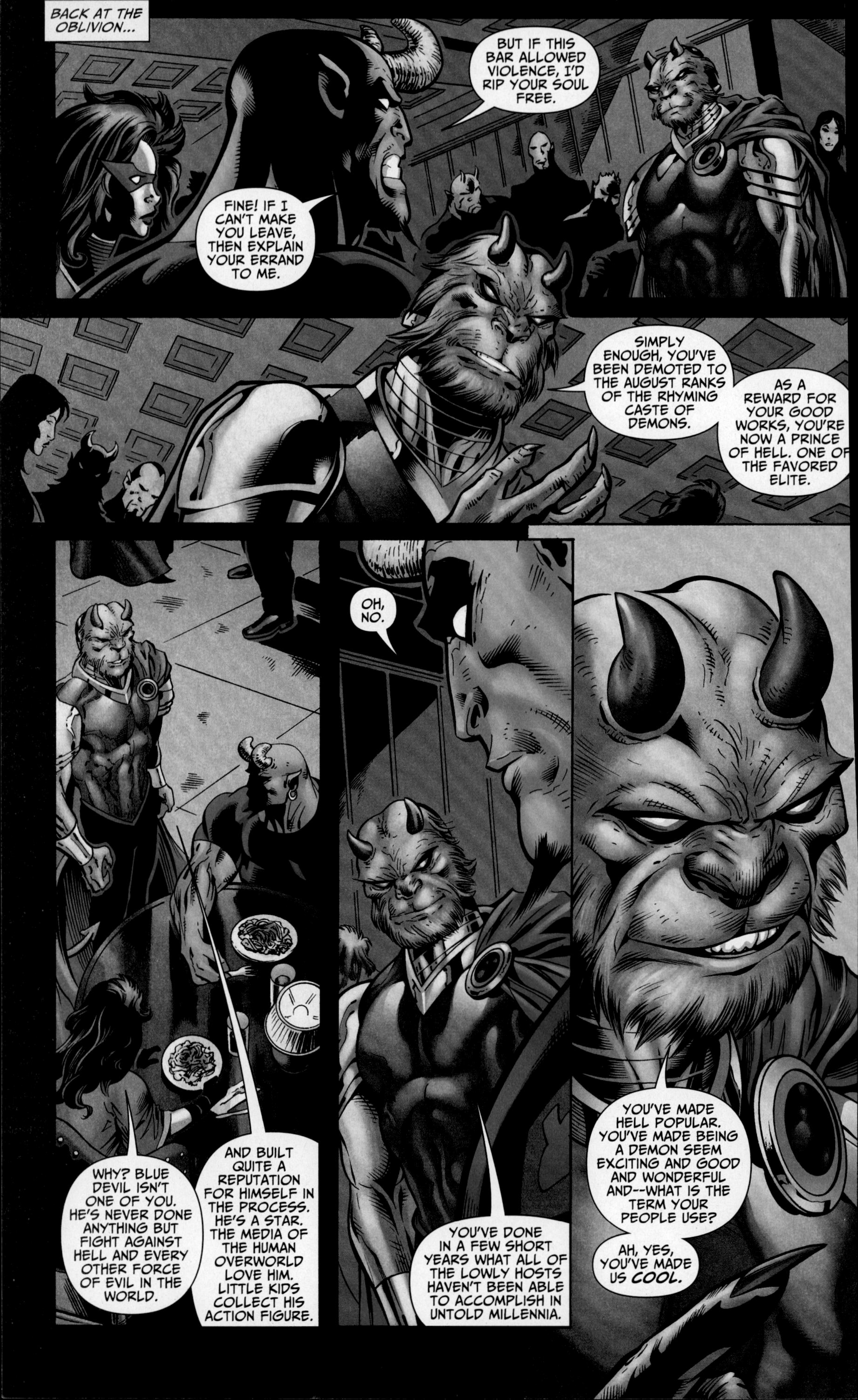
BACK AT THE OBLIVION...
BUT IF THIS BAR ALLOWED VIOLENCE, I'D RIP YOUR SOUL FREE.
FINE! IF I CAN'T MAKE YOU LEAVE, THEN EXPLAIN YOUR ERRAND TO ME.
SIMPLY ENOUGH, YOU'VE BEEN DEMOTED TO THE AUGUST RANKS OF THE RHYMING CASTE OF DEMONS.
AS A REWARD FOR YOUR GOOD WORKS, YOU'RE NOW A PRINCE OF HELL. ONE OF THE FAVORED ELITE.
WHY? BLUE DEVIL ISN'T ONE OF YOU. HE'S NEVER DONE ANYTHING BUT FIGHT AGAINST HELL AND EVERY OTHER FORCE OF EVIL IN THE WORLD.
AND BUILT QUITE A REPUTATION FOR HIMSELF IN THE PROCESS. HE'S A STAR. THE MEDIA OF THE HUMAN OVERWORLD LOVE HIM. LITTLE KIDS COLLECT HIS ACTION FIGURE.
OH, NO.
YOU'VE DONE IN A FEW SHORT YEARS WHAT ALL OF THE LOWLY HOSTS HAVEN'T BEEN ABLE TO ACCOMPLISH IN UNTOLD MILLENNIA.
YOU'VE MADE HELL POPULAR. YOU'VE MADE BEING A DEMON SEEM EXCITING AND GOOD AND WONDERFUL AND--WHAT IS THE TERM YOUR PEOPLE USE?
AH, YES, YOU'VE MADE US *COOL*.

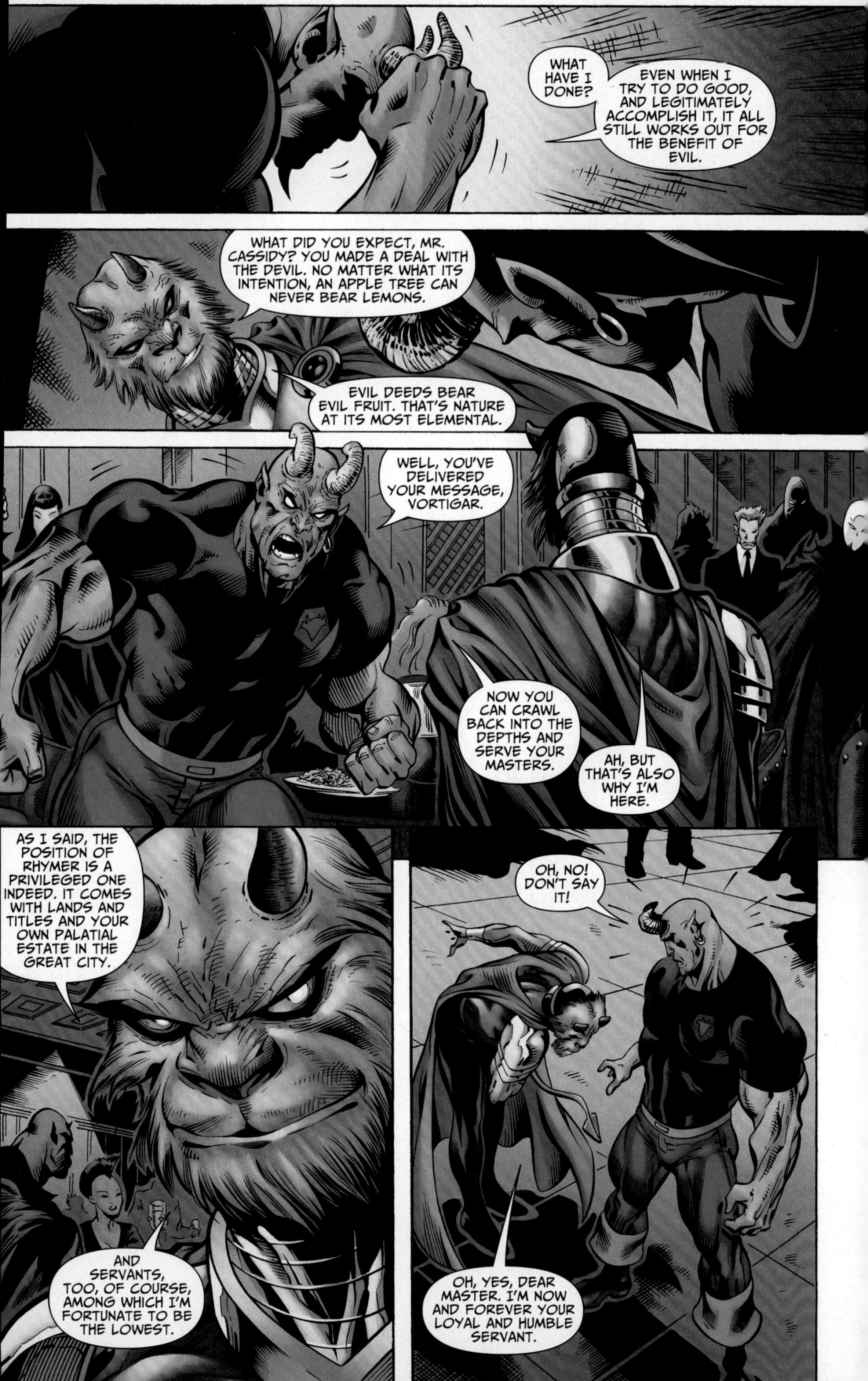
WHAT HAVE I DONE?
EVEN WHEN I TRY TO DO GOOD, AND LEGITIMATELY ACCOMPLISH IT, IT ALL STILL WORKS OUT FOR THE BENEFIT OF EVIL.
WHAT DID YOU EXPECT, MR. CASSIDY? YOU MADE A DEAL WITH THE DEVIL. NO MATTER WHAT ITS INTENTION, AN APPLE TREE CAN NEVER BEAR LEMONS.
EVIL DEEDS BEAR EVIL FRUIT. THAT'S NATURE AT ITS MOST ELEMENTAL.
WELL, YOU'VE DELIVERED YOUR MESSAGE, VORTIGAR.
NOW YOU CAN CRAWL BACK INTO THE DEPTHS AND SERVE YOUR MASTERS.
AH, BUT THAT'S ALSO WHY I'M HERE.
AS I SAID, THE POSITION OF RHYMER IS A PRIVILEGED ONE INDEED. IT COMES WITH LANDS AND TITLES AND YOUR OWN PALATIAL ESTATE IN THE GREAT CITY.
AND SERVANTS, TOO, OF COURSE, AMONG WHICH I'M FORTUNATE TO BE THE LOWEST.
OH, NO! DON'T SAY IT!
OH, YES, DEAR MASTER. I'M NOW AND FOREVER YOUR LOYAL AND HUMBLE SERVANT.

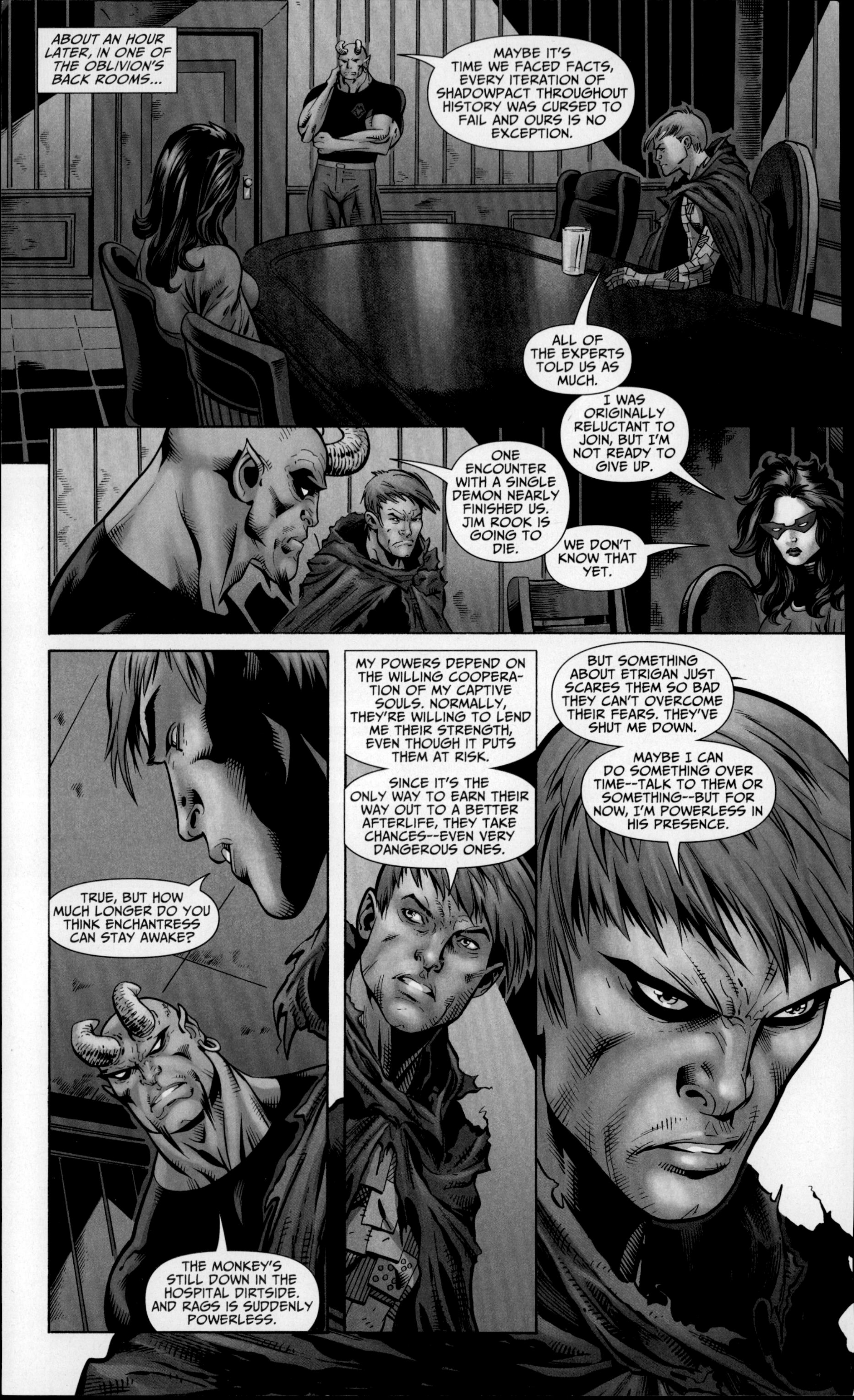
ABOUT AN HOUR LATER, IN ONE OF THE OBLIVION'S BACK ROOMS...
MAYBE IT'S TIME WE FACED FACTS, EVERY ITERATION OF SHADOWPACT THROUGHOUT HISTORY WAS CURSED TO FAIL AND OURS IS NO EXCEPTION.
ALL OF THE EXPERTS TOLD US AS MUCH.
I WAS ORIGINALLY RELUCTANT TO JOIN, BUT I'M NOT READY TO GIVE UP.
ONE ENCOUNTER WITH A SINGLE DEMON NEARLY FINISHED US. JIM ROOK IS GOING TO DIE.
WE DON'T KNOW THAT YET.
TRUE, BUT HOW MUCH LONGER DO YOU THINK ENCHANTRESS CAN STAY AWAKE?
THE MONKEY'S STILL DOWN IN THE HOSPITAL DIRTSIDE. AND RAGS IS SUDDENLY POWERLESS.
MY POWERS DEPEND ON THE WILLING COOPERATION OF MY CAPTIVE SOULS. NORMALLY, THEY'RE WILLING TO LEND ME THEIR STRENGTH, EVEN THOUGH IT PUTS THEM AT RISK.
SINCE IT'S THE ONLY WAY TO EARN THEIR WAY OUT TO A BETTER AFTERLIFE, THEY TAKE CHANCES--EVEN VERY DANGEROUS ONES.
BUT SOMETHING ABOUT ETRIGAN JUST SCARES THEM SO BAD THEY CAN'T OVERCOME THEIR FEARS. THEY'VE SHUT ME DOWN.
MAYBE I CAN DO SOMETHING OVER TIME--TALK TO THEM OR SOMETHING--BUT FOR NOW, I'M POWERLESS IN HIS PRESENCE.

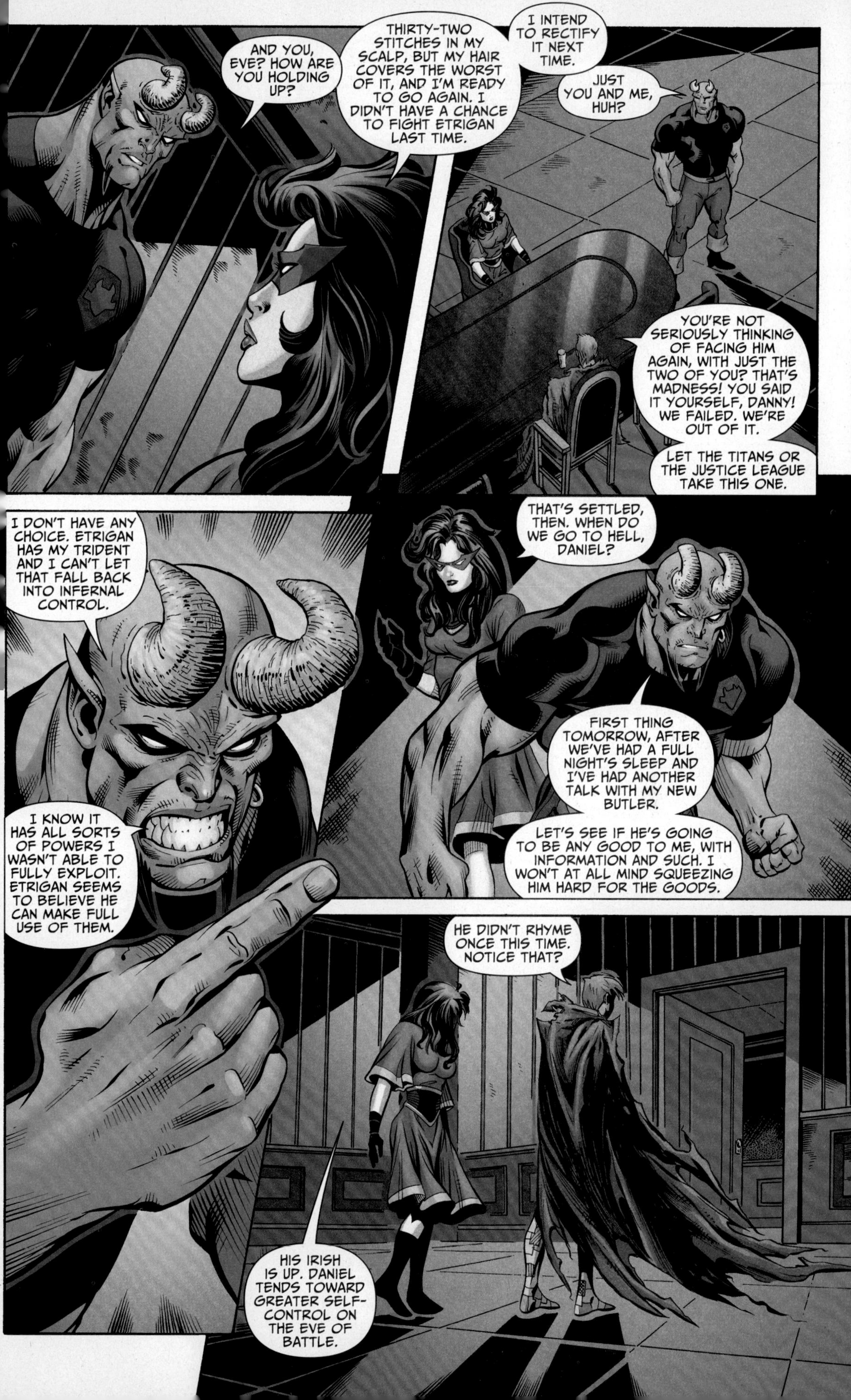
AND YOU, EVE? HOW ARE YOU HOLDING UP?
THIRTY-TWO STITCHES IN MY SCALP, BUT MY HAIR COVERS THE WORST OF IT, AND I'M READY TO GO AGAIN. I DIDN'T HAVE A CHANCE TO FIGHT ETRIGAN LAST TIME.
I INTEND TO RECTIFY IT NEXT TIME.
JUST YOU AND ME, HUH?
YOU'RE NOT SERIOUSLY THINKING OF FACING HIM AGAIN, WITH JUST THE TWO OF YOU? THAT'S MADNESS! YOU SAID IT YOURSELF, DANNY! WE FAILED. WE'RE OUT OF IT.
LET THE TITANS OR THE JUSTICE LEAGUE TAKE THIS ONE.
I DON'T HAVE ANY CHOICE. ETRIGAN HAS MY TRIDENT AND I CAN'T LET THAT FALL BACK INTO INFERNAL CONTROL.
I KNOW IT HAS ALL SORTS OF POWERS I WASN'T ABLE TO FULLY EXPLOIT. ETRIGAN SEEMS TO BELIEVE HE CAN MAKE FULL USE OF THEM.
THAT'S SETTLED, THEN. WHEN DO WE GO TO HELL, DANIEL?
FIRST THING TOMORROW, AFTER WE'VE HAD A FULL NIGHT'S SLEEP AND I'VE HAD ANOTHER TALK WITH MY NEW BUTLER.
LET'S SEE IF HE'S GOING TO BE ANY GOOD TO ME, WITH INFORMATION AND SUCH. I WON'T AT ALL MIND SQUEEZING HIM HARD FOR THE GOODS.
HE DIDN'T RHYME ONCE THIS TIME. NOTICE THAT?
HIS IRISH IS UP. DANIEL TENDS TOWARD GREATER SELF-CONTROL ON THE EVE OF BATTLE.

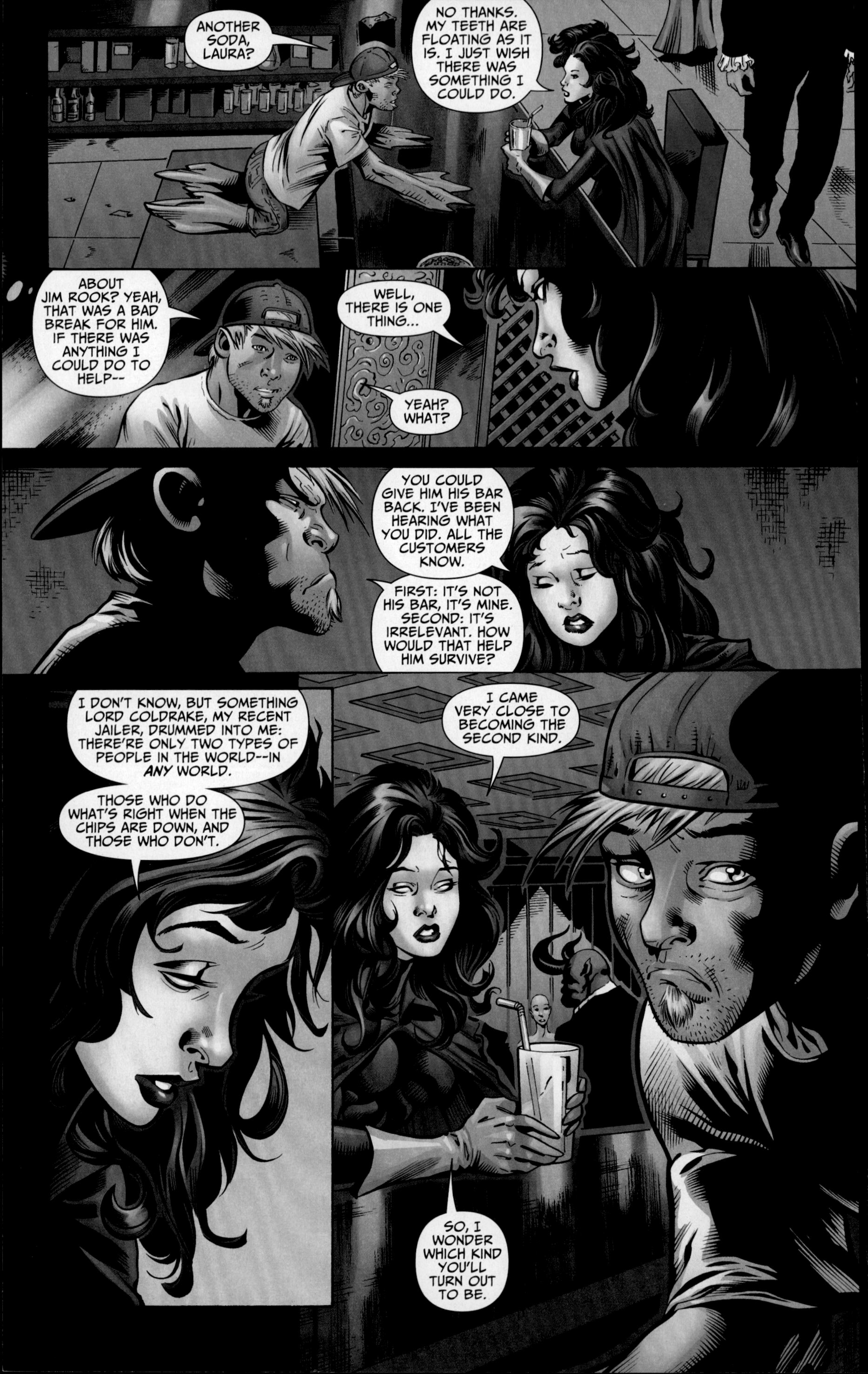
ANOTHER SODA, LAURA?
NO THANKS. MY TEETH ARE FLOATING AS IT IS. I JUST WISH THERE WAS SOMETHING I COULD DO.
ABOUT JIM ROOK? YEAH, THAT WAS A BAD BREAK FOR HIM. IF THERE WAS ANYTHING I COULD DO TO HELP--
WELL, THERE IS ONE THING...
YEAH? WHAT?
YOU COULD GIVE HIM HIS BAR BACK. I'VE BEEN HEARING WHAT YOU DID. ALL THE CUSTOMERS KNOW.
FIRST: IT'S NOT HIS BAR, IT'S MINE. SECOND: IT'S IRRELEVANT. HOW WOULD THAT HELP HIM SURVIVE?
I DON'T KNOW, BUT SOMETHING LORD COLDRAKE, MY RECENT JAILER, DRUMMED INTO ME: THERE'RE ONLY TWO TYPES OF PEOPLE IN THE WORLD--IN *ANY* WORLD.
THOSE WHO DO WHAT'S RIGHT WHEN THE CHIPS ARE DOWN, AND THOSE WHO DON'T.
I CAME VERY CLOSE TO BECOMING THE SECOND KIND.
SO, I WONDER WHICH KIND YOU'LL TURN OUT TO BE.

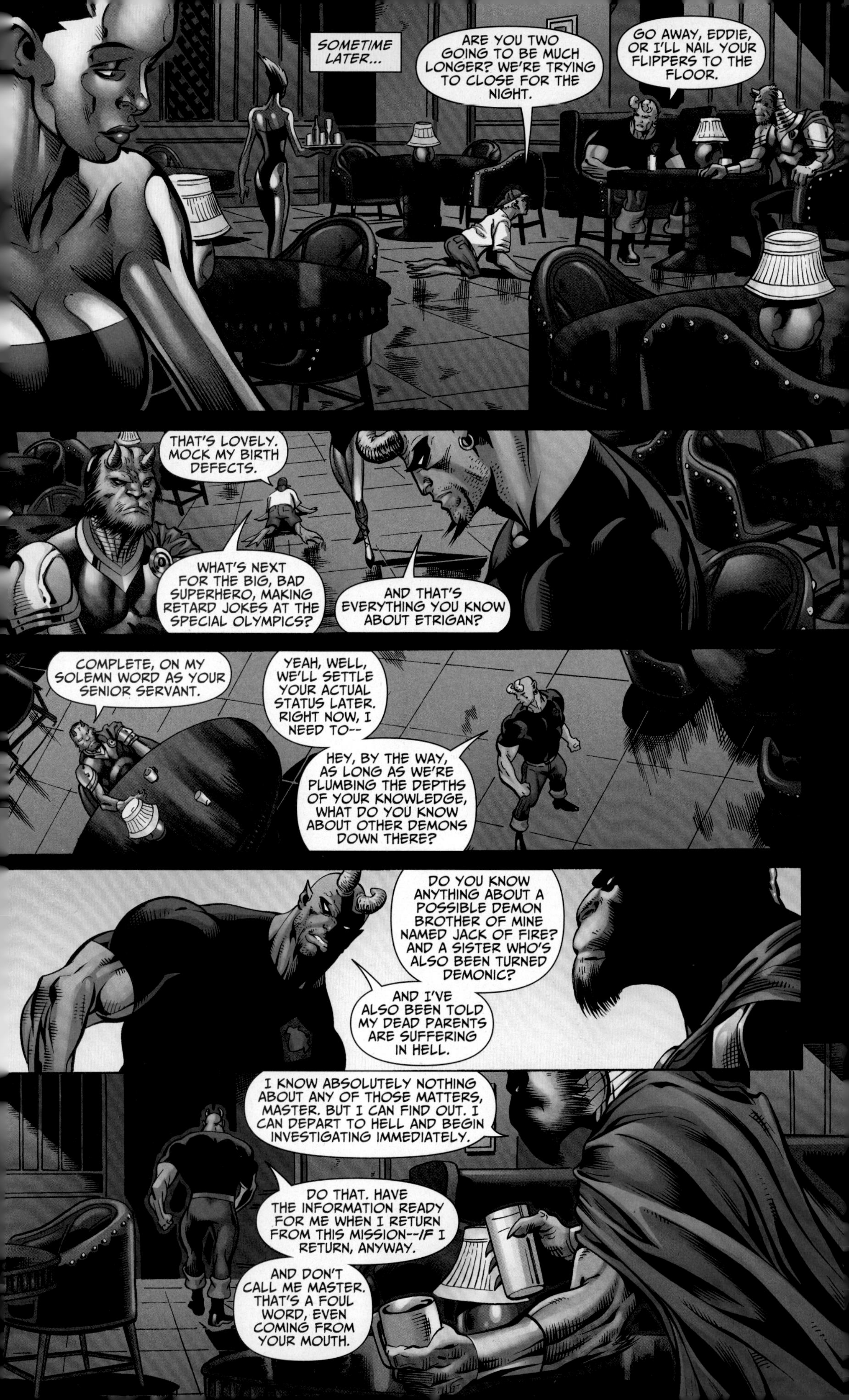
SOMETIME LATER...
ARE YOU TWO GOING TO BE MUCH LONGER? WE'RE TRYING TO CLOSE FOR THE NIGHT.
GO AWAY, EDDIE, OR I'LL NAIL YOUR FLIPPERS TO THE FLOOR.
THAT'S LOVELY. MOCK MY BIRTH DEFECTS.
WHAT'S NEXT FOR THE BIG, BAD SUPERHERO, MAKING RETARD JOKES AT THE SPECIAL OLYMPICS?
AND THAT'S EVERYTHING YOU KNOW ABOUT ETRIGAN?
COMPLETE, ON MY SOLEMN WORD AS YOUR SENIOR SERVANT.
YEAH, WELL, WE'LL SETTLE YOUR ACTUAL STATUS LATER. RIGHT NOW, I NEED TO--
HEY, BY THE WAY, AS LONG AS WE'RE PLUMBING THE DEPTHS OF YOUR KNOWLEDGE, WHAT DO YOU KNOW ABOUT OTHER DEMONS DOWN THERE?
DO YOU KNOW ANYTHING ABOUT A POSSIBLE DEMON BROTHER OF MINE NAMED JACK OF FIRE? AND A SISTER WHO'S ALSO BEEN TURNED DEMONIC?
AND I'VE ALSO BEEN TOLD MY DEAD PARENTS ARE SUFFERING IN HELL.
I KNOW ABSOLUTELY NOTHING ABOUT ANY OF THOSE MATTERS, MASTER. BUT I CAN FIND OUT. I CAN DEPART TO HELL AND BEGIN INVESTIGATING IMMEDIATELY.
DO THAT. HAVE THE INFORMATION READY FOR ME WHEN I RETURN FROM THIS MISSION--*IF* I RETURN, ANYWAY.
AND DON'T CALL ME MASTER. THAT'S A FOUL WORD, EVEN COMING FROM YOUR MOUTH.

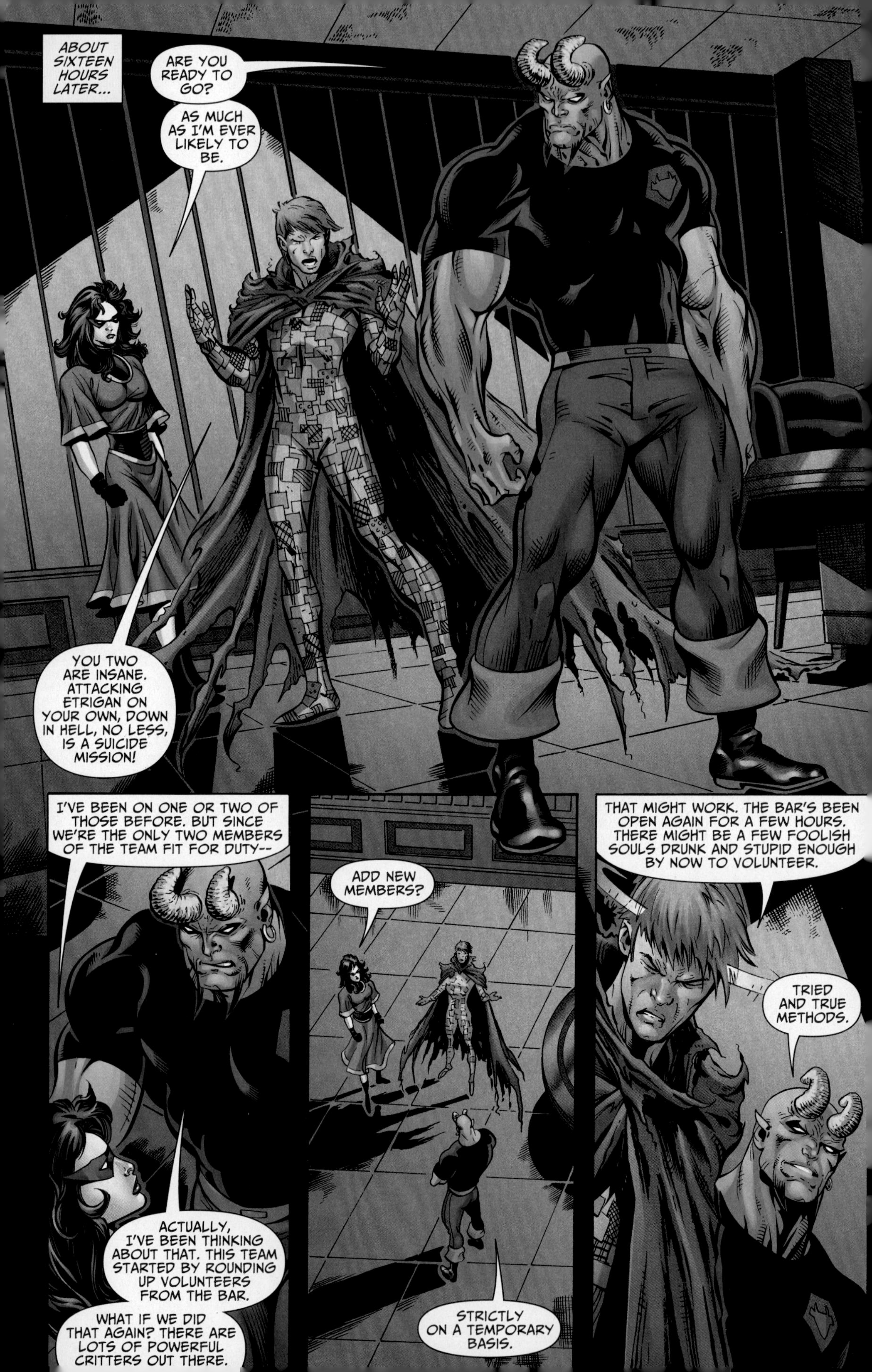
ABOUT SIXTEEN HOURS LATER...
ARE YOU READY TO GO?
AS MUCH AS I'M EVER LIKELY TO BE.
YOU TWO ARE INSANE. ATTACKING ETRIGAN ON YOUR OWN, DOWN IN HELL, NO LESS, IS A SUICIDE MISSION!
I'VE BEEN ON ONE OR TWO OF THOSE BEFORE. BUT SINCE WE'RE THE ONLY TWO MEMBERS OF THE TEAM FIT FOR DUTY--
ACTUALLY, I'VE BEEN THINKING ABOUT THAT. THIS TEAM STARTED BY ROUNDING UP VOLUNTEERS FROM THE BAR.
WHAT IF WE DID THAT AGAIN? THERE ARE LOTS OF POWERFUL CRITTERS OUT THERE.
ADD NEW MEMBERS?
STRICTLY ON A TEMPORARY BASIS.
THAT MIGHT WORK. THE BAR'S BEEN OPEN AGAIN FOR A FEW HOURS. THERE MIGHT BE A FEW FOOLISH SOULS DRUNK AND STUPID ENOUGH BY NOW TO VOLUNTEER.
TRIED AND TRUE METHODS.

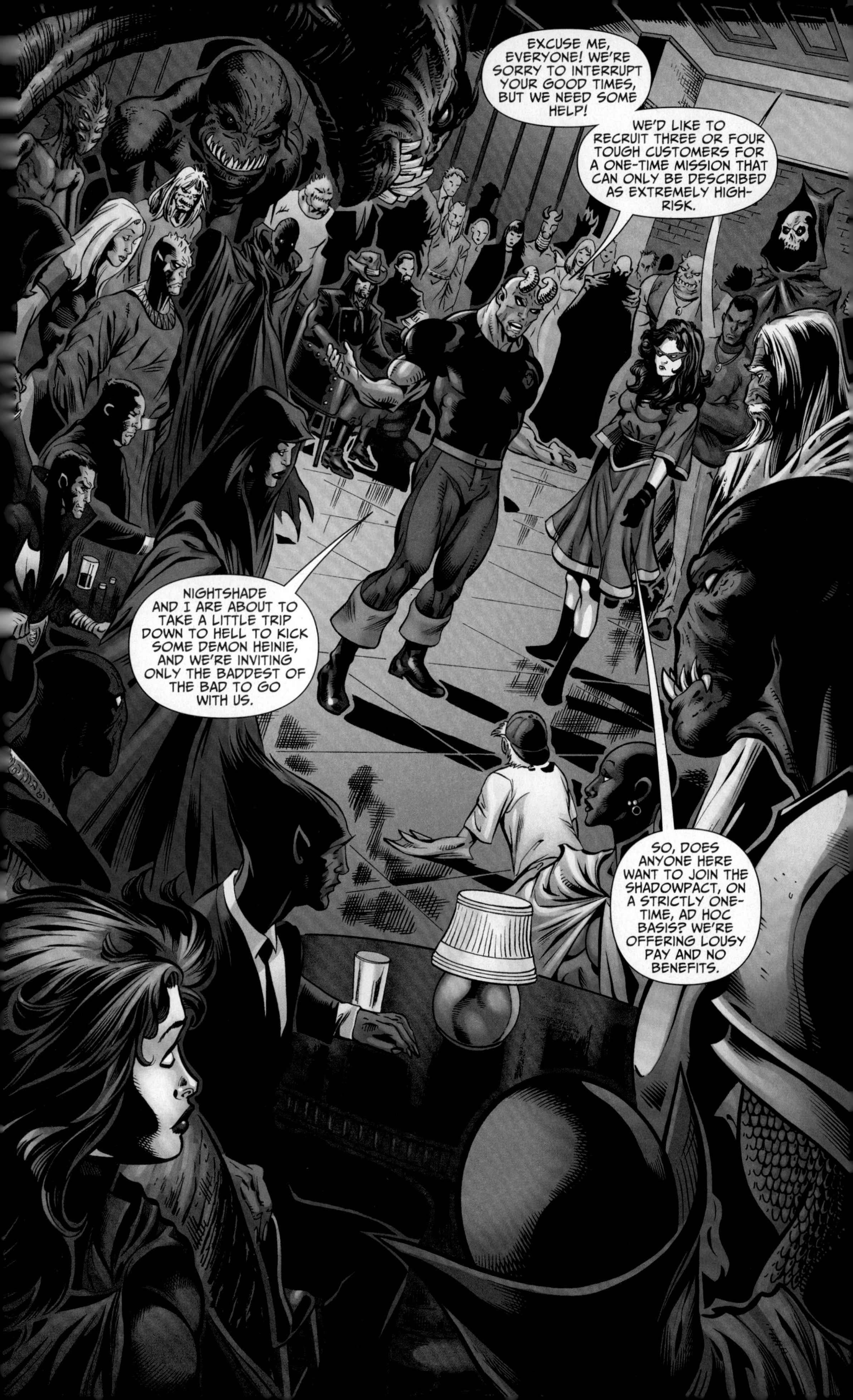
EXCUSE ME, EVERYONE! WE'RE SORRY TO INTERRUPT YOUR GOOD TIMES, BUT WE NEED SOME HELP!
WE'D LIKE TO RECRUIT THREE OR FOUR TOUGH CUSTOMERS FOR A ONE-TIME MISSION THAT CAN ONLY BE DESCRIBED AS EXTREMELY HIGH-RISK.
NIGHTSHADE AND I ARE ABOUT TO TAKE A LITTLE TRIP DOWN TO HELL TO KICK SOME DEMON HEINIE, AND WE'RE INVITING ONLY THE BADDEST OF THE BAD TO GO WITH US.
SO, DOES ANYONE HERE WANT TO JOIN THE SHADOWPACT, ON A STRICTLY ONE-TIME, AD HOC BASIS? WE'RE OFFERING LOUSY PAY AND NO BENEFITS.

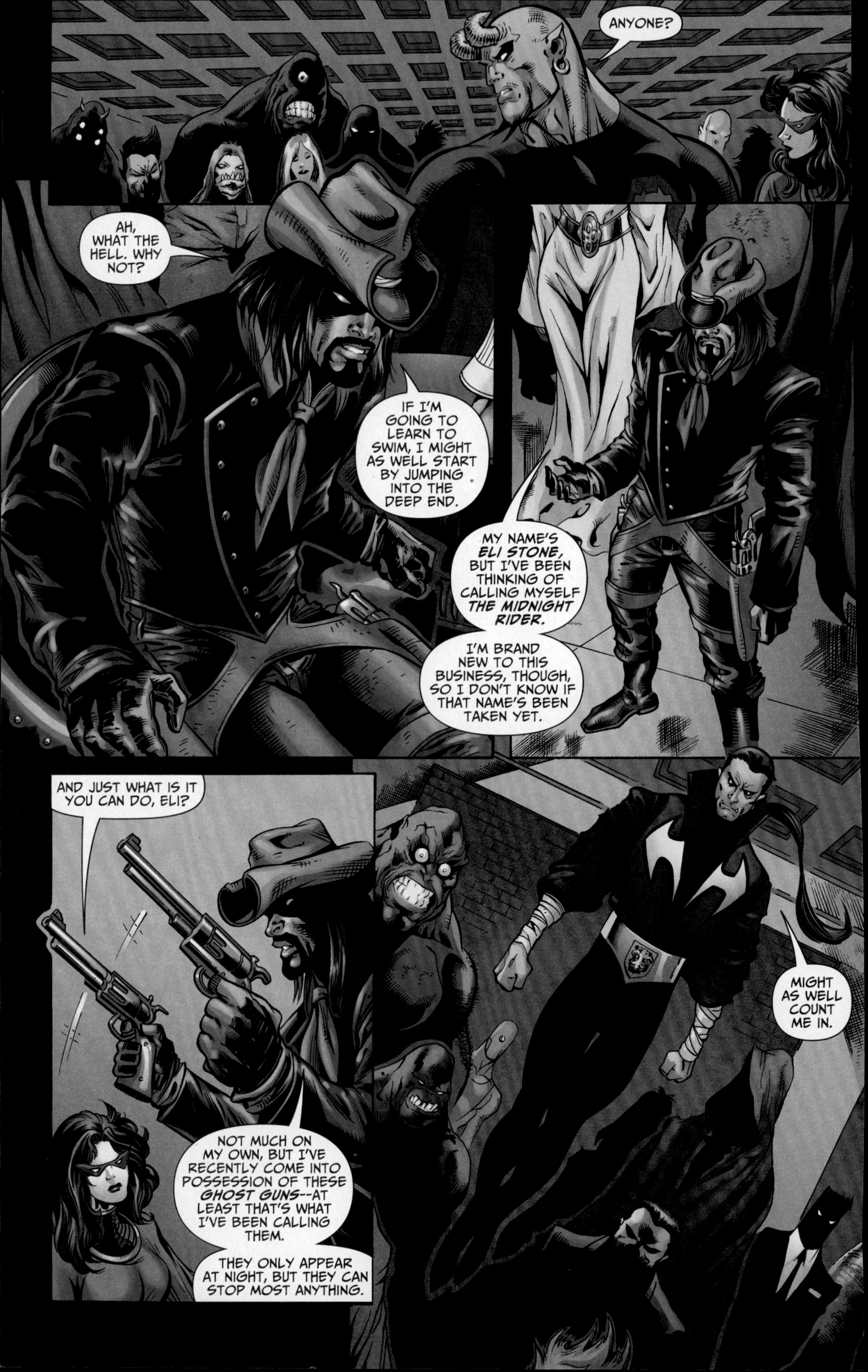
ANYONE?
AH, WHAT THE HELL. WHY NOT?
IF I'M GOING TO LEARN TO SWIM, I MIGHT AS WELL START BY JUMPING INTO THE DEEP END.
MY NAME'S ELI STONE, BUT I'VE BEEN THINKING OF CALLING MYSELF THE MIDNIGHT RIDER.
I'M BRAND NEW TO THIS BUSINESS, THOUGH, SO I DON'T KNOW IF THAT NAME'S BEEN TAKEN YET.
AND JUST WHAT IS IT YOU CAN DO, ELI?
NOT MUCH ON MY OWN, BUT I'VE RECENTLY COME INTO POSSESSION OF THESE GHOST GUNS--AT LEAST THAT'S WHAT I'VE BEEN CALLING THEM.
THEY ONLY APPEAR AT NIGHT, BUT THEY CAN STOP MOST ANYTHING.
MIGHT AS WELL COUNT ME IN.

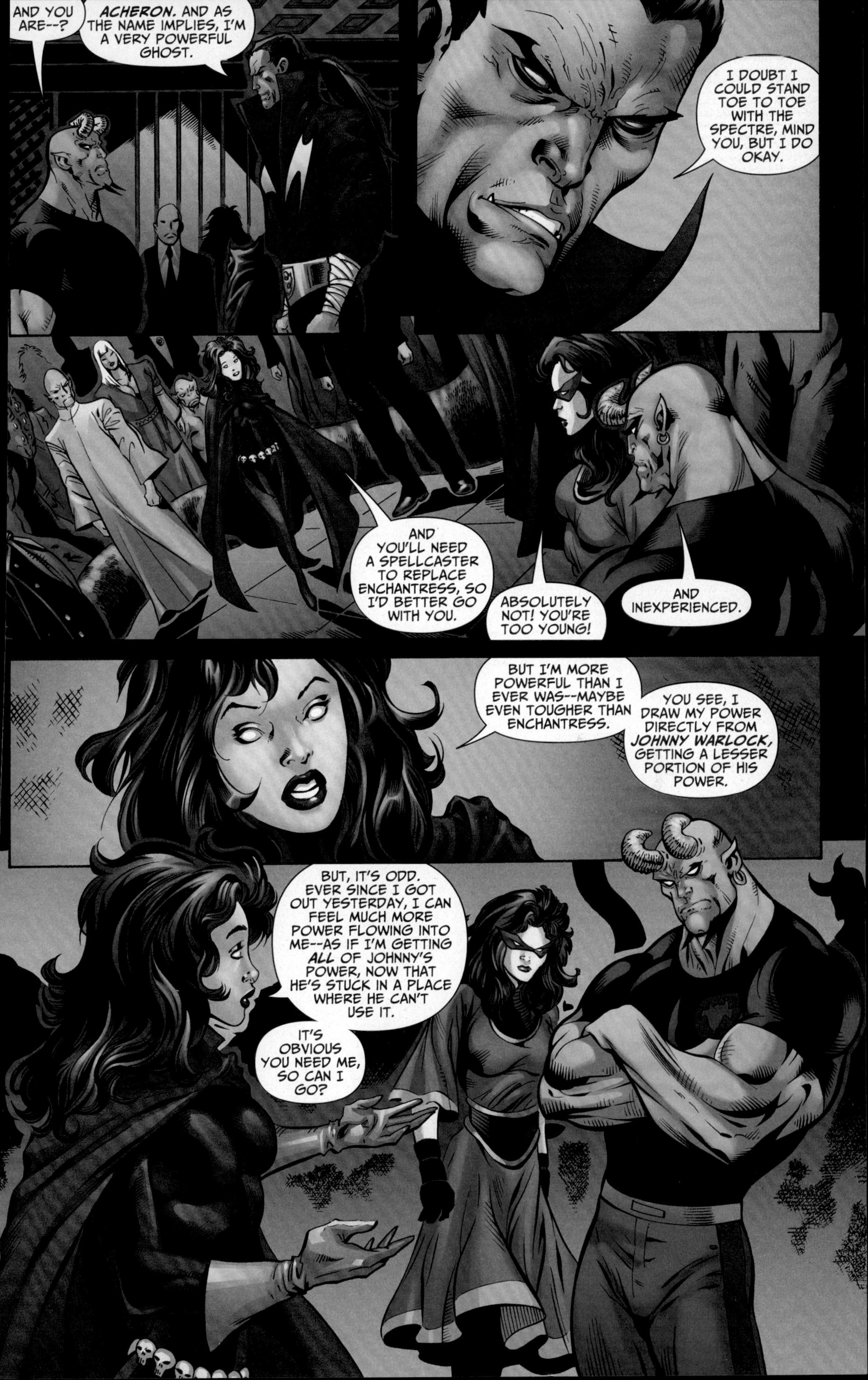
AND YOU ARE--?
ACHERON. AND AS THE NAME IMPLIES, I'M A VERY POWERFUL GHOST.
I DOUBT I COULD STAND TOE TO TOE WITH THE SPECTRE, MIND YOU, BUT I DO OKAY.
AND YOU'LL NEED A SPELLCASTER TO REPLACE ENCHANTRESS, SO I'D BETTER GO WITH YOU.
ABSOLUTELY NOT! YOU'RE TOO YOUNG!
AND INEXPERIENCED.
BUT I'M MORE POWERFUL THAN I EVER WAS--MAYBE EVEN TOUGHER THAN ENCHANTRESS.
YOU SEE, I DRAW MY POWER DIRECTLY FROM JOHNNY WARLOCK, GETTING A LESSER PORTION OF HIS POWER.
BUT, IT'S ODD. EVER SINCE I GOT OUT YESTERDAY, I CAN FEEL MUCH MORE POWER FLOWING INTO ME--AS IF I'M GETTING ALL OF JOHNNY'S POWER, NOW THAT HE'S STUCK IN A PLACE WHERE HE CAN'T USE IT.
IT'S OBVIOUS YOU NEED ME, SO CAN I GO?

THE DEMON TRIPTYCH: PART 3
THE LUCIFER TRIDENT

cover art by **TOM DERENICK** *and* **WAYNE FAUCHER**
colored by **MIKE ATIYEH**

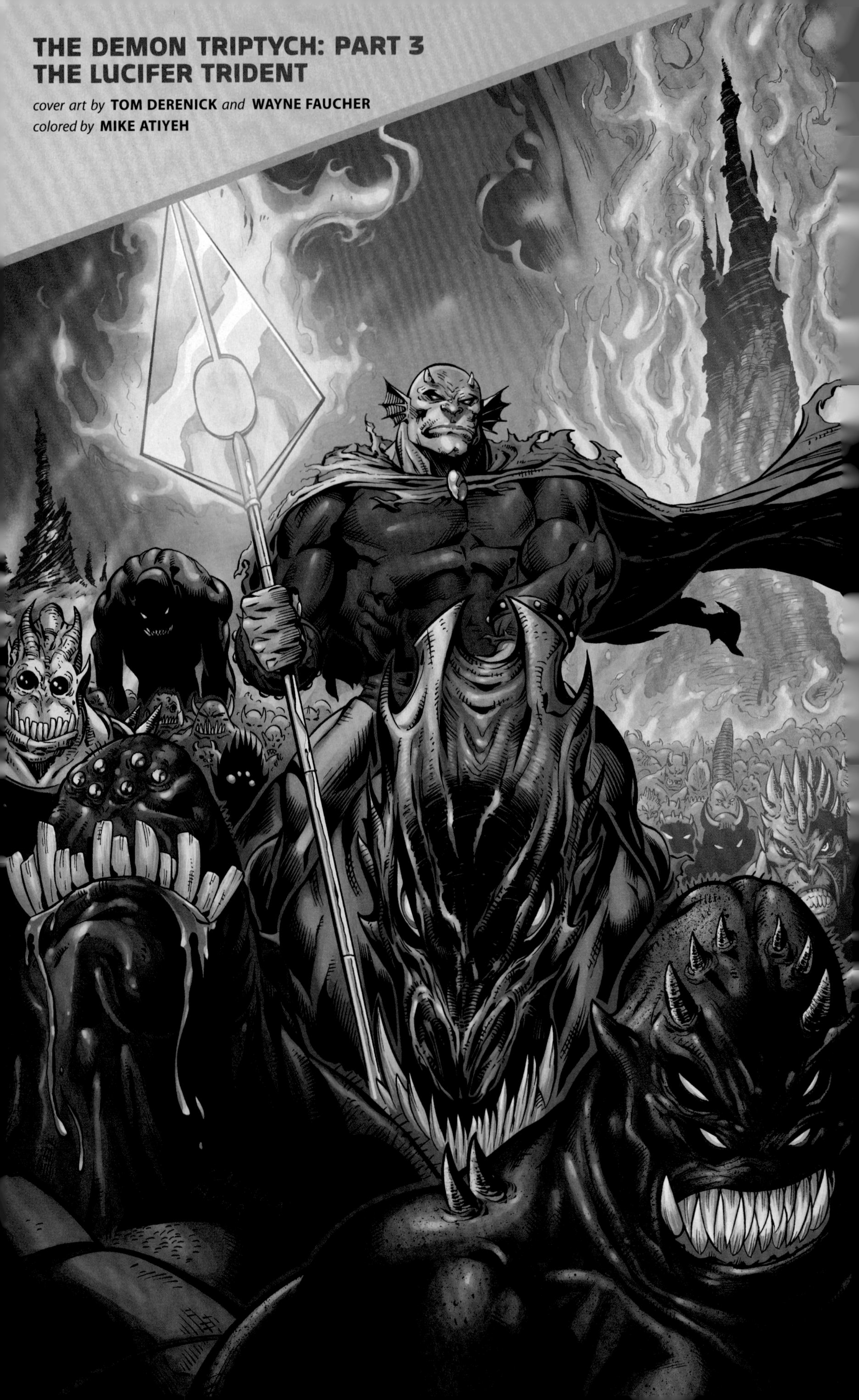

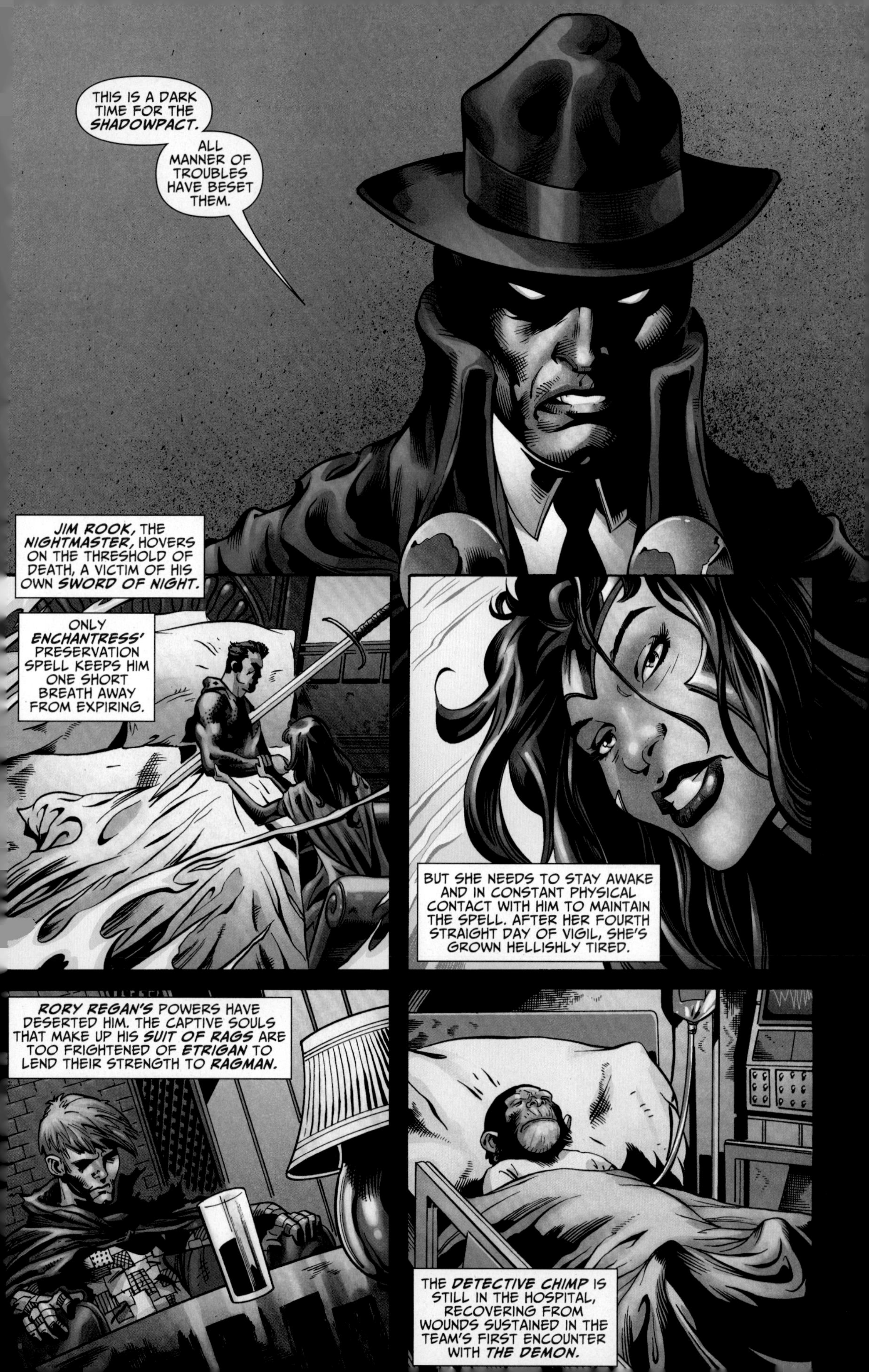
THIS IS A DARK TIME FOR THE SHADOWPACT.
ALL MANNER OF TROUBLES HAVE BESET THEM.
JIM ROOK, THE NIGHTMASTER, HOVERS ON THE THRESHOLD OF DEATH, A VICTIM OF HIS OWN SWORD OF NIGHT.
ONLY ENCHANTRESS' PRESERVATION SPELL KEEPS HIM ONE SHORT BREATH AWAY FROM EXPIRING.
BUT SHE NEEDS TO STAY AWAKE AND IN CONSTANT PHYSICAL CONTACT WITH HIM TO MAINTAIN THE SPELL. AFTER HER FOURTH STRAIGHT DAY OF VIGIL, SHE'S GROWN HELLISHLY TIRED.
RORY REGAN'S POWERS HAVE DESERTED HIM. THE CAPTIVE SOULS THAT MAKE UP HIS SUIT OF RAGS ARE TOO FRIGHTENED OF ETRIGAN TO LEND THEIR STRENGTH TO RAGMAN.
THE DETECTIVE CHIMP IS STILL IN THE HOSPITAL, RECOVERING FROM WOUNDS SUSTAINED IN THE TEAM'S FIRST ENCOUNTER WITH THE DEMON.

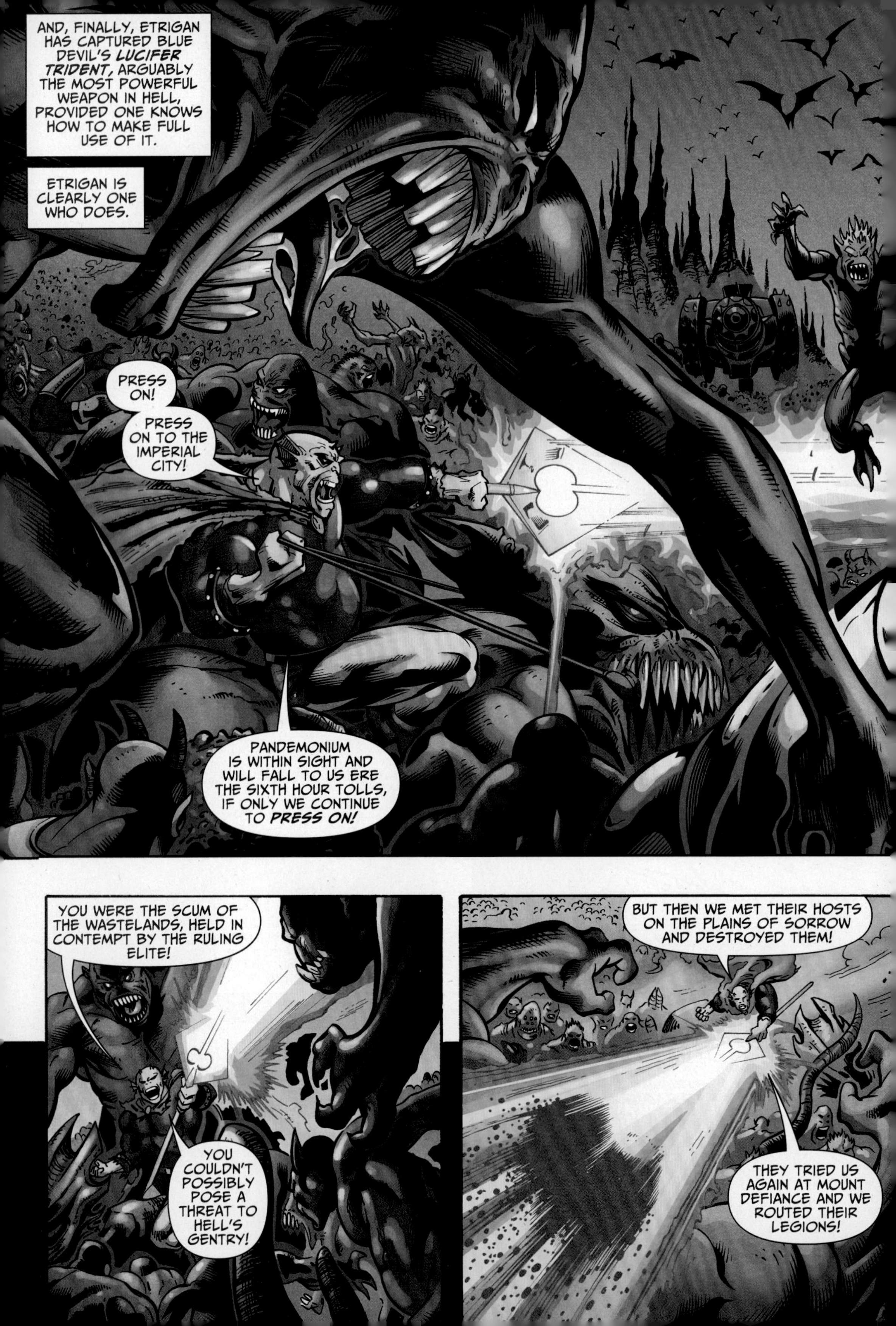

AND, FINALLY, ETRIGAN HAS CAPTURED BLUE DEVIL'S *LUCIFER TRIDENT*, ARGUABLY THE MOST POWERFUL WEAPON IN HELL, PROVIDED ONE KNOWS HOW TO MAKE FULL USE OF IT.
ETRIGAN IS CLEARLY ONE WHO DOES.
PRESS ON!
PRESS ON TO THE IMPERIAL CITY!
PANDEMONIUM IS WITHIN SIGHT AND WILL FALL TO US ERE THE SIXTH HOUR TOLLS, IF ONLY WE CONTINUE TO *PRESS ON!*
YOU WERE THE SCUM OF THE WASTELANDS, HELD IN CONTEMPT BY THE RULING ELITE!
YOU COULDN'T POSSIBLY POSE A THREAT TO HELL'S GENTRY!
BUT THEN WE MET THEIR HOSTS ON THE PLAINS OF SORROW AND DESTROYED THEM!
THEY TRIED US AGAIN AT MOUNT DEFIANCE AND WE ROUTED THEIR LEGIONS!

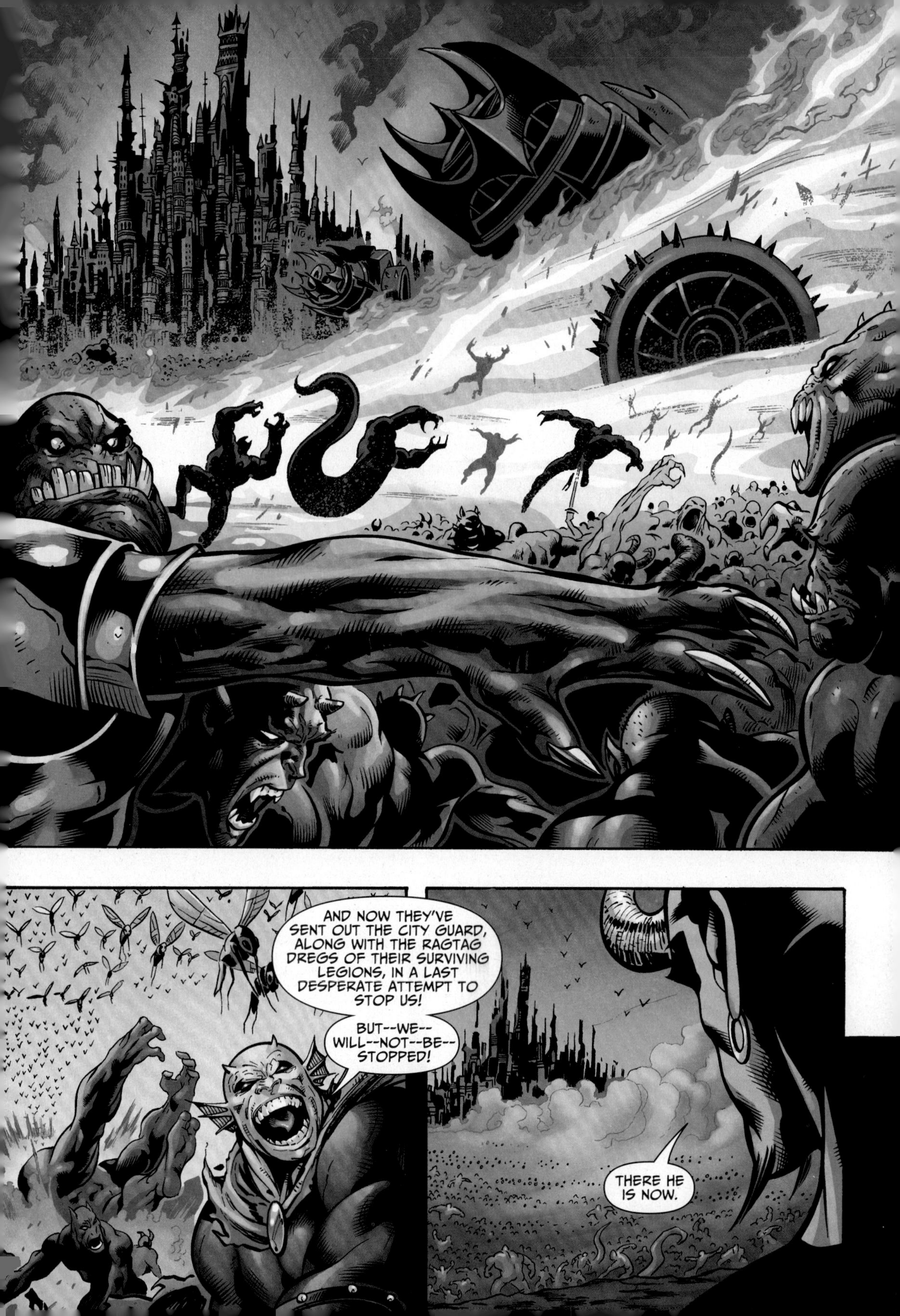
AND NOW THEY'VE SENT OUT THE CITY GUARD, ALONG WITH THE RAGTAG DREGS OF THEIR SURVIVING LEGIONS, IN A LAST DESPERATE ATTEMPT TO STOP US!
BUT--WE-- WILL--NOT--BE-- STOPPED!
THERE HE IS NOW.

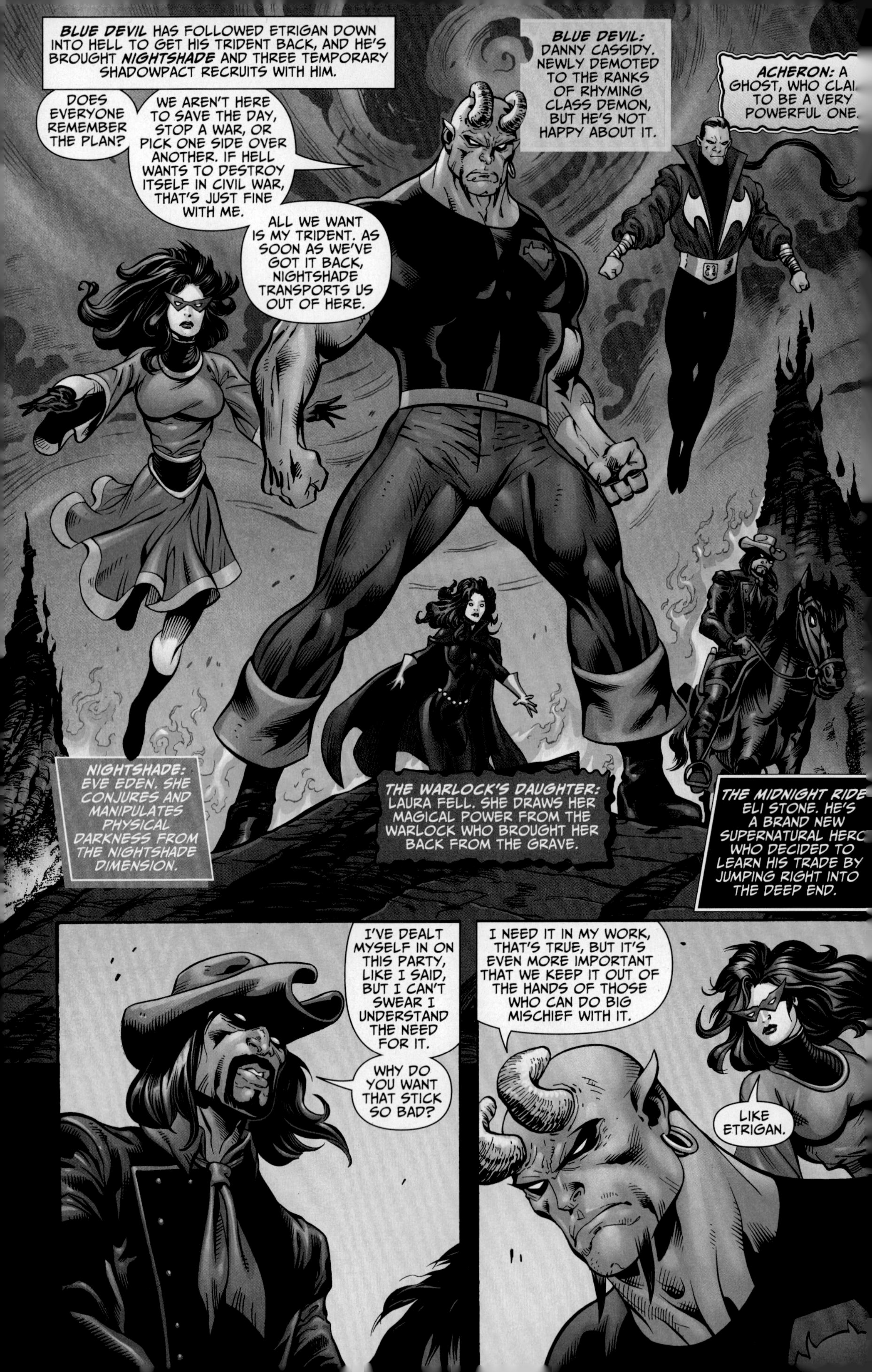
BLUE DEVIL HAS FOLLOWED ETRIGAN DOWN INTO HELL TO GET HIS TRIDENT BACK, AND HE'S BROUGHT NIGHTSHADE AND THREE TEMPORARY SHADOWPACT RECRUITS WITH HIM.
DOES EVERYONE REMEMBER THE PLAN?
WE AREN'T HERE TO SAVE THE DAY, STOP A WAR, OR PICK ONE SIDE OVER ANOTHER. IF HELL WANTS TO DESTROY ITSELF IN CIVIL WAR, THAT'S JUST FINE WITH ME.
ALL WE WANT IS MY TRIDENT. AS SOON AS WE'VE GOT IT BACK, NIGHTSHADE TRANSPORTS US OUT OF HERE.
BLUE DEVIL: DANNY CASSIDY. NEWLY DEMOTED TO THE RANKS OF RHYMING CLASS DEMON, BUT HE'S NOT HAPPY ABOUT IT.
ACHERON: A GHOST, WHO CLAI TO BE A VERY POWERFUL ONE.
NIGHTSHADE: EVE EDEN. SHE CONJURES AND MANIPULATES PHYSICAL DARKNESS FROM THE NIGHTSHADE DIMENSION.
THE WARLOCK'S DAUGHTER: LAURA FELL. SHE DRAWS HER MAGICAL POWER FROM THE WARLOCK WHO BROUGHT HER BACK FROM THE GRAVE.
THE MIDNIGHT RIDE ELI STONE. HE'S A BRAND NEW SUPERNATURAL HERO WHO DECIDED TO LEARN HIS TRADE BY JUMPING RIGHT INTO THE DEEP END.
I'VE DEALT MYSELF IN ON THIS PARTY, LIKE I SAID, BUT I CAN'T SWEAR I UNDERSTAND THE NEED FOR IT.
WHY DO YOU WANT THAT STICK SO BAD?
I NEED IT IN MY WORK, THAT'S TRUE, BUT IT'S EVEN MORE IMPORTANT THAT WE KEEP IT OUT OF THE HANDS OF THOSE WHO CAN DO BIG MISCHIEF WITH IT.
LIKE ETRIGAN.

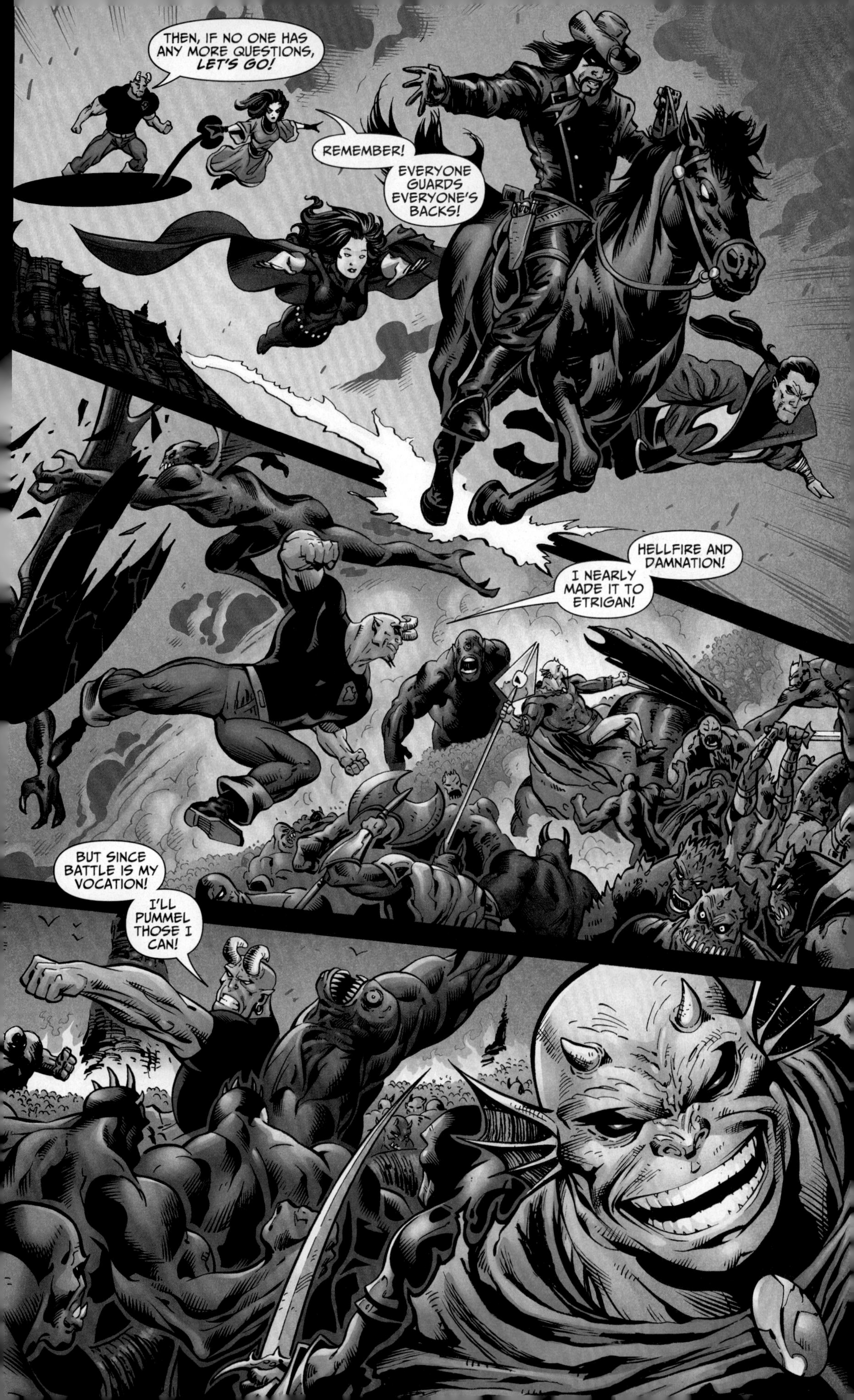
THEN, IF NO ONE HAS ANY MORE QUESTIONS, LET'S GO!
REMEMBER!
EVERYONE GUARDS EVERYONE'S BACKS!
HELLFIRE AND DAMNATION!
I NEARLY MADE IT TO ETRIGAN!
BUT SINCE BATTLE IS MY VOCATION!
I'LL PUMMEL THOSE I CAN!

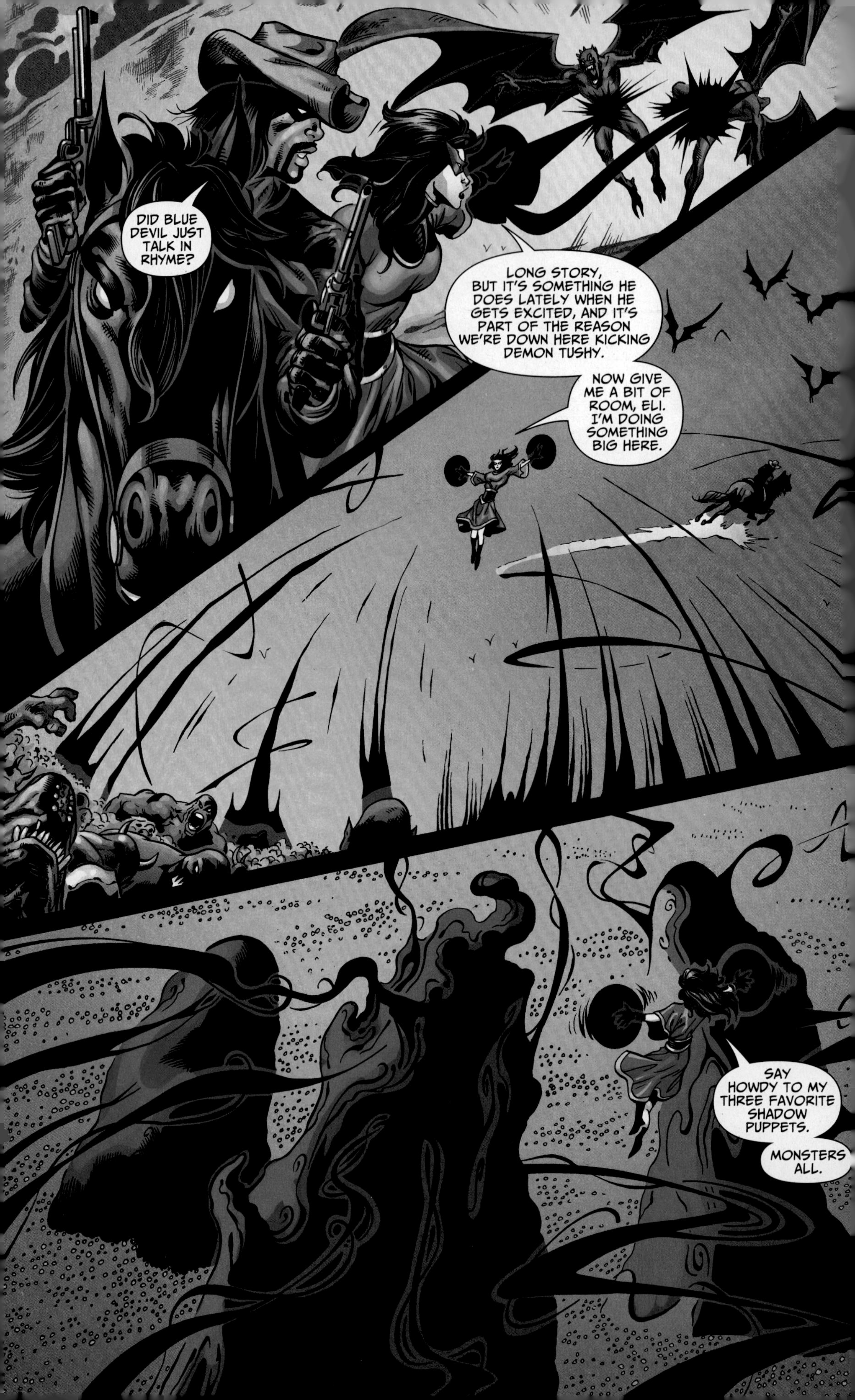
DID BLUE DEVIL JUST TALK IN RHYME?
LONG STORY, BUT IT'S SOMETHING HE DOES LATELY WHEN HE GETS EXCITED, AND IT'S PART OF THE REASON WE'RE DOWN HERE KICKING DEMON TUSHY.
NOW GIVE ME A BIT OF ROOM, ELI. I'M DOING SOMETHING BIG HERE.
SAY HOWDY TO MY THREE FAVORITE SHADOW PUPPETS.
MONSTERS ALL.

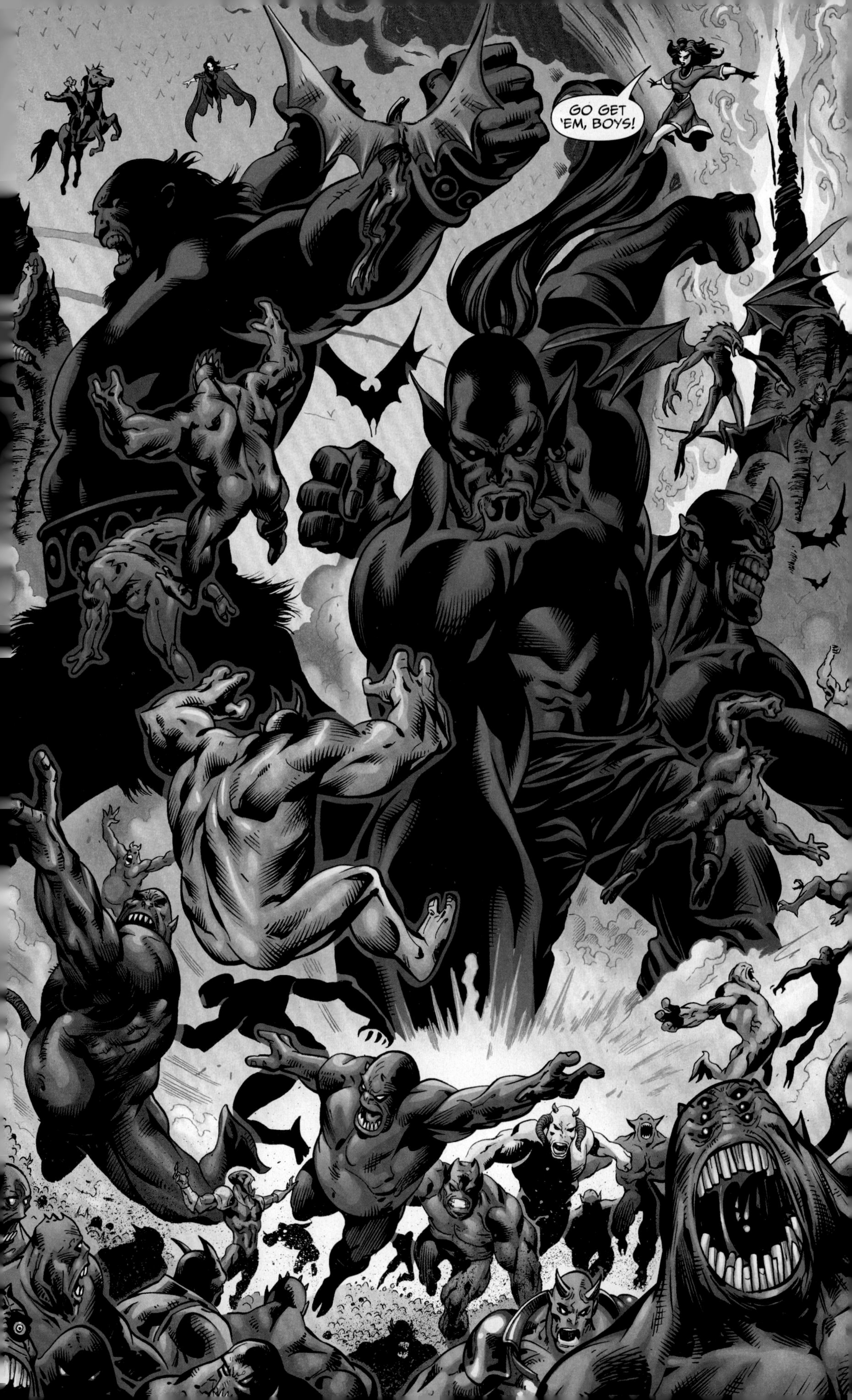
GO GET
'EM, BOYS!

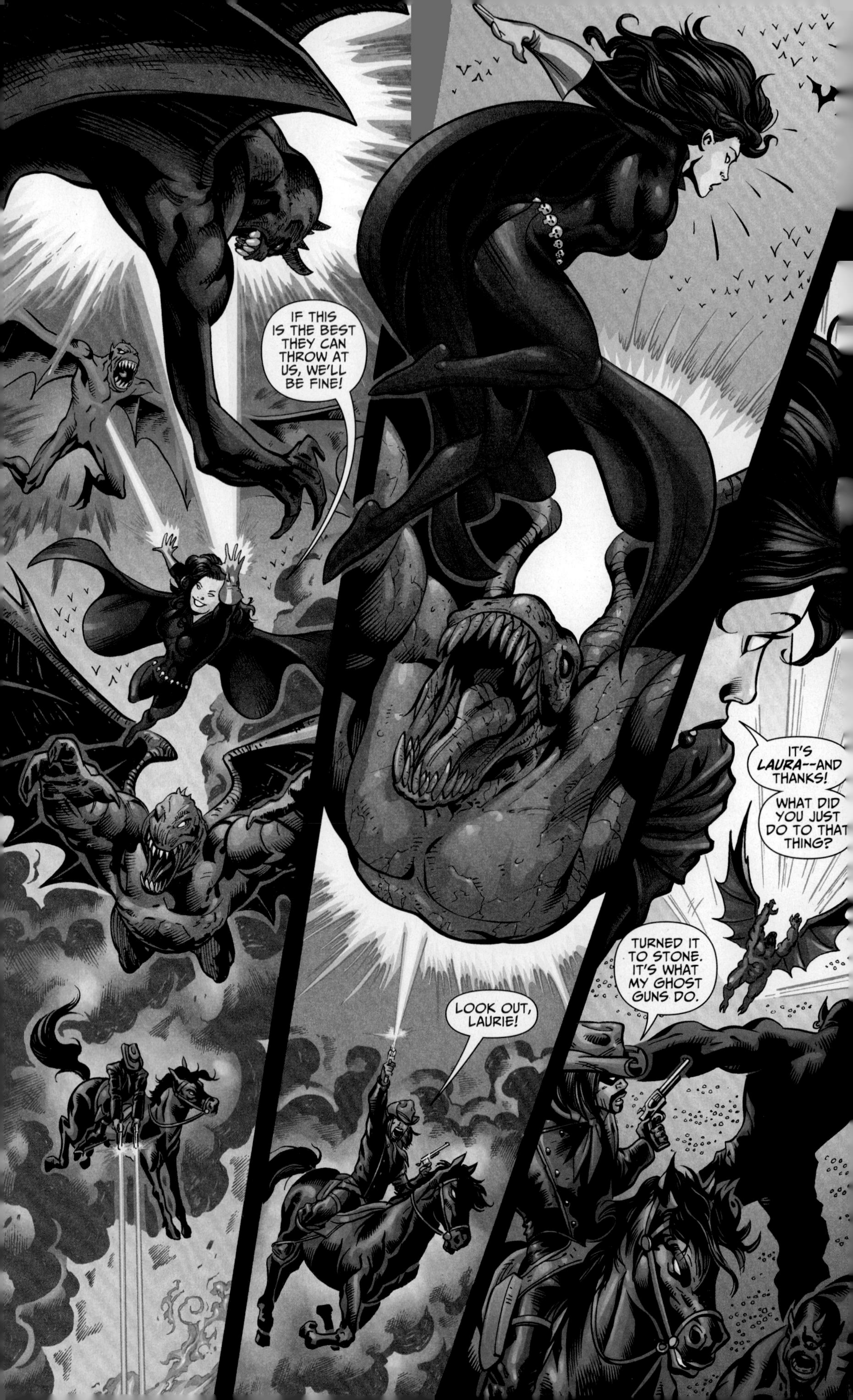
IF THIS IS THE BEST THEY CAN THROW AT US, WE'LL BE FINE!
LOOK OUT, LAURIE!
IT'S LAURA--AND THANKS!
WHAT DID YOU JUST DO TO THAT THING?
TURNED IT TO STONE. IT'S WHAT MY GHOST GUNS DO.

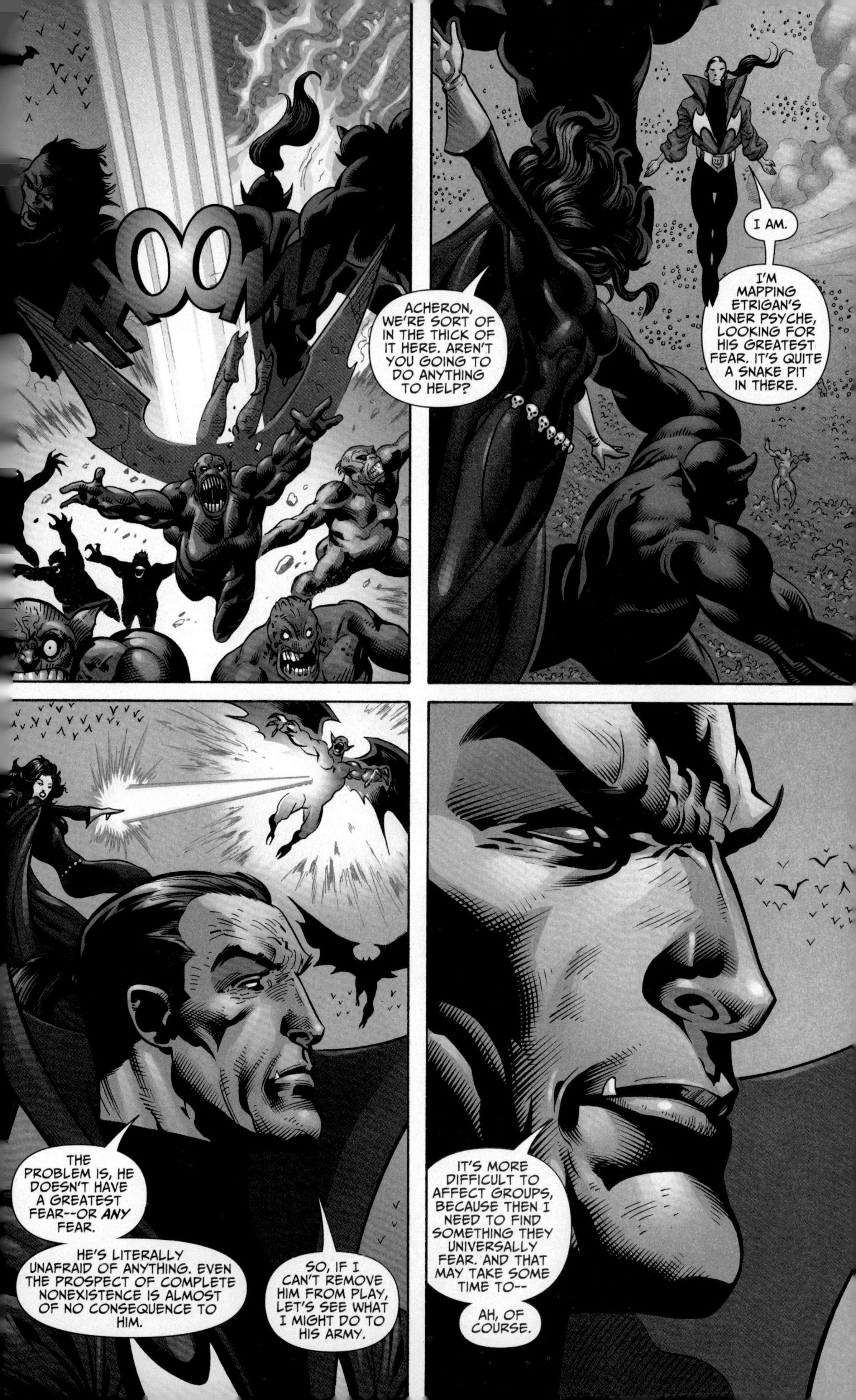

THOOM
ACHERON, WE'RE SORT OF IN THE THICK OF IT HERE. AREN'T YOU GOING TO DO ANYTHING TO HELP?
I AM.
I'M MAPPING ETRIGAN'S INNER PSYCHE, LOOKING FOR HIS GREATEST FEAR. IT'S QUITE A SNAKE PIT IN THERE.
THE PROBLEM IS, HE DOESN'T HAVE A GREATEST FEAR--OR ANY FEAR.
HE'S LITERALLY UNAFRAID OF ANYTHING. EVEN THE PROSPECT OF COMPLETE NONEXISTENCE IS ALMOST OF NO CONSEQUENCE TO HIM.
SO, IF I CAN'T REMOVE HIM FROM PLAY, LET'S SEE WHAT I MIGHT DO TO HIS ARMY.
IT'S MORE DIFFICULT TO AFFECT GROUPS, BECAUSE THEN I NEED TO FIND SOMETHING THEY UNIVERSALLY FEAR. AND THAT MAY TAKE SOME TIME TO--
AH, OF COURSE.

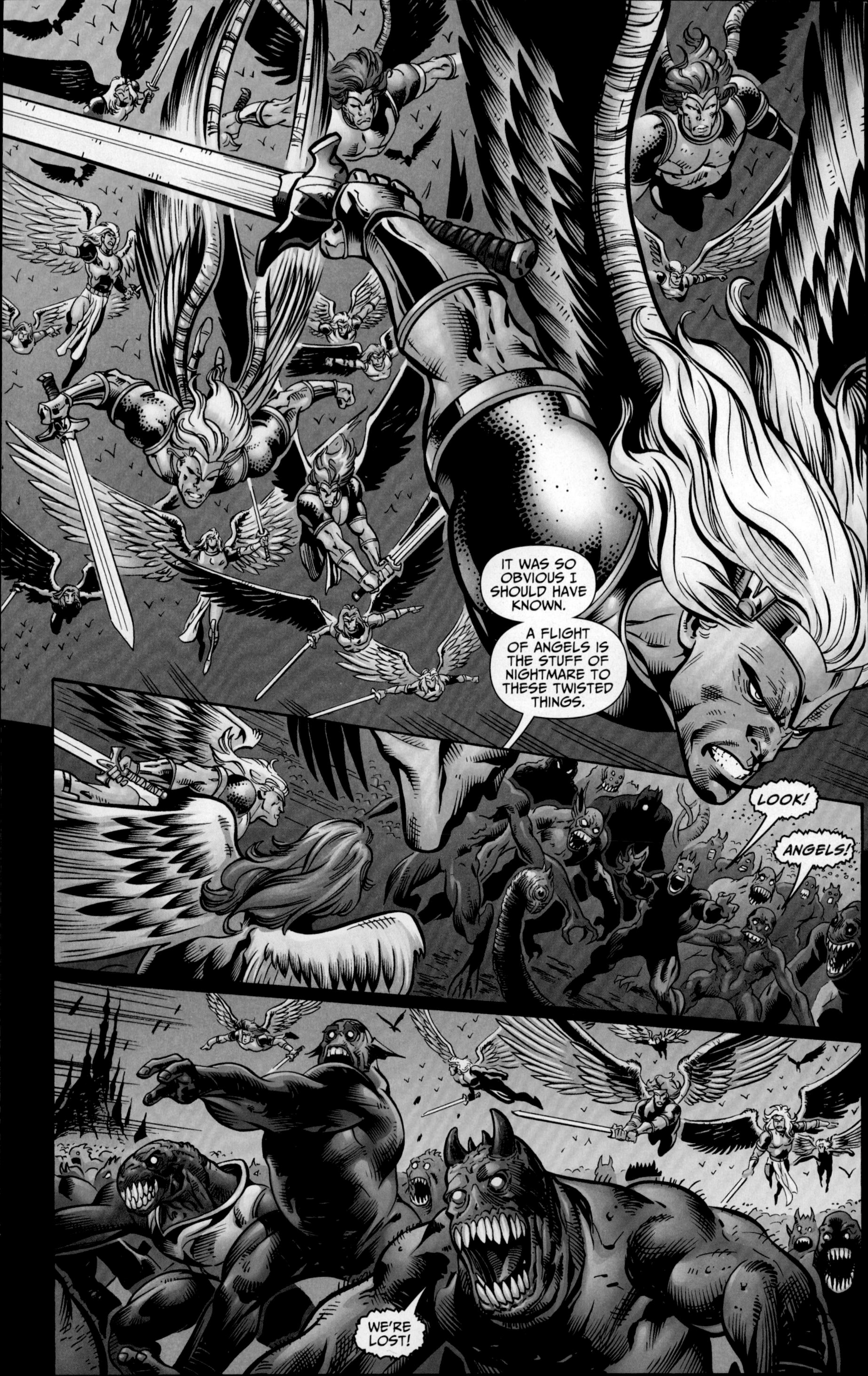
IT WAS SO OBVIOUS I SHOULD HAVE KNOWN.
A FLIGHT OF ANGELS IS THE STUFF OF NIGHTMARE TO THESE TWISTED THINGS.
LOOK!
ANGELS!
WE'RE LOST!

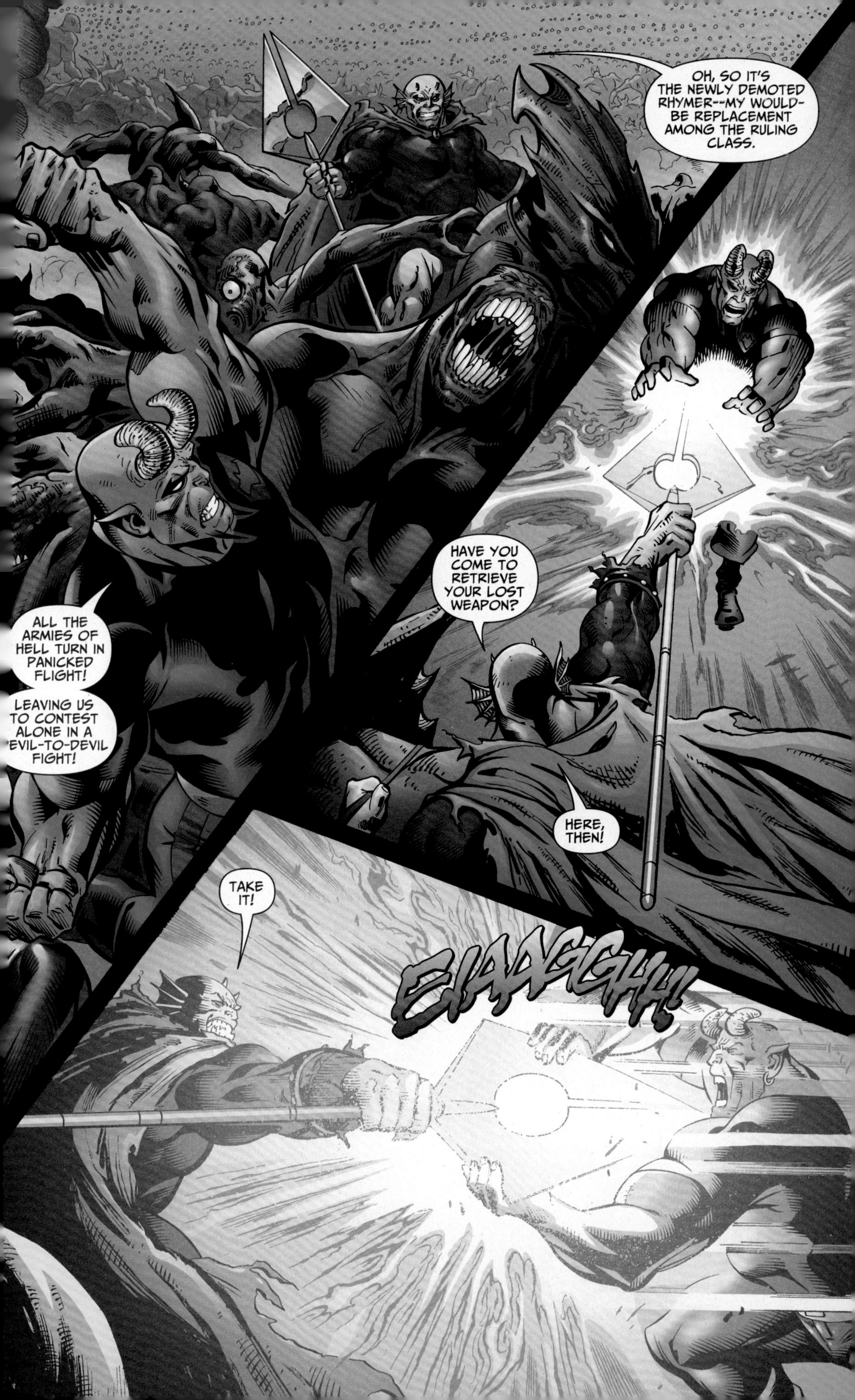
ALL THE ARMIES OF HELL TURN IN PANICKED FLIGHT!
LEAVING US TO CONTEST ALONE IN A EVIL-TO-DEVIL FIGHT!
OH, SO IT'S THE NEWLY DEMOTED RHYMER--MY WOULD-BE REPLACEMENT AMONG THE RULING CLASS.
HAVE YOU COME TO RETRIEVE YOUR LOST WEAPON?
HERE, THEN!
TAKE IT!
EIAAGGHH!

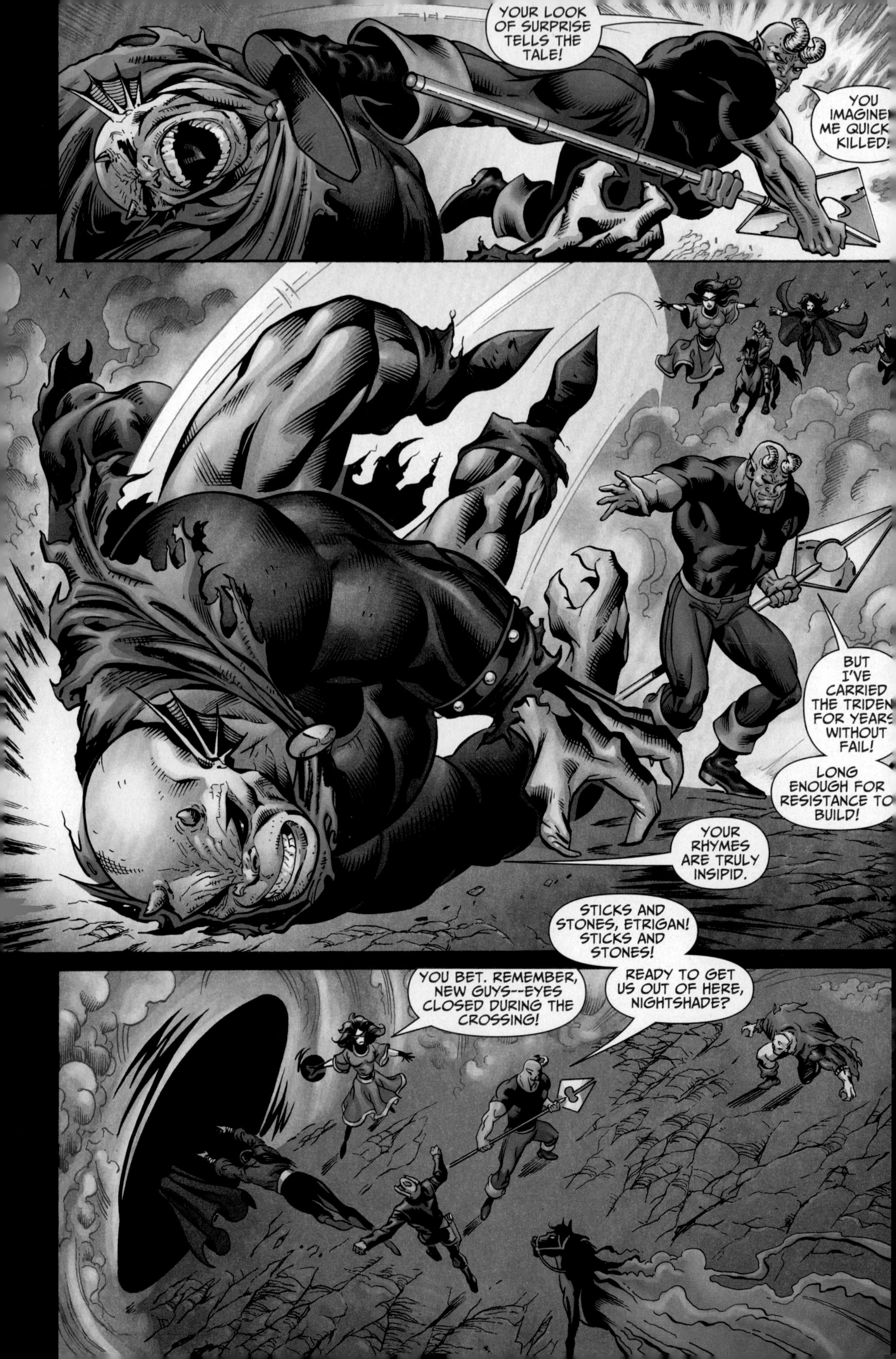
YOUR LOOK OF SURPRISE TELLS THE TALE!
YOU IMAGINED ME QUICK KILLED!
BUT I'VE CARRIED THE TRIDENT FOR YEARS WITHOUT FAIL!
LONG ENOUGH FOR RESISTANCE TO BUILD!
YOUR RHYMES ARE TRULY INSIPID.
STICKS AND STONES, ETRIGAN! STICKS AND STONES!
READY TO GET US OUT OF HERE, NIGHTSHADE?
YOU BET. REMEMBER, NEW GUYS--EYES CLOSED DURING THE CROSSING!

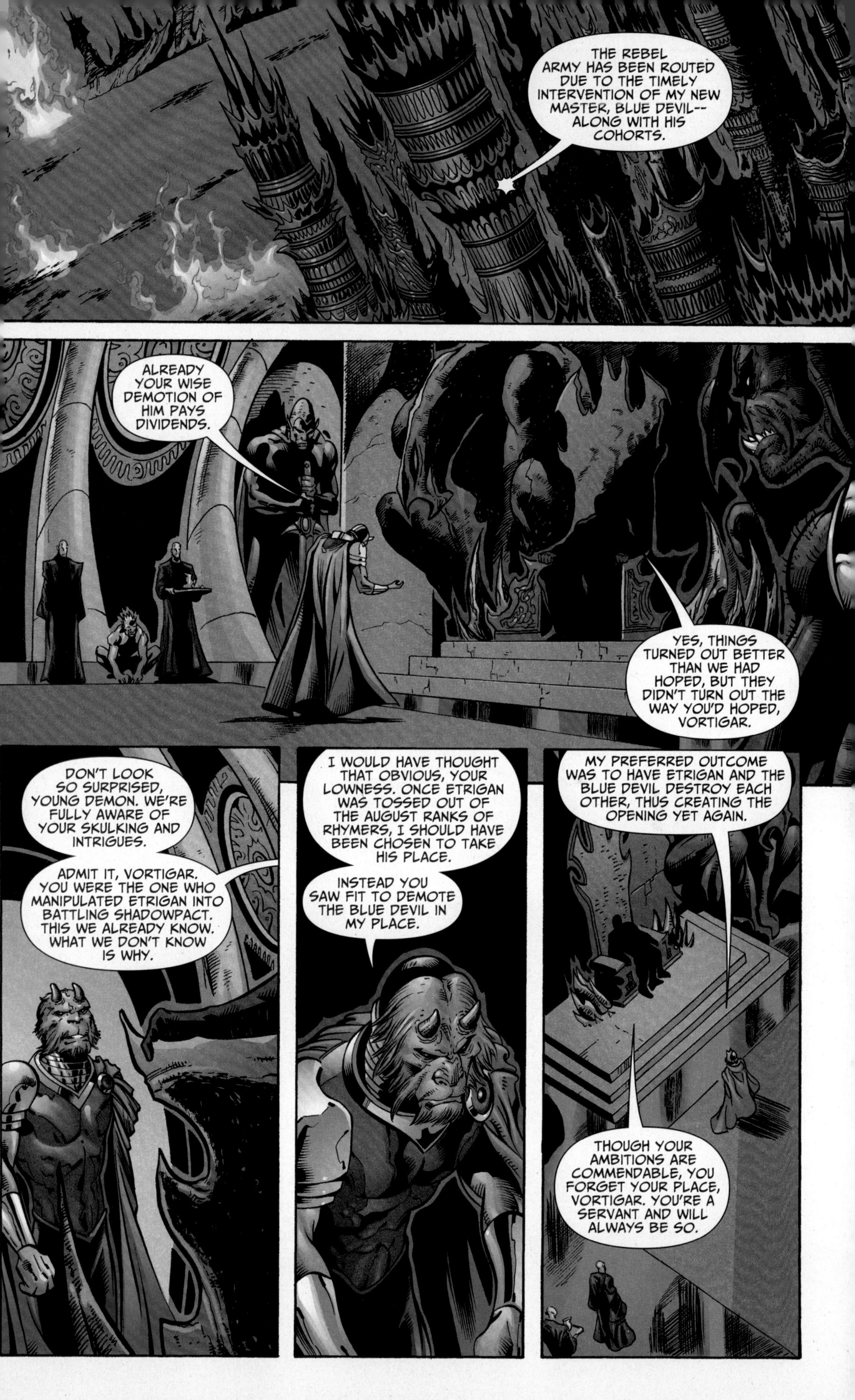
THE REBEL ARMY HAS BEEN ROUTED DUE TO THE TIMELY INTERVENTION OF MY NEW MASTER, BLUE DEVIL-- ALONG WITH HIS COHORTS.
ALREADY YOUR WISE DEMOTION OF HIM PAYS DIVIDENDS.
YES, THINGS TURNED OUT BETTER THAN WE HAD HOPED, BUT THEY DIDN'T TURN OUT THE WAY YOU'D HOPED, VORTIGAR.
DON'T LOOK SO SURPRISED, YOUNG DEMON. WE'RE FULLY AWARE OF YOUR SKULKING AND INTRIGUES.
ADMIT IT, VORTIGAR. YOU WERE THE ONE WHO MANIPULATED ETRIGAN INTO BATTLING SHADOWPACT. THIS WE ALREADY KNOW. WHAT WE DON'T KNOW IS WHY.
I WOULD HAVE THOUGHT THAT OBVIOUS, YOUR LOWNESS. ONCE ETRIGAN WAS TOSSED OUT OF THE AUGUST RANKS OF RHYMERS, I SHOULD HAVE BEEN CHOSEN TO TAKE HIS PLACE.
INSTEAD YOU SAW FIT TO DEMOTE THE BLUE DEVIL IN MY PLACE.
MY PREFERRED OUTCOME WAS TO HAVE ETRIGAN AND THE BLUE DEVIL DESTROY EACH OTHER, THUS CREATING THE OPENING YET AGAIN.
THOUGH YOUR AMBITIONS ARE COMMENDABLE, YOU FORGET YOUR PLACE, VORTIGAR. YOU'RE A SERVANT AND WILL ALWAYS BE SO.

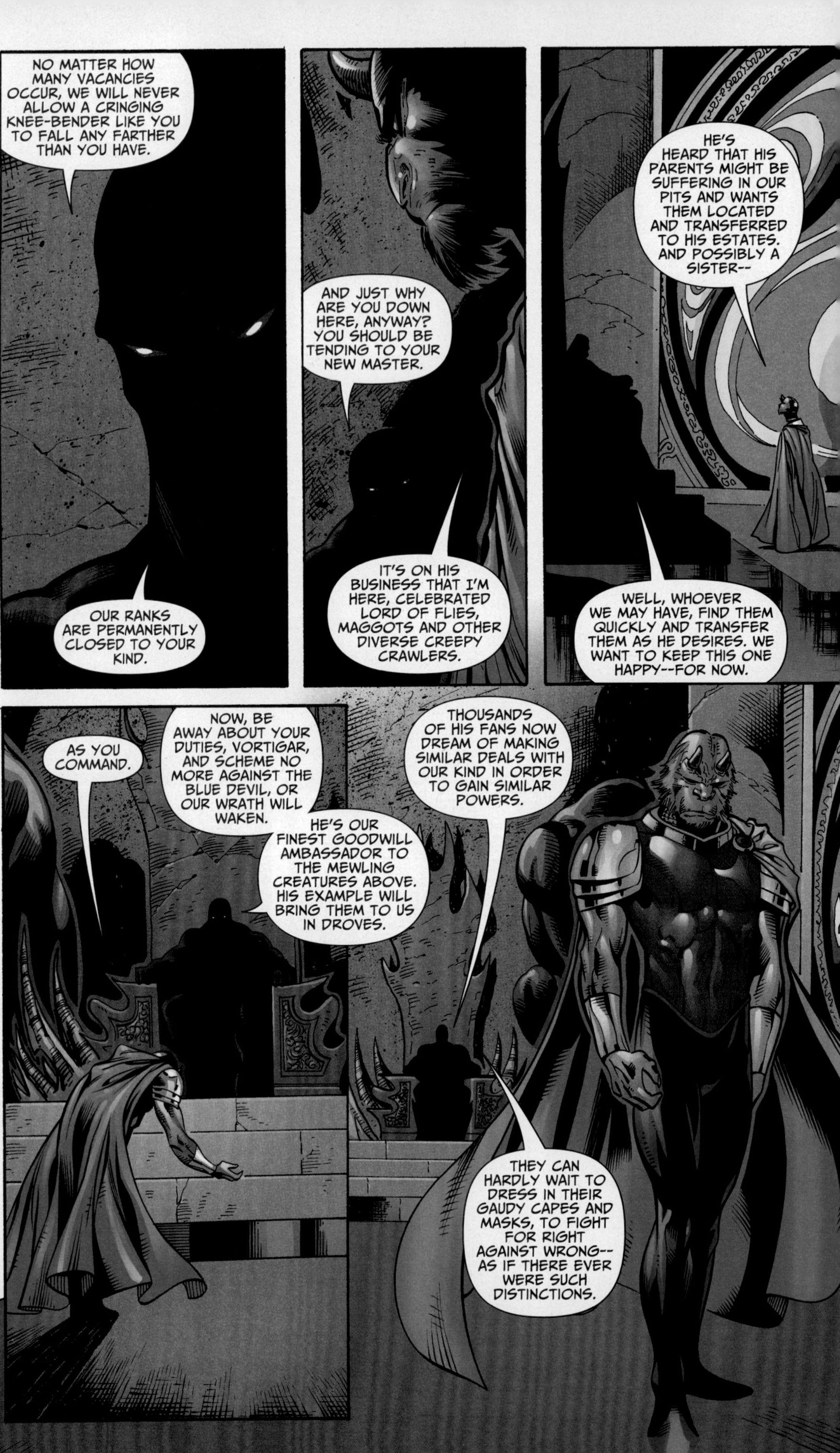
NO MATTER HOW MANY VACANCIES OCCUR, WE WILL NEVER ALLOW A CRINGING KNEE-BENDER LIKE YOU TO FALL ANY FARTHER THAN YOU HAVE.
OUR RANKS ARE PERMANENTLY CLOSED TO YOUR KIND.
AND JUST WHY ARE YOU DOWN HERE, ANYWAY? YOU SHOULD BE TENDING TO YOUR NEW MASTER.
IT'S ON HIS BUSINESS THAT I'M HERE, CELEBRATED LORD OF FLIES, MAGGOTS AND OTHER DIVERSE CREEPY CRAWLERS.
HE'S HEARD THAT HIS PARENTS MIGHT BE SUFFERING IN OUR PITS AND WANTS THEM LOCATED AND TRANSFERRED TO HIS ESTATES. AND POSSIBLY A SISTER--
WELL, WHOEVER WE MAY HAVE, FIND THEM QUICKLY AND TRANSFER THEM AS HE DESIRES. WE WANT TO KEEP THIS ONE HAPPY--FOR NOW.
THOUSANDS OF HIS FANS NOW DREAM OF MAKING SIMILAR DEALS WITH OUR KIND IN ORDER TO GAIN SIMILAR POWERS.
THEY CAN HARDLY WAIT TO DRESS IN THEIR GAUDY CAPES AND MASKS, TO FIGHT FOR RIGHT AGAINST WRONG-- AS IF THERE EVER WERE SUCH DISTINCTIONS.
HE'S OUR FINEST GOODWILL AMBASSADOR TO THE MEWLING CREATURES ABOVE. HIS EXAMPLE WILL BRING THEM TO US IN DROVES.
NOW, BE AWAY ABOUT YOUR DUTIES, VORTIGAR, AND SCHEME NO MORE AGAINST THE BLUE DEVIL, OR OUR WRATH WILL WAKEN.
AS YOU COMMAND.

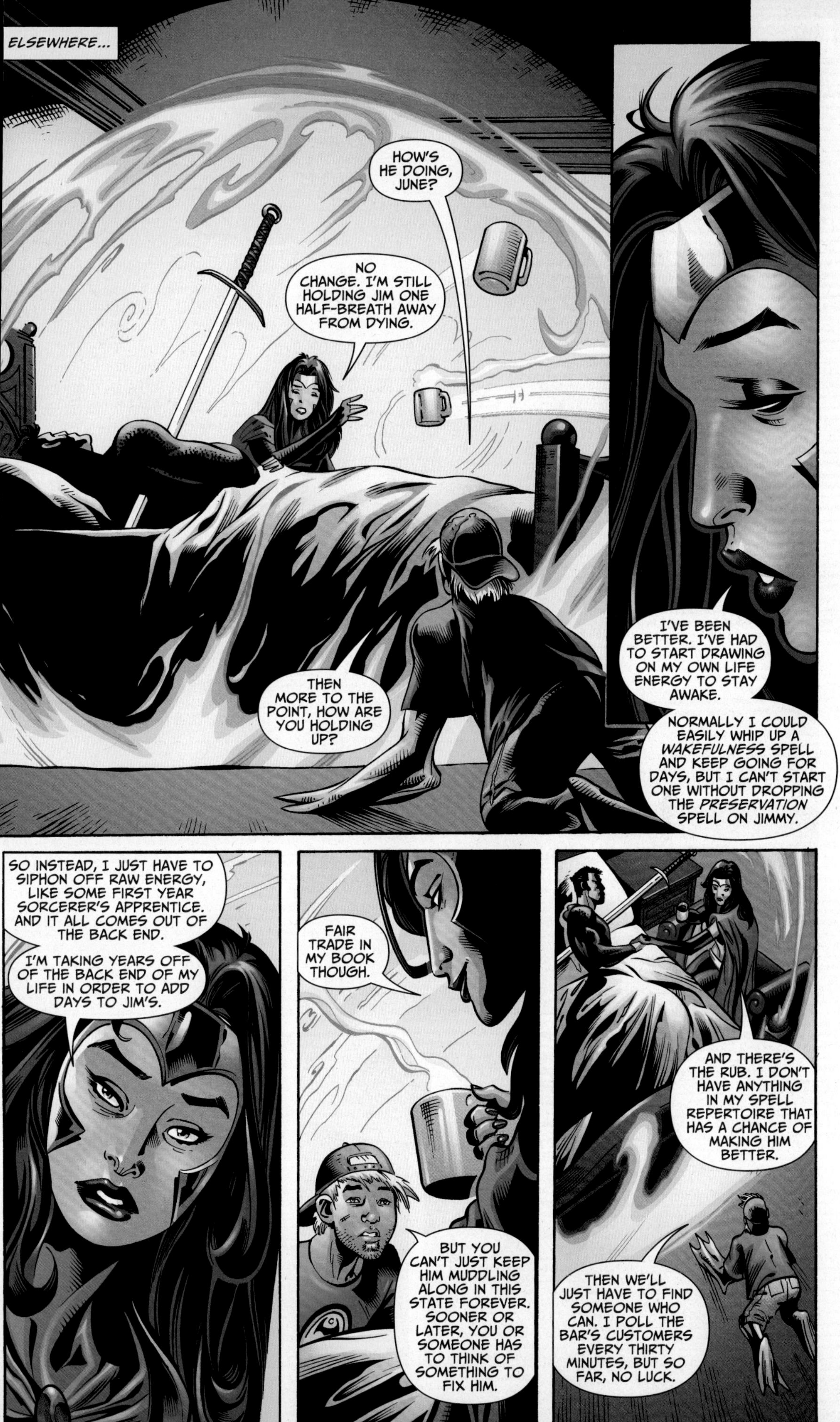
ELSEWHERE...
HOW'S HE DOING, JUNE?
NO CHANGE. I'M STILL HOLDING JIM ONE HALF-BREATH AWAY FROM DYING.
THEN MORE TO THE POINT, HOW ARE YOU HOLDING UP?
I'VE BEEN BETTER. I'VE HAD TO START DRAWING ON MY OWN LIFE ENERGY TO STAY AWAKE.
NORMALLY I COULD EASILY WHIP UP A *WAKEFULNESS* SPELL AND KEEP GOING FOR DAYS, BUT I CAN'T START ONE WITHOUT DROPPING THE *PRESERVATION* SPELL ON JIMMY.
SO INSTEAD, I JUST HAVE TO SIPHON OFF RAW ENERGY, LIKE SOME FIRST YEAR SORCERER'S APPRENTICE. AND IT ALL COMES OUT OF THE BACK END.
I'M TAKING YEARS OFF OF THE BACK END OF MY LIFE IN ORDER TO ADD DAYS TO JIM'S.
FAIR TRADE IN MY BOOK THOUGH.
BUT YOU CAN'T JUST KEEP HIM MUDDLING ALONG IN THIS STATE FOREVER. SOONER OR LATER, YOU OR SOMEONE HAS TO THINK OF SOMETHING TO FIX HIM.
AND THERE'S THE RUB. I DON'T HAVE ANYTHING IN MY SPELL REPERTOIRE THAT HAS A CHANCE OF MAKING HIM BETTER.
THEN WE'LL JUST HAVE TO FIND SOMEONE WHO CAN. I POLL THE BAR'S CUSTOMERS EVERY THIRTY MINUTES, BUT SO FAR, NO LUCK.

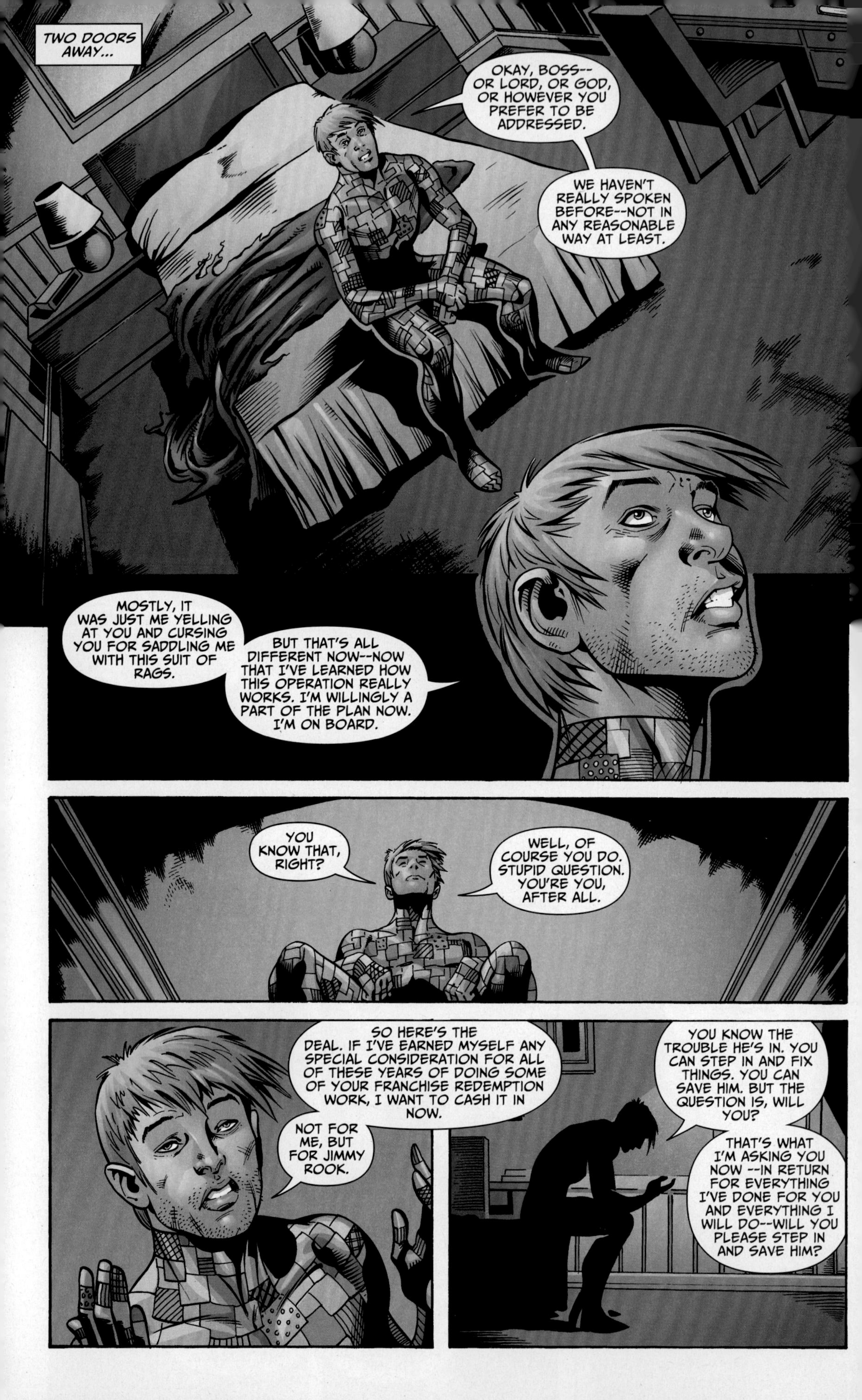
TWO DOORS AWAY...
OKAY, BOSS--OR LORD, OR GOD, OR HOWEVER YOU PREFER TO BE ADDRESSED.
WE HAVEN'T REALLY SPOKEN BEFORE--NOT IN ANY REASONABLE WAY AT LEAST.
MOSTLY, IT WAS JUST ME YELLING AT YOU AND CURSING YOU FOR SADDLING ME WITH THIS SUIT OF RAGS.
BUT THAT'S ALL DIFFERENT NOW--NOW THAT I'VE LEARNED HOW THIS OPERATION REALLY WORKS. I'M WILLINGLY A PART OF THE PLAN NOW. I'M ON BOARD.
YOU KNOW THAT, RIGHT?
WELL, OF COURSE YOU DO. STUPID QUESTION. YOU'RE YOU, AFTER ALL.
SO HERE'S THE DEAL. IF I'VE EARNED MYSELF ANY SPECIAL CONSIDERATION FOR ALL OF THESE YEARS OF DOING SOME OF YOUR FRANCHISE REDEMPTION WORK, I WANT TO CASH IT IN NOW.
NOT FOR ME, BUT FOR JIMMY ROOK.
YOU KNOW THE TROUBLE HE'S IN. YOU CAN STEP IN AND FIX THINGS. YOU CAN SAVE HIM. BUT THE QUESTION IS, WILL YOU?
THAT'S WHAT I'M ASKING YOU NOW --IN RETURN FOR EVERYTHING I'VE DONE FOR YOU AND EVERYTHING I WILL DO--WILL YOU PLEASE STEP IN AND SAVE HIM?

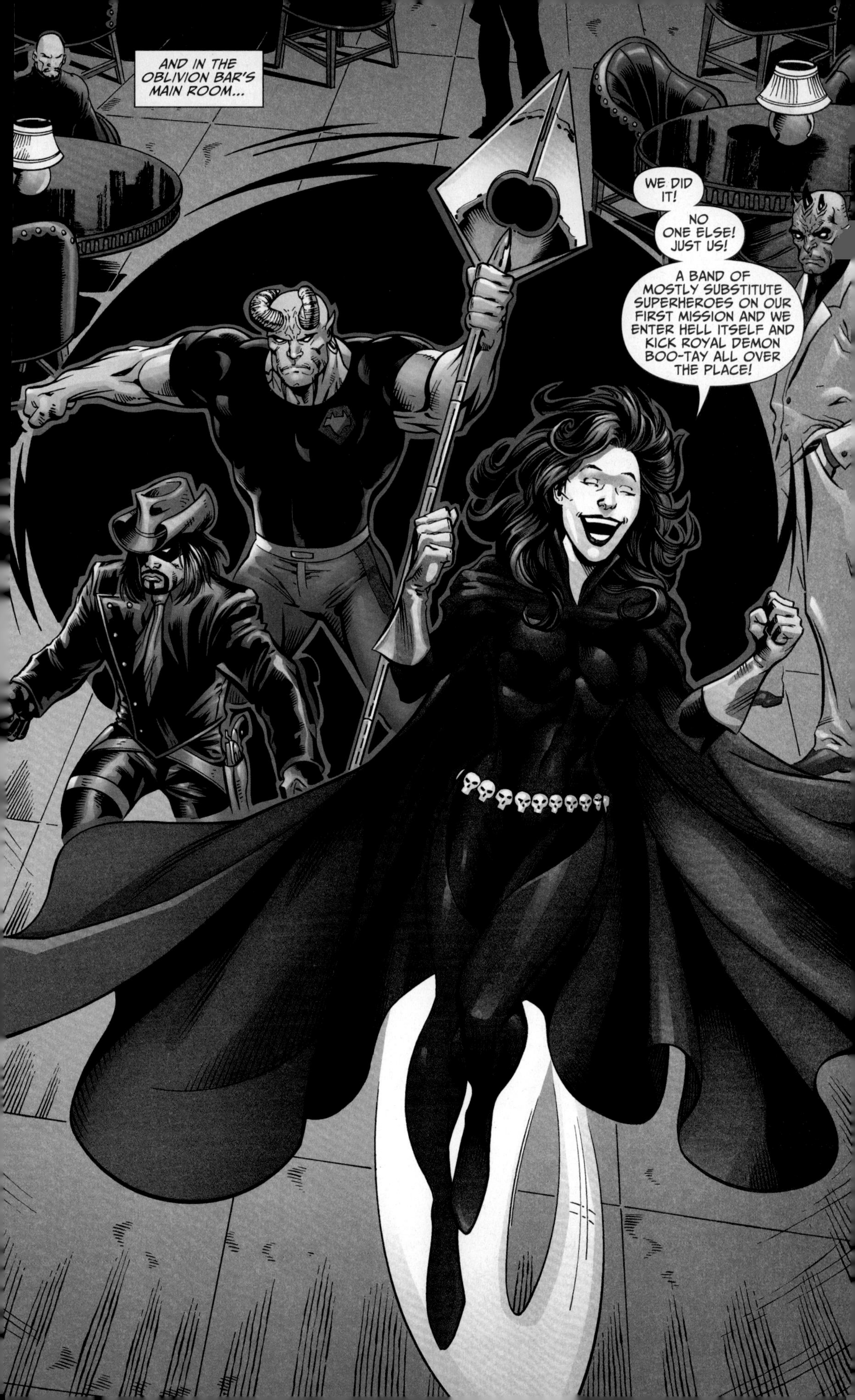
AND IN THE OBLIVION BAR'S MAIN ROOM...
WE DID IT!
NO ONE ELSE! JUST US!
A BAND OF MOSTLY SUBSTITUTE SUPERHEROES ON OUR FIRST MISSION AND WE ENTER HELL ITSELF AND KICK ROYAL DEMON BOO-TAY ALL OVER THE PLACE!

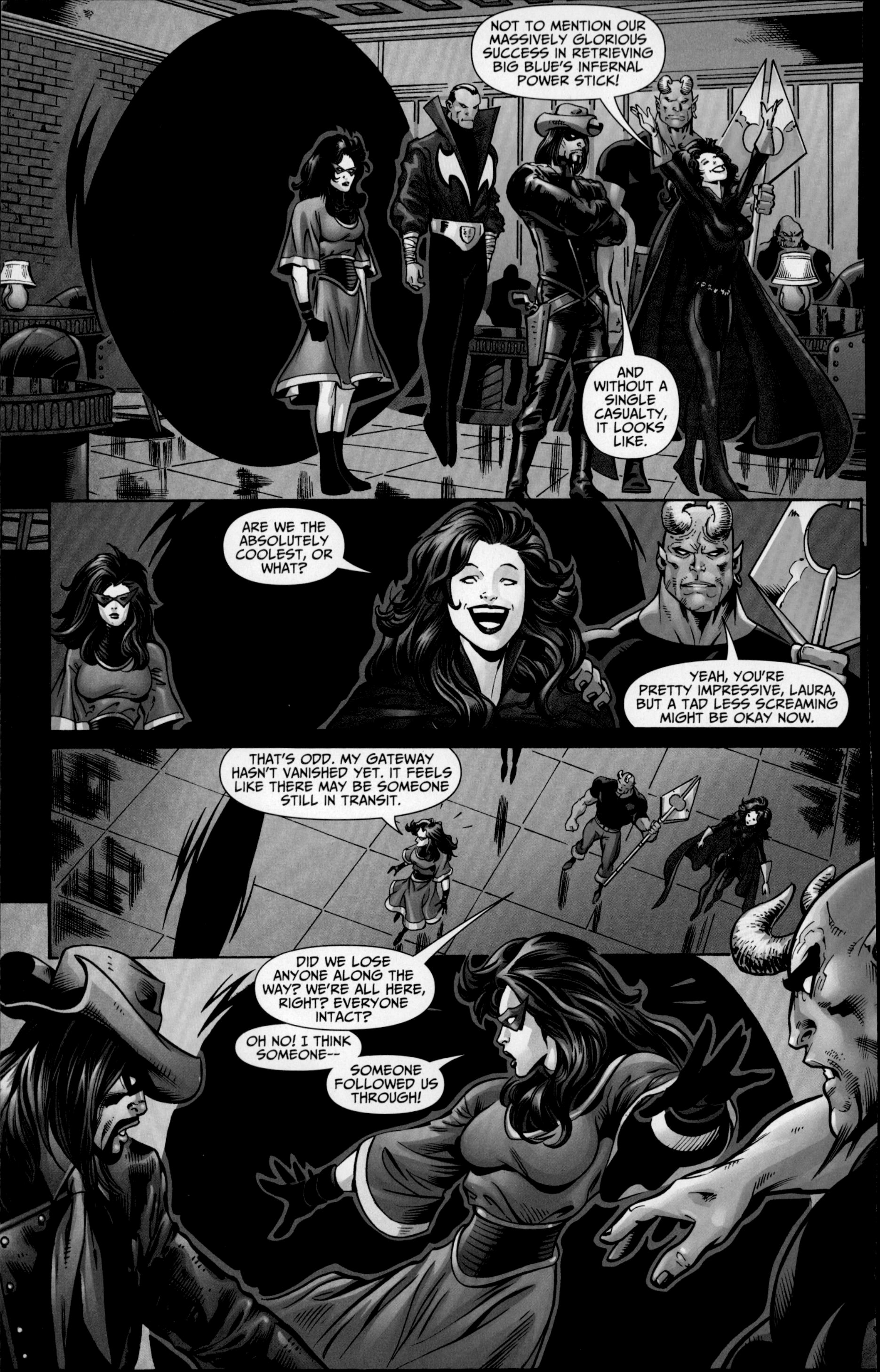
NOT TO MENTION OUR MASSIVELY GLORIOUS SUCCESS IN RETRIEVING BIG BLUE'S INFERNAL POWER STICK!
AND WITHOUT A SINGLE CASUALTY, IT LOOKS LIKE.
ARE WE THE ABSOLUTELY COOLEST, OR WHAT?
YEAH, YOU'RE PRETTY IMPRESSIVE, LAURA, BUT A TAD LESS SCREAMING MIGHT BE OKAY NOW.
THAT'S ODD. MY GATEWAY HASN'T VANISHED YET. IT FEELS LIKE THERE MAY BE SOMEONE STILL IN TRANSIT.
DID WE LOSE ANYONE ALONG THE WAY? WE'RE ALL HERE, RIGHT? EVERYONE INTACT?
OH NO! I THINK SOMEONE--
SOMEONE FOLLOWED US THROUGH!

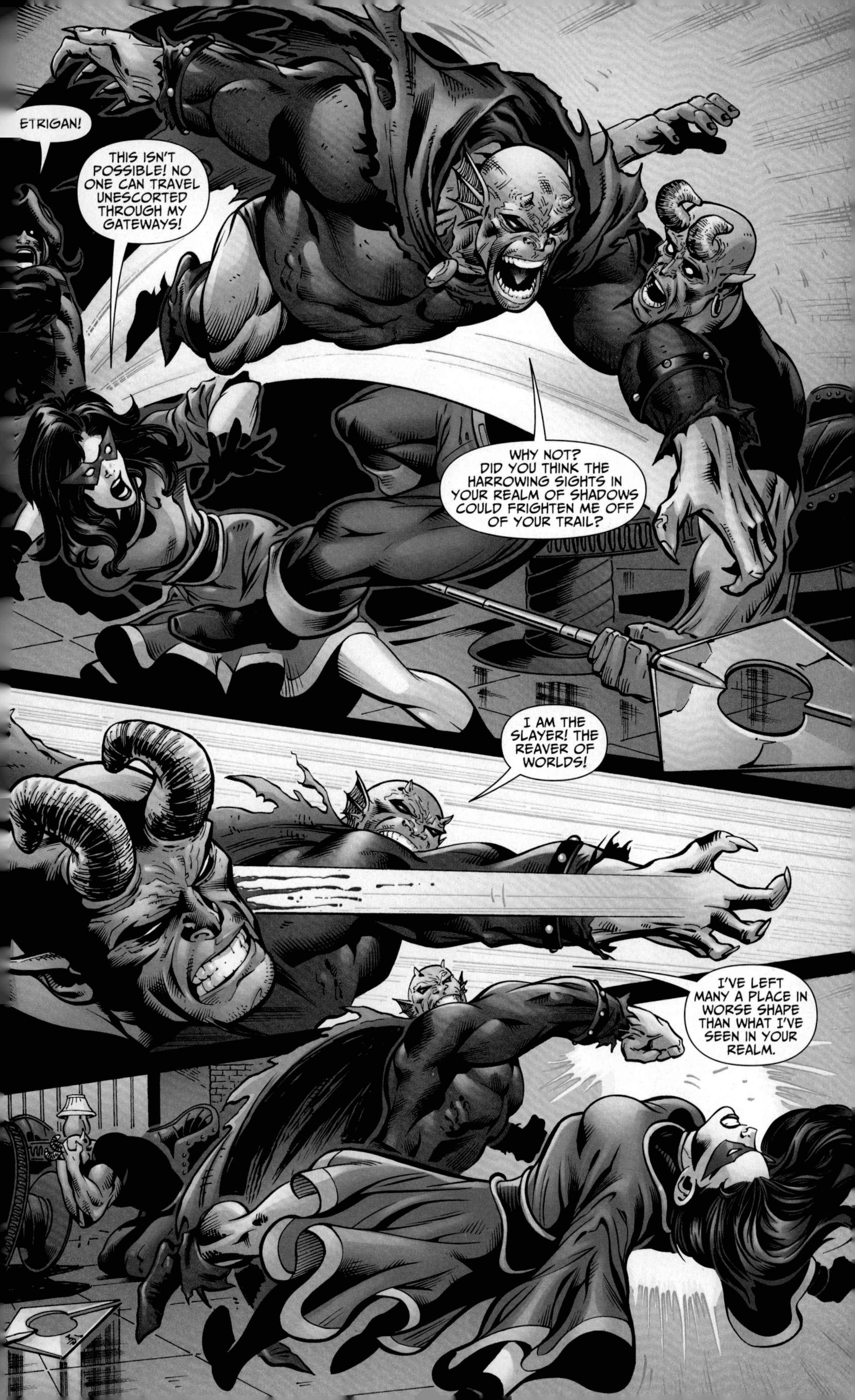
ETRIGAN!
THIS ISN'T POSSIBLE! NO ONE CAN TRAVEL UNESCORTED THROUGH MY GATEWAYS!
WHY NOT? DID YOU THINK THE HARROWING SIGHTS IN YOUR REALM OF SHADOWS COULD FRIGHTEN ME OFF OF YOUR TRAIL?
I AM THE SLAYER! THE REAVER OF WORLDS!
I'VE LEFT MANY A PLACE IN WORSE SHAPE THAN WHAT I'VE SEEN IN YOUR REALM.

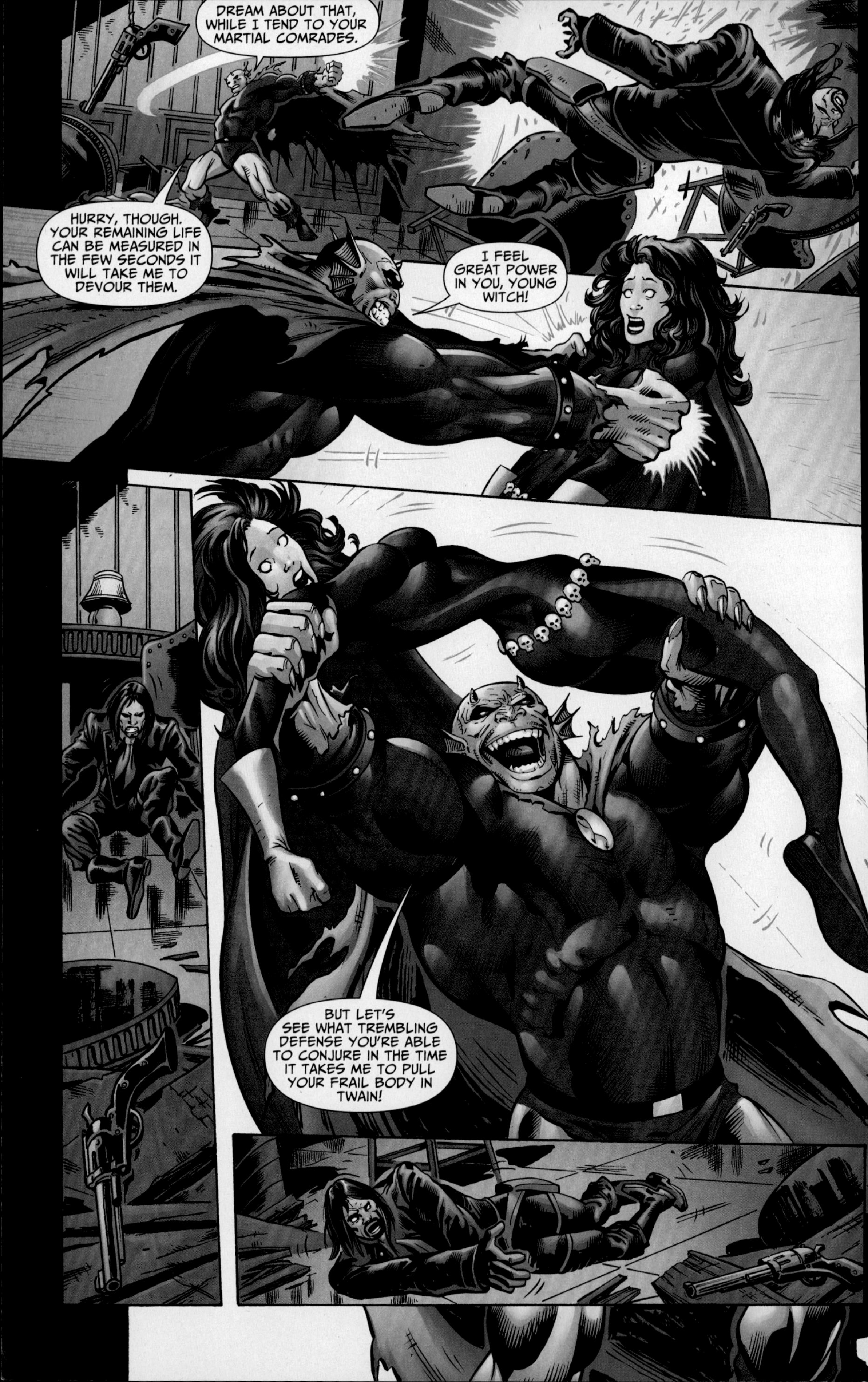
DREAM ABOUT THAT, WHILE I TEND TO YOUR MARTIAL COMRADES.
HURRY, THOUGH. YOUR REMAINING LIFE CAN BE MEASURED IN THE FEW SECONDS IT WILL TAKE ME TO DEVOUR THEM.
I FEEL GREAT POWER IN YOU, YOUNG WITCH!
BUT LET'S SEE WHAT TREMBLING DEFENSE YOU'RE ABLE TO CONJURE IN THE TIME IT TAKES ME TO PULL YOUR FRAIL BODY IN TWAIN!

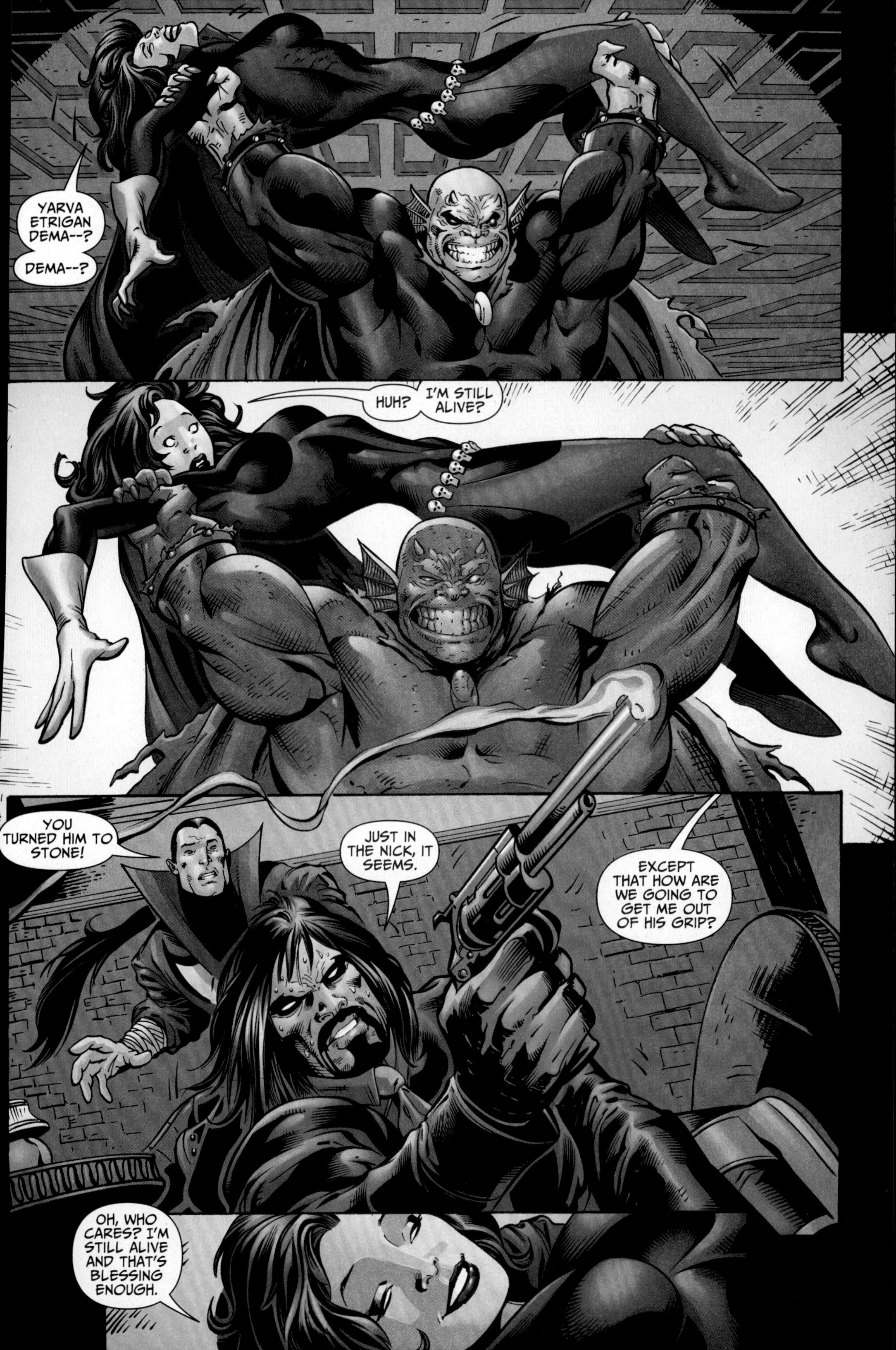
YARVA ETRIGAN DEMA--?
DEMA--?
HUH?
I'M STILL ALIVE?
YOU TURNED HIM TO STONE!
JUST IN THE NICK, IT SEEMS.
EXCEPT THAT HOW ARE WE GOING TO GET ME OUT OF HIS GRIP?
OH, WHO CARES? I'M STILL ALIVE AND THAT'S BLESSING ENOUGH.

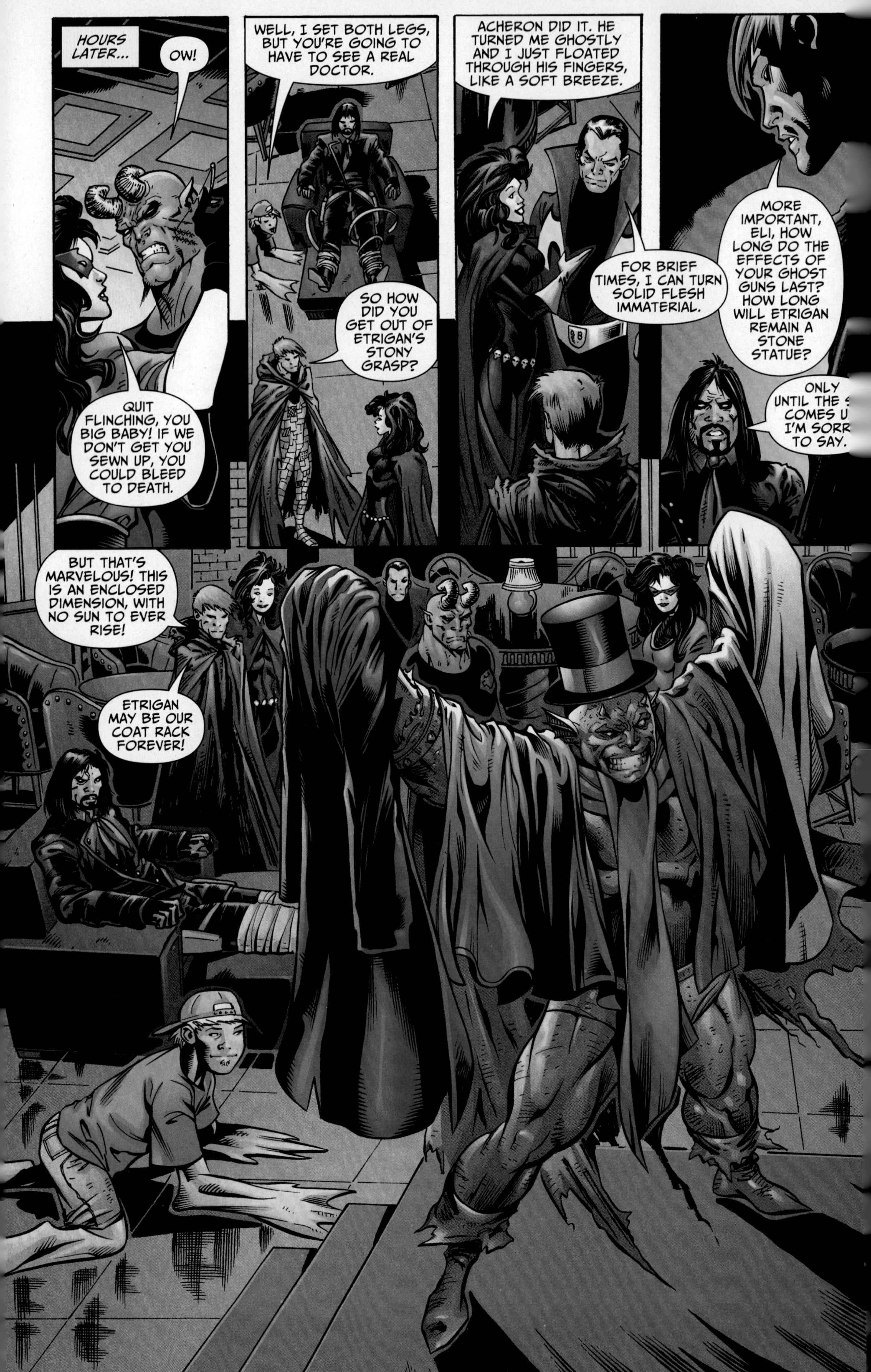
HOURS LATER...
OW!
QUIT FLINCHING, YOU BIG BABY! IF WE DON'T GET YOU SEWN UP, YOU COULD BLEED TO DEATH.
WELL, I SET BOTH LEGS, BUT YOU'RE GOING TO HAVE TO SEE A REAL DOCTOR.
SO HOW DID YOU GET OUT OF ETRIGAN'S STONY GRASP?
ACHERON DID IT. HE TURNED ME GHOSTLY AND I JUST FLOATED THROUGH HIS FINGERS, LIKE A SOFT BREEZE.
FOR BRIEF TIMES, I CAN TURN SOLID FLESH IMMATERIAL.
MORE IMPORTANT, ELI, HOW LONG DO THE EFFECTS OF YOUR GHOST GUNS LAST? HOW LONG WILL ETRIGAN REMAIN A STONE STATUE?
ONLY UNTIL THE S COMES U I'M SORR TO SAY.
BUT THAT'S MARVELOUS! THIS IS AN ENCLOSED DIMENSION, WITH NO SUN TO EVER RISE!
ETRIGAN MAY BE OUR COAT RACK FOREVER!

LIVE BY THE SWORD, DIE BY THE SWORD

cover art by **TOM DERENICK** *and* **WAYNE FAUCHER**

colored by **MIKE ATIYEH**

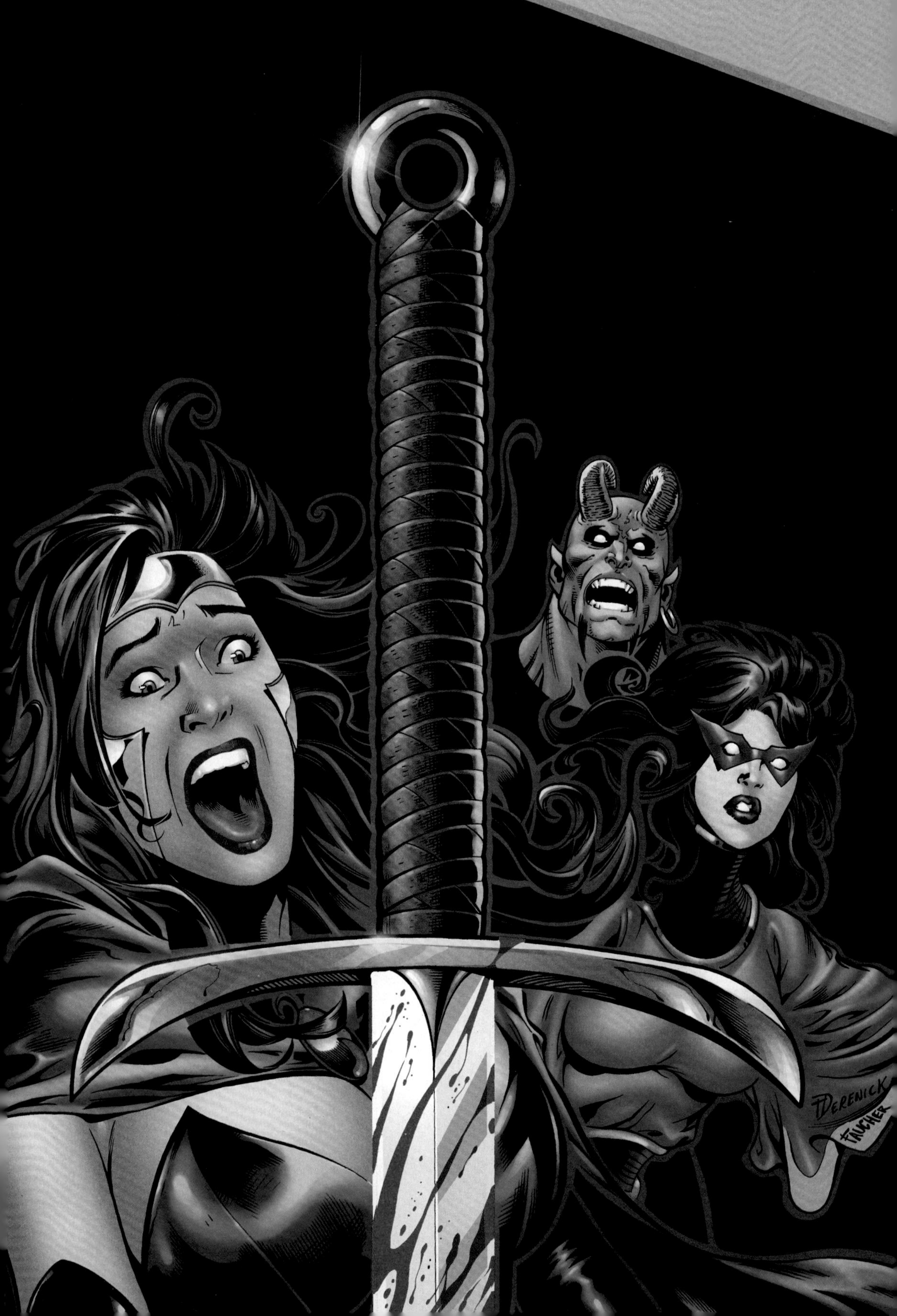
DERENICK
FAUCHER

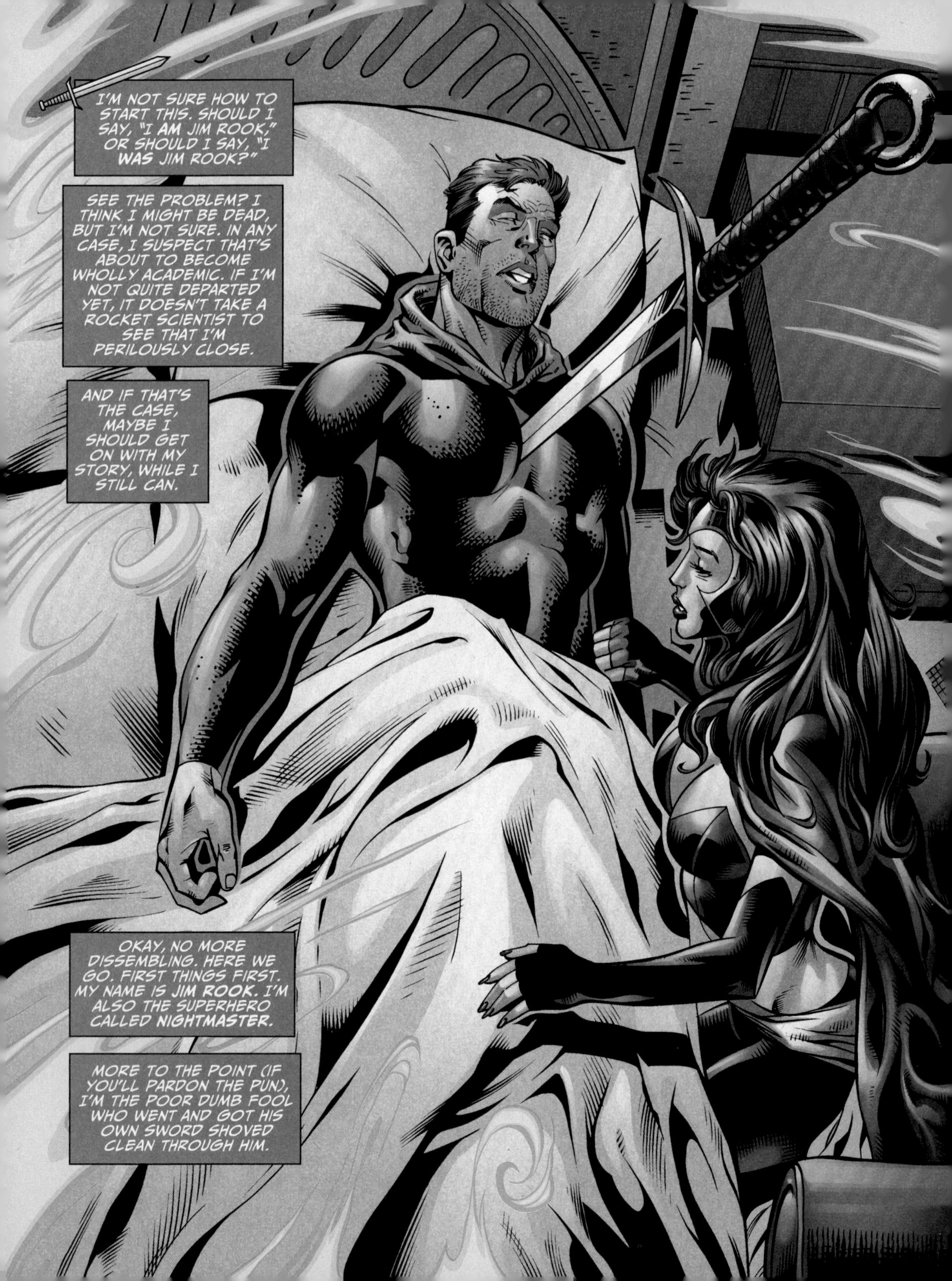
I'M NOT SURE HOW TO START THIS. SHOULD I SAY, "I **AM** JIM ROOK," OR SHOULD I SAY, "I **WAS** JIM ROOK?"
SEE THE PROBLEM? I THINK I MIGHT BE DEAD, BUT I'M NOT SURE. IN ANY CASE, I SUSPECT THAT'S ABOUT TO BECOME WHOLLY ACADEMIC. IF I'M NOT QUITE DEPARTED YET, IT DOESN'T TAKE A ROCKET SCIENTIST TO SEE THAT I'M PERILOUSLY CLOSE.
AND IF THAT'S THE CASE, MAYBE I SHOULD GET ON WITH MY STORY, WHILE I STILL CAN.
OKAY, NO MORE DISSEMBLING. HERE WE GO. FIRST THINGS FIRST. MY NAME IS **JIM ROOK**. I'M ALSO THE SUPERHERO CALLED **NIGHTMASTER**.
MORE TO THE POINT (IF YOU'LL PARDON THE PUN), I'M THE POOR DUMB FOOL WHO WENT AND GOT HIS OWN SWORD SHOVED CLEAN THROUGH HIM.

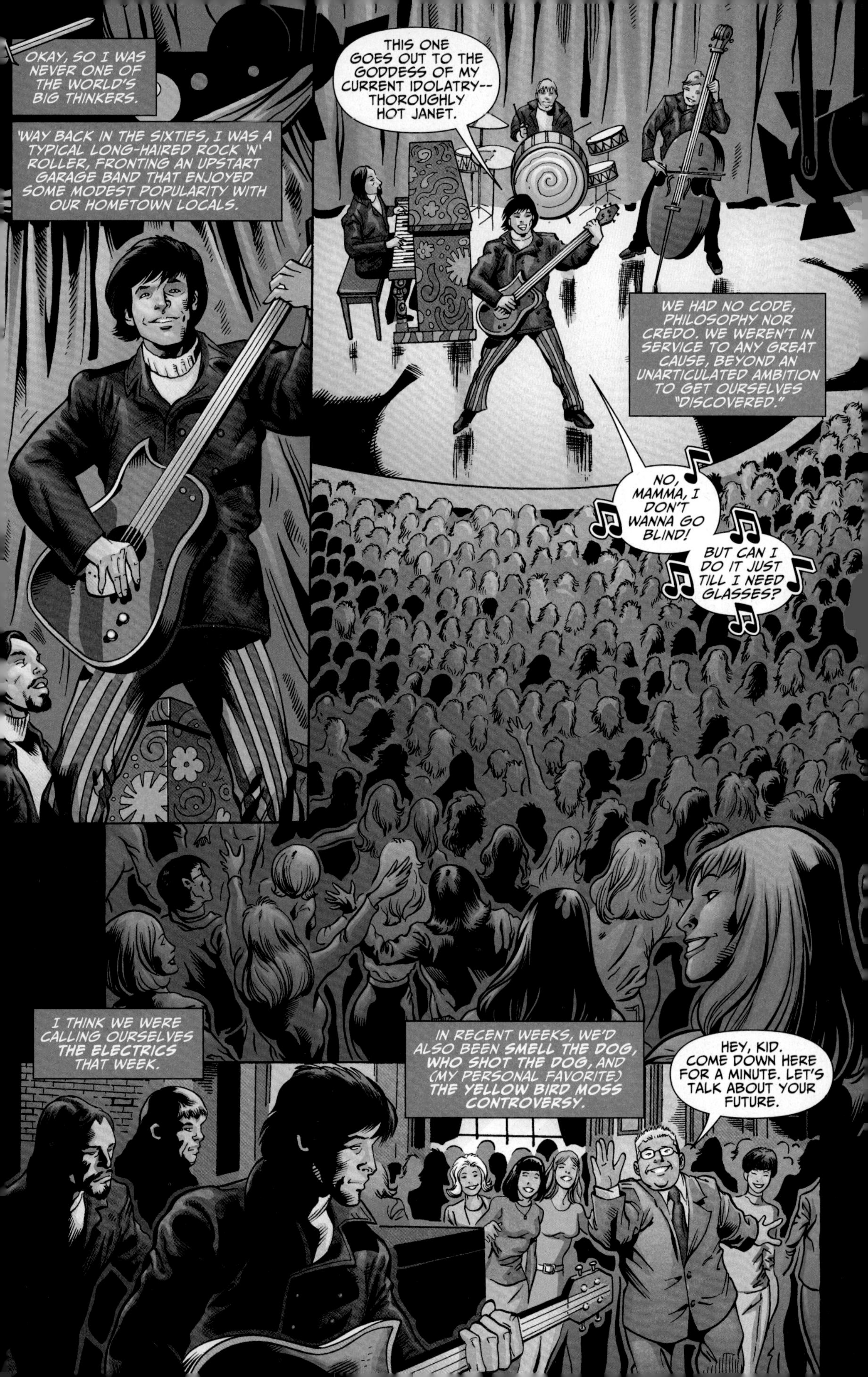

OKAY, SO I WAS NEVER ONE OF THE WORLD'S BIG THINKERS.
'WAY BACK IN THE SIXTIES, I WAS A TYPICAL LONG-HAIRED ROCK 'N' ROLLER, FRONTING AN UPSTART GARAGE BAND THAT ENJOYED SOME MODEST POPULARITY WITH OUR HOMETOWN LOCALS.
THIS ONE GOES OUT TO THE GODDESS OF MY CURRENT IDOLATRY-- THOROUGHLY HOT JANET.
WE HAD NO CODE, PHILOSOPHY NOR CREDO. WE WEREN'T IN SERVICE TO ANY GREAT CAUSE, BEYOND AN UNARTICULATED AMBITION TO GET OURSELVES "DISCOVERED."
NO, MAMMA, I DON'T WANNA GO BLIND!
BUT CAN I DO IT JUST TILL I NEED GLASSES?
I THINK WE WERE CALLING OURSELVES THE ELECTRICS THAT WEEK.
IN RECENT WEEKS, WE'D ALSO BEEN SMELL THE DOG, WHO SHOT THE DOG, AND (MY PERSONAL FAVORITE) THE YELLOW BIRD MOSS CONTROVERSY.
HEY, KID. COME DOWN HERE FOR A MINUTE. LET'S TALK ABOUT YOUR FUTURE.

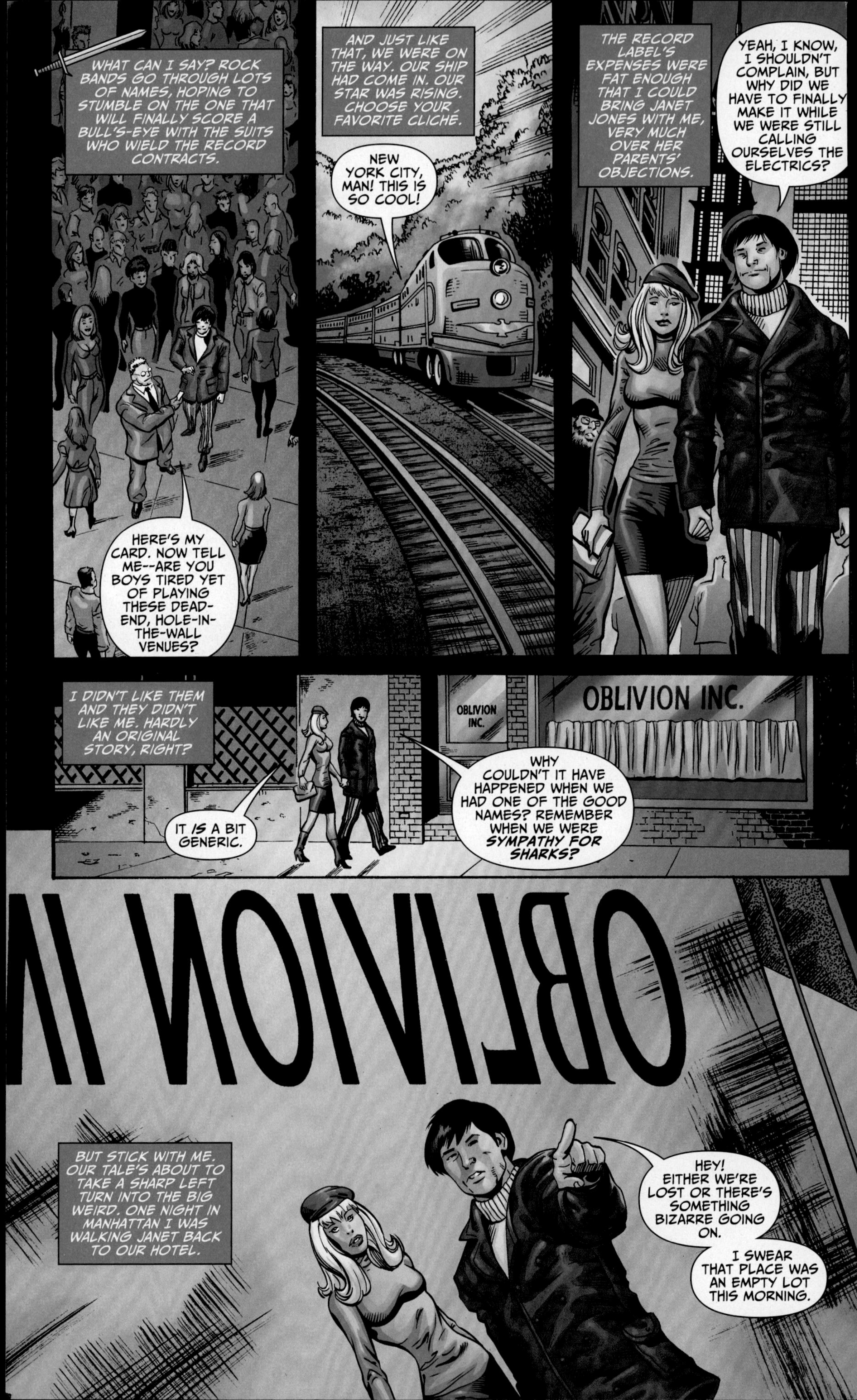
WHAT CAN I SAY? ROCK BANDS GO THROUGH LOTS OF NAMES, HOPING TO STUMBLE ON THE ONE THAT WILL FINALLY SCORE A BULL'S-EYE WITH THE SUITS WHO WIELD THE RECORD CONTRACTS.
HERE'S MY CARD. NOW TELL ME--ARE YOU BOYS TIRED YET OF PLAYING THESE DEAD-END, HOLE-IN-THE-WALL VENUES?
AND JUST LIKE THAT, WE WERE ON THE WAY. OUR SHIP HAD COME IN. OUR STAR WAS RISING. CHOOSE YOUR FAVORITE CLICHÉ.
NEW YORK CITY, MAN! THIS IS SO COOL!
THE RECORD LABEL'S EXPENSES WERE FAT ENOUGH THAT I COULD BRING JANET JONES WITH ME, VERY MUCH OVER HER PARENTS' OBJECTIONS.
YEAH, I KNOW, I SHOULDN'T COMPLAIN, BUT WHY DID WE HAVE TO FINALLY MAKE IT WHILE WE WERE STILL CALLING OURSELVES THE ELECTRICS?
I DIDN'T LIKE THEM AND THEY DIDN'T LIKE ME. HARDLY AN ORIGINAL STORY, RIGHT?
IT *IS* A BIT GENERIC.
OBLIVION INC.
OBLIVION INC.
WHY COULDN'T IT HAVE HAPPENED WHEN WE HAD ONE OF THE GOOD NAMES? REMEMBER WHEN WE WERE *SYMPATHY FOR SHARKS?*
OBLIVION IN
BUT STICK WITH ME. OUR TALE'S ABOUT TO TAKE A SHARP LEFT TURN INTO THE BIG WEIRD. ONE NIGHT IN MANHATTAN I WAS WALKING JANET BACK TO OUR HOTEL.
HEY! EITHER WE'RE LOST OR THERE'S SOMETHING BIZARRE GOING ON.
I SWEAR THAT PLACE WAS AN EMPTY LOT THIS MORNING.

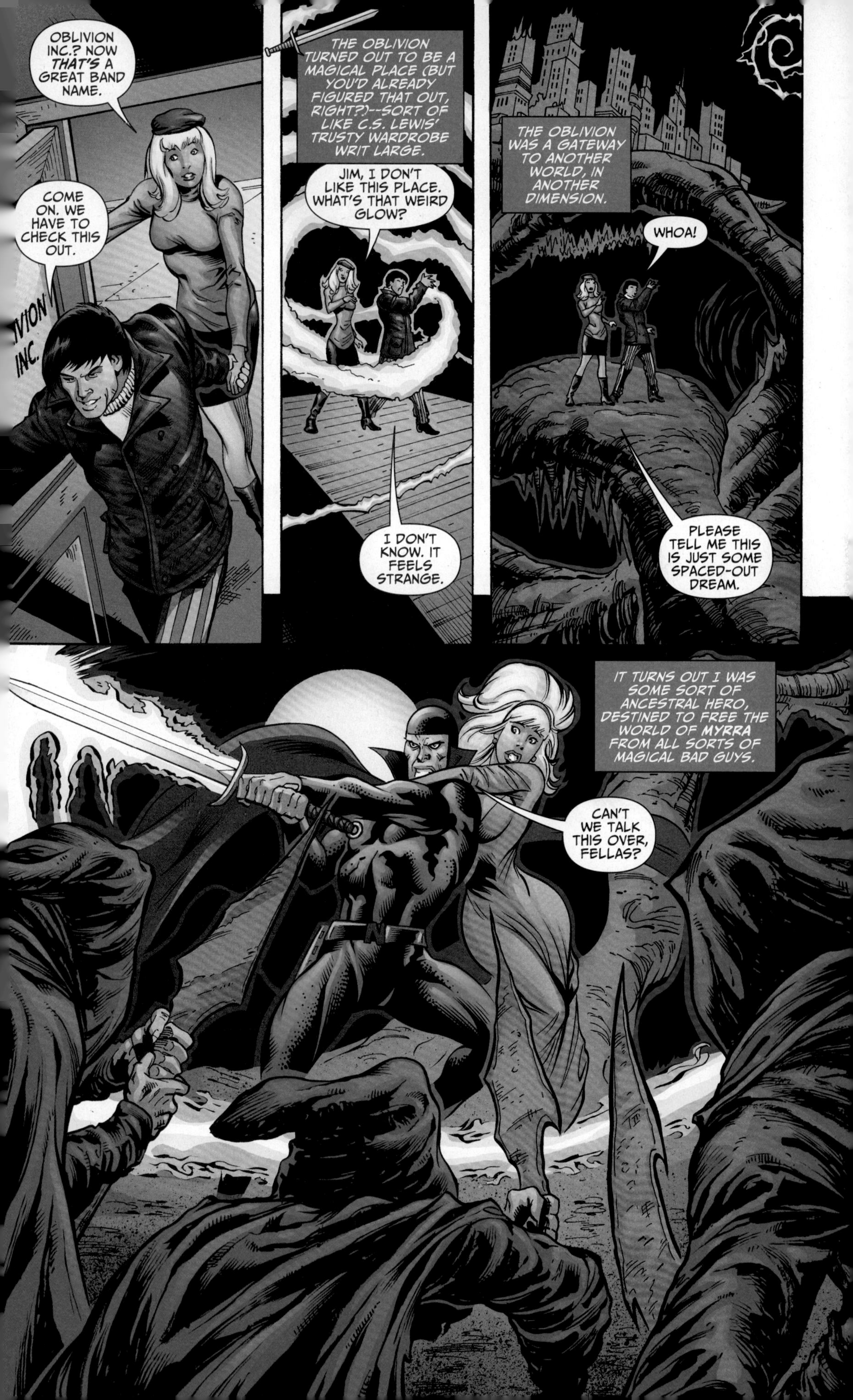
OBLIVION INC.? NOW THAT'S A GREAT BAND NAME.
COME ON. WE HAVE TO CHECK THIS OUT.
OBLIVION INC.
THE OBLIVION TURNED OUT TO BE A MAGICAL PLACE (BUT YOU'D ALREADY FIGURED THAT OUT, RIGHT?)--SORT OF LIKE C.S. LEWIS' TRUSTY WARDROBE WRIT LARGE.
JIM, I DON'T LIKE THIS PLACE. WHAT'S THAT WEIRD GLOW?
I DON'T KNOW. IT FEELS STRANGE.
THE OBLIVION WAS A GATEWAY TO ANOTHER WORLD, IN ANOTHER DIMENSION.
WHOA!
PLEASE TELL ME THIS IS JUST SOME SPACED-OUT DREAM.
IT TURNS OUT I WAS SOME SORT OF ANCESTRAL HERO, DESTINED TO FREE THE WORLD OF MYRRA FROM ALL SORTS OF MAGICAL BAD GUYS.
CAN'T WE TALK THIS OVER, FELLAS?

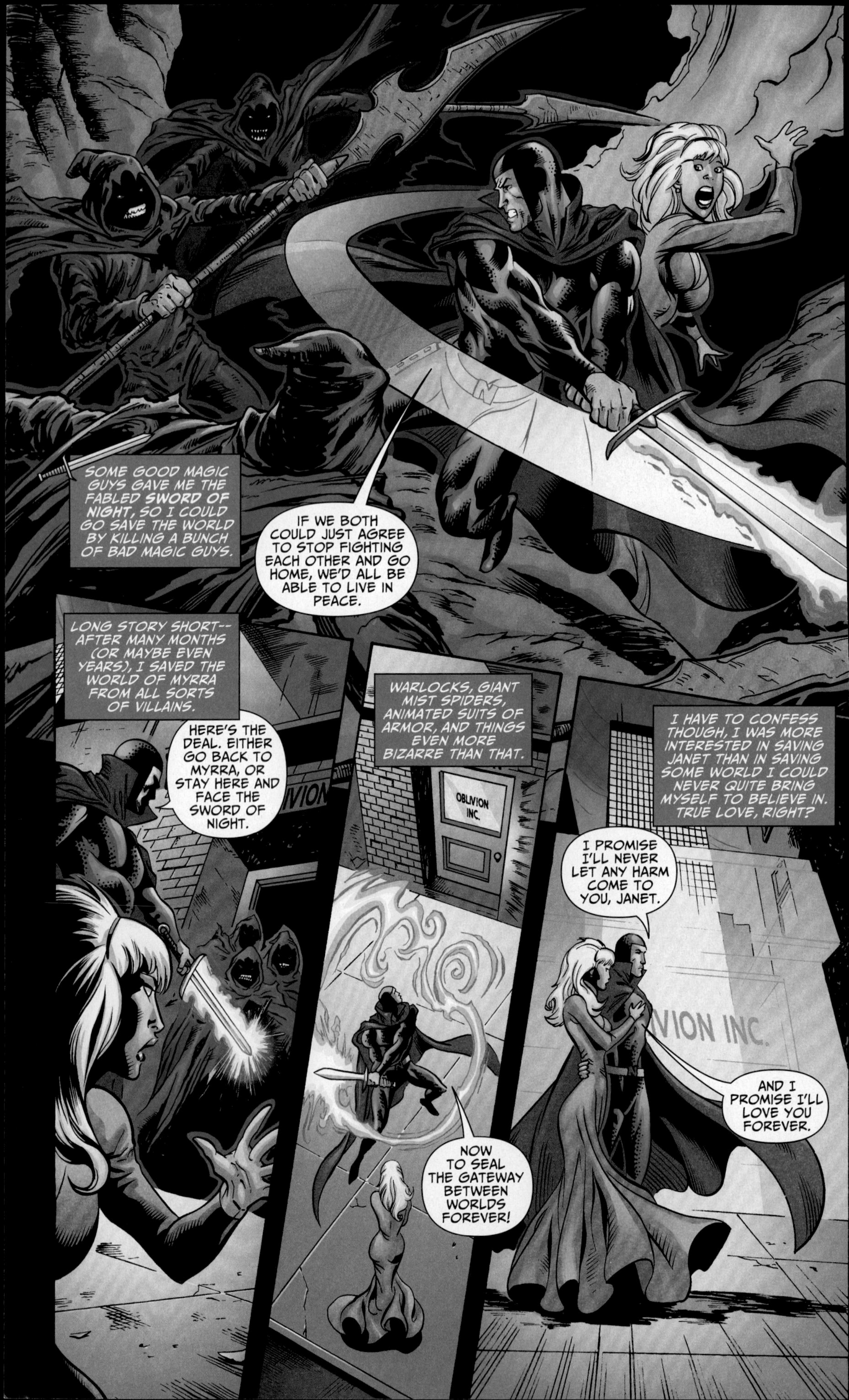
SOME GOOD MAGIC GUYS GAVE ME THE FABLED **SWORD OF NIGHT**, SO I COULD GO SAVE THE WORLD BY KILLING A BUNCH OF BAD MAGIC GUYS.
IF WE BOTH COULD JUST AGREE TO STOP FIGHTING EACH OTHER AND GO HOME, WE'D ALL BE ABLE TO LIVE IN PEACE.
LONG STORY SHORT-- AFTER MANY MONTHS (OR MAYBE EVEN YEARS), I SAVED THE WORLD OF MYRRA FROM ALL SORTS OF VILLAINS.
HERE'S THE DEAL. EITHER GO BACK TO MYRRA, OR STAY HERE AND FACE THE SWORD OF NIGHT.
WARLOCKS, GIANT MIST SPIDERS, ANIMATED SUITS OF ARMOR, AND THINGS EVEN MORE BIZARRE THAN THAT.
OBLIVION INC.
NOW TO SEAL THE GATEWAY BETWEEN WORLDS FOREVER!
I HAVE TO CONFESS THOUGH, I WAS MORE INTERESTED IN SAVING JANET THAN IN SAVING SOME WORLD I COULD NEVER QUITE BRING MYSELF TO BELIEVE IN. TRUE LOVE, RIGHT?
I PROMISE I'LL NEVER LET ANY HARM COME TO YOU, JANET.
AND I PROMISE I'LL LOVE YOU FOREVER.

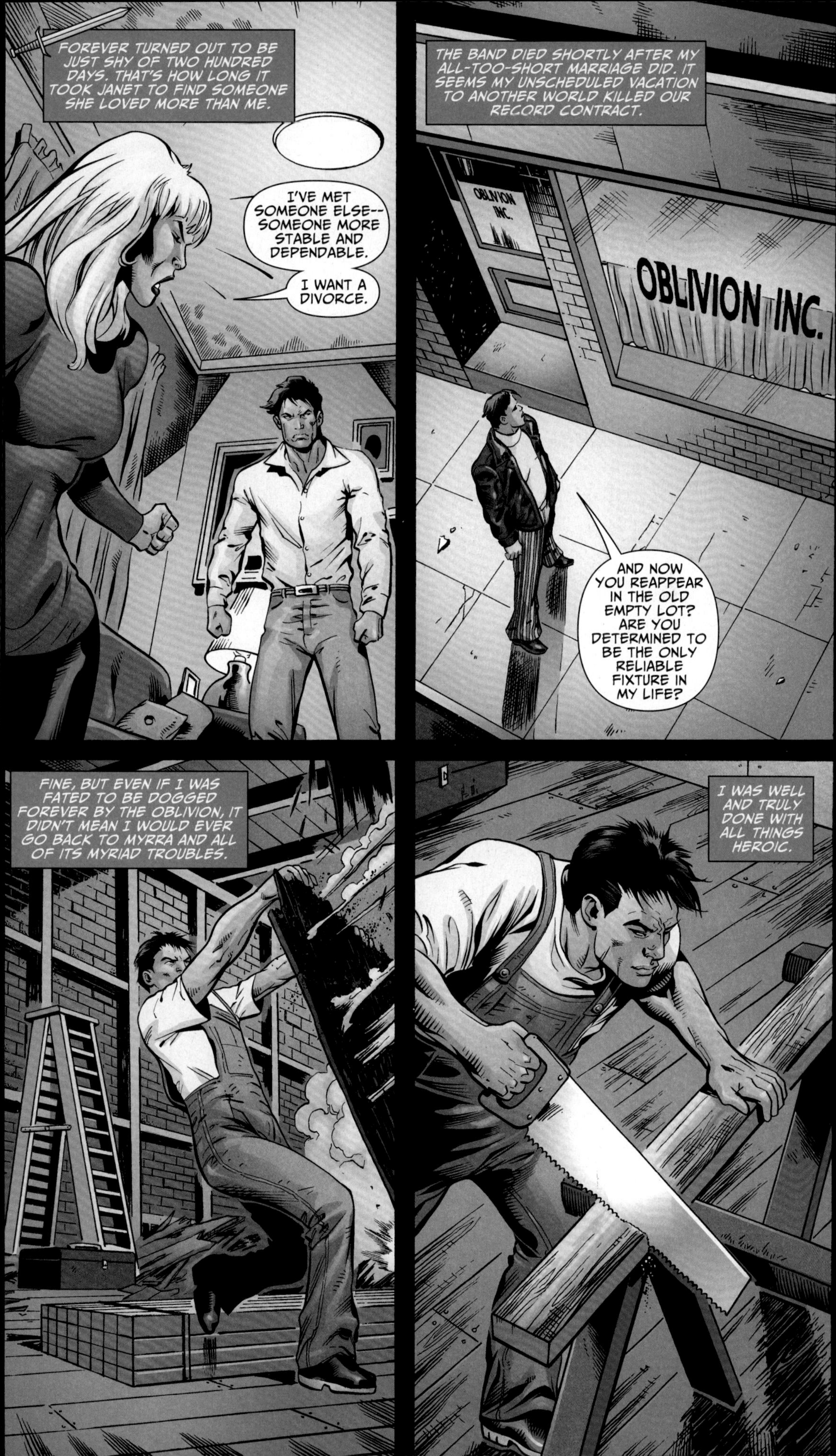
FOREVER TURNED OUT TO BE JUST SHY OF TWO HUNDRED DAYS. THAT'S HOW LONG IT TOOK JANET TO FIND SOMEONE SHE LOVED MORE THAN ME.
I'VE MET SOMEONE ELSE-- SOMEONE MORE STABLE AND DEPENDABLE.
I WANT A DIVORCE.
THE BAND DIED SHORTLY AFTER MY ALL-TOO-SHORT MARRIAGE DID. IT SEEMS MY UNSCHEDULED VACATION TO ANOTHER WORLD KILLED OUR RECORD CONTRACT.
OBLIVION INC.
OBLIVION INC.
AND NOW YOU REAPPEAR IN THE OLD EMPTY LOT? ARE YOU DETERMINED TO BE THE ONLY RELIABLE FIXTURE IN MY LIFE?
FINE, BUT EVEN IF I WAS FATED TO BE DOGGED FOREVER BY THE OBLIVION, IT DIDN'T MEAN I WOULD EVER GO BACK TO MYRRA AND ALL OF ITS MYRIAD TROUBLES.
I WAS WELL AND TRULY DONE WITH ALL THINGS HEROIC.

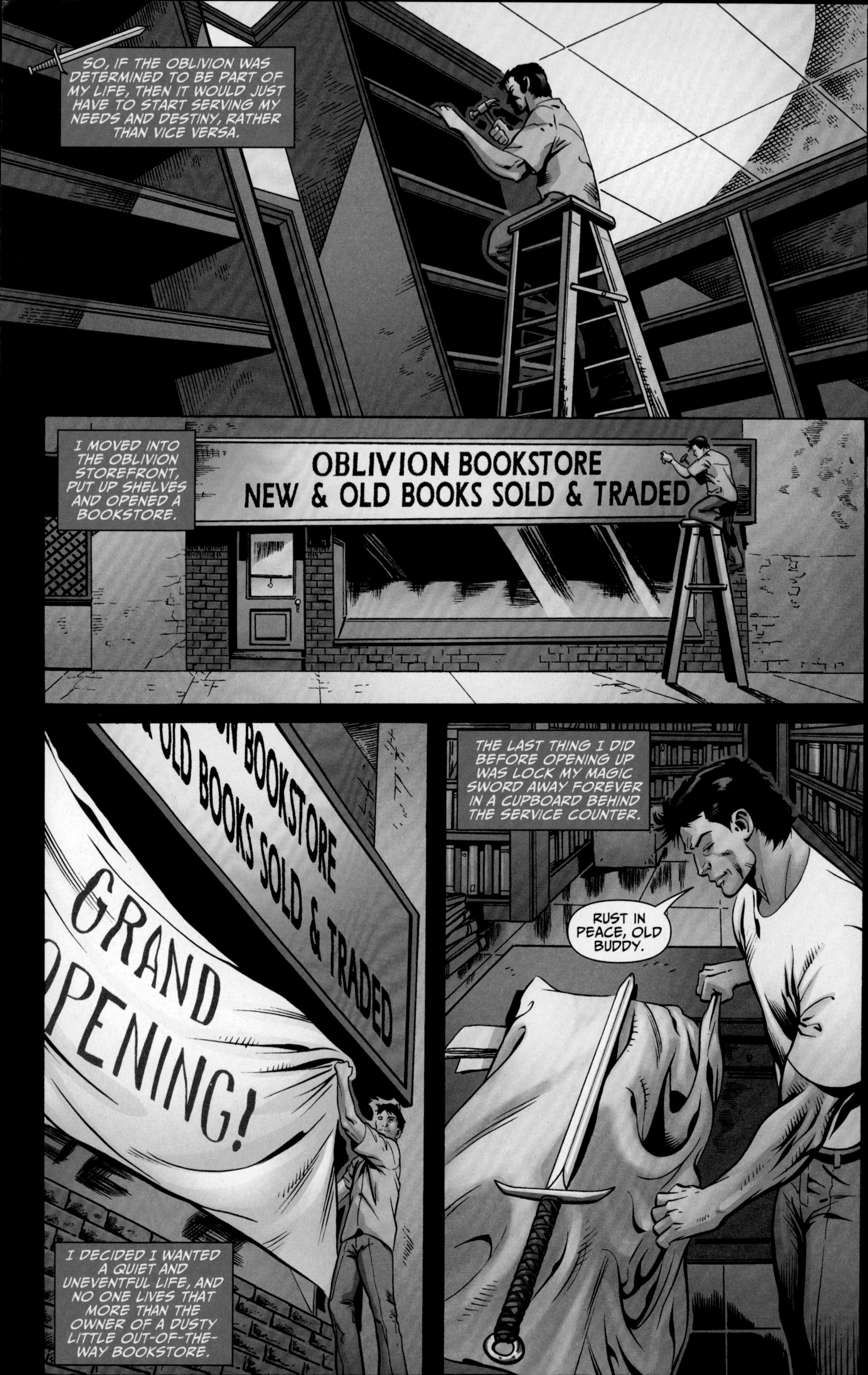
SO, IF THE OBLIVION WAS DETERMINED TO BE PART OF MY LIFE, THEN IT WOULD JUST HAVE TO START SERVING MY NEEDS AND DESTINY, RATHER THAN VICE VERSA.
I MOVED INTO THE OBLIVION STOREFRONT, PUT UP SHELVES AND OPENED A BOOKSTORE.
OBLIVION BOOKSTORE
NEW & OLD BOOKS SOLD & TRADED
GRAND OPENING!
I DECIDED I WANTED A QUIET AND UNEVENTFUL LIFE, AND NO ONE LIVES THAT MORE THAN THE OWNER OF A DUSTY LITTLE OUT-OF-THE-WAY BOOKSTORE.
THE LAST THING I DID BEFORE OPENING UP WAS LOCK MY MAGIC SWORD AWAY FOREVER IN A CUPBOARD BEHIND THE SERVICE COUNTER.
RUST IN PEACE, OLD BUDDY.

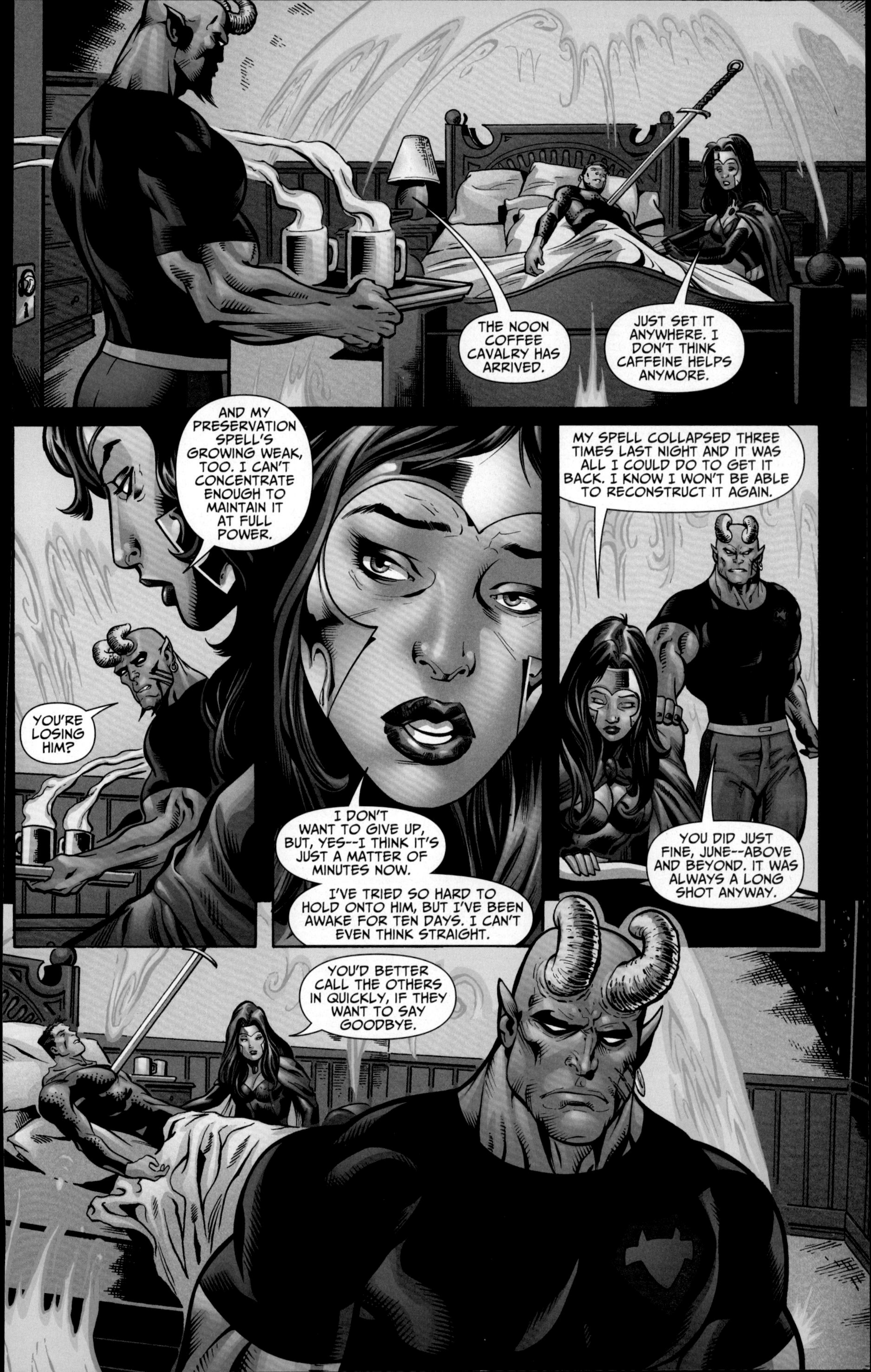
THE NOON COFFEE CAVALRY HAS ARRIVED.
JUST SET IT ANYWHERE. I DON'T THINK CAFFEINE HELPS ANYMORE.
AND MY PRESERVATION SPELL'S GROWING WEAK, TOO. I CAN'T CONCENTRATE ENOUGH TO MAINTAIN IT AT FULL POWER.
YOU'RE LOSING HIM?
I DON'T WANT TO GIVE UP, BUT, YES--I THINK IT'S JUST A MATTER OF MINUTES NOW.
I'VE TRIED SO HARD TO HOLD ONTO HIM, BUT I'VE BEEN AWAKE FOR TEN DAYS. I CAN'T EVEN THINK STRAIGHT.
MY SPELL COLLAPSED THREE TIMES LAST NIGHT AND IT WAS ALL I COULD DO TO GET IT BACK. I KNOW I WON'T BE ABLE TO RECONSTRUCT IT AGAIN.
YOU DID JUST FINE, JUNE--ABOVE AND BEYOND. IT WAS ALWAYS A LONG SHOT ANYWAY.
YOU'D BETTER CALL THE OTHERS IN QUICKLY, IF THEY WANT TO SAY GOODBYE.

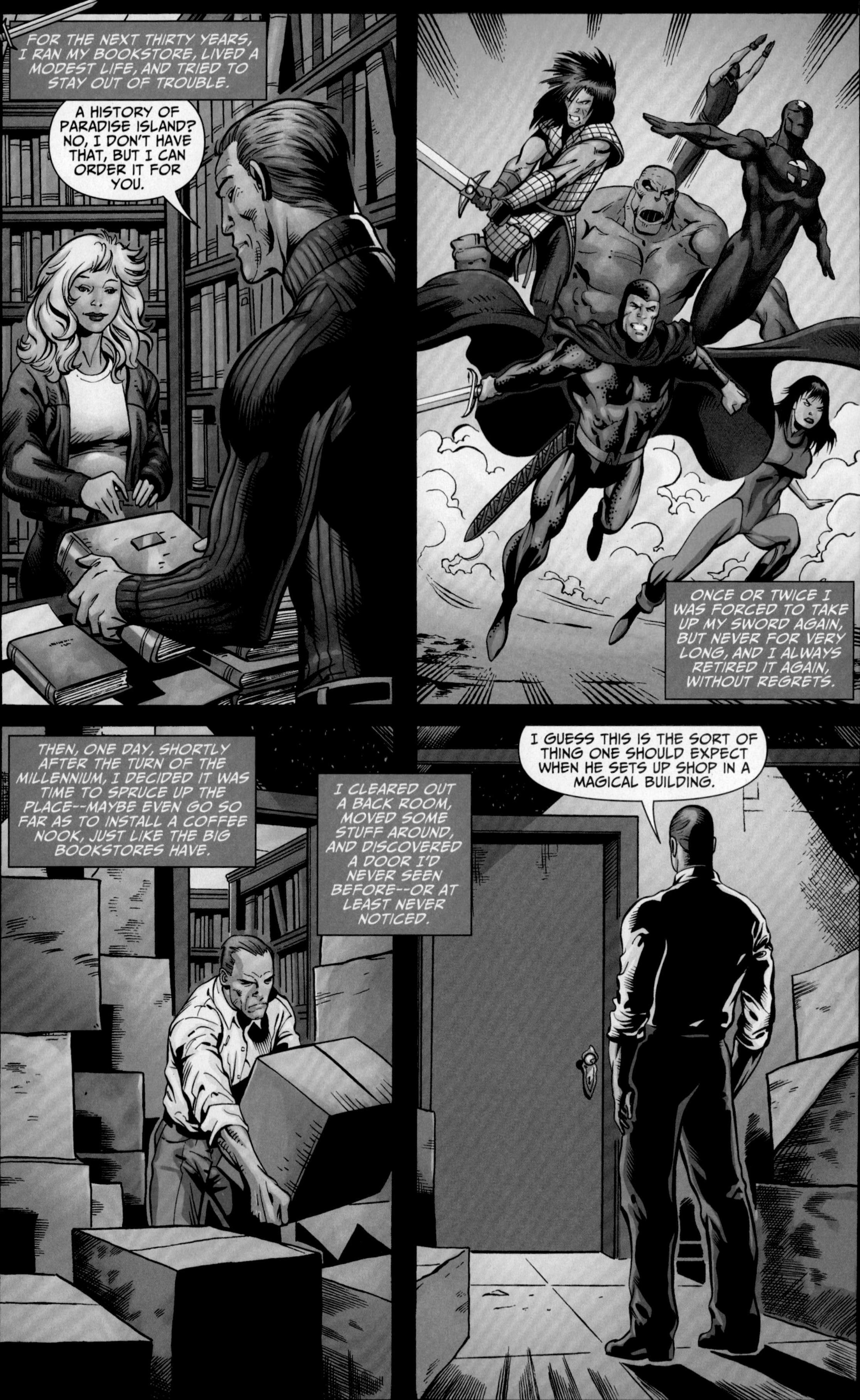
FOR THE NEXT THIRTY YEARS, I RAN MY BOOKSTORE, LIVED A MODEST LIFE, AND TRIED TO STAY OUT OF TROUBLE.
A HISTORY OF PARADISE ISLAND? NO, I DON'T HAVE THAT, BUT I CAN ORDER IT FOR YOU.
ONCE OR TWICE I WAS FORCED TO TAKE UP MY SWORD AGAIN, BUT NEVER FOR VERY LONG, AND I ALWAYS RETIRED IT AGAIN, WITHOUT REGRETS.
THEN, ONE DAY, SHORTLY AFTER THE TURN OF THE MILLENNIUM, I DECIDED IT WAS TIME TO SPRUCE UP THE PLACE--MAYBE EVEN GO SO FAR AS TO INSTALL A COFFEE NOOK, JUST LIKE THE BIG BOOKSTORES HAVE.
I CLEARED OUT A BACK ROOM, MOVED SOME STUFF AROUND, AND DISCOVERED A DOOR I'D NEVER SEEN BEFORE--OR AT LEAST NEVER NOTICED.
I GUESS THIS IS THE SORT OF THING ONE SHOULD EXPECT WHEN HE SETS UP SHOP IN A MAGICAL BUILDING.

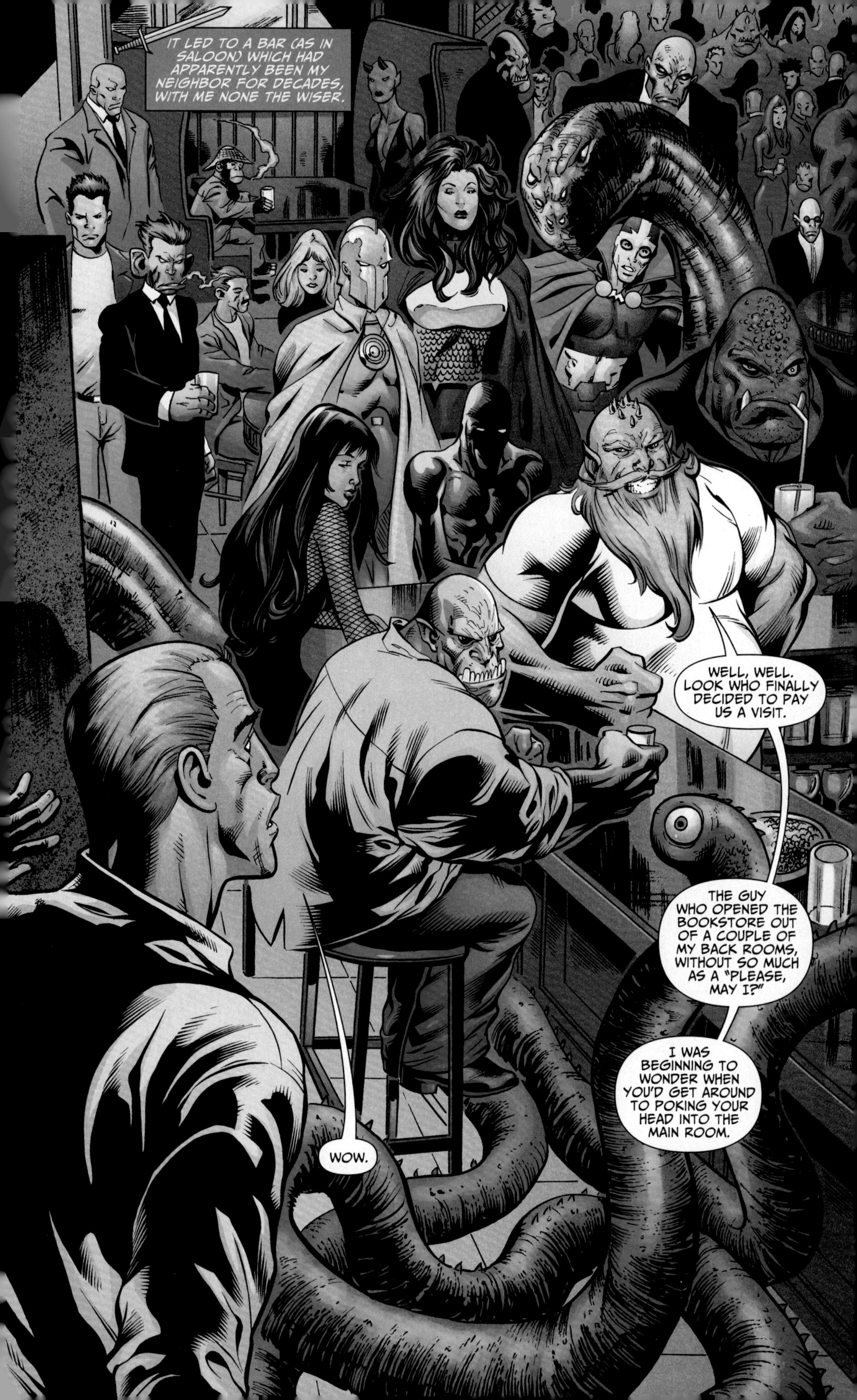
IT LED TO A BAR (AS IN SALOON) WHICH HAD APPARENTLY BEEN MY NEIGHBOR FOR DECADES, WITH ME NONE THE WISER.
WELL, WELL. LOOK WHO FINALLY DECIDED TO PAY US A VISIT.
THE GUY WHO OPENED THE BOOKSTORE OUT OF A COUPLE OF MY BACK ROOMS, WITHOUT SO MUCH AS A "PLEASE, MAY I?"
I WAS BEGINNING TO WONDER WHEN YOU'D GET AROUND TO POKING YOUR HEAD INTO THE MAIN ROOM.
WOW.

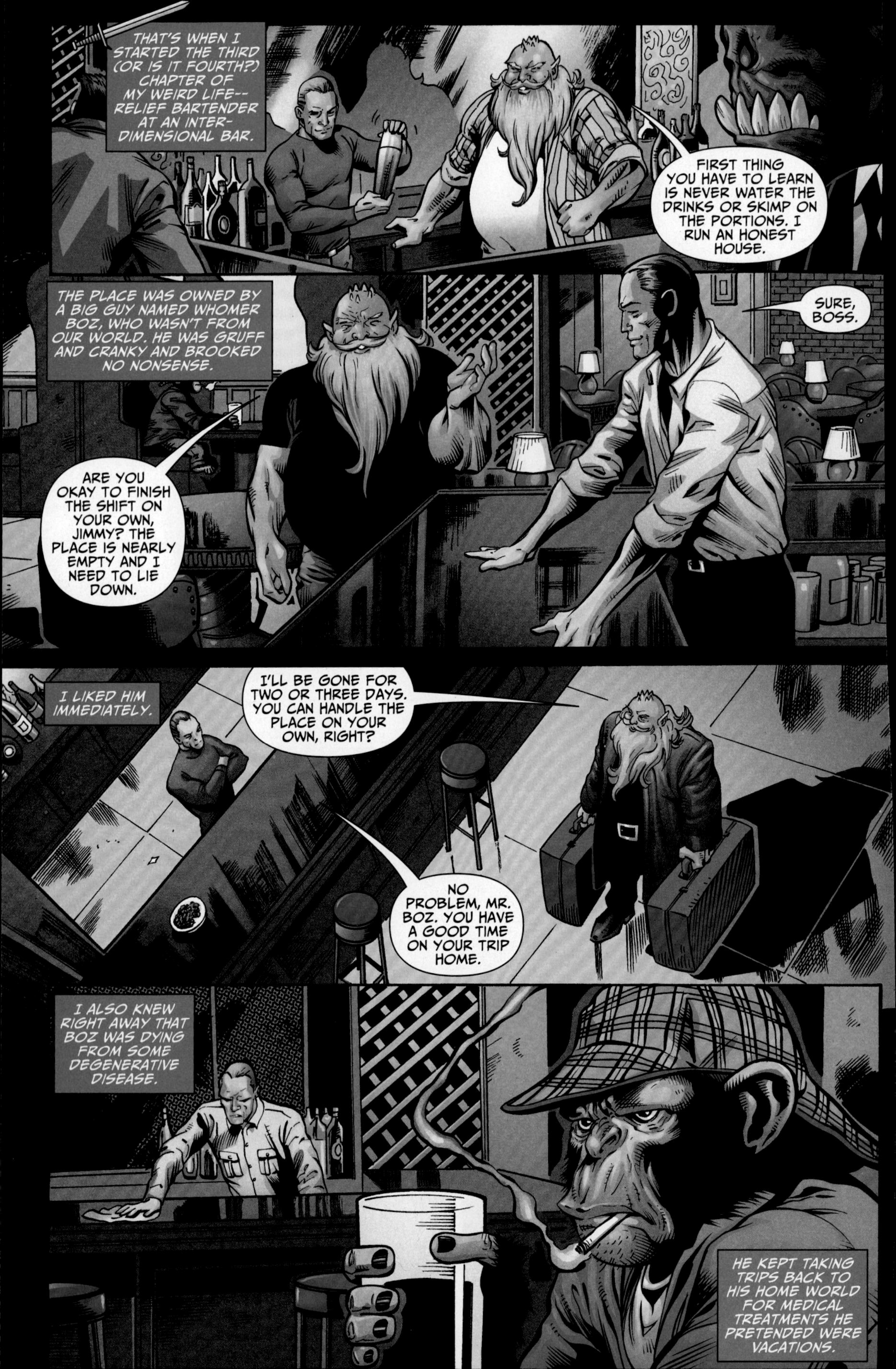
THAT'S WHEN I STARTED THE THIRD (OR IS IT FOURTH?) CHAPTER OF MY WEIRD LIFE-- RELIEF BARTENDER AT AN INTER-DIMENSIONAL BAR.
FIRST THING YOU HAVE TO LEARN IS NEVER WATER THE DRINKS OR SKIMP ON THE PORTIONS. I RUN AN HONEST HOUSE.
THE PLACE WAS OWNED BY A BIG GUY NAMED WHOMER BOZ, WHO WASN'T FROM OUR WORLD. HE WAS GRUFF AND CRANKY AND BROOKED NO NONSENSE.
SURE, BOSS.
ARE YOU OKAY TO FINISH THE SHIFT ON YOUR OWN, JIMMY? THE PLACE IS NEARLY EMPTY AND I NEED TO LIE DOWN.
I LIKED HIM IMMEDIATELY.
I'LL BE GONE FOR TWO OR THREE DAYS. YOU CAN HANDLE THE PLACE ON YOUR OWN, RIGHT?
NO PROBLEM, MR. BOZ. YOU HAVE A GOOD TIME ON YOUR TRIP HOME.
I ALSO KNEW RIGHT AWAY THAT BOZ WAS DYING FROM SOME DEGENERATIVE DISEASE.
HE KEPT TAKING TRIPS BACK TO HIS HOME WORLD FOR MEDICAL TREATMENTS HE PRETENDED WERE VACATIONS.

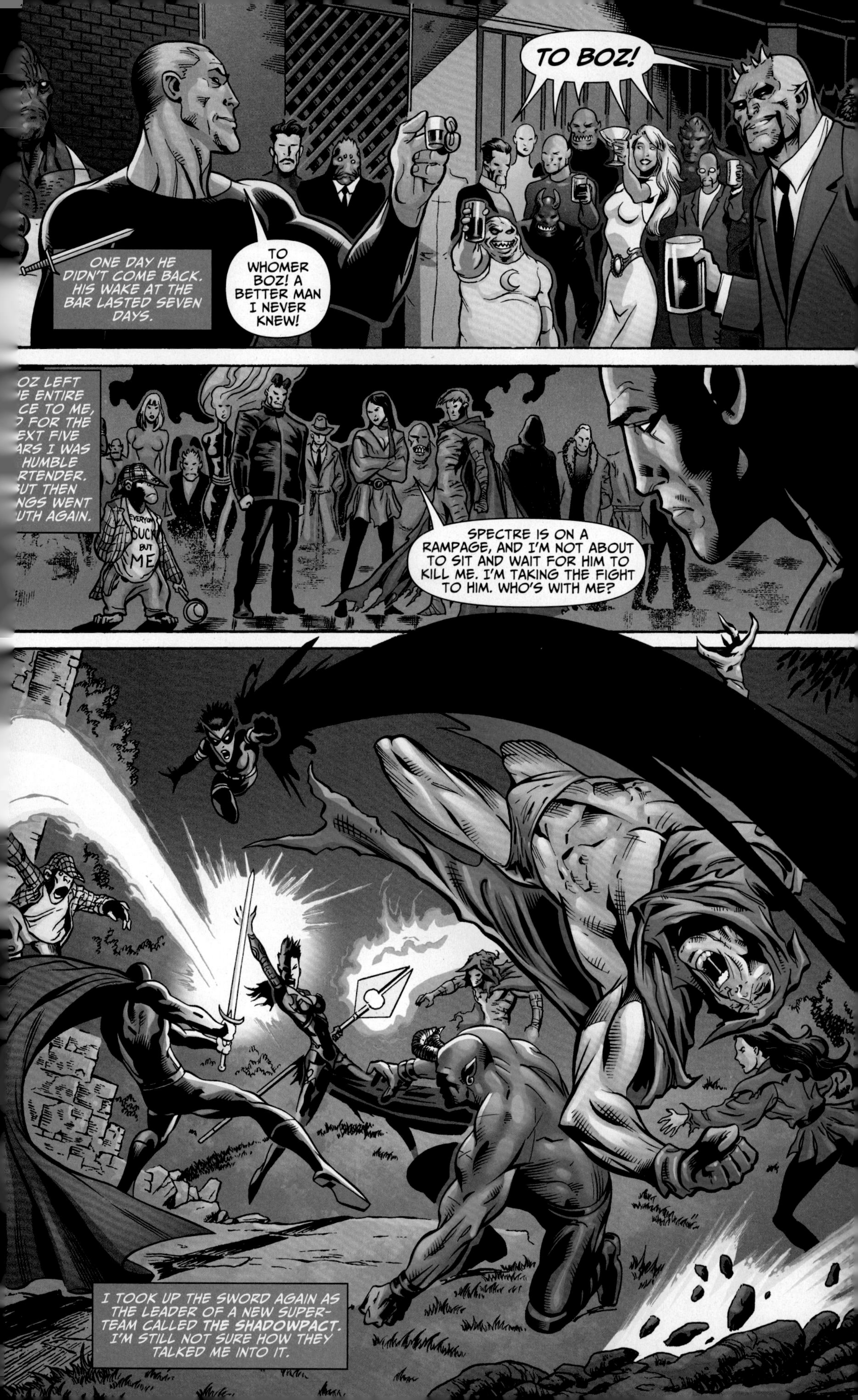

TO BOZ!
ONE DAY HE DIDN'T COME BACK. HIS WAKE AT THE BAR LASTED SEVEN DAYS.
TO WHOMER BOZ! A BETTER MAN I NEVER KNEW!
OZ LEFT E ENTIRE CE TO ME, FOR THE EXT FIVE ARS I WAS HUMBLE RTENDER. BUT THEN NGS WENT UTH AGAIN.
SPECTRE IS ON A RAMPAGE, AND I'M NOT ABOUT TO SIT AND WAIT FOR HIM TO KILL ME. I'M TAKING THE FIGHT TO HIM. WHO'S WITH ME?
I TOOK UP THE SWORD AGAIN AS THE LEADER OF A NEW SUPER-TEAM CALLED THE SHADOWPACT. I'M STILL NOT SURE HOW THEY TALKED ME INTO IT.

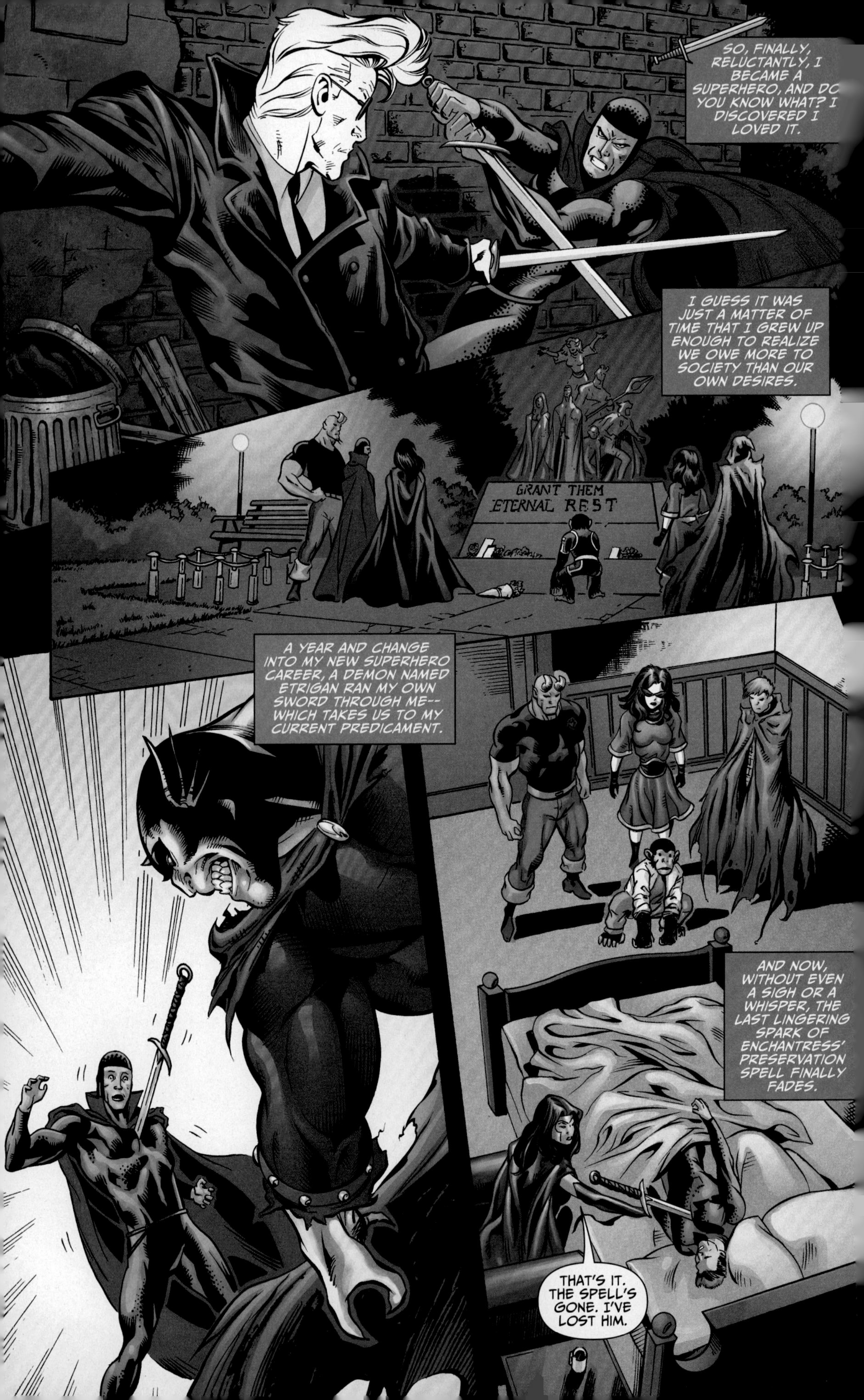
SO, FINALLY, RELUCTANTLY, I BECAME A SUPERHERO, AND DO YOU KNOW WHAT? I DISCOVERED I LOVED IT.
I GUESS IT WAS JUST A MATTER OF TIME THAT I GREW UP ENOUGH TO REALIZE WE OWE MORE TO SOCIETY THAN OUR OWN DESIRES.
GRANT THEM ETERNAL REST
A YEAR AND CHANGE INTO MY NEW SUPERHERO CAREER, A DEMON NAMED ETRIGAN RAN MY OWN SWORD THROUGH ME-- WHICH TAKES US TO MY CURRENT PREDICAMENT.
AND NOW, WITHOUT EVEN A SIGH OR A WHISPER, THE LAST LINGERING SPARK OF ENCHANTRESS' PRESERVATION SPELL FINALLY FADES.
THAT'S IT. THE SPELL'S GONE. I'VE LOST HIM.

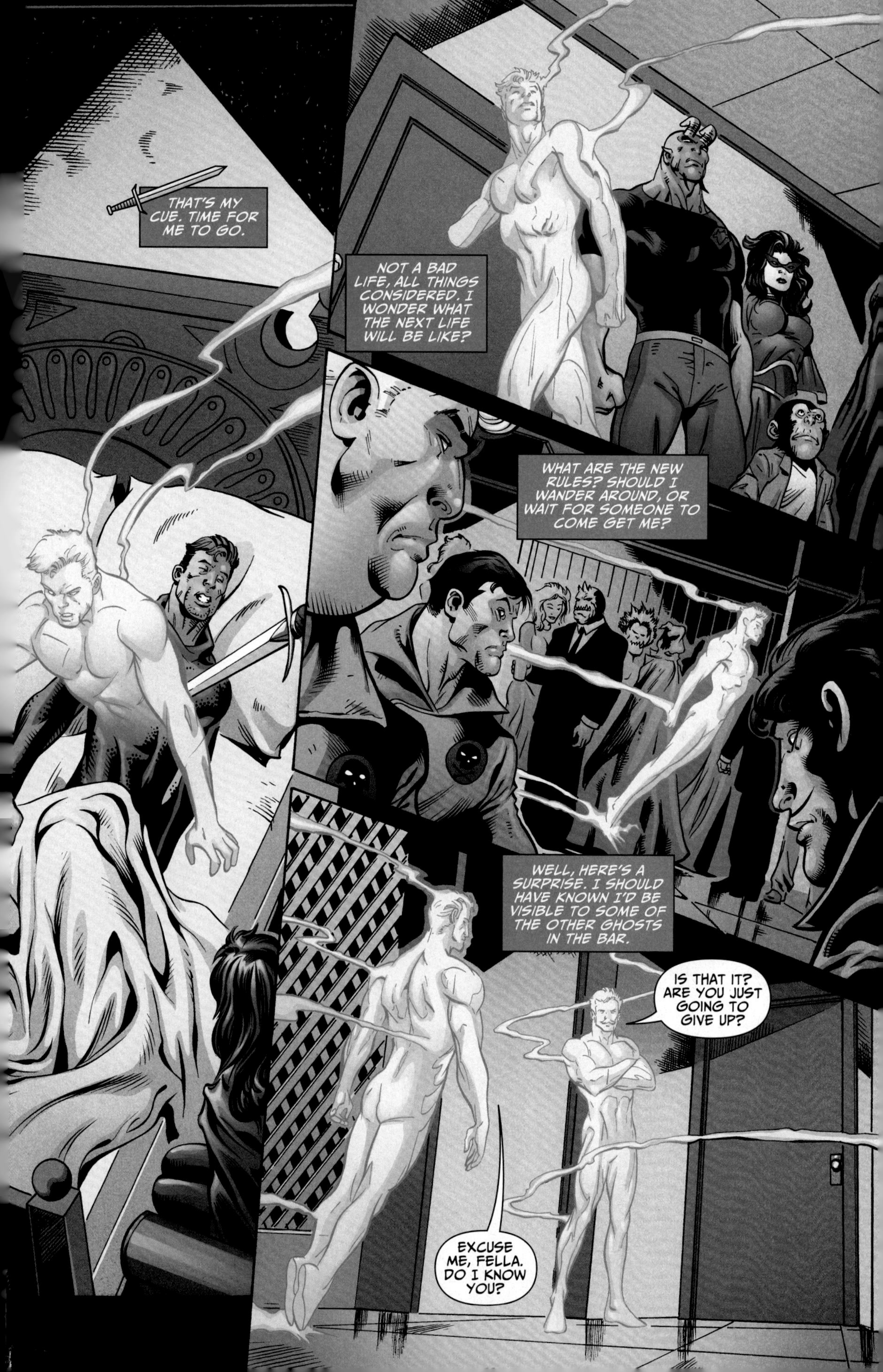
THAT'S MY CUE. TIME FOR ME TO GO.
NOT A BAD LIFE, ALL THINGS CONSIDERED. I WONDER WHAT THE NEXT LIFE WILL BE LIKE?
WHAT ARE THE NEW RULES? SHOULD I WANDER AROUND, OR WAIT FOR SOMEONE TO COME GET ME?
WELL, HERE'S A SURPRISE. I SHOULD HAVE KNOWN I'D BE VISIBLE TO SOME OF THE OTHER GHOSTS IN THE BAR.
IS THAT IT? ARE YOU JUST GOING TO GIVE UP?
EXCUSE ME, FELLA. DO I KNOW YOU?

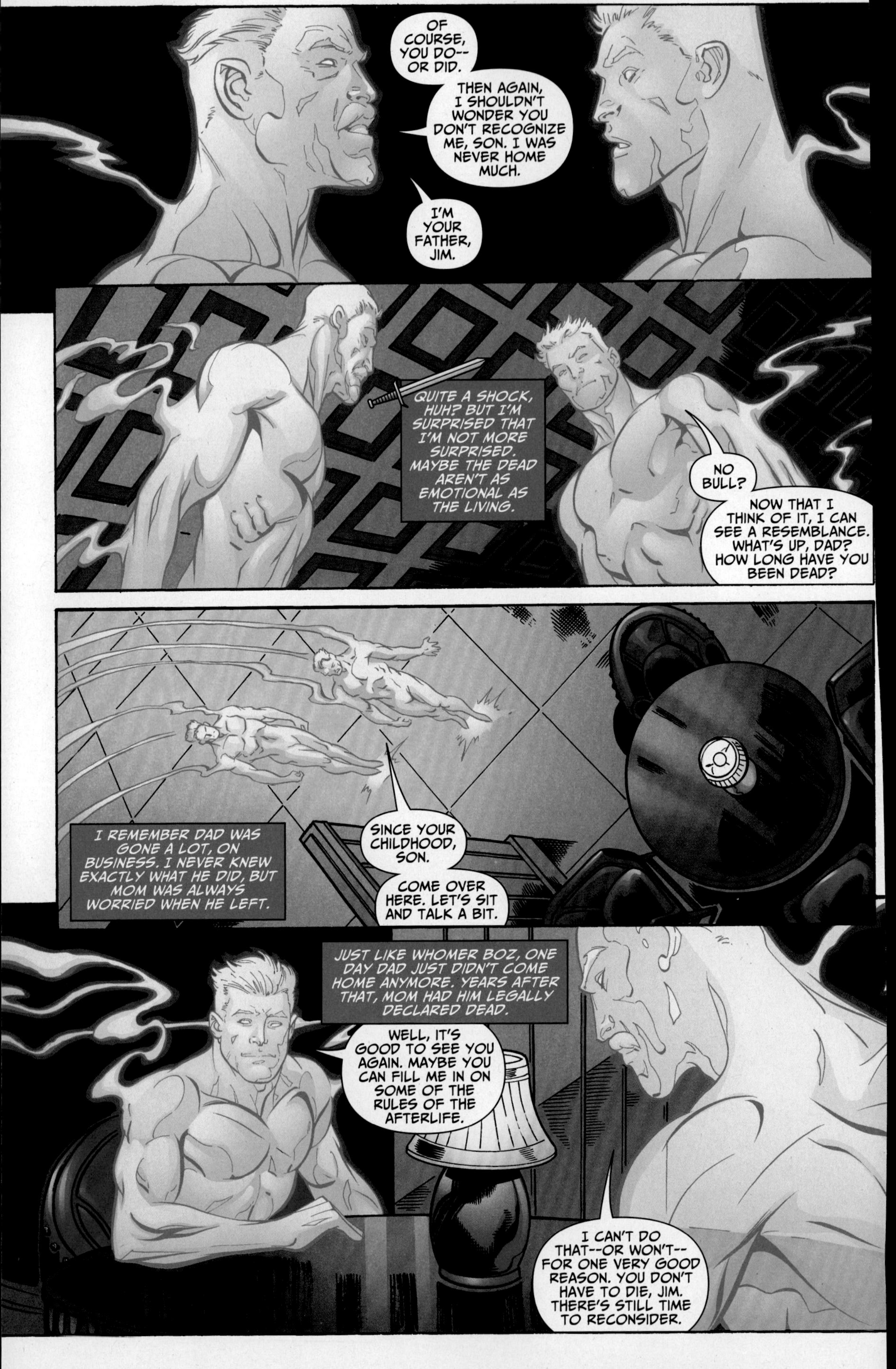

OF COURSE, YOU DO-- OR DID.
THEN AGAIN, I SHOULDN'T WONDER YOU DON'T RECOGNIZE ME, SON. I WAS NEVER HOME MUCH.
I'M YOUR FATHER, JIM.
QUITE A SHOCK, HUH? BUT I'M SURPRISED THAT I'M NOT MORE SURPRISED. MAYBE THE DEAD AREN'T AS EMOTIONAL AS THE LIVING.
NO BULL?
NOW THAT I THINK OF IT, I CAN SEE A RESEMBLANCE. WHAT'S UP, DAD? HOW LONG HAVE YOU BEEN DEAD?
I REMEMBER DAD WAS GONE A LOT, ON BUSINESS. I NEVER KNEW EXACTLY WHAT HE DID, BUT MOM WAS ALWAYS WORRIED WHEN HE LEFT.
SINCE YOUR CHILDHOOD, SON.
COME OVER HERE. LET'S SIT AND TALK A BIT.
JUST LIKE WHOMER BOZ, ONE DAY DAD JUST DIDN'T COME HOME ANYMORE. YEARS AFTER THAT, MOM HAD HIM LEGALLY DECLARED DEAD.
WELL, IT'S GOOD TO SEE YOU AGAIN. MAYBE YOU CAN FILL ME IN ON SOME OF THE RULES OF THE AFTERLIFE.
I CAN'T DO THAT--OR WON'T-- FOR ONE VERY GOOD REASON. YOU DON'T HAVE TO DIE, JIM. THERE'S STILL TIME TO RECONSIDER.

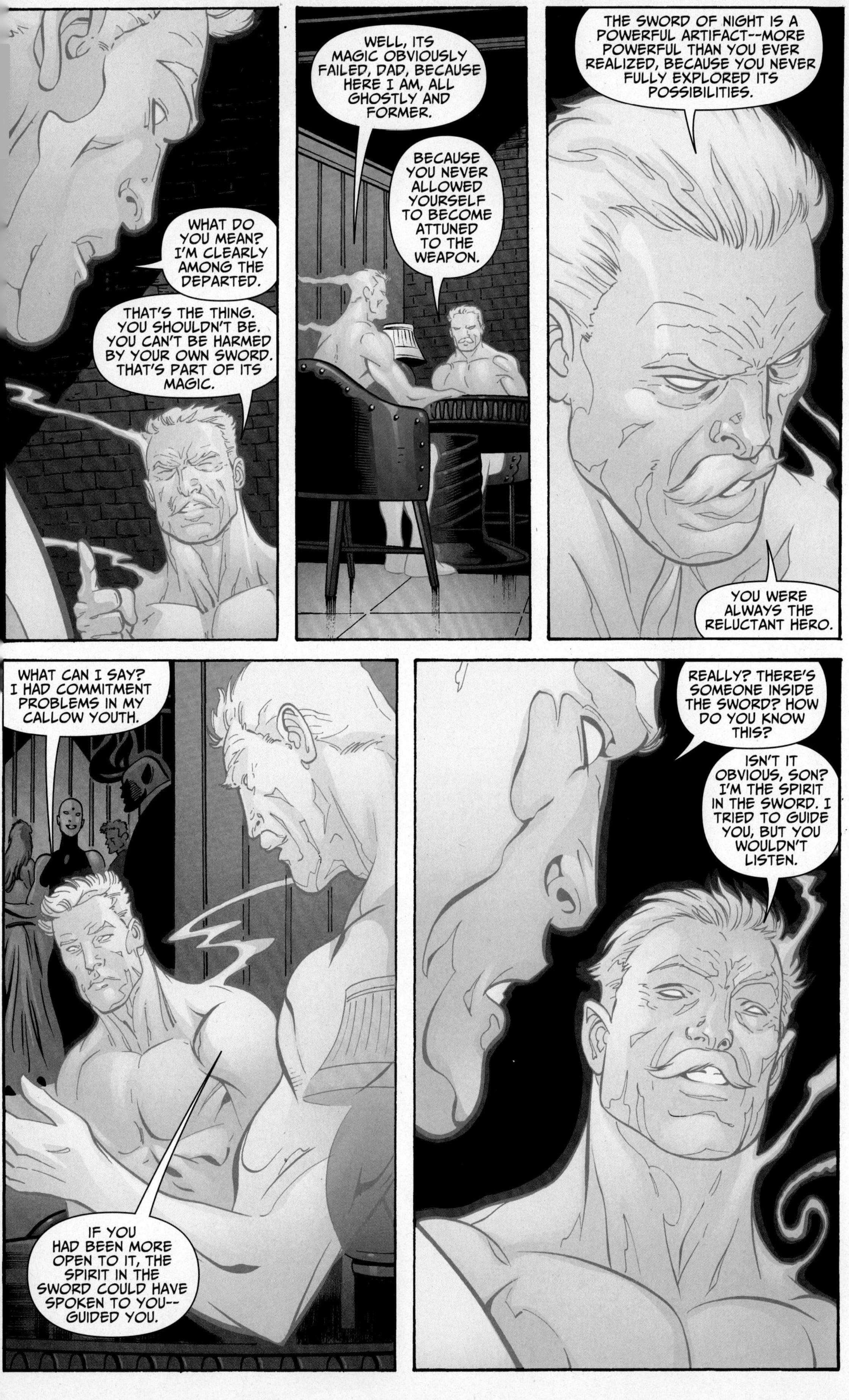
WHAT DO YOU MEAN? I'M CLEARLY AMONG THE DEPARTED.
THAT'S THE THING. YOU SHOULDN'T BE. YOU CAN'T BE HARMED BY YOUR OWN SWORD. THAT'S PART OF ITS MAGIC.
WELL, ITS MAGIC OBVIOUSLY FAILED, DAD, BECAUSE HERE I AM, ALL GHOSTLY AND FORMER.
BECAUSE YOU NEVER ALLOWED YOURSELF TO BECOME ATTUNED TO THE WEAPON.
THE SWORD OF NIGHT IS A POWERFUL ARTIFACT--MORE POWERFUL THAN YOU EVER REALIZED, BECAUSE YOU NEVER FULLY EXPLORED ITS POSSIBILITIES.
YOU WERE ALWAYS THE RELUCTANT HERO.
WHAT CAN I SAY? I HAD COMMITMENT PROBLEMS IN MY CALLOW YOUTH.
IF YOU HAD BEEN MORE OPEN TO IT, THE SPIRIT IN THE SWORD COULD HAVE SPOKEN TO YOU-- GUIDED YOU.
REALLY? THERE'S SOMEONE INSIDE THE SWORD? HOW DO YOU KNOW THIS?
ISN'T IT OBVIOUS, SON? I'M THE SPIRIT IN THE SWORD. I TRIED TO GUIDE YOU, BUT YOU WOULDN'T LISTEN.

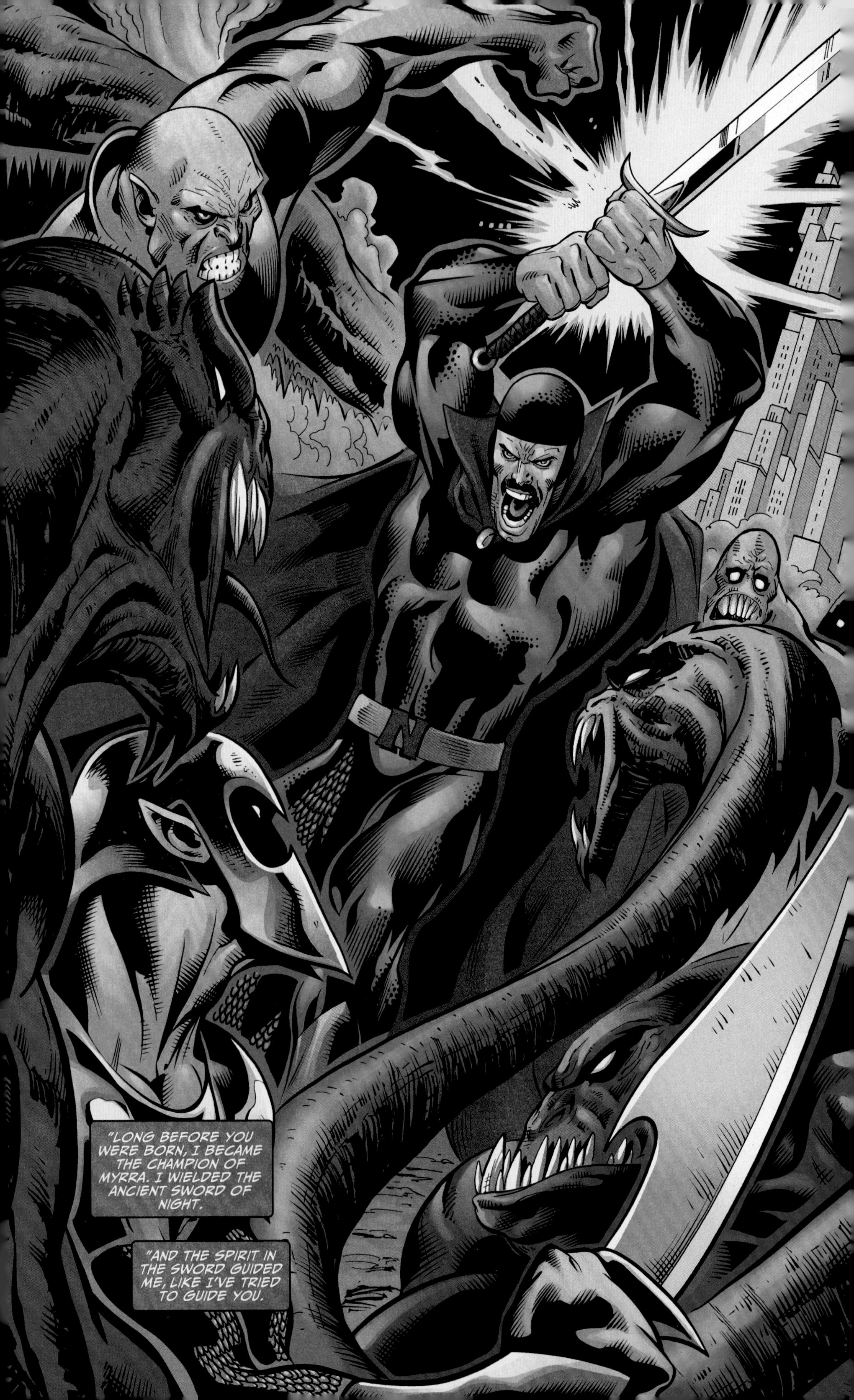
"LONG BEFORE YOU WERE BORN, I BECAME THE CHAMPION OF MYRRA. I WIELDED THE ANCIENT SWORD OF NIGHT.
"AND THE SPIRIT IN THE SWORD GUIDED ME, LIKE I'VE TRIED TO GUIDE YOU.

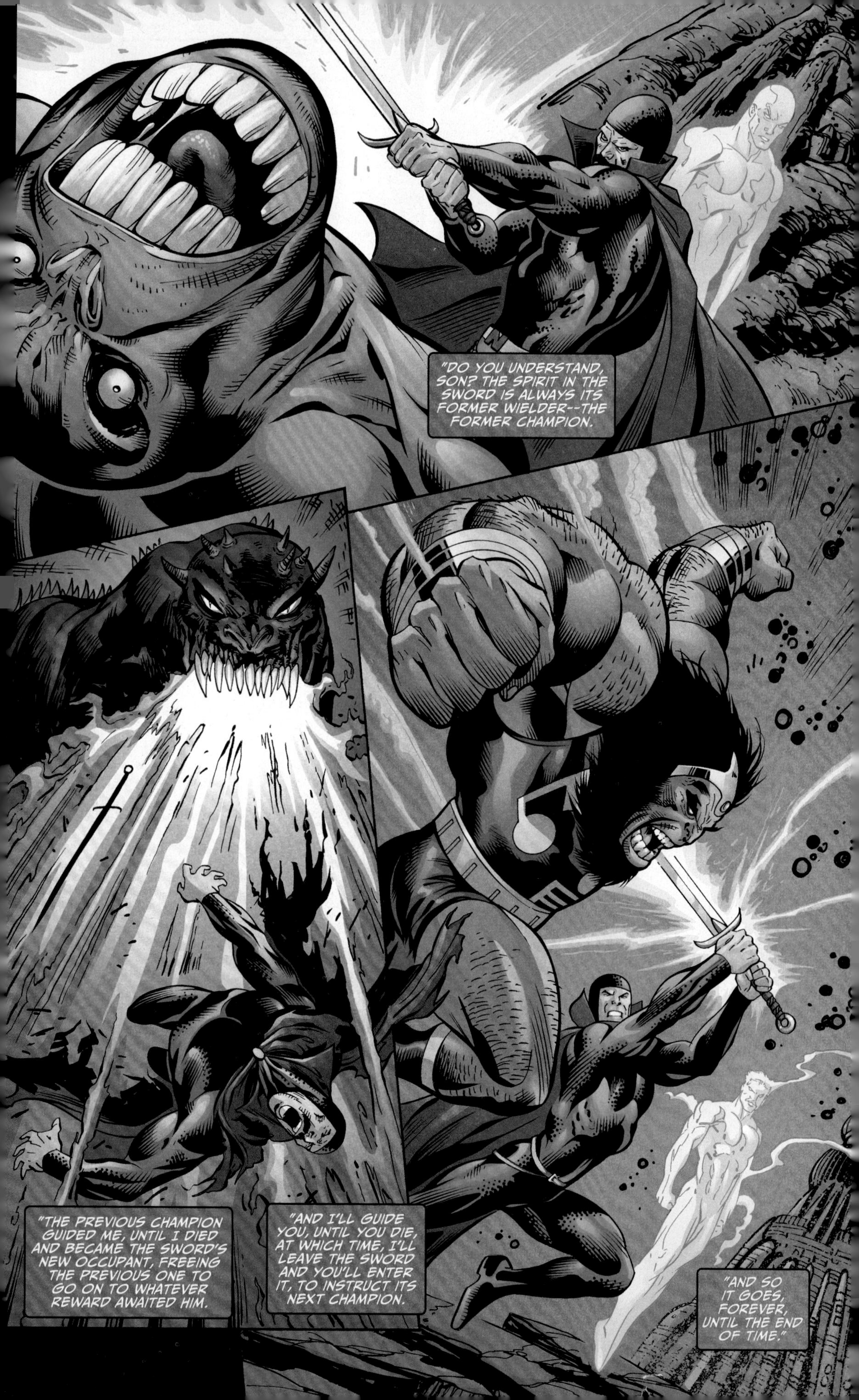
"DO YOU UNDERSTAND, SON? THE SPIRIT IN THE SWORD IS ALWAYS ITS FORMER WIELDER--THE FORMER CHAMPION.
"THE PREVIOUS CHAMPION GUIDED ME, UNTIL I DIED AND BECAME THE SWORD'S NEW OCCUPANT, FREEING THE PREVIOUS ONE TO GO ON TO WHATEVER REWARD AWAITED HIM.
"AND I'LL GUIDE YOU, UNTIL YOU DIE, AT WHICH TIME, I'LL LEAVE THE SWORD AND YOU'LL ENTER IT, TO INSTRUCT ITS NEXT CHAMPION.
"AND SO IT GOES, FOREVER, UNTIL THE END OF TIME."

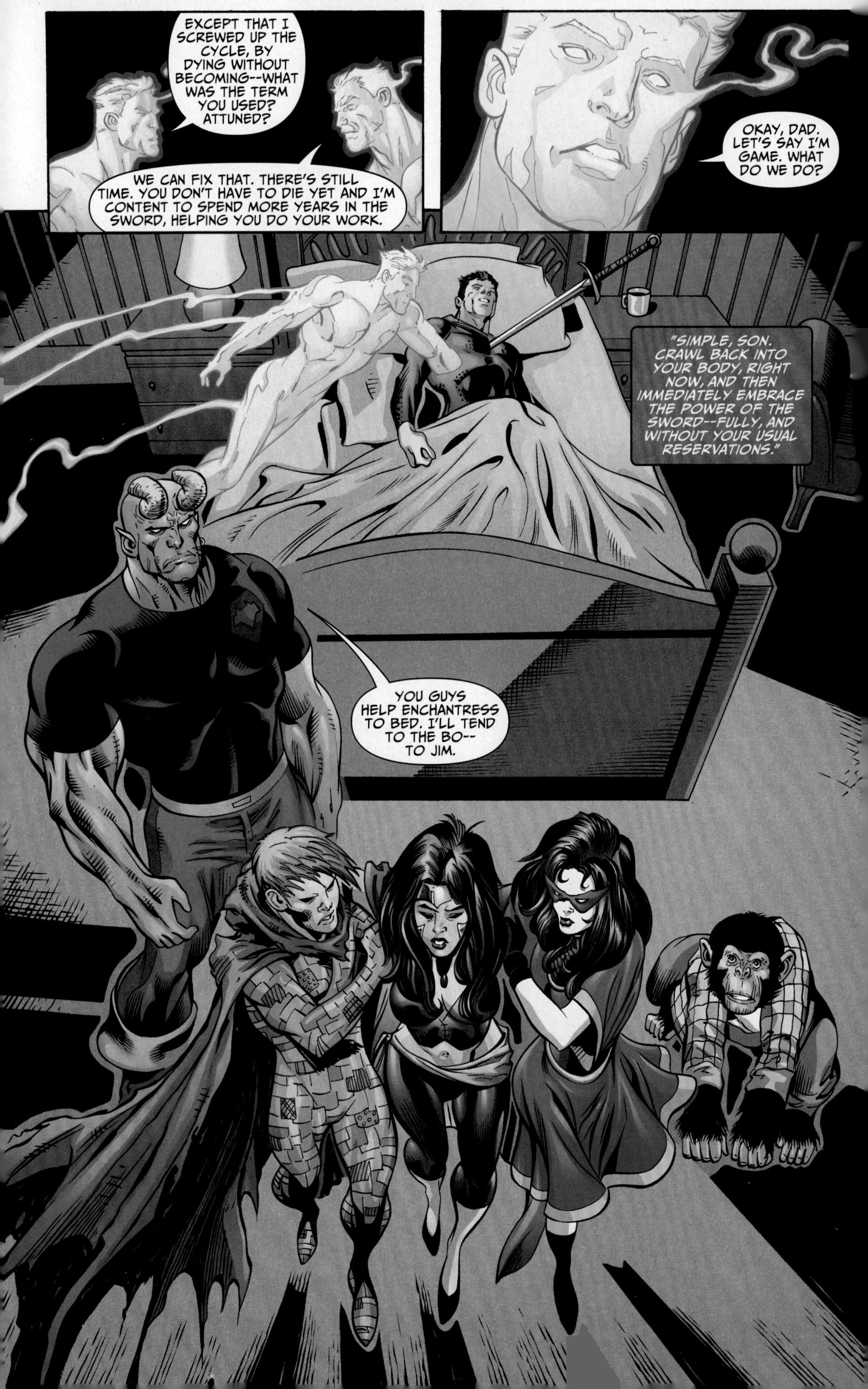

EXCEPT THAT I SCREWED UP THE CYCLE, BY DYING WITHOUT BECOMING--WHAT WAS THE TERM YOU USED? ATTUNED?
WE CAN FIX THAT. THERE'S STILL TIME. YOU DON'T HAVE TO DIE YET AND I'M CONTENT TO SPEND MORE YEARS IN THE SWORD, HELPING YOU DO YOUR WORK.
OKAY, DAD. LET'S SAY I'M GAME. WHAT DO WE DO?
"SIMPLE, SON. CRAWL BACK INTO YOUR BODY, RIGHT NOW, AND THEN IMMEDIATELY EMBRACE THE POWER OF THE SWORD--FULLY, AND WITHOUT YOUR USUAL RESERVATIONS."
YOU GUYS HELP ENCHANTRESS TO BED. I'LL TEND TO THE BO-- TO JIM.

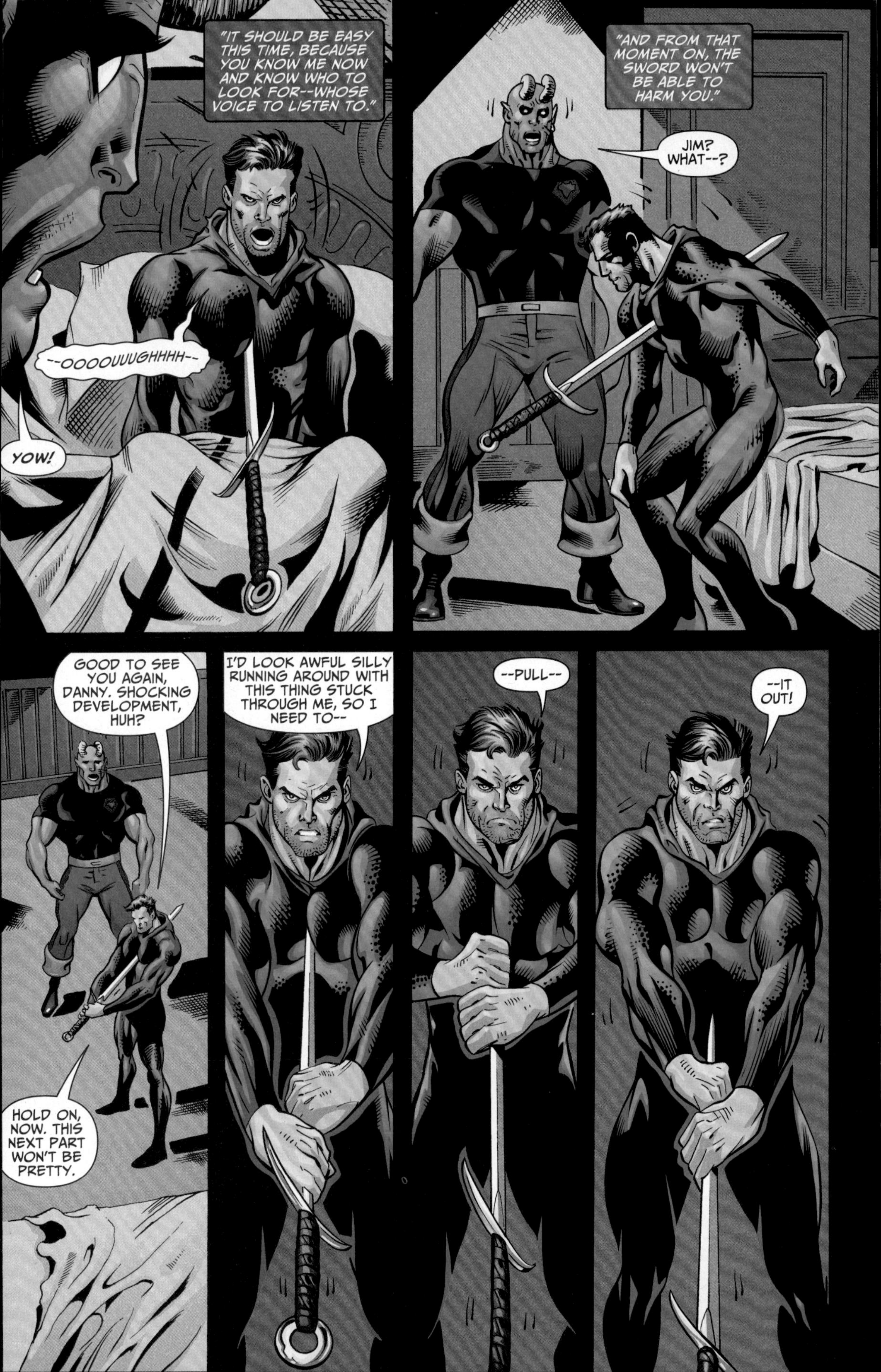
"IT SHOULD BE EASY THIS TIME, BECAUSE YOU KNOW ME NOW AND KNOW WHO TO LOOK FOR--WHOSE VOICE TO LISTEN TO."
--OOOOUUUGHHHH--
YOW!
"AND FROM THAT MOMENT ON, THE SWORD WON'T BE ABLE TO HARM YOU."
JIM? WHAT--?
GOOD TO SEE YOU AGAIN, DANNY. SHOCKING DEVELOPMENT, HUH?
HOLD ON, NOW. THIS NEXT PART WON'T BE PRETTY.
I'D LOOK AWFUL SILLY RUNNING AROUND WITH THIS THING STUCK THROUGH ME, SO I NEED TO--
--PULL--
--IT OUT!

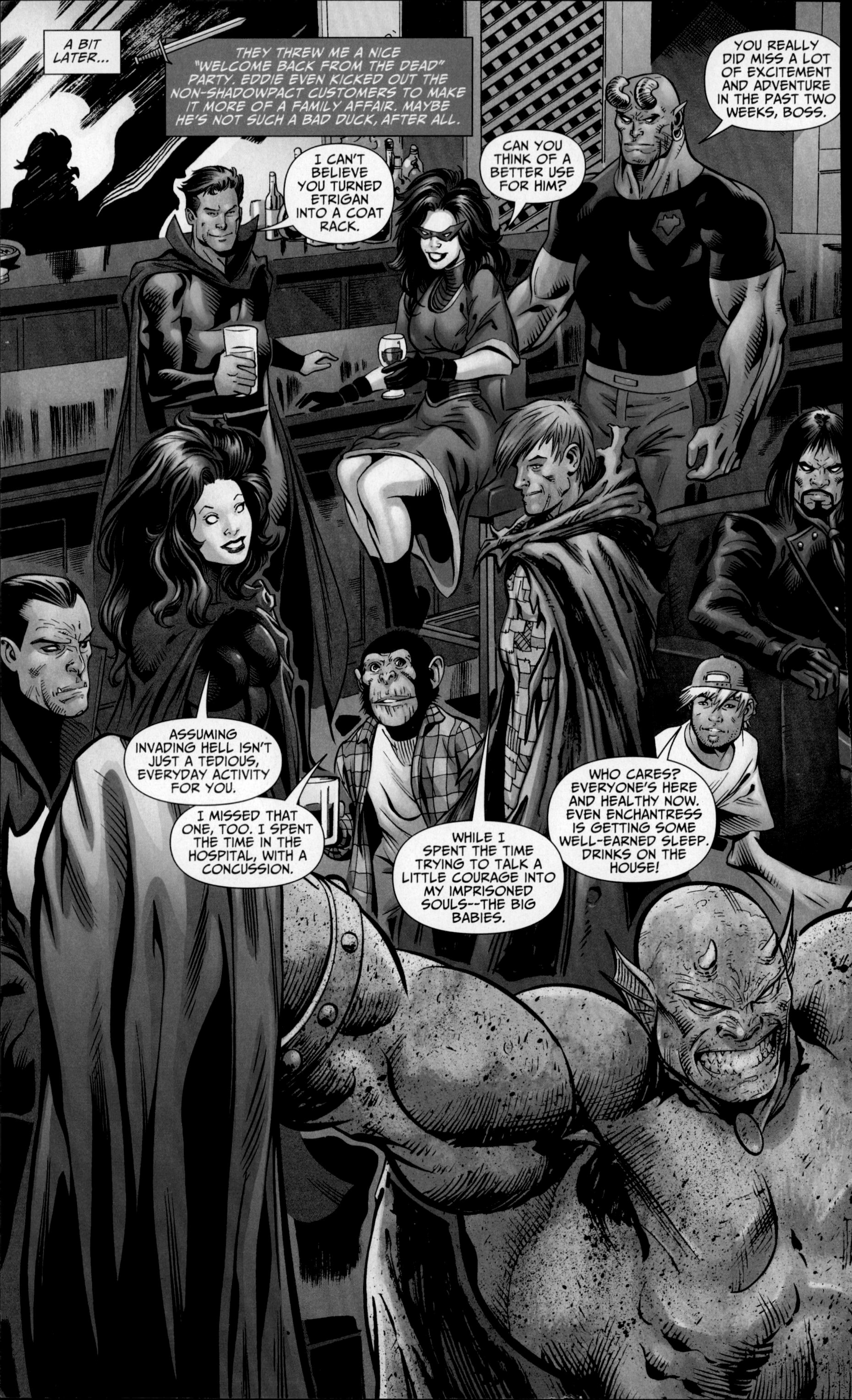
A BIT LATER...
THEY THREW ME A NICE "WELCOME BACK FROM THE DEAD" PARTY. EDDIE EVEN KICKED OUT THE NON-SHADOWPACT CUSTOMERS TO MAKE IT MORE OF A FAMILY AFFAIR. MAYBE HE'S NOT SUCH A BAD DUCK, AFTER ALL.
I CAN'T BELIEVE YOU TURNED ETRIGAN INTO A COAT RACK.
CAN YOU THINK OF A BETTER USE FOR HIM?
YOU REALLY DID MISS A LOT OF EXCITEMENT AND ADVENTURE IN THE PAST TWO WEEKS, BOSS.
ASSUMING INVADING HELL ISN'T JUST A TEDIOUS, EVERYDAY ACTIVITY FOR YOU.
I MISSED THAT ONE, TOO. I SPENT THE TIME IN THE HOSPITAL, WITH A CONCUSSION.
WHILE I SPENT THE TIME TRYING TO TALK A LITTLE COURAGE INTO MY IMPRISONED SOULS--THE BIG BABIES.
WHO CARES? EVERYONE'S HERE AND HEALTHY NOW. EVEN ENCHANTRESS IS GETTING SOME WELL-EARNED SLEEP. DRINKS ON THE HOUSE!

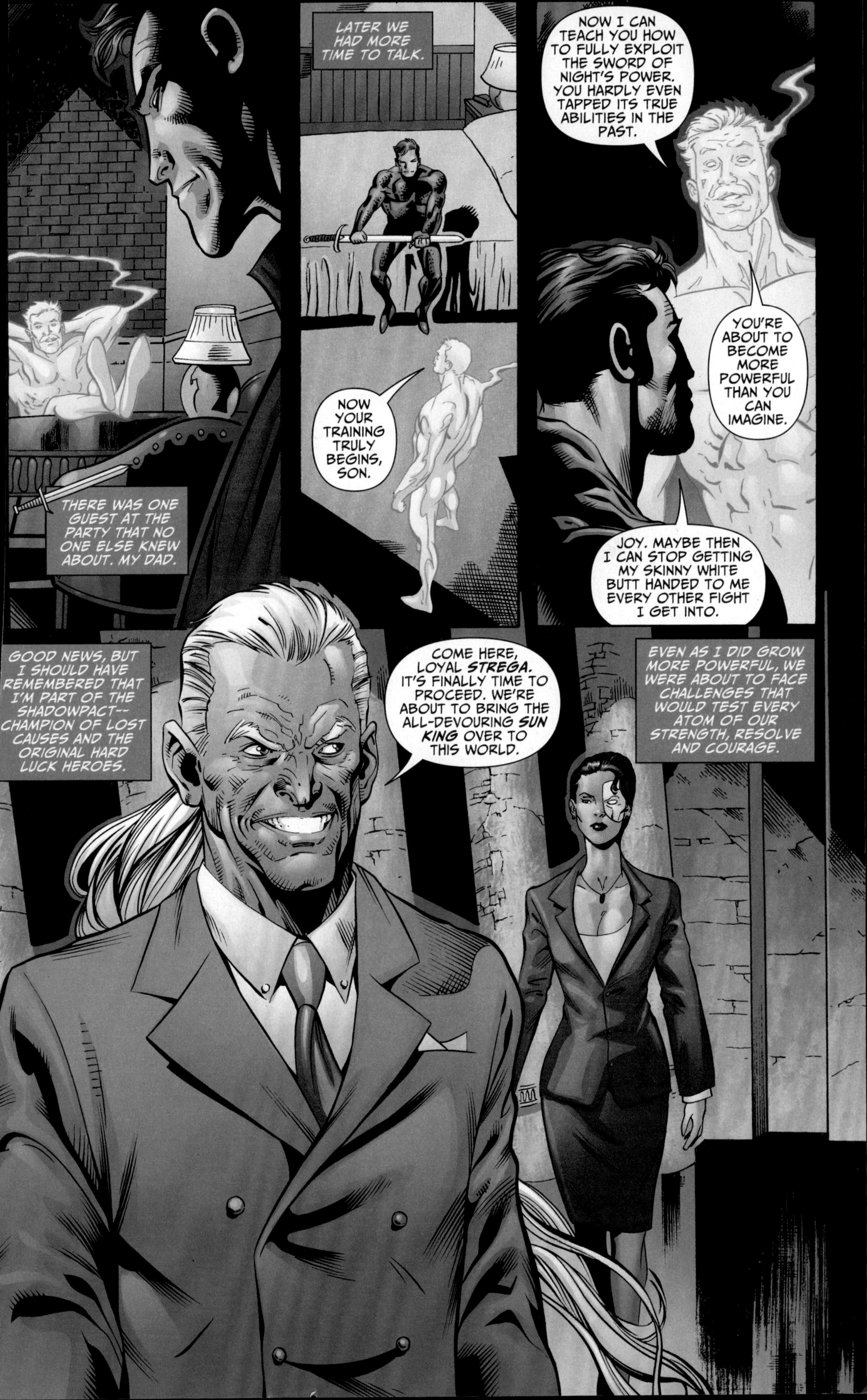
THERE WAS ONE GUEST AT THE PARTY THAT NO ONE ELSE KNEW ABOUT. MY DAD.
LATER WE HAD MORE TIME TO TALK.
NOW YOUR TRAINING TRULY BEGINS, SON.
NOW I CAN TEACH YOU HOW TO FULLY EXPLOIT THE SWORD OF NIGHT'S POWER. YOU HARDLY EVEN TAPPED ITS TRUE ABILITIES IN THE PAST.
YOU'RE ABOUT TO BECOME MORE POWERFUL THAN YOU CAN IMAGINE.
JOY. MAYBE THEN I CAN STOP GETTING MY SKINNY WHITE BUTT HANDED TO ME EVERY OTHER FIGHT I GET INTO.
GOOD NEWS, BUT I SHOULD HAVE REMEMBERED THAT I'M PART OF THE SHADOWPACT--CHAMPION OF LOST CAUSES AND THE ORIGINAL HARD LUCK HEROES.
COME HERE, LOYAL STREGA. IT'S FINALLY TIME TO PROCEED. WE'RE ABOUT TO BRING THE ALL-DEVOURING SUN KING OVER TO THIS WORLD.
EVEN AS I DID GROW MORE POWERFUL, WE WERE ABOUT TO FACE CHALLENGES THAT WOULD TEST EVERY ATOM OF OUR STRENGTH, RESOLVE AND COURAGE.

BAD TIDINGS & EVIL DEEDS

cover art by **SCOTT HAMPTON**
colored by **MIKE ATIYEH**

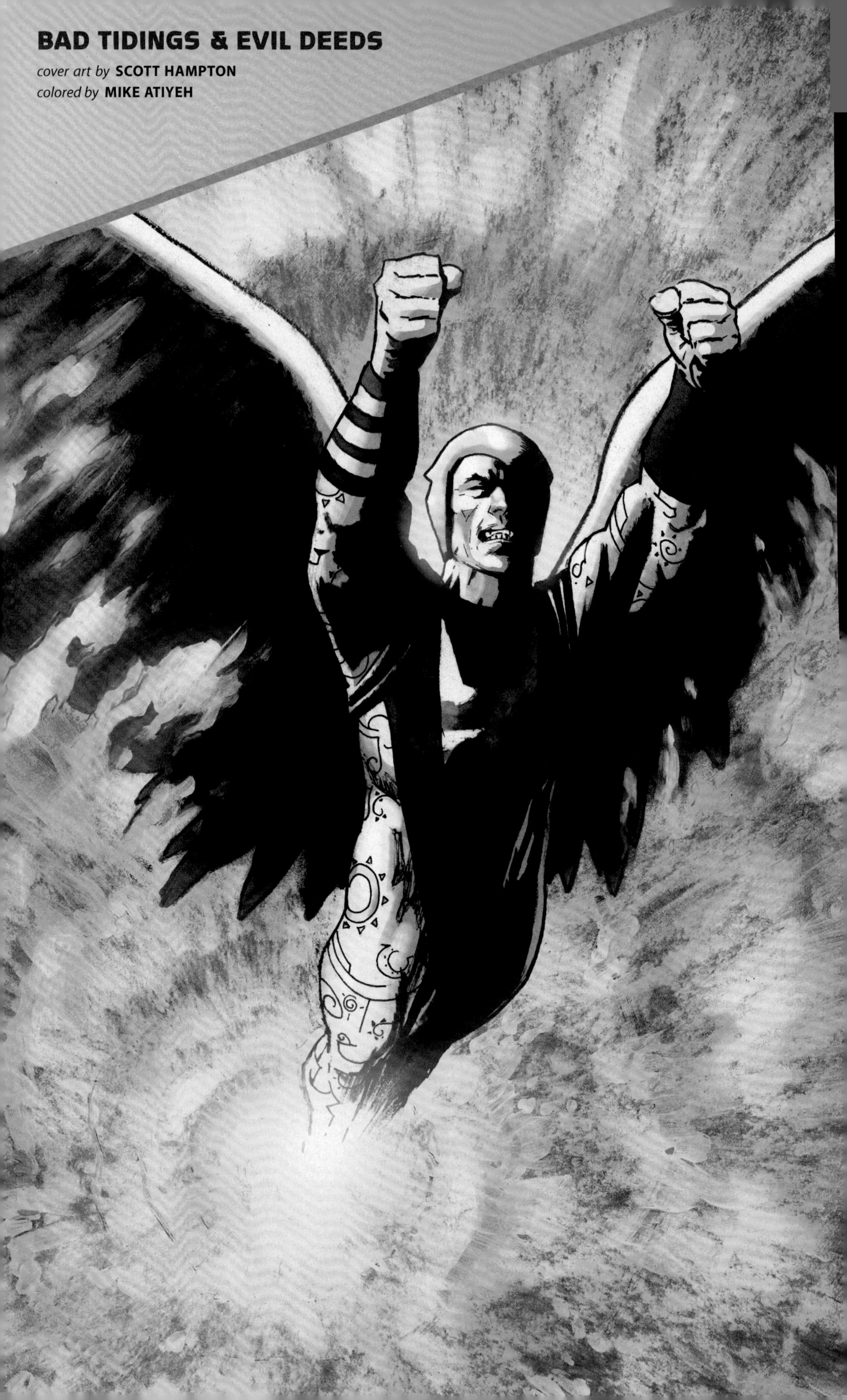

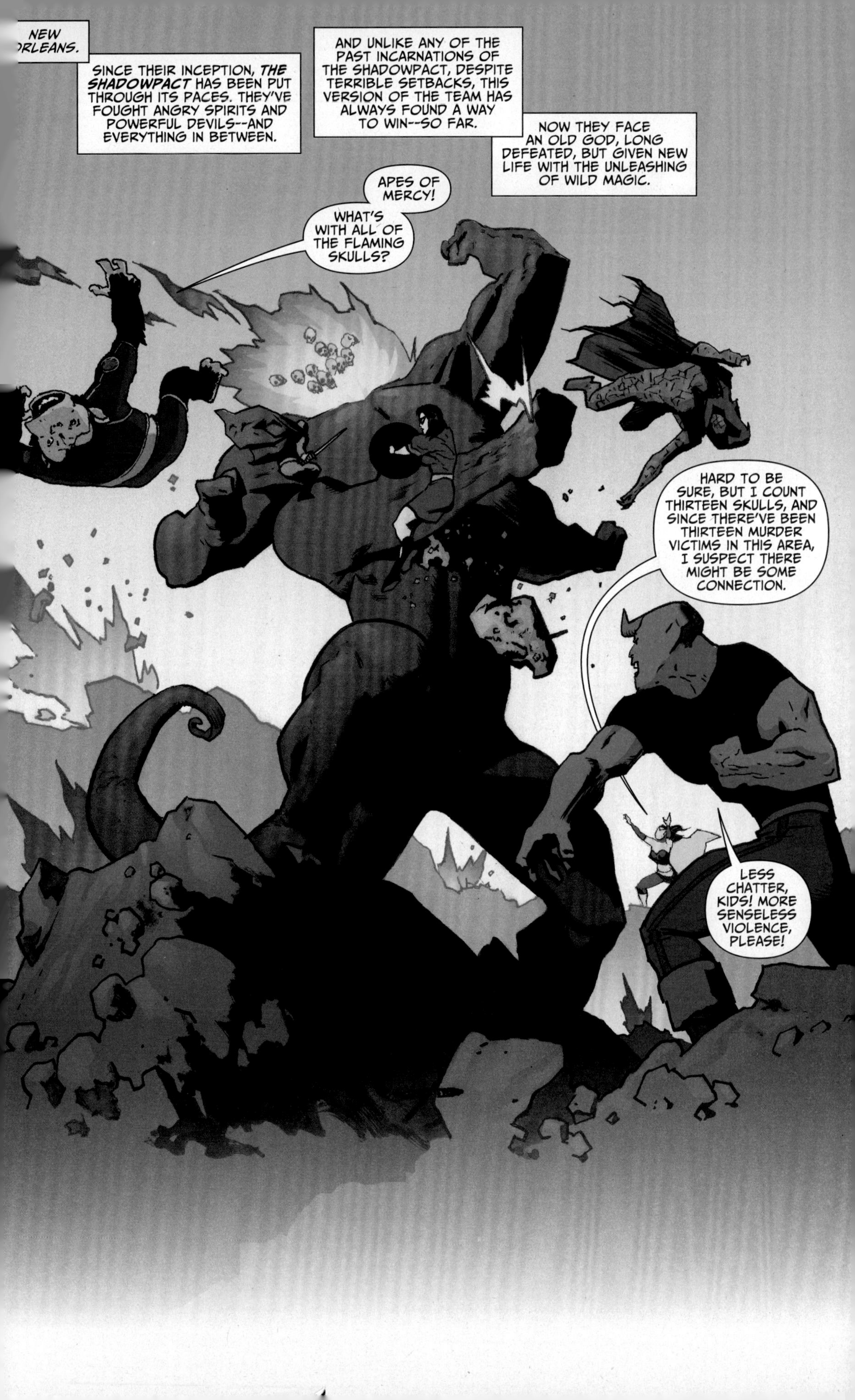
NEW ORLEANS.
SINCE THEIR INCEPTION, THE SHADOWPACT HAS BEEN PUT THROUGH ITS PACES. THEY'VE FOUGHT ANGRY SPIRITS AND POWERFUL DEVILS--AND EVERYTHING IN BETWEEN.
AND UNLIKE ANY OF THE PAST INCARNATIONS OF THE SHADOWPACT, DESPITE TERRIBLE SETBACKS, THIS VERSION OF THE TEAM HAS ALWAYS FOUND A WAY TO WIN--SO FAR.
NOW THEY FACE AN OLD GOD, LONG DEFEATED, BUT GIVEN NEW LIFE WITH THE UNLEASHING OF WILD MAGIC.
APES OF MERCY!
WHAT'S WITH ALL OF THE FLAMING SKULLS?
HARD TO BE SURE, BUT I COUNT THIRTEEN SKULLS, AND SINCE THERE'VE BEEN THIRTEEN MURDER VICTIMS IN THIS AREA, I SUSPECT THERE MIGHT BE SOME CONNECTION.
LESS CHATTER, KIDS! MORE SENSELESS VIOLENCE, PLEASE!

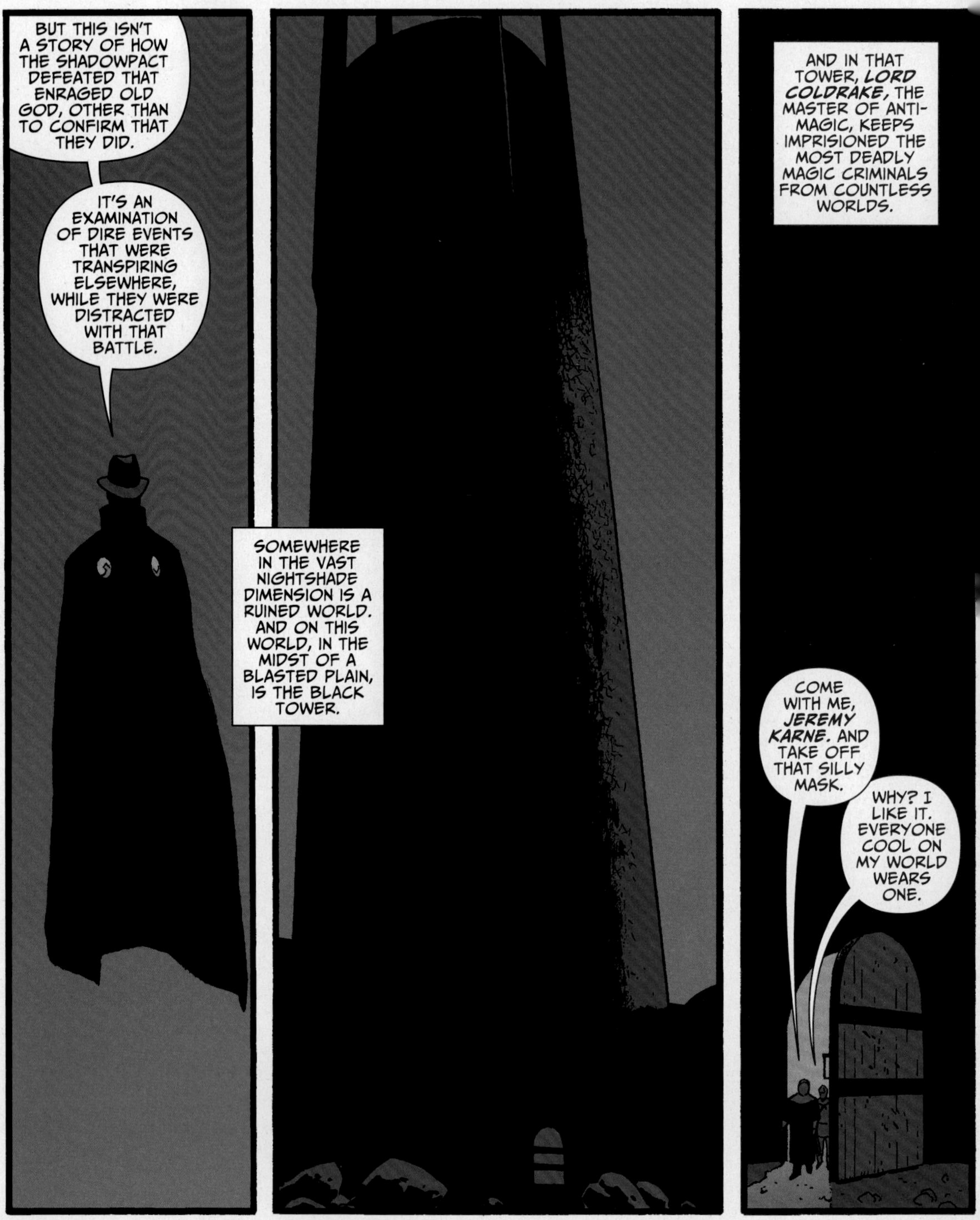

BUT THIS ISN'T A STORY OF HOW THE SHADOWPACT DEFEATED THAT ENRAGED OLD GOD, OTHER THAN TO CONFIRM THAT THEY DID.
IT'S AN EXAMINATION OF DIRE EVENTS THAT WERE TRANSPIRING ELSEWHERE, WHILE THEY WERE DISTRACTED WITH THAT BATTLE.
SOMEWHERE IN THE VAST NIGHTSHADE DIMENSION IS A RUINED WORLD. AND ON THIS WORLD, IN THE MIDST OF A BLASTED PLAIN, IS THE BLACK TOWER.
AND IN THAT TOWER, LORD COLDRAKE, THE MASTER OF ANTI-MAGIC, KEEPS IMPRISIONED THE MOST DEADLY MAGIC CRIMINALS FROM COUNTLESS WORLDS.
COME WITH ME, JEREMY KARNE. AND TAKE OFF THAT SILLY MASK.
WHY? I LIKE IT. EVERYONE COOL ON MY WORLD WEARS ONE.

SOME NEW SUPPLY WAGONS ARE IN AND YOU'RE GOING TO UNLOAD THEM.

ALONE? WHAT HAVE I DONE TO MAKE YOU SO MAD AT ME, JUVO? I THOUGHT WE'D BECOME FRIENDS.

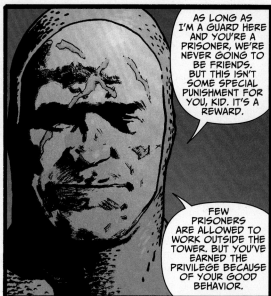

AS LONG AS I'M A GUARD HERE AND YOU'RE A PRISONER, WE'RE NEVER GOING TO BE FRIENDS. BUT THIS ISN'T SOME SPECIAL PUNISHMENT FOR YOU, KID. IT'S A REWARD.

FEW PRISONERS ARE ALLOWED TO WORK OUTSIDE THE TOWER. BUT YOU'VE EARNED THE PRIVILEGE BECAUSE OF YOUR GOOD BEHAVIOR.

IF MORE OF THE OTHERS BEHAVED AS WELL AS YOU, YOU'D HAVE MORE HELP UNLOADING THE SUPPLIES.

LUCKY ME. THIS ISN'T EASY WORK, YOU KNOW. THESE WAGONS COME EVERY DAY. AND THEY STAY WAY OUT AWAY FROM THE TOWER.

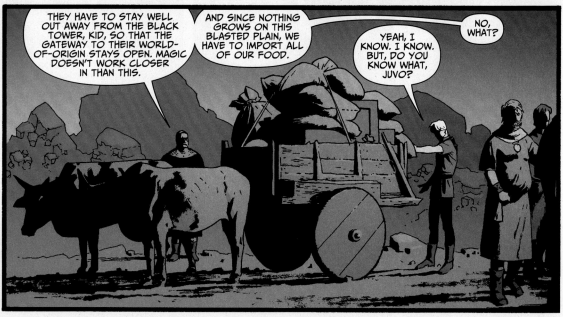

THEY HAVE TO STAY WELL OUT AWAY FROM THE BLACK TOWER, KID, SO THAT THE GATEWAY TO THEIR WORLD-OF-ORIGIN STAYS OPEN. MAGIC DOESN'T WORK CLOSER IN THAN THIS.

AND SINCE NOTHING GROWS ON THIS BLASTED PLAIN, WE HAVE TO IMPORT ALL OF OUR FOOD.

YEAH, I KNOW. I KNOW. BUT, DO YOU KNOW WHAT, JUVO?

NO, WHAT?

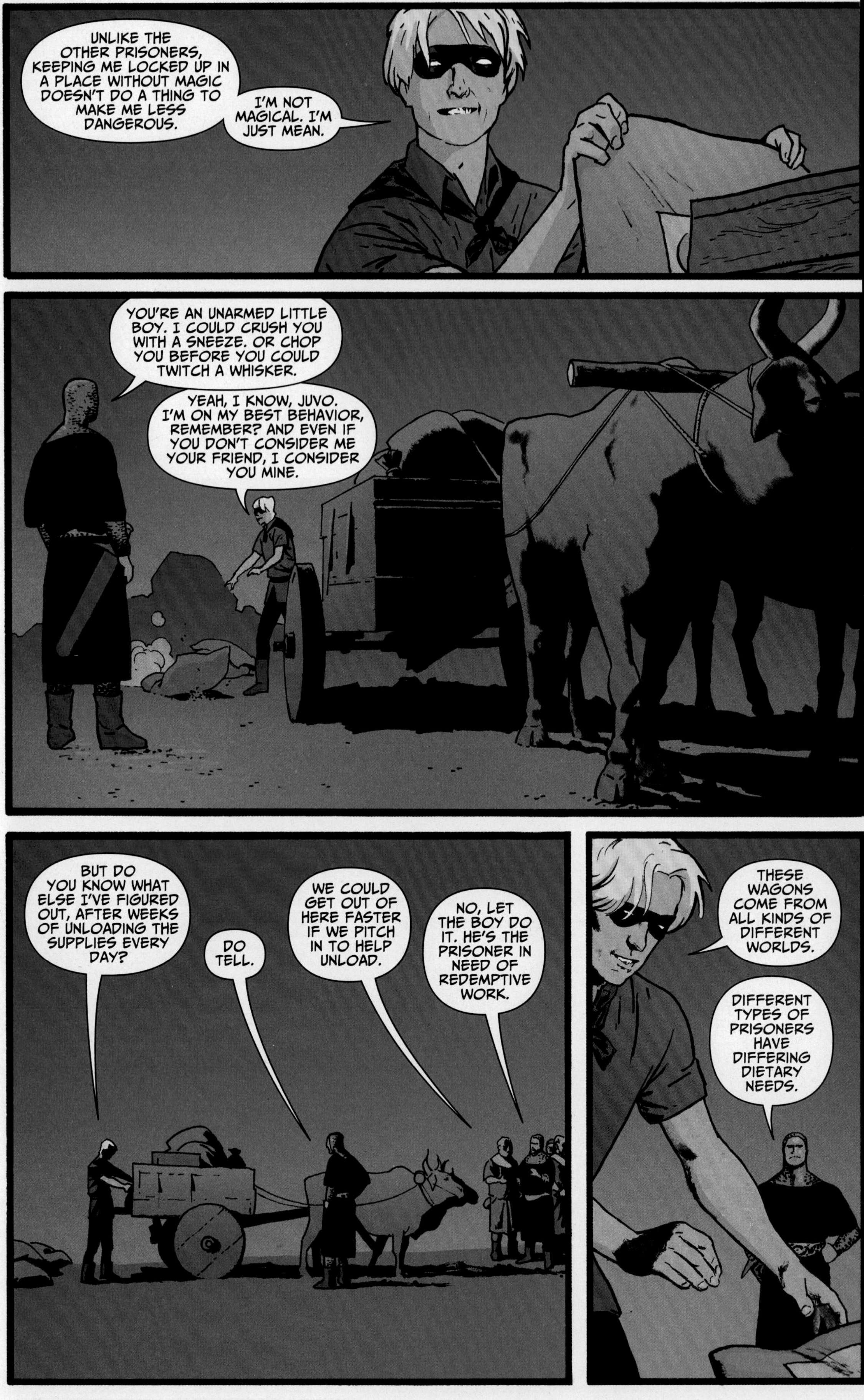
UNLIKE THE OTHER PRISONERS, KEEPING ME LOCKED UP IN A PLACE WITHOUT MAGIC DOESN'T DO A THING TO MAKE ME LESS DANGEROUS.
I'M NOT MAGICAL. I'M JUST MEAN.
YOU'RE AN UNARMED LITTLE BOY. I COULD CRUSH YOU WITH A SNEEZE. OR CHOP YOU BEFORE YOU COULD TWITCH A WHISKER.
YEAH, I KNOW, JUVO. I'M ON MY BEST BEHAVIOR, REMEMBER? AND EVEN IF YOU DON'T CONSIDER ME YOUR FRIEND, I CONSIDER YOU MINE.
BUT DO YOU KNOW WHAT ELSE I'VE FIGURED OUT, AFTER WEEKS OF UNLOADING THE SUPPLIES EVERY DAY?
DO TELL.
WE COULD GET OUT OF HERE FASTER IF WE PITCH IN TO HELP UNLOAD.
NO, LET THE BOY DO IT. HE'S THE PRISONER IN NEED OF REDEMPTIVE WORK.
THESE WAGONS COME FROM ALL KINDS OF DIFFERENT WORLDS.
DIFFERENT TYPES OF PRISONERS HAVE DIFFERING DIETARY NEEDS.

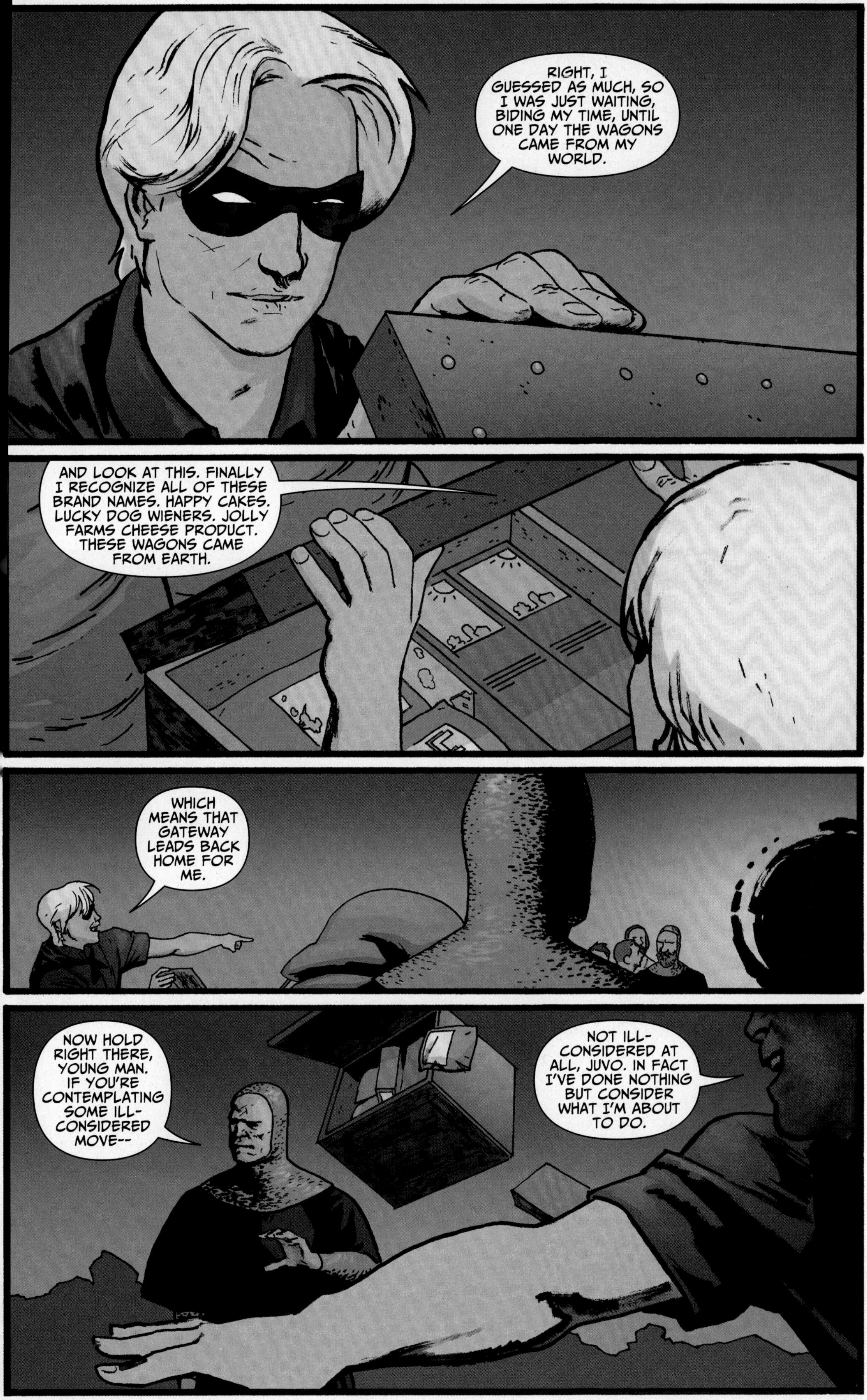
RIGHT, I GUESSED AS MUCH, SO I WAS JUST WAITING, BIDING MY TIME, UNTIL ONE DAY THE WAGONS CAME FROM MY WORLD.
AND LOOK AT THIS. FINALLY I RECOGNIZE ALL OF THESE BRAND NAMES. HAPPY CAKES. LUCKY DOG WIENERS. JOLLY FARMS CHEESE PRODUCT. THESE WAGONS CAME FROM EARTH.
WHICH MEANS THAT GATEWAY LEADS BACK HOME FOR ME.
NOW HOLD RIGHT THERE, YOUNG MAN. IF YOU'RE CONTEMPLATING SOME ILL-CONSIDERED MOVE--
NOT ILL-CONSIDERED AT ALL, JUVO. IN FACT I'VE DONE NOTHING BUT CONSIDER WHAT I'M ABOUT TO DO.

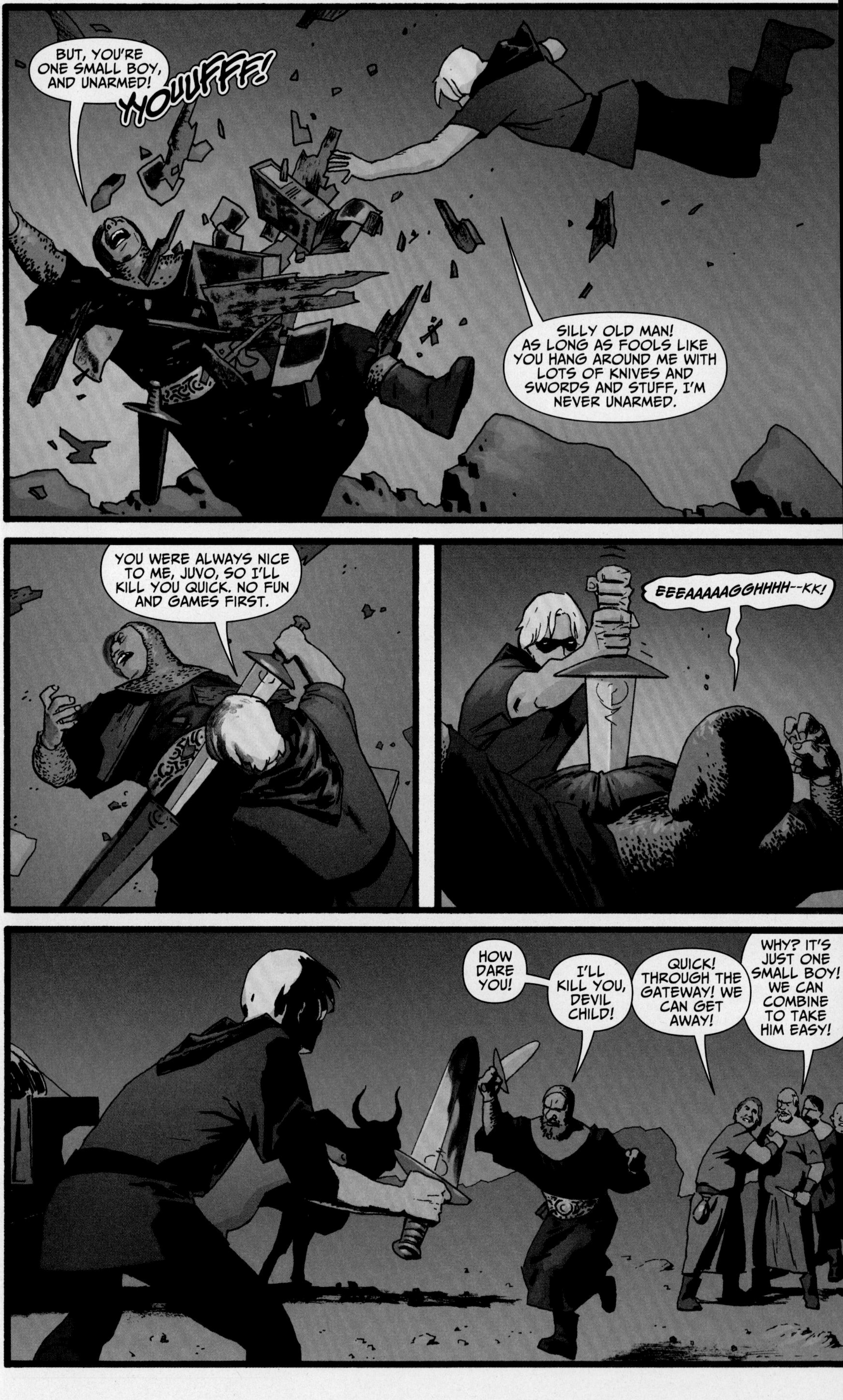
BUT, YOU'RE ONE SMALL BOY, AND UNARMED!
YOUUFFF!
SILLY OLD MAN! AS LONG AS FOOLS LIKE YOU HANG AROUND ME WITH LOTS OF KNIVES AND SWORDS AND STUFF, I'M NEVER UNARMED.
YOU WERE ALWAYS NICE TO ME, JUVO, SO I'LL KILL YOU QUICK. NO FUN AND GAMES FIRST.
EEEAAAAAGGHHHH--KK!
HOW DARE YOU!
I'LL KILL YOU, DEVIL CHILD!
QUICK! THROUGH THE GATEWAY! WE CAN GET AWAY!
WHY? IT'S JUST ONE SMALL BOY! WE CAN COMBINE TO TAKE HIM EASY!

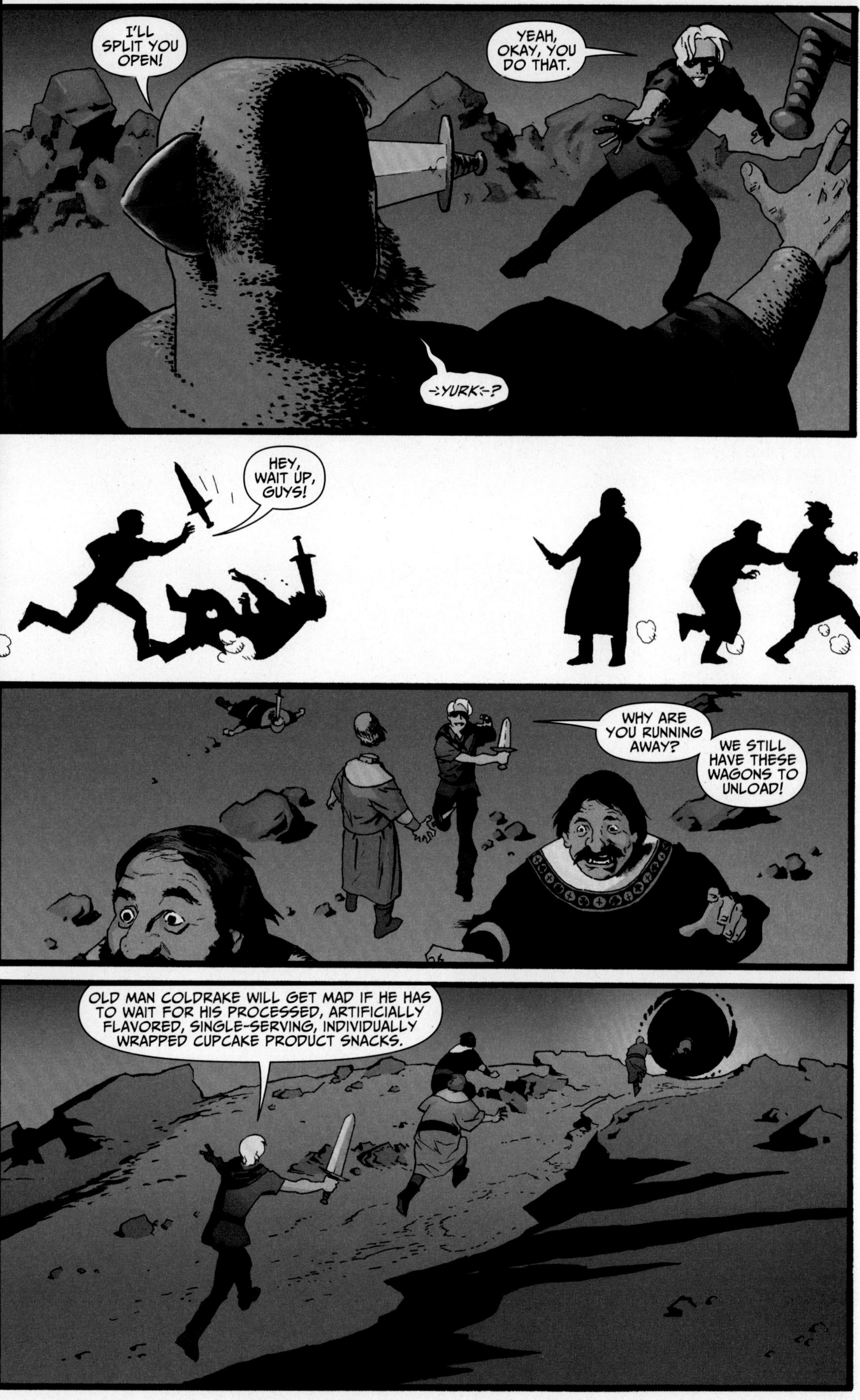
I'LL SPLIT YOU OPEN!
YEAH, OKAY, YOU DO THAT.
-YURK-?
HEY, WAIT UP, GUYS!
WHY ARE YOU RUNNING AWAY?
WE STILL HAVE THESE WAGONS TO UNLOAD!
OLD MAN COLDRAKE WILL GET MAD IF HE HAS TO WAIT FOR HIS PROCESSED, ARTIFICIALLY FLAVORED, SINGLE-SERVING, INDIVIDUALLY WRAPPED CUPCAKE PRODUCT SNACKS.

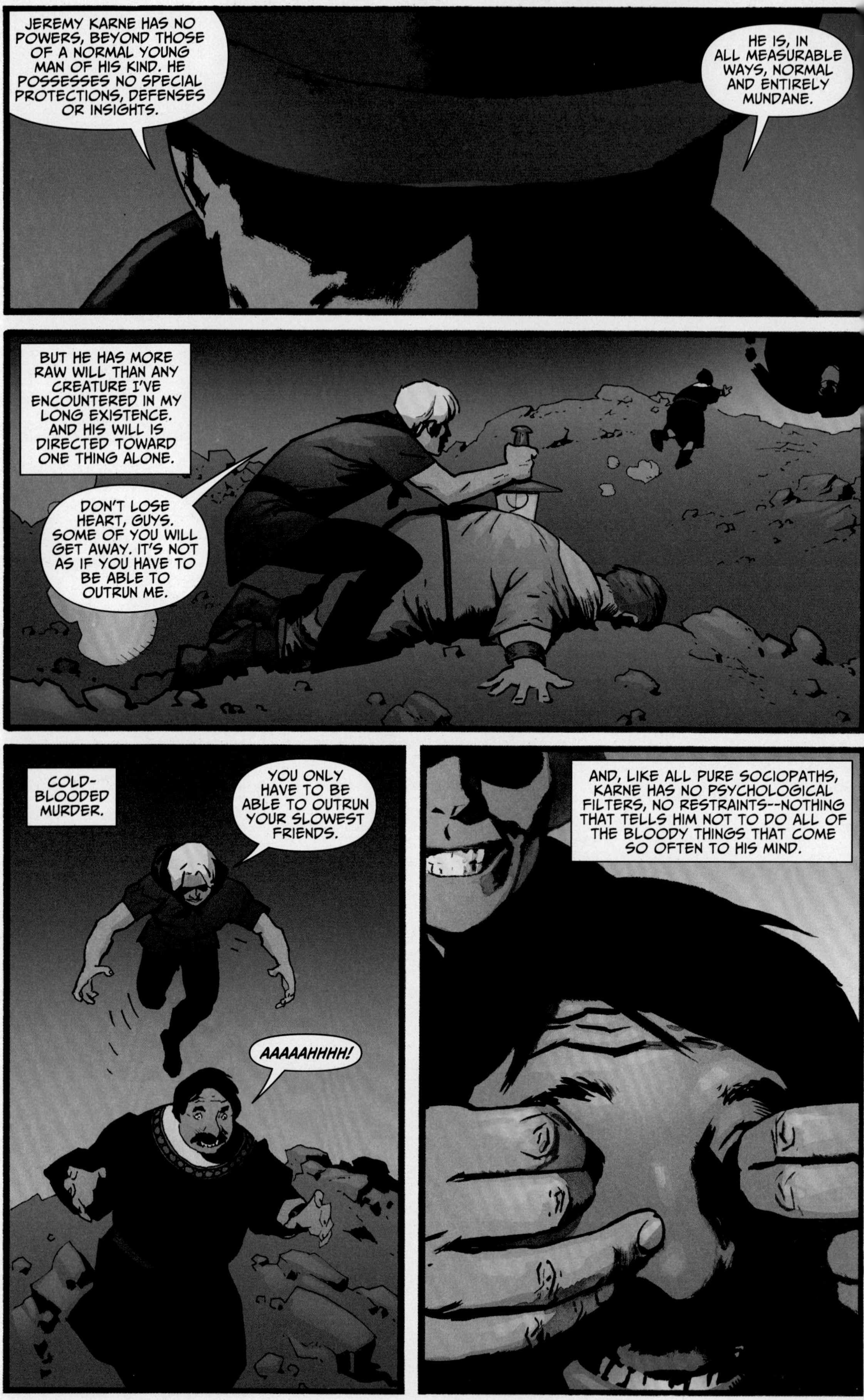
JEREMY KARNE HAS NO POWERS, BEYOND THOSE OF A NORMAL YOUNG MAN OF HIS KIND. HE POSSESSES NO SPECIAL PROTECTIONS, DEFENSES OR INSIGHTS.
HE IS, IN ALL MEASURABLE WAYS, NORMAL AND ENTIRELY MUNDANE.
BUT HE HAS MORE RAW WILL THAN ANY CREATURE I'VE ENCOUNTERED IN MY LONG EXISTENCE. AND HIS WILL IS DIRECTED TOWARD ONE THING ALONE.
DON'T LOSE HEART, GUYS. SOME OF YOU WILL GET AWAY. IT'S NOT AS IF YOU HAVE TO BE ABLE TO OUTRUN ME.
COLD-BLOODED MURDER.
YOU ONLY HAVE TO BE ABLE TO OUTRUN YOUR SLOWEST FRIENDS.
AAAAAHHHH!
AND, LIKE ALL PURE SOCIOPATHS, KARNE HAS NO PSYCHOLOGICAL FILTERS, NO RESTRAINTS--NOTHING THAT TELLS HIM NOT TO DO ALL OF THE BLOODY THINGS THAT COME SO OFTEN TO HIS MIND.

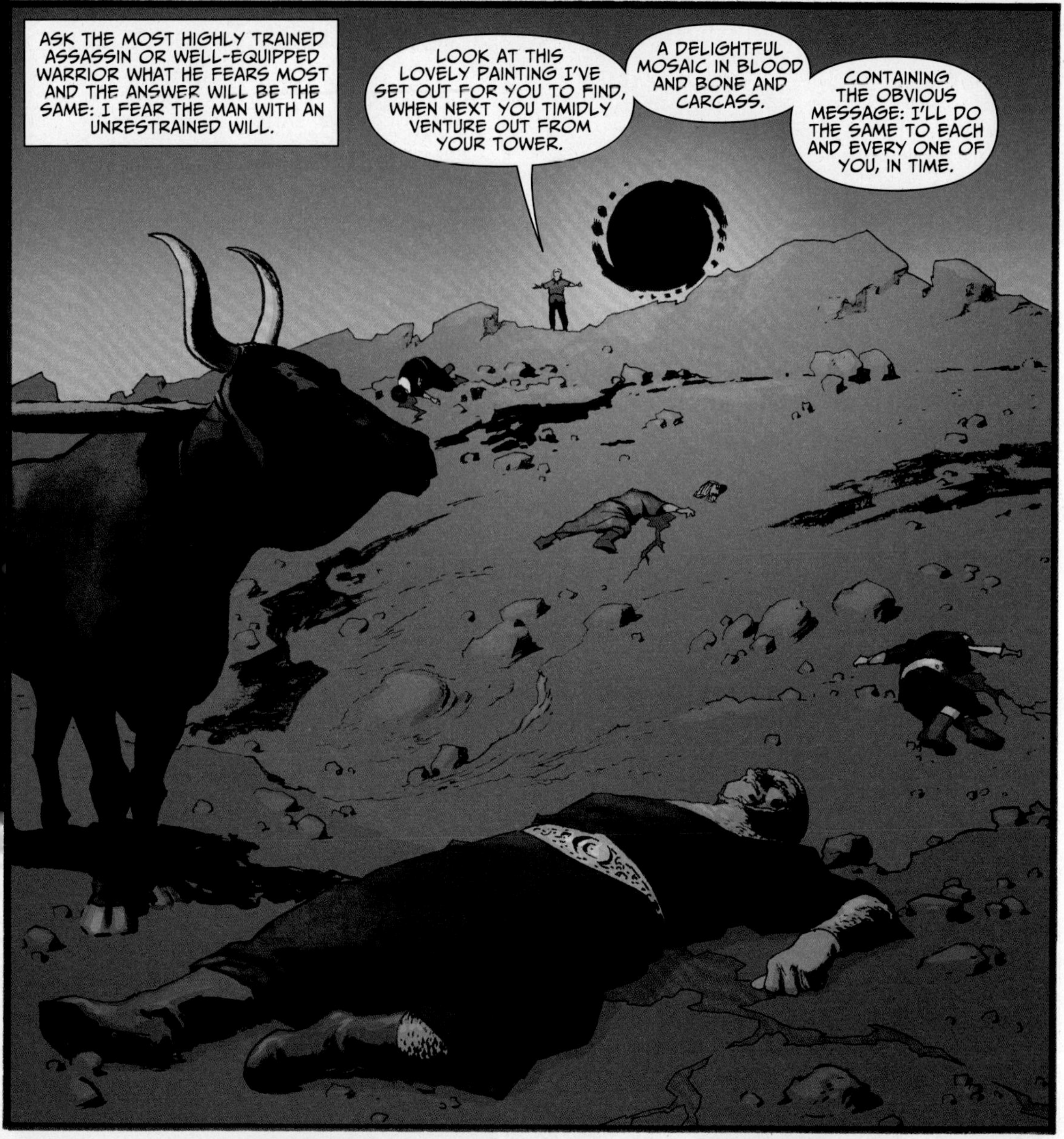
ASK THE MOST HIGHLY TRAINED ASSASSIN OR WELL-EQUIPPED WARRIOR WHAT HE FEARS MOST AND THE ANSWER WILL BE THE SAME: I FEAR THE MAN WITH AN UNRESTRAINED WILL.
LOOK AT THIS LOVELY PAINTING I'VE SET OUT FOR YOU TO FIND, WHEN NEXT YOU TIMIDLY VENTURE OUT FROM YOUR TOWER.
A DELIGHTFUL MOSAIC IN BLOOD AND BONE AND CARCASS.
CONTAINING THE OBVIOUS MESSAGE: I'LL DO THE SAME TO EACH AND EVERY ONE OF YOU, IN TIME.

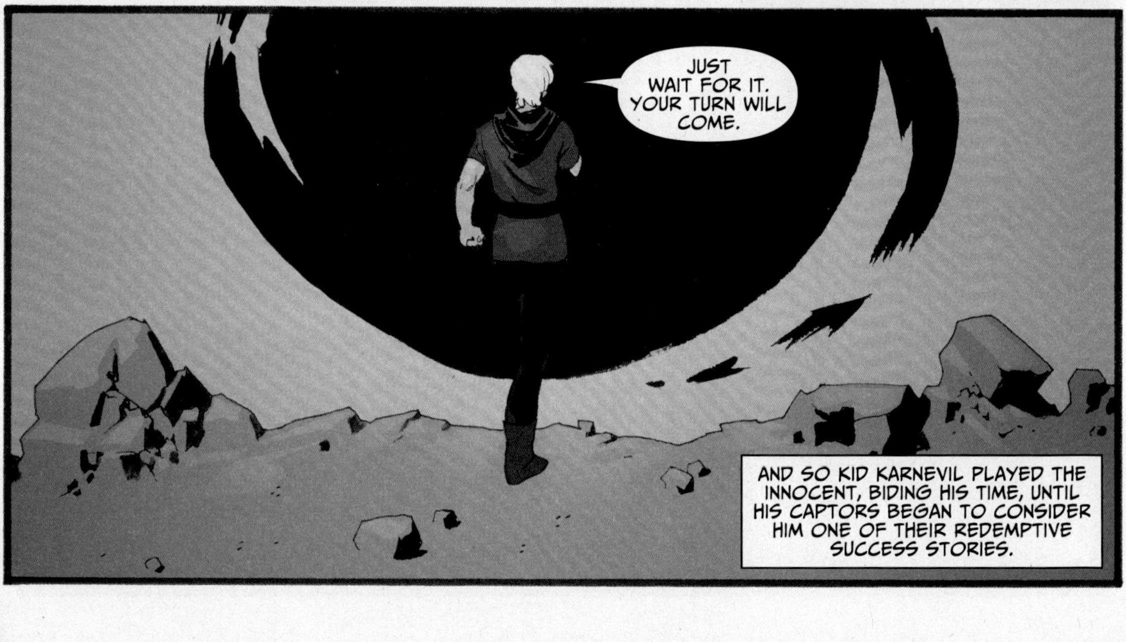
JUST WAIT FOR IT. YOUR TURN WILL COME.
AND SO KID KARNEVIL PLAYED THE INNOCENT, BIDING HIS TIME, UNTIL HIS CAPTORS BEGAN TO CONSIDER HIM ONE OF THEIR REDEMPTIVE SUCCESS STORIES.

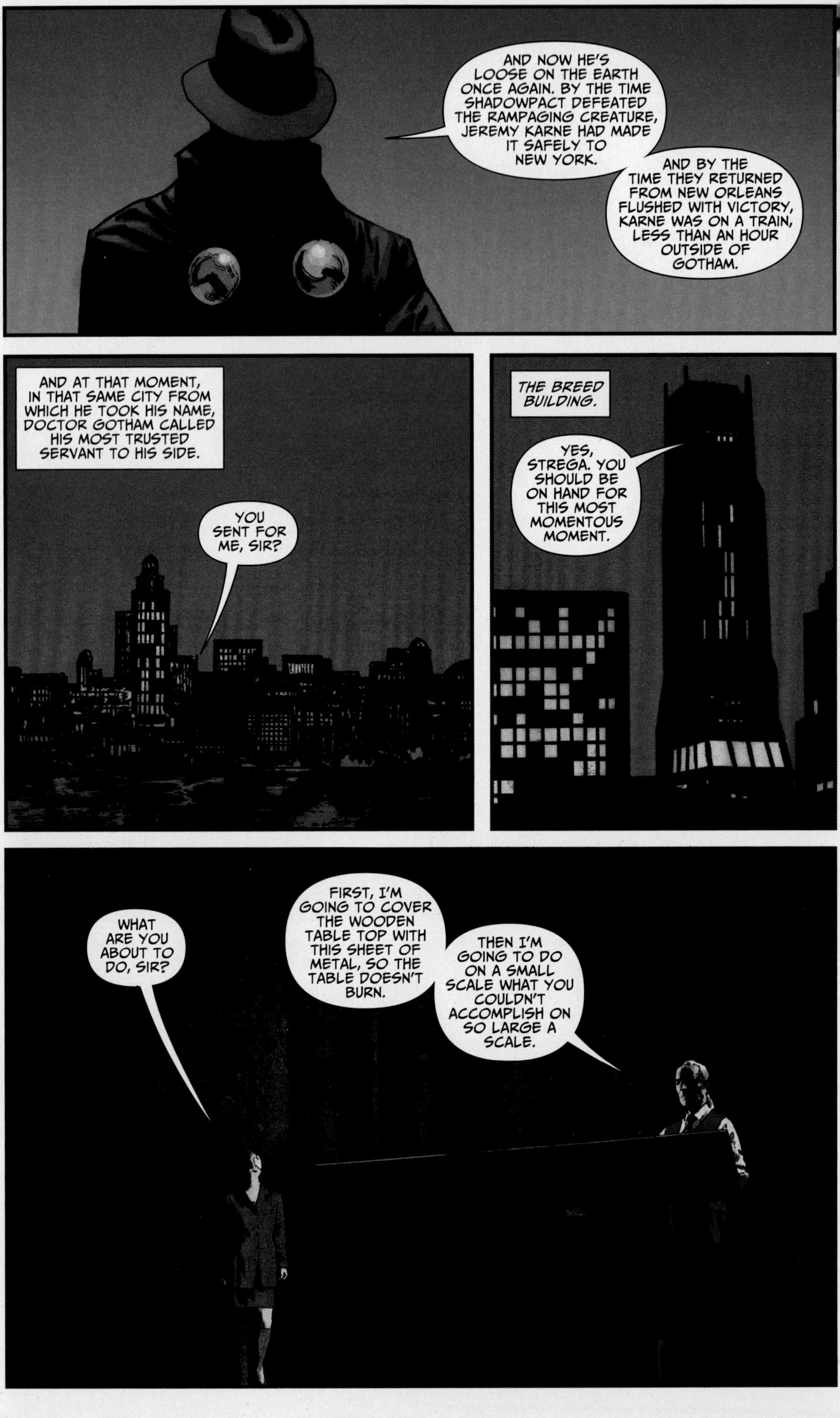

AND NOW HE'S LOOSE ON THE EARTH ONCE AGAIN. BY THE TIME SHADOWPACT DEFEATED THE RAMPAGING CREATURE, JEREMY KARNE HAD MADE IT SAFELY TO NEW YORK.
AND BY THE TIME THEY RETURNED FROM NEW ORLEANS FLUSHED WITH VICTORY, KARNE WAS ON A TRAIN, LESS THAN AN HOUR OUTSIDE OF GOTHAM.
AND AT THAT MOMENT, IN THAT SAME CITY FROM WHICH HE TOOK HIS NAME, DOCTOR GOTHAM CALLED HIS MOST TRUSTED SERVANT TO HIS SIDE.
YOU SENT FOR ME, SIR?
THE BREED BUILDING.
YES, STREGA. YOU SHOULD BE ON HAND FOR THIS MOST MOMENTOUS MOMENT.
WHAT ARE YOU ABOUT TO DO, SIR?
FIRST, I'M GOING TO COVER THE WOODEN TABLE TOP WITH THIS SHEET OF METAL, SO THE TABLE DOESN'T BURN.
THEN I'M GOING TO DO ON A SMALL SCALE WHAT YOU COULDN'T ACCOMPLISH ON SO LARGE A SCALE.

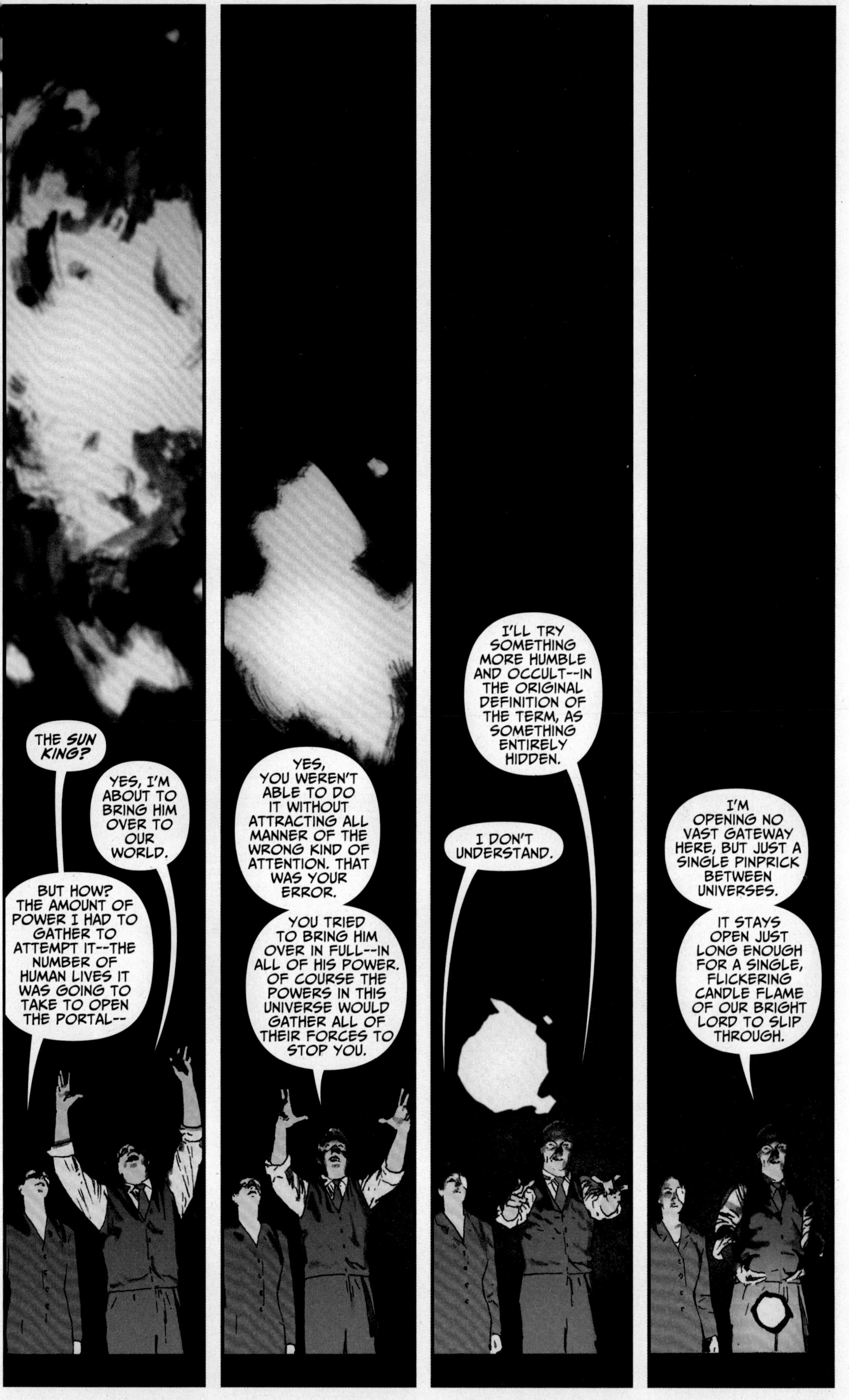
THE SUN KING?
YES, I'M ABOUT TO BRING HIM OVER TO OUR WORLD.
BUT HOW? THE AMOUNT OF POWER I HAD TO GATHER TO ATTEMPT IT--THE NUMBER OF HUMAN LIVES IT WAS GOING TO TAKE TO OPEN THE PORTAL--
YES, YOU WEREN'T ABLE TO DO IT WITHOUT ATTRACTING ALL MANNER OF THE WRONG KIND OF ATTENTION. THAT WAS YOUR ERROR.
YOU TRIED TO BRING HIM OVER IN FULL--IN ALL OF HIS POWER. OF COURSE THE POWERS IN THIS UNIVERSE WOULD GATHER ALL OF THEIR FORCES TO STOP YOU.
I DON'T UNDERSTAND.
I'LL TRY SOMETHING MORE HUMBLE AND OCCULT--IN THE ORIGINAL DEFINITION OF THE TERM, AS SOMETHING ENTIRELY HIDDEN.
I'M OPENING NO VAST GATEWAY HERE, BUT JUST A SINGLE PINPRICK BETWEEN UNIVERSES.
IT STAYS OPEN JUST LONG ENOUGH FOR A SINGLE, FLICKERING CANDLE FLAME OF OUR BRIGHT LORD TO SLIP THROUGH.

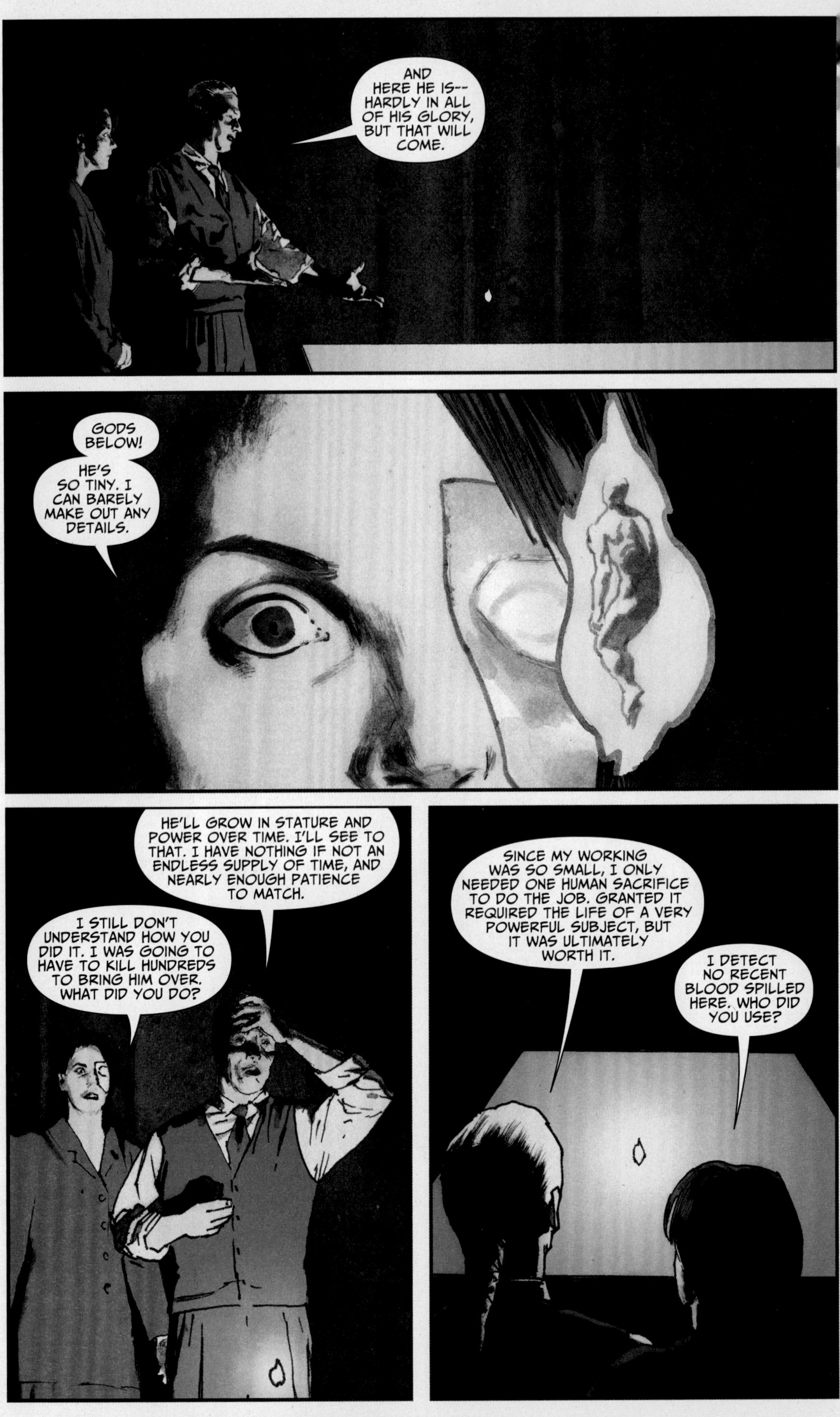
AND HERE HE IS-- HARDLY IN ALL OF HIS GLORY, BUT THAT WILL COME.
GODS BELOW!
HE'S SO TINY. I CAN BARELY MAKE OUT ANY DETAILS.
HE'LL GROW IN STATURE AND POWER OVER TIME. I'LL SEE TO THAT. I HAVE NOTHING IF NOT AN ENDLESS SUPPLY OF TIME, AND NEARLY ENOUGH PATIENCE TO MATCH.
I STILL DON'T UNDERSTAND HOW YOU DID IT. I WAS GOING TO HAVE TO KILL HUNDREDS TO BRING HIM OVER. WHAT DID YOU DO?
SINCE MY WORKING WAS SO SMALL, I ONLY NEEDED ONE HUMAN SACRIFICE TO DO THE JOB. GRANTED IT REQUIRED THE LIFE OF A VERY POWERFUL SUBJECT, BUT IT WAS ULTIMATELY WORTH IT.
I DETECT NO RECENT BLOOD SPILLED HERE. WHO DID YOU USE?

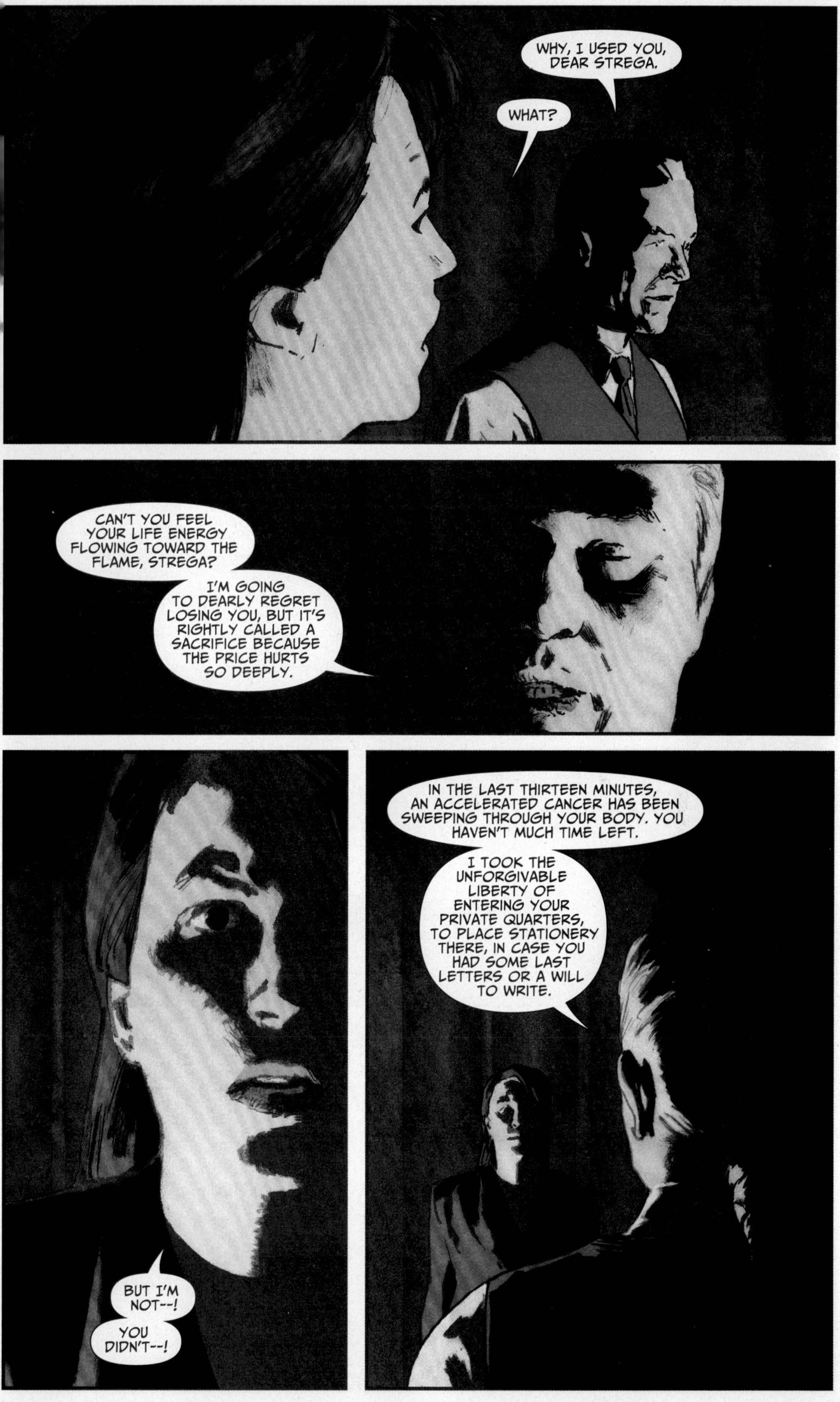
WHY, I USED YOU, DEAR STREGA.
WHAT?
CAN'T YOU FEEL YOUR LIFE ENERGY FLOWING TOWARD THE FLAME, STREGA?
I'M GOING TO DEARLY REGRET LOSING YOU, BUT IT'S RIGHTLY CALLED A SACRIFICE BECAUSE THE PRICE HURTS SO DEEPLY.
BUT I'M NOT--!
YOU DIDN'T--!
IN THE LAST THIRTEEN MINUTES, AN ACCELERATED CANCER HAS BEEN SWEEPING THROUGH YOUR BODY. YOU HAVEN'T MUCH TIME LEFT.
I TOOK THE UNFORGIVABLE LIBERTY OF ENTERING YOUR PRIVATE QUARTERS, TO PLACE STATIONERY THERE, IN CASE YOU HAD SOME LAST LETTERS OR A WILL TO WRITE.

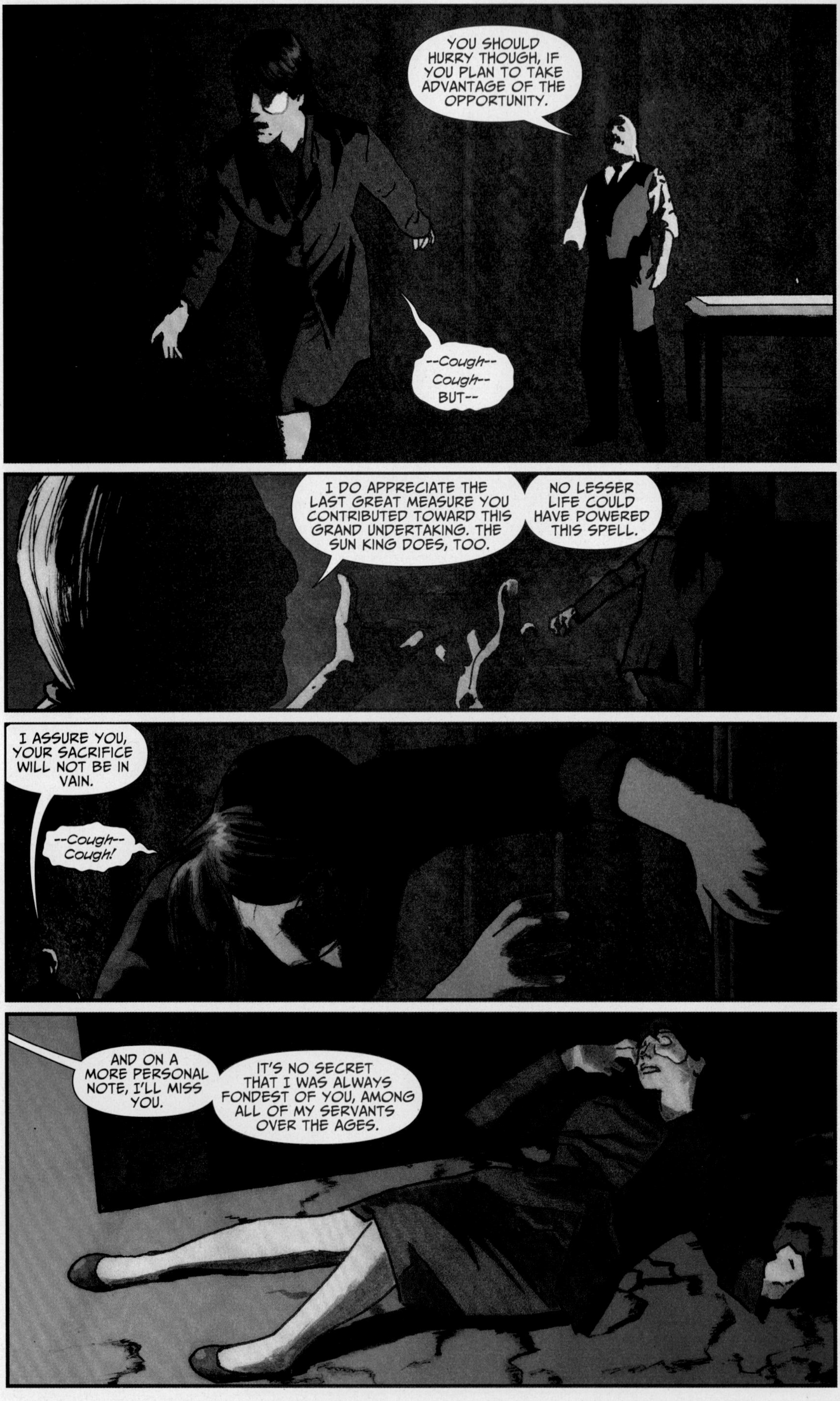
YOU SHOULD HURRY THOUGH, IF YOU PLAN TO TAKE ADVANTAGE OF THE OPPORTUNITY.
--Cough-- Cough-- BUT--
I DO APPRECIATE THE LAST GREAT MEASURE YOU CONTRIBUTED TOWARD THIS GRAND UNDERTAKING. THE SUN KING DOES, TOO.
NO LESSER LIFE COULD HAVE POWERED THIS SPELL.
I ASSURE YOU, YOUR SACRIFICE WILL NOT BE IN VAIN.
--Cough-- Cough!
AND ON A MORE PERSONAL NOTE, I'LL MISS YOU.
IT'S NO SECRET THAT I WAS ALWAYS FONDEST OF YOU, AMONG ALL OF MY SERVANTS OVER THE AGES.

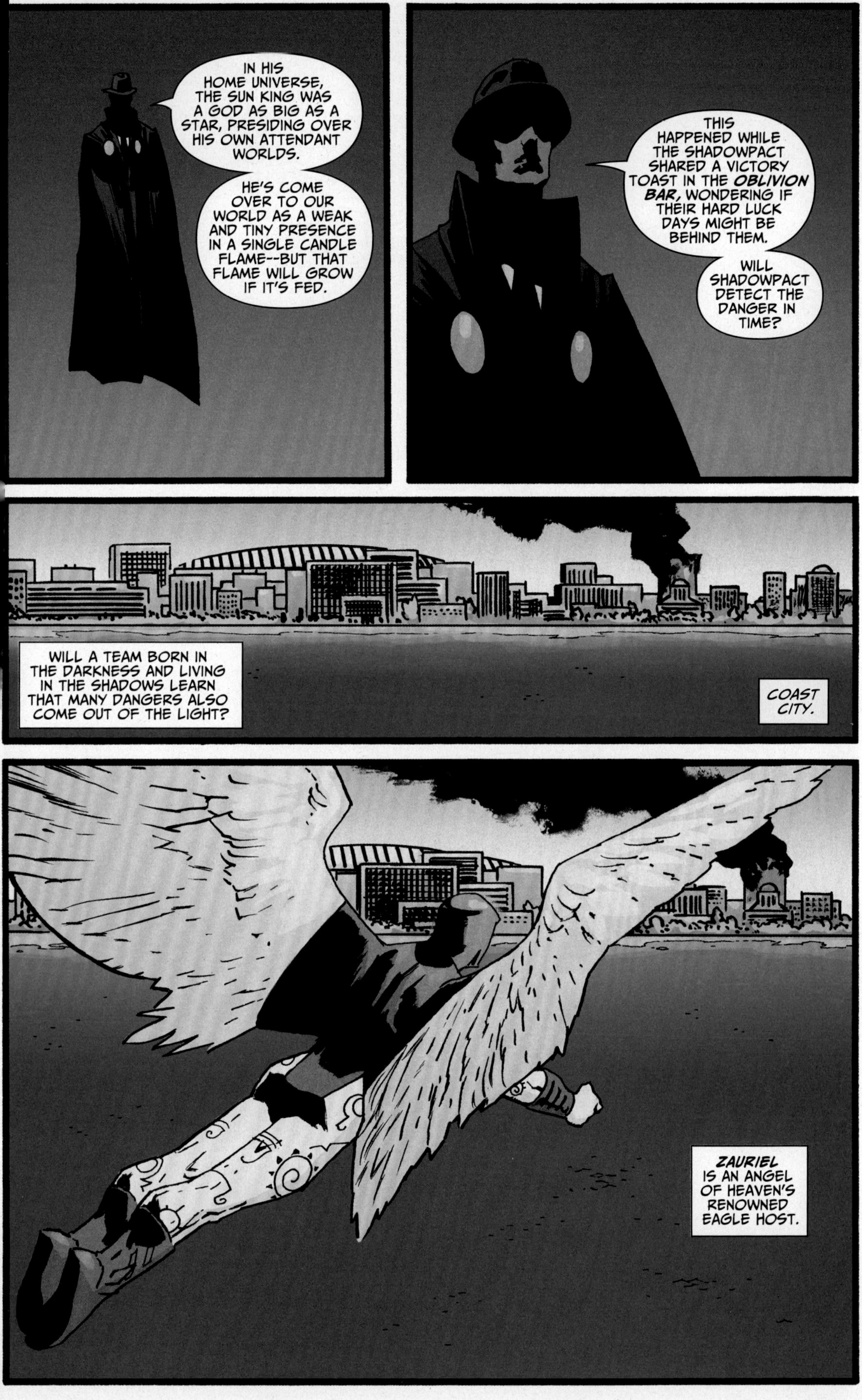
IN HIS HOME UNIVERSE, THE SUN KING WAS A GOD AS BIG AS A STAR, PRESIDING OVER HIS OWN ATTENDANT WORLDS.
HE'S COME OVER TO OUR WORLD AS A WEAK AND TINY PRESENCE IN A SINGLE CANDLE FLAME--BUT THAT FLAME WILL GROW IF IT'S FED.
THIS HAPPENED WHILE THE SHADOWPACT SHARED A VICTORY TOAST IN THE OBLIVION BAR, WONDERING IF THEIR HARD LUCK DAYS MIGHT BE BEHIND THEM.
WILL SHADOWPACT DETECT THE DANGER IN TIME?
WILL A TEAM BORN IN THE DARKNESS AND LIVING IN THE SHADOWS LEARN THAT MANY DANGERS ALSO COME OUT OF THE LIGHT?
COAST CITY.
ZAURIEL IS AN ANGEL OF HEAVEN'S RENOWNED EAGLE HOST.

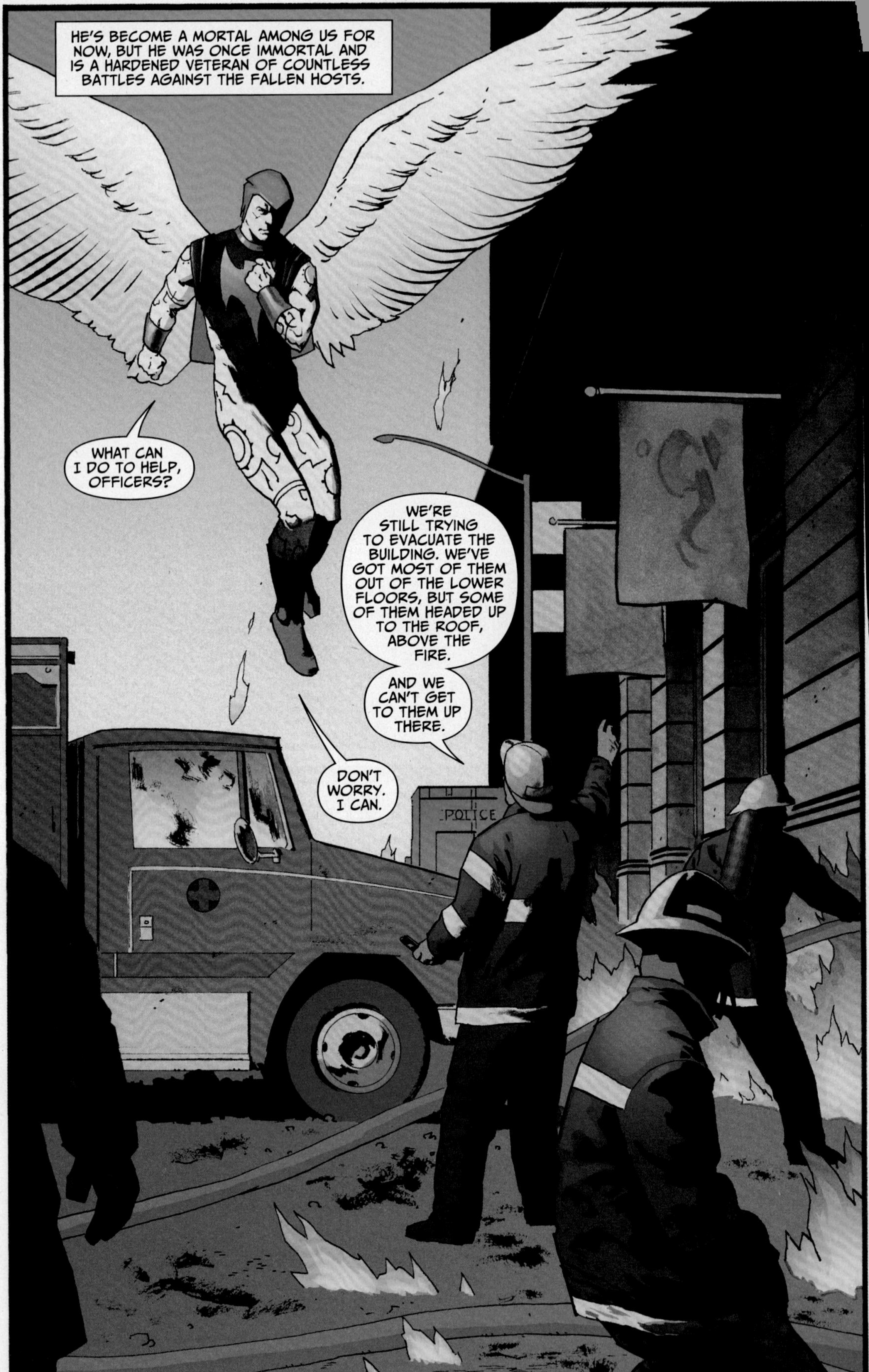
HE'S BECOME A MORTAL AMONG US FOR NOW, BUT HE WAS ONCE IMMORTAL AND IS A HARDENED VETERAN OF COUNTLESS BATTLES AGAINST THE FALLEN HOSTS.
WHAT CAN I DO TO HELP, OFFICERS?
WE'RE STILL TRYING TO EVACUATE THE BUILDING. WE'VE GOT MOST OF THEM OUT OF THE LOWER FLOORS, BUT SOME OF THEM HEADED UP TO THE ROOF, ABOVE THE FIRE.
AND WE CAN'T GET TO THEM UP THERE.
DON'T WORRY. I CAN.
POLICE

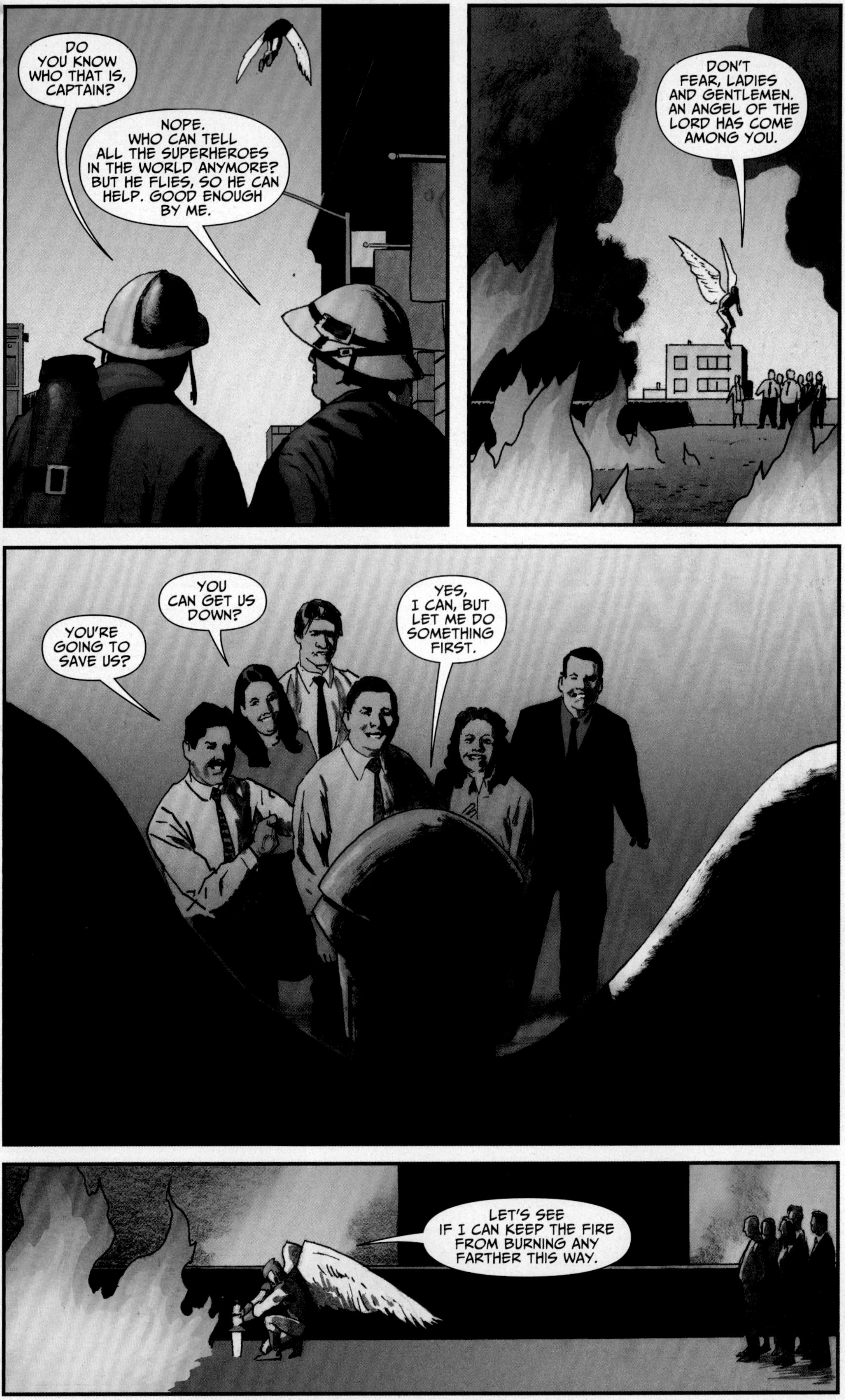

DO YOU KNOW WHO THAT IS, CAPTAIN?
NOPE. WHO CAN TELL ALL THE SUPERHEROES IN THE WORLD ANYMORE? BUT HE FLIES, SO HE CAN HELP. GOOD ENOUGH BY ME.
DON'T FEAR, LADIES AND GENTLEMEN. AN ANGEL OF THE LORD HAS COME AMONG YOU.
YOU'RE GOING TO SAVE US?
YOU CAN GET US DOWN?
YES, I CAN, BUT LET ME DO SOMETHING FIRST.
LET'S SEE IF I CAN KEEP THE FIRE FROM BURNING ANY FARTHER THIS WAY.

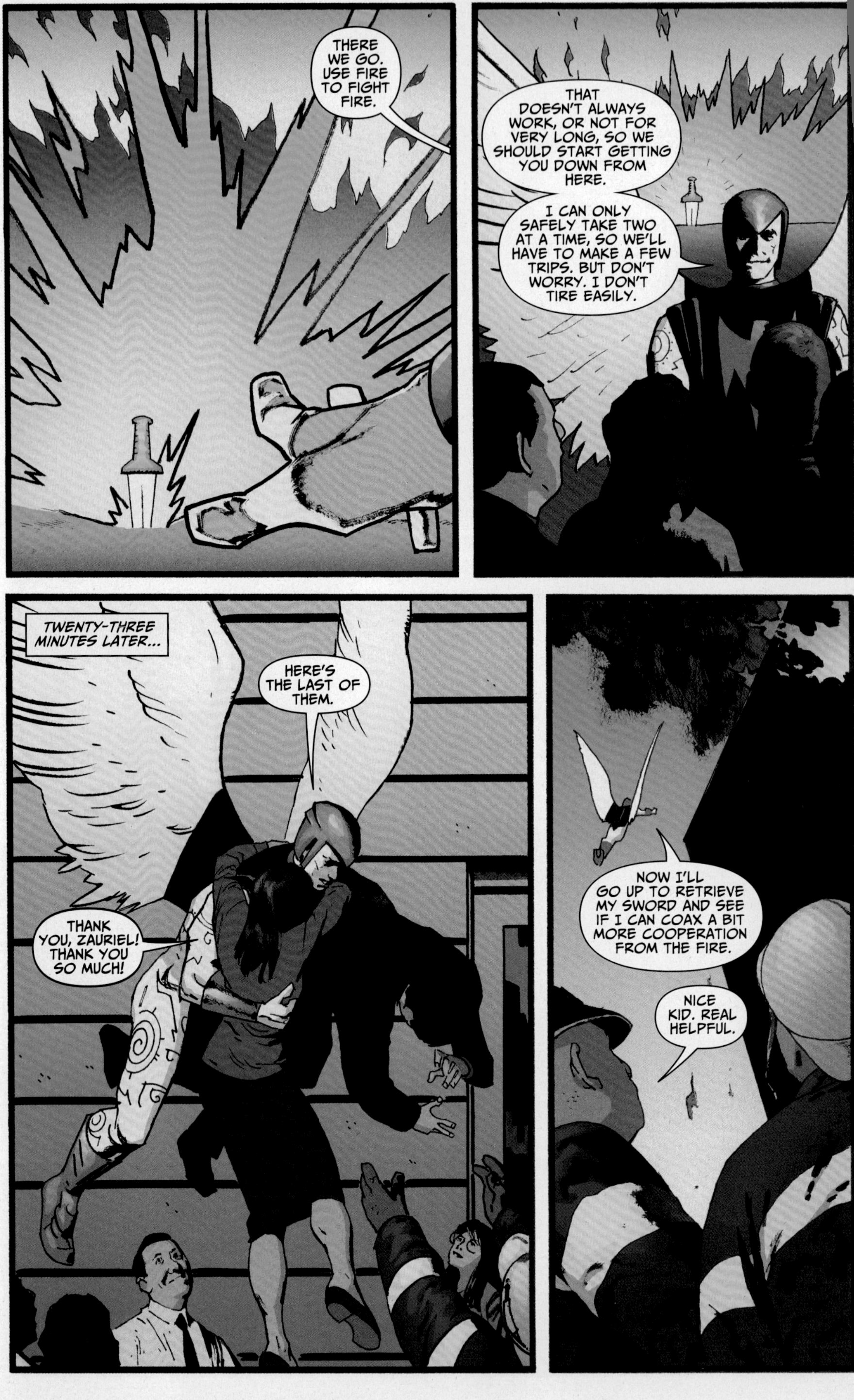
THERE WE GO. USE FIRE TO FIGHT FIRE.
THAT DOESN'T ALWAYS WORK, OR NOT FOR VERY LONG, SO WE SHOULD START GETTING YOU DOWN FROM HERE.
I CAN ONLY SAFELY TAKE TWO AT A TIME, SO WE'LL HAVE TO MAKE A FEW TRIPS. BUT DON'T WORRY. I DON'T TIRE EASILY.
TWENTY-THREE MINUTES LATER...
HERE'S THE LAST OF THEM.
THANK YOU, ZAURIEL! THANK YOU SO MUCH!
NOW I'LL GO UP TO RETRIEVE MY SWORD AND SEE IF I CAN COAX A BIT MORE COOPERATION FROM THE FIRE.
NICE KID. REAL HELPFUL.

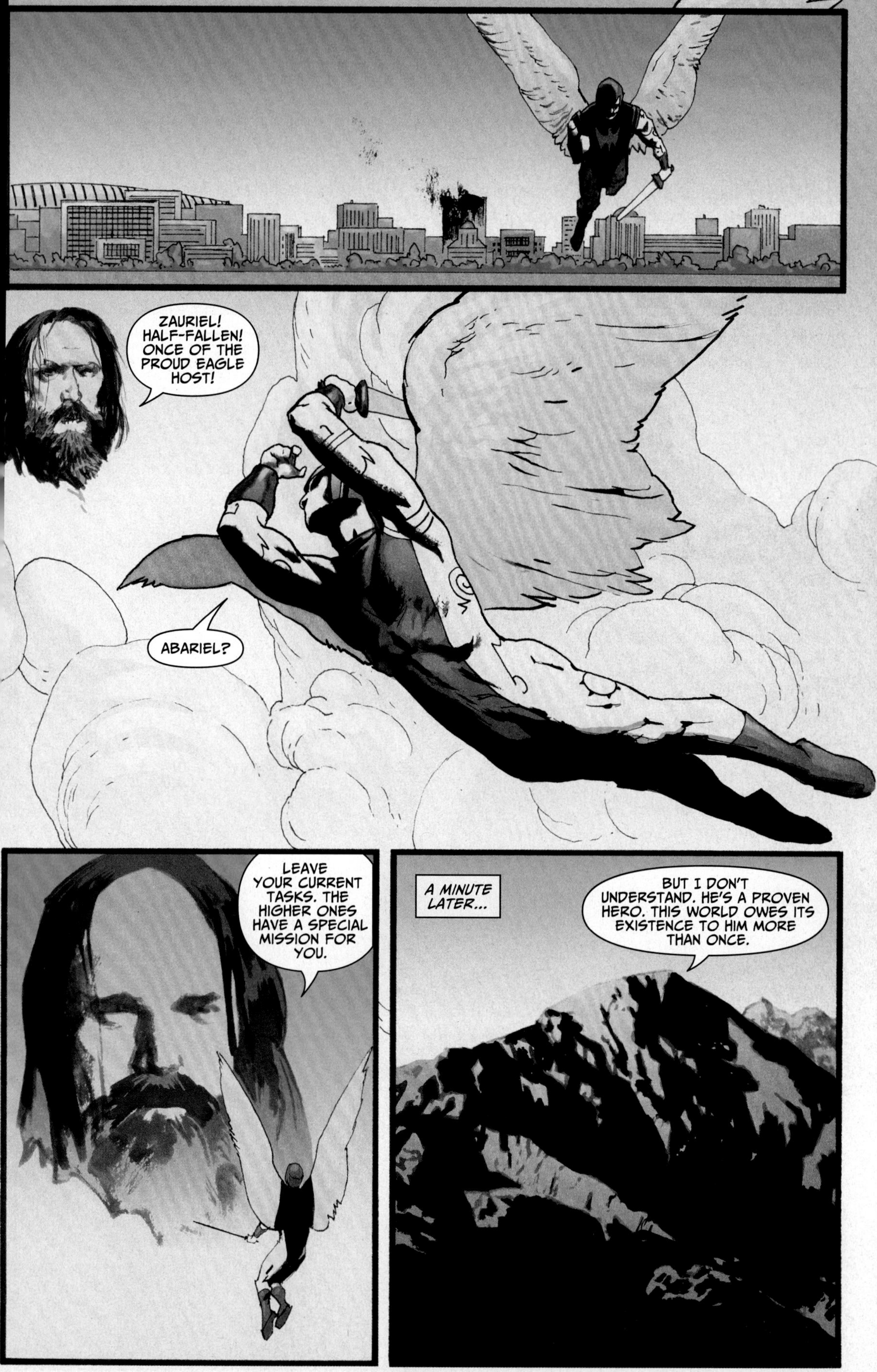
ZAURIEL! HALF-FALLEN! ONCE OF THE PROUD EAGLE HOST!
ABARIEL?
LEAVE YOUR CURRENT TASKS. THE HIGHER ONES HAVE A SPECIAL MISSION FOR YOU.
A MINUTE LATER...
BUT I DON'T UNDERSTAND. HE'S A PROVEN HERO. THIS WORLD OWES ITS EXISTENCE TO HIM MORE THAN ONCE.

IRRELEVANT. THE LOW POWERS OFTEN SEEM TO DO GOOD WORKS, BUT ALWAYS IN SERVICE TO TERRIBLE GOALS.

YOUR SO-CALLED HERO HAS BEEN MADE A RHYMER NOW AND IS THE TOAST OF THE DEPTHS. HE MAINTAINS ESTATES AND SERVANTS IN THE INFERNAL CITY.

IN WHAT WAY DOES THAT SEEM GOOD AND HEROIC AND DECENT TO YOU?

HE SOLD HIS SOUL, NOT TO SAVE ANOTHER, NOT IN SOME GRAND BUT MISGUIDED ATTEMPT TO ACCOMPLISH ANY GREAT DEED. HE SIMPLY WANTED MORE FAME.

HE TRADED HIS GREATEST GIFT FROM THE MOST HIGH IN RETURN FOR MORE POPULARITY AMONG THE MOST TERMINALLY INANE OF MANKIND.

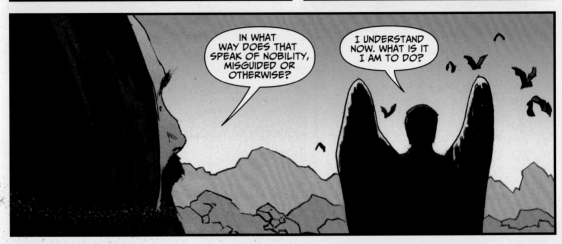

IN WHAT WAY DOES THAT SPEAK OF NOBILITY, MISGUIDED OR OTHERWISE?

I UNDERSTAND NOW. WHAT IS IT I AM TO DO?

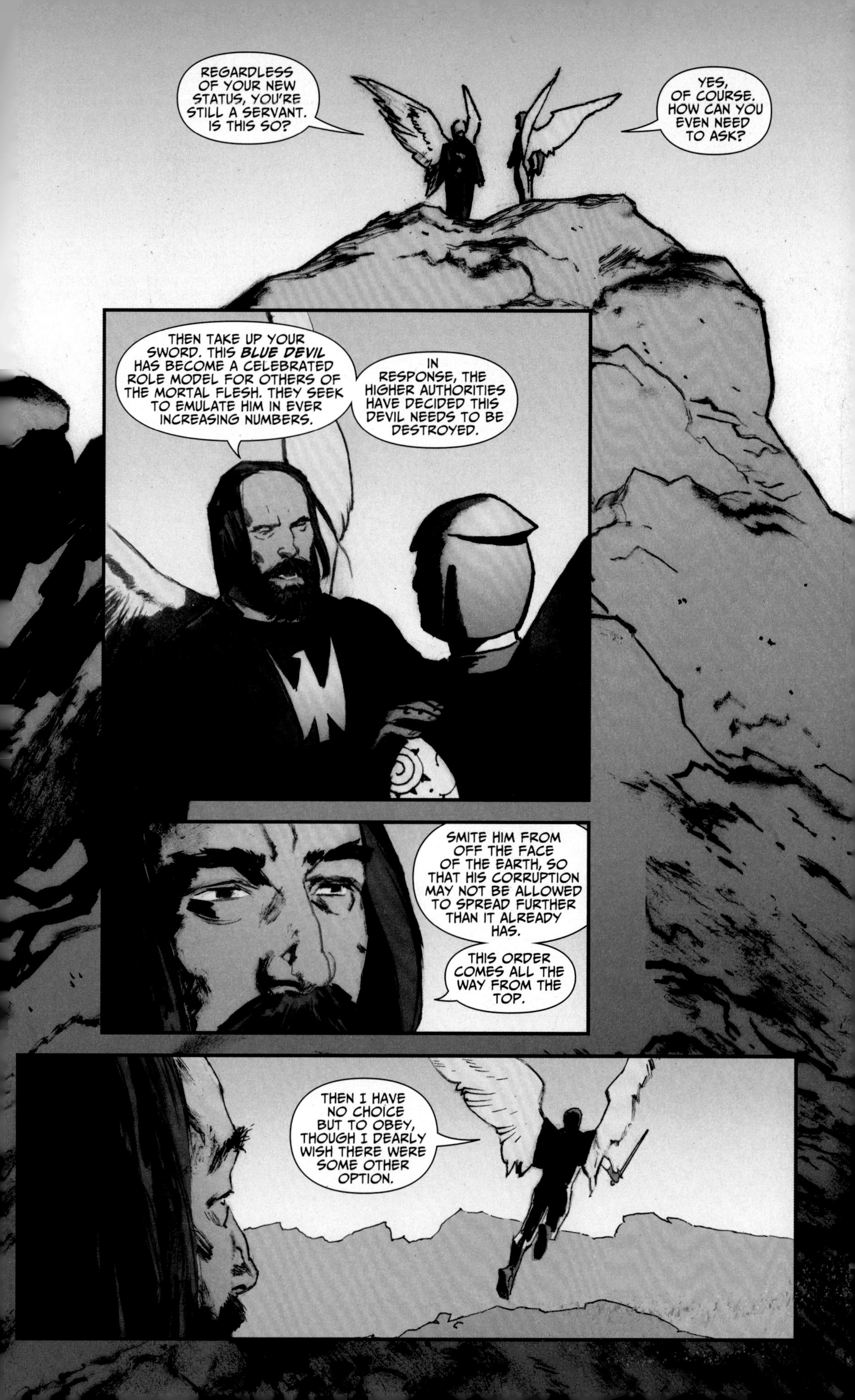
REGARDLESS OF YOUR NEW STATUS, YOU'RE STILL A SERVANT. IS THIS SO?
YES, OF COURSE. HOW CAN YOU EVEN NEED TO ASK?
THEN TAKE UP YOUR SWORD. THIS BLUE DEVIL HAS BECOME A CELEBRATED ROLE MODEL FOR OTHERS OF THE MORTAL FLESH. THEY SEEK TO EMULATE HIM IN EVER INCREASING NUMBERS.
IN RESPONSE, THE HIGHER AUTHORITIES HAVE DECIDED THIS DEVIL NEEDS TO BE DESTROYED.
SMITE HIM FROM OFF THE FACE OF THE EARTH, SO THAT HIS CORRUPTION MAY NOT BE ALLOWED TO SPREAD FURTHER THAN IT ALREADY HAS.
THIS ORDER COMES ALL THE WAY FROM THE TOP.
THEN I HAVE NO CHOICE BUT TO OBEY, THOUGH I DEARLY WISH THERE WERE SOME OTHER OPTION.

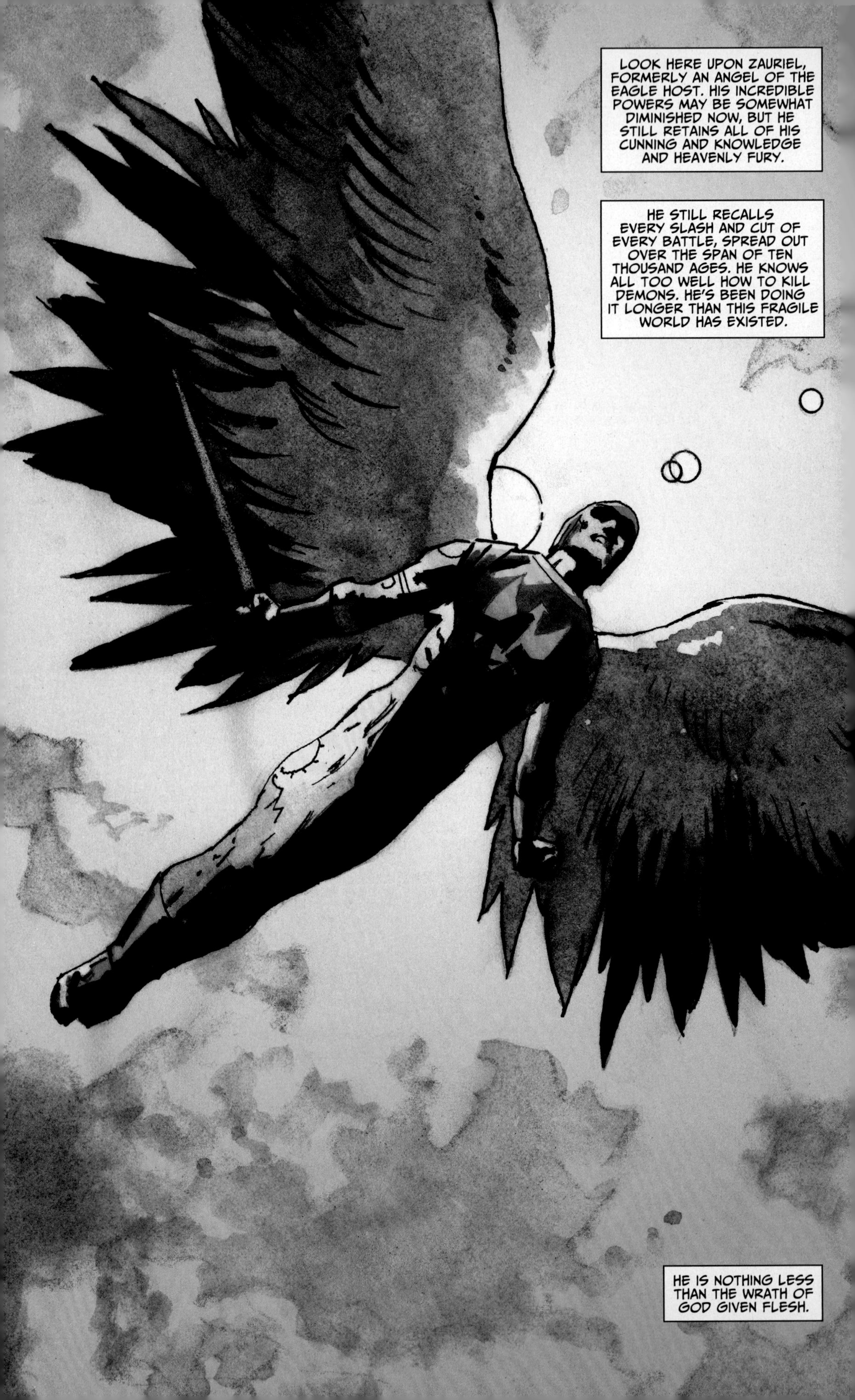
LOOK HERE UPON ZAURIEL, FORMERLY AN ANGEL OF THE EAGLE HOST. HIS INCREDIBLE POWERS MAY BE SOMEWHAT DIMINISHED NOW, BUT HE STILL RETAINS ALL OF HIS CUNNING AND KNOWLEDGE AND HEAVENLY FURY.
HE STILL RECALLS EVERY SLASH AND CUT OF EVERY BATTLE, SPREAD OUT OVER THE SPAN OF TEN THOUSAND AGES. HE KNOWS ALL TOO WELL HOW TO KILL DEMONS. HE'S BEEN DOING IT LONGER THAN THIS FRAGILE WORLD HAS EXISTED.
HE IS NOTHING LESS THAN THE WRATH OF GOD GIVEN FLESH.

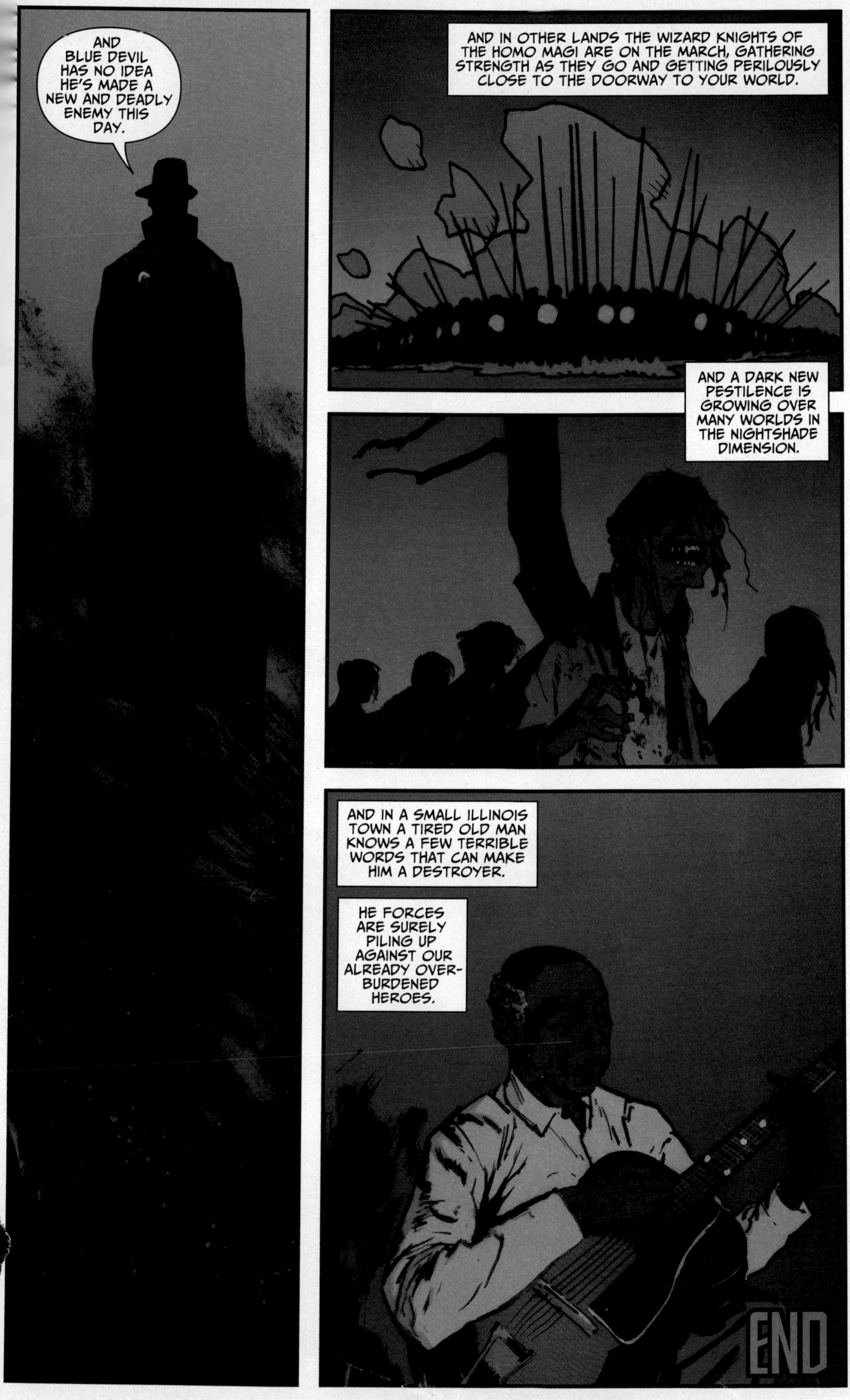
AND BLUE DEVIL HAS NO IDEA HE'S MADE A NEW AND DEADLY ENEMY THIS DAY.
AND IN OTHER LANDS THE WIZARD KNIGHTS OF THE HOMO MAGI ARE ON THE MARCH, GATHERING STRENGTH AS THEY GO AND GETTING PERILOUSLY CLOSE TO THE DOORWAY TO YOUR WORLD.
AND A DARK NEW PESTILENCE IS GROWING OVER MANY WORLDS IN THE NIGHTSHADE DIMENSION.
AND IN A SMALL ILLINOIS TOWN A TIRED OLD MAN KNOWS A FEW TERRIBLE WORDS THAT CAN MAKE HIM A DESTROYER.
HE FORCES ARE SURELY PILING UP AGAINST OUR ALREADY OVER-BURDENED HEROES.
END

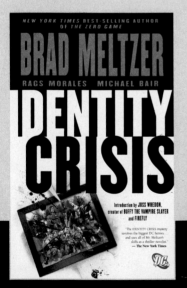